101
FREQUENTLY ASKED
QUESTIONS
ABOUT
HOMOSEXUALITY

MIKE HALEY

HARVEST HOUSE PUBLISHERS

EUGENE, OREGON

Cover by Koechel Peterson & Associates, Minneapolis, Minnesota

Back cover author photo by Don Jones

101 FREQUENTLY ASKED QUESTIONS ABOUT HOMOSEXUALITY
Copyright © 2004 by Mike Haley
Published by Harvest House Publishers
Eugene, Oregon 97402
www.harvesthousepublishers.com

Library of Congress Cataloging-in-Publication Data

Haley, Mike, 1962-
    101 frequently asked questions about homosexuality / Mike Haley.
       p. cm.
    Includes bibliographical references.
    ISBN 0-7369-1470-6 (pbk.)
    1. Homosexuality in the Bible—Miscellanea.   I. Title: One hundred one frequently asked questions about homosexuality.   II. Title: One hundred and one frequently asked questions about homosexuality.   III. Title.
    BR115.H6H35 2004
    261.8'35766—dc22

2004005163

Printed in the United States of America

04 05 06 07 08 09 10 11 12 / BP-CF / 10 9 8 7 6 5 4 3 2 1

"101 Frequently Asked Questions About Homosexuality is brilliant! Mike Haley has encapsulated psychological, spiritual, and practical answers to the most pressing questions of our time in this invaluable and biblically sound resource. I believe that this book could revolutionize a culture in need of being accurately educated about the issues surrounding homosexuality."

Alan Chambers,
Executive Director, Exodus International

"101 Frequently Asked Questions About Homosexuality reads like a series of personal letters from a good friend. Mike Haley provides godly, straightforward, thought-provoking perspective, and compassionate insights to the subject of homosexuality. A must read!"

Jeff Konrad,
author of *You Don't Have To Be Gay*

"Everyone's talking about homosexuality, but so few are speaking about it from an informed, biblically based perspective. Mike Haley provides this and much more in this comprehensive, user-friendly apologetic. If you're looking for practical, intelligent answers on *the* hot button issue of our time, pick up *101 Questions.* You'll be grateful, as I am, that Haley sorted the issues and has given us the tools with which to address them."

Joe Dallas,
author of *Desires in Conflict* and
When Homosexuality Hits Home

"Mike Haley's many years of experience in ministry well qualify him to write this book—a kind of "everything you always wanted to know" about same-sex attractions—for Christian strugglers and the clergy, counselors, and family members who would help them. Don't miss this solid, information-packed book. It's a first-rate contribution to the literature."

Dr. Joseph Nicolosi
President, National Association for
Research and Therapy of Homosexuality

"Mike's book is a timely, insightful and thought-provoking text. He covers a multitude of questions that inevitably arise and are often asked by family, friends, pastors, neighbors, and same-sex attracted men and women. Thank you, Mike, for providing us with this much-needed resource."

Anne Paulk
author of *Restoring Sexual Identity: Hope for Women Who Struggle with Same-Sex Attraction*

"As a former homosexual, Mike Haley has 'been there, done that.' He knows first-hand the pain and emptiness experienced by many homosexual men and women. Mike speaks the truth about homosexuality, but does so with a compassionate voice. This book explores the latest scientific findings about homosexuality as well as the timeless wisdom of Scripture. If you or someone you love is struggling with same-sex attraction, this book will start you on the road to hope and healing."

Dr. Bill Maier
Vice-President, Psychologist in Residence
Focus on the Family

"Because of my own deliverance from homosexuality, I often have the opportunity to talk with many men and women who desire that same freedom…and I also meet many parents, siblings, and friends of homosexuals who want advice on how to deal with the issue. So many times I have wished there was a comprehensive resource I could place in their hands…and now there is!"

Dennis Jernigan
Recording Artist, Worship Leader

This book is dedicated to my wife, Angie
You raise me up…to more than I can be

and my sons

Bennett Michael and Brenner Hamilton
who bring me joy unspeakable

Acknowledgments

First I must thank my best friend, Jeff Konrad, the man who encouraged me to take a chance at freedom, loved me when I was unlovable, and stood beside me as my best man on one of the first days I truly realized the Lord desired to restore "the years the locusts had stolen." You showed me that an endeavor like this book was possible and cheered me on when I was ready to quit. That possibility became a reality with the help of my two capable editors, Gary and Karla Schneeberger. Thank you both—I will be forever grateful to you for helping my heart find its voice. Our friendship was forged through this project, and that alone made it worth every ounce of effort.

Few are as precious to me as my coworkers on the Love Won Out team who for years have lifted my tired arms and allowed me to walk in the fullness of my giftings. I take great comfort knowing that you labor alongside me to reach those who desperately need God's touch. Karen, Linda, and Melissa: I will forever be thankful. You are true sisters in the faith.

I remember years ago praying alongside John Smid and John Paulk—two men who believed in me enough to help me believe in myself—that someone in the Christian community would come alongside the ex-gay movement and give it the attention it lacked for so many years. Little did we know that a decade later, Dr. James Dobson would be that man. He, the board of Focus on the Family, and the Executive Cabinet have endured much heat for taking on this ministry. They've done so knowing that the true source of that heat is the purifying fire of God's truth. Thank you all for being willing to stand in the gap for those who need the healing balm of His Word.

Thanks also to Tom Minnery and my family in Public Policy who have touched my life by your examples, prayers, and encouragement.

I can't wait to get to heaven and see just how my life was spared from many evils because of the prayers of faithful people—especially those at Focus on the Family, like my friends in Human Resources, Operations, and Accounting prayer teams, the men and women of Public Affairs and Master Writers, and all those who've labored in obscurity on my family's behalf.

Also, my bros, Ken Lane, Kurt Leander, and Victor Marx, who care enough to become uncomfortable in order to make a difference in one another's lives. Thanks for sharpening my rough edges.

To two churches who cherished the unwanted harvest, Church of the Open Door in San Rafael and Central Church in Memphis: You walked out a godly example of the difference a true body of Christ can make in people's lives.

Some people support this ministry for no reason other than to be vessels of healing to those often forgotten by the church. Thank you, Don and Diana Schmierer and Phil and Vicki Burress, for not only helping but giving of your own resources, time, and efforts to make sure no one falls by the wayside who has been adversely affected by homosexuality.

Thank you to Alan and Leslie Chambers and those on the Exodus board I've had the privilege to work with. Few others on this planet have felt so much like family.

To Bob Davies, Frank and Anita Worthen, Dr. Nicolosi, Joe Dallas, and the countless others who've forged a path through very dark and desolate places to make this possible for thousands who've needed the light: My thanks are nothing compared to what you will receive from the Lord, but thank you on behalf of all those you've shown the way.

Angie's family has become my own: Mom, Pops, Sheryl, Tom, Laena, Saen, Tracye, Adam, Rachel, Ryan, and Jared. Thanks for accepting me with never a hint of judgment.

I doubt the freedom I possess today would be as full had my family not stuck with me—even when it may have seemed impossible. You've each given me something to cherish. Jeff and Robin, your consistency and availability have meant the world; I've learned so much through your commitment to each other, your family, and me. My niece (Cori) and nephews (Christopher, Taylor, and Kyle)—the preciousness of each of your births and lives gave me solace even in the darkest time of my life as a "gay man." You gave me hope that maybe someday I would be able to fulfill my dreams of being a dad as well. Thanks for never being embarrassed or ashamed of your Uncle Mike. Tony and Debbie, you took me in and brought me home. May my firstborn son—your namesake—always remind you of the respect, admiration, and appreciation I have for you both. But few can own the reason for my healing like Grammy Cross. I know that the blame for the arthritis in those knees falls on me. Thank you for enduring the pain and staying on them on my behalf.

And last, but definitely not least, Dad. Thanks for being a man who always sought to provide and love, even when my expectations blinded me to the reality of your expressions of each.

Contents

Chapter 3: Answers for Friends

Chapter 4: Answers for the Church

Chapter 5: Answers for Men

Chapter 8: Answering Theology

Chapter 9: Answering Culture

Chapter 11: Answering Science

Chapter 12: Answering Your Need

Introduction

YOU DIDN'T BUY A BOOK CALLED *101 Frequently Asked Questions About Homosexuality* for the questions. You bought it for the answers. But how do you know you can trust the 101 answers contained on these pages?

My hope is that you will trust me. Every day, I work on issues related to homosexuality in my job as manager of the Gender Issues Department at Focus on the Family. I also serve on the board of Exodus International, North America, a worldwide ministry dedicated to helping those affected by homosexuality.

But this issue is important to me for personal reasons. For 12 years, I lived as an active homosexual. I know the subculture. I've felt what homosexuals feel—the hurt, rejection, anger, broken relationships, and the intense desire to be loved for who they are. I also know how their friends and loved ones feel when someone close to them "comes out" about their homosexuality. I know how the church often seems like the last place to go for help. And I know how families suffer and pray through the pain—as my own dear family did.

My story is not that different from the story of many homosexuals. My family includes men and women of faith on both sides, and as a young boy I asked Christ to be my Savior. But I was the only son of a father who owned a chain of sporting goods stores—the ultimate "man's man." I was expected to be the best football player, the best basketball player, the best baseball player, and the best of everything my father could possibly make me. But I could not live up to those expectations.

Instead of identifying with my father and emulating him, I gravitated to the security and acceptance my mother and sisters provided, and soon my father began to angrily label me as "sissy" and "worthless" in front of his macho friends. Sometimes he would ask me, "Why don't you just go in the house and be with your mom and sisters? That's where you'd rather be anyway!"

Before long, one of my dad's employees began to show me some much needed attention. This man took me to Disneyland and to the beach. He affirmed who I was and provided the male attention I so desperately craved. When I was 11 years old, that attention turned sexual. My need to be affirmed by a man was met in the most inappropriate way imaginable.

I was too young to recognize this misguided attention for what it really was—sexual abuse. The relationship continued through junior high and high school, and by the time I graduated, I'd jumped headfirst into the homosexual lifestyle. But realizing that my same-sex attractions and relationships didn't jibe with the things I heard at church, I confided my homosexual struggle to a high school counselor. Her response? "You just need to realize you were born gay. Get rid of your internalized homophobia and embrace your homosexuality."

A year or so later, a youth worker at church told me I simply needed to read my Bible and pray more. But the more I read and prayed, the more frustrated and angry I became at the God I had grown up loving, because change was not happening for me.

I moved away, chasing the carrot of happiness with a new partner, a new city, and a new identity. But through it all, I remained in close contact with my two sisters, who showed me unconditional love.

One day in 1985, I went to a gay gym and found myself attracted to a man I'd seen there before. I followed him out to the parking lot, where he abruptly told me that he was a Christian walking out of homosexuality. *This guy is crazy,* I thought. *God wouldn't do that for you—I tried it, and He didn't do it for me.*

As we continued to debate whether change was possible, the man made several references to another man named Jeff Konrad. Jeff had left the lifestyle and was studying the root causes of homosexuality and writing a book. As we talked, the man's eyes suddenly widened, and he shouted, "Oh my gosh—there's Jeff right now!"

I then heard a voice saying, *Was My arm too short to rescue you?*

From then on, Jeff Konrad became a symbol of hope in my search for wholeness. Over the next four years we corresponded, discussed, and argued—and all the while, he reassured me of God's love for me. (The letters we wrote over the years were eventually published in his book *You Don't Have to Be Gay*.)

I began a journey back to a wholeness I hadn't known since I was 11. I left the gay lifestyle, moved in with one of my sisters, and attended an Exodus International conference not long afterward. At that conference, I found 800 other men and women with the same hurts and wounds, who wanted to know Jesus in a way that would help deliver them from this life-dominating sin. It was the most unbelievable thing I had ever experienced.

While there, I learned about a residential program for men and women struggling with homosexuality. Because of my sexual addiction, I knew I needed that type of 24-hour care. Before I left the conference, several men and women gathered to pray over me. One of the men read Jeremiah 15:19 (NASB):

> Therefore, thus says the LORD, "If you return, then I will restore you—Before Me you will stand; and if you extract the precious from the worthless, you will become My spokesman."

I began to realize that God thought of me as precious and not "worthless"—as my father had.

The night I got home from the conference, I met a girl named Angie through a mutual acquaintance. She and I quickly became fast friends. When I moved to Northern California in December 1990 for the residential ministry, Angie stayed close to me emotionally, providing long-distance support while I walked out of homosexuality. During that time of healing, mountains of hurt and rejection melted as I found a freedom I hadn't known before.

I had always dreamed of being a youth pastor, but because of my past—I actually had a police record, having been booked for prostitution in 1987—I believed it would be impossible. So I earned a degree in Christian Education from Biola University and applied for my teaching credential. At the same time, I found myself growing closer to Angie. In fact, it was love—and on December 4, 1994, we were married.

Within a short time, God allowed me to work with a reparative therapy ministry, helping bring many men and women out of homosexuality. And then, amazingly, God allowed me to fulfill my calling to be a youth pastor—despite my record.

Angie and I thrived in our God-given callings; we loved the kids to whom we ministered, and the kids and their parents loved us. Through it all, the Lord showed me that some churches still believe in the complete, life-changing power of Jesus Christ.

I was a youth pastor for almost three years. Then, in May 1998, I received a phone call from an old friend who was working for Focus on the Family. Another formerly gay man, John Paulk, encouraged me to apply for a position in Focus on the Family's new gender-identity outreach ministry, Love Won Out. I said, "Thank you, but no." John offered the position to me two more times, and two more times I turned it down.

But God had other ideas. One morning at 4:30 A.M., as I was sleeplessly skimming a book entitled *Spiritual Leadership,* I heard the Lord say, *I want to sound the note through you.* He reminded me of the Jeremiah verse and His desire to use me as His spokesman.

So we moved to Colorado Springs, and I began the job at Focus on the Family in October 1998. Instead of just ministering to kids at my church, I was now able to speak with youth all over the country—and to enjoy a fulfillment I never expected as I help men and women walk out of homosexuality.

The Lord has continued the blessings. The first—our son Bennett—was born in December, 1999. The second, Brenner, was born in April, 2002.

Fifteen years have passed since I made that life-changing decision to leave homosexuality. Today, I'm secure in who I am. I'm not going back. I was there for 12 years. I know what that lifestyle has to offer me. And what I have now I wouldn't trade for the world.

God has been good to me. And He extends that same goodness to all who will come to Him—just as they are. My hope is that you or your loved one will come to experience that goodness for yourselves. My prayer is that this book will help you find it.

Mike Haley
April 2004

1

Answering the Basics

THIS BOOK MAY BE YOUR FIRST SERIOUS INQUIRY into homosexuality. Perhaps a friend or loved one has recently admitted a same-sex attraction. Or maybe the nightly news or morning paper has caused your concern. Perhaps you, yourself, have experienced attractions to your own sex and are wondering, *Am I a homosexual? And if I am, can I do anything to change my sexual orientation?*

For whatever reason you've picked up this book, you have questions. And some of them may be the most basic queries imaginable, such as *What is homosexuality?*

This first chapter deals with some of these most basic questions.

1. What is homosexuality?

Most people assume homosexuality to be little more than a sexual act between two individuals of the same gender. This is far too simplistic a view of this multifaceted topic. Anyone interested in this subject must take four areas into account: physiological psychic response, identity, behavior, and lifestyle options.

Learned Responses

God created each of us as a complex creature. We have needs that must be met in order for us to grow and mature. When these needs are not met, we establish immature coping mechanisms that often work directly against God's original intent for us. Frank Worthen, the founder of Exodus International, explains this phenomenon this way:

> *Psychic response* is a technical term for what many people refer to as a "homosexual orientation." Though many people claim that they have experienced visual or sexual attraction for the same sex

"as long as they can remember," there is a progression in a person's life that leads to a homosexual psychic response. A child may start out with a need to compare himself with others to see if he measures up to societal standards. When he feels he doesn't compare favorably with others, he develops admiration for those traits and physical characteristics he feels he does not possess. Admiration, which is normal, may turn to envy. Envy leads to the desire to possess others and finally, to consume others. This strong desire becomes eroticized somewhere along the way, eventually leading to homosexual psychic response (also known as sexual thought life or fantasy).*

Behavior

When these psychic responses take root, some people carry out these fantasies first through masturbation and later in actual sexual behavior with another male or female. But the physical act itself does not indicate a homosexual orientation. Many young boys who engage in homosexual behavior later end up with no vestiges of homosexuality.

Identity

The problem in today's social climate is that more and more individuals are taking on a gay identity simply because they need to find their place. Many who would rarely have experienced a struggle with homosexuality find themselves comfortable in this identity because of society's "anything goes" mentality.

Other people embrace a gay identity after years of physiological psychic response. Their behaviors create an identity in which they take comfort or even pride.

Lifestyle

Homosexuality includes varying lifestyles. Some gays only engage in anonymous and relatively rare sexual encounters and tend to live in constant fear of being found out. Others "come out" and become

---

* From Frank Worthen, "What Is Homosexuality," www.exodus-international.org/library_additionalarti-cles_08.shtml.

active, politically motivated members of the gay community and associate only with those favorable to like causes.

As you can see, homosexuality is multidimensional, and individuals can land anywhere on the spectrum of these four basic components. What does this information mean for you? Don't just take a friend or loved one's confession or proclamation of homosexuality as evidence that he or she is engaging in same-sex sexual behavior. Talk to him or her to develop a deeper understanding of what the admission means.

2. Do homosexuals choose to be gay?

Let me answer this one directly: *No!* And in case you didn't hear me, let me speak up: NO!

This continues to be one of the myths of homosexuality that uninformed people perpetuate. Christians or conservatives may say to a homosexual, "I have a heart for those in your community, and I love *you*." And then as if to drive a splinter under the fingernail of the hand they've just reached out to hold, they add: "But you and your friends have to realize that homosexuality was your choice."

Ouch.

I can tell you from personal experience that virtually *no one* chooses homosexuality and the resulting pain and rejection that comes with it. No child or adolescent approaches the smorgasbord of sexual orientations and says, "Hmm…I think I'll take that one." On the contrary, most homosexuals try to deny the existence of their same-sex attractions, to pray it away, or to repress it until they become so discouraged by their inability to master the desires that they "come out." Attributing this struggle to the willing choice of any individual not only conveys a lack of understanding but adds to the tremendous shame seared into many homosexuals' hearts.

So let me say clearly again: *No one chooses to feel attracted to someone of the same sex.* However, men and women do choose how they will act on those feelings. When the pain of this struggle captivates the heart, some people believe their only option is a homosexual identity and lifestyle. That's where choice comes into play: actively participating in a homosexual act.

One last important note on this subject: As harmful as the "you chose to be gay" argument is another oft-repeated phrase, all too frequently seen on the signs of conservative protesters at gay events: "God didn't create Adam and Steve, He created Adam and Eve." Anyone who thinks this is cute or helpful couldn't be more wrong. Flippant expressions like this make whoever's saying them look foolish, and their underlying malice directly contradicts Scripture. Remember Solomon's advice: "He who winks maliciously causes grief, and a chattering fool comes to ruin. The mouth of the righteous is a fountain of life" (Proverbs 10:10-11). Excise this quip from your vocabulary and instead choose to offer life!

3. What is the difference between the terms "gay" and "homosexual"?

These terms are often used interchangeably, but they have some very real differences. Knowing what they are can help you offer advice and counsel to those who seek your input.

There really is no such thing as a homosexual. As strange as that may sound, it's true. We are all biological heterosexuals. To be sure, some heterosexuals, through a combination of factors, find themselves dealing with a homosexual problem—and when I use the term "homosexual" in my answers, I'm referring to men and women who, because of these various factors, find themselves attracted to members of their own sex. But to firmly identify oneself as a homosexual is to buy into the false idea that two distinct, valid, immutable orientations exist.

Still society will continue to use the term "homosexual," so here are some basic differences between that word and "gay": Men and women who experience homoerotic desires, fantasies, and attractions are those most likely to identify themselves as homosexual. However, not all homosexuals think of or classify themselves as "gay"—a term with decidedly sociopolitical overtones, one that is as much about identifying oneself as a member of a community than identifying oneself by sexual orientation. As Dr. Joseph Nicolosi explains, some men "experience conflict between their values and their sexual orientation."[1] These individuals would never be comfortable claiming a gay identity.

The ultimate rule of thumb? All gays are homosexual but not all homosexuals choose to identify themselves as gay. Another helpful distinction is that those who seek to walk away from homosexuality can be referred to as "non-gay homosexuals."[2]

4. If I'm having homosexual fantasies, does that mean I'm gay?

Fantasies alone don't make you homosexual. A homosexual is a person who consciously accepts that label and begins to act out on his or her feelings. Many, many people have engaged in fleeting same-sex experimentation, but that doesn't make them homosexual, either. On the other hand, some people who have never engaged in homosexual behavior have a tremendous homosexual problem.

Regarding your personal situation, the first relevant question is this: How often do these fantasies occur? A single episode does not mean you're homosexual. However, if these fantasies persist, the potential for a serious homosexual problem exists, especially if they go unchecked or if you encourage them through pornography or masturbation.

Some Native Americans believe that each of us has within our hearts a white dog (good) and a black dog (evil) fighting for control. As would be the case in real life, the dog that is nurtured has the best chance of thriving. The same is true of the fight for your heart. Whichever dog you are feeding is going to become dominant and take over. You need to do all you can to overcome the undesired "dog." Find someone knowledgeable about the root causes of homosexuality if you find these fantasies continuing and becoming increasingly frequent. But please don't allow one (or even a few) episodes of homosexual fantasy to paralyze you from living as God has created you—heterosexually.

5. Is homosexuality preventable?

The prevention of homosexuality in children has become one of the primary emphases of research within the ex-gay movement. That represents a shift from the traditional focus, undertaken by Exodus International and like-minded ministries, which have spent most of their energies spreading the message of redemption. These ministries have often been the only hope people struggling with homosexuality (and their family members) have had when seeking answers and assistance.

In recent years, however, attention has shifted from not only redeeming homosexuals but also preventing homosexuality. At the leading edge of this movement are Dr. Joseph and Linda Nicolosi, authors of *A Parent's Guide to Preventing Homosexuality,* in which they spell out some important steps parents can take to offer an atmosphere in the home that will increase the chances of their children growing up secure in their gender identity. "Gender nonconformity in childhood," the Nicolisis note, "most researchers agree, is the single most common factor associated with homosexuality....Unfortunately, many members of the mental health profession—psychiatrists, psychologists, and social workers—think it is unnecessary to inform parents of the possibility of a homosexual outcome."[3]

They continue by warning that "despite parents' key role in forming the gender identity of their sons and daughters, many of them are astonishingly unaware not only of their own behavior with an emotionally vulnerable son but also of their child's resulting deficits."[4]

Unfortunately, parents' most common responses when faced with their children's gender nonconformity are not helpful.

1. *Denial*

The Nicolosis warn that many parents erroneously express sentiments such as " 'It's just a phase; he'll probably outgrow it.'...Or they claim, 'It's no big deal. He looks so cute—he's just trying to get attention when he dresses up like a little girl.' " This mentality "stems, in part, from the fact that our culture has made it increasingly hard for parents to determine what gender development is normal and what is abnormal, what is worth worrying about and what is not."

So when do you need to start worrying? "The answer is," the authors suggest, "a certain amount of cross-gender play is tolerable. However, if your son does not give it up quickly, you will need to take a look not only at his behavior but also at yours."

2. Confusion

Mixed messages regarding gender saturate our culture, and many parents don't know what to think. They often feel confused and paralyzed by the conflicting values and opinions.

The Nicolosis have documented this phenomenon well. One teacher, they note, assured a mother who was confused by her son's gender nonconformity not to worry because "it's perfectly healthy—he's getting in touch with his feminine side." Another off-base adviser said, "Don't intervene. What he's doing is in no way a problem. You don't want your child to be a stereotyped macho man, do you?" Yet most mothers intuitively know something is askew.

3. Avoidance

The Nicolosis note: "Many parents who do finally consult a psychologist have been worried about their [child] for months, and many of them for years, but have done nothing about it."

So what are parents to do?

The Nicolosis suggest that "the first step in intervention is for parents to educate themselves. This often means correcting false information. Gender—our sense of maleness and femaleness—is not merely an arbitrary social construct. It is, rather, a basic and essential way in which we humans participate in society and express ourselves within the real world."

The next step would be to assess the health of your marriage. "[Most] couples who come to a therapist looking for help with their child are experiencing disharmony in their relationship. The wife will complain, 'My husband is so hard to reach. He's just not emotionally connected to me or the kids.' The husband will respond, 'The truth is that she's a major control freak! If she would just back off, I'd get more involved.'"

Now, let's take a more in-depth look at how parents should handle issues of gender nonconformity in their children.

Parents with Sons

Since our children first learn what it means to be male or female from familial interactions, moms and dads must carefully consider how their efforts, dysfunctions, emotions, and affirmations can affect their sons—both positively and negatively.

Everyone knows that moms are important, yet moms must be aware of their level of involvement. In fact, the Nicolosis suggest,

> without realizing it, mothers can become overinvolved in their son's lives. In some cases, this behavior may have arisen because of a mother's need to attend to her son's childhood illnesses. In fact, a number of studies have shown a higher than average correlation between adult homosexuality and early childhood medical problems. Mothers of homosexual men tend, in our experience, to be expressive, extroverted, emotionally accessible, engaging, and highly involved in the boy's life. The mother's problem might be that she is too invested; the boundaries between her and her son are not clear....Sometimes mothers overinvest in their sons for their own needs, because they have not found emotional intimacy in their marriage.

Parents should also consider what the Nicolosis refer to as

> the Classic Triadic Relationship....Repeatedly, researchers have found the classic triadic (three-way) relationship in the family backgrounds of homosexual men. In this situation, the mother often has a poor or limited relationship with her husband, so she shifts her emotional needs to her son. The father is usually non-expressive and detached and often is critical as well. So in the triadic family pattern we have the detached father, the overinvolved mother, and the temperamentally sensitive, emotionally attuned boy who fills in for the father where the father falls short.

Like mothers, fathers must be aware of the impact they can have on the healthy formation of their son's gender indentity.

> Psychoanalysts have long recognized the importance of the father in the boy's development and in his separation from his mother. Some analysts have referred to the father as a "breath of fresh air" from overinvolvement with the mother. Dad can be the knight in shining armor with whom the child can play, while being distinctively different from his mother.

The Nicolosis suggest that the best type of father is "salient (which is…being benevolent and strong)" and one "worthy of emulation."

The Nicolosis go on to address four key things fathers can do to help solidify a relationship with their sons that can promote a healthy gender identity. First, dads need to be keenly aware of not rejecting their sons if the sons have rejected them. "Many fathers of gender-confused sons simply give up and leave the boy to his mother. This is a big mistake.…Your task is to pursue your son, push through his defensive detachment, and with steady and consistent efforts, to become an important person in his life." Secondly, "Dads must remain committed. Maintaining the parental team is very important, but generally the most challenging problem is keeping the father involved on a consistent basis. In fact, the difficulty of maintaining Dad's active, daily participation is the most common obstacle to successful therapy." Next, dads must learn to listen for feelings. The Nicolosis want to make sure their readers understand that "while we have been placing much of the focus of intervention on gender-appropriate behavioral change, we must not forget the true task, which is emotional bonding with the same-sex parent. And in this focus on achieving behavioral change, the child's feelings can easily be overlooked." And lastly, they suggest four ways for fathers to develop closer relationships with their sons.

> 1. A dad needs to play physically with his boys, remembering occasionally to let them win. "By 'playing weak,' the dad allows the son to feel tough, strong, and aggressive."

2. "Showering with Dad is good for small boys and can sometimes include brothers....Showering with Dad and other males in the house fosters a common, relaxed, anatomically based identity and breaks down the fascination and sense of mystery around male anatomy which will fuel male eroticism when puberty arrives."

3. "Trips out of the house with just father and son are very helpful."

4. "Dad should be the last person to tuck the son into bed."

Much is involved in imparting healthy gender identities in boys, but this brief overview can aid you as you assess the atmosphere in your home.

Parents with Daughters

Many of the same family dynamics that impart a healthy gender identity in boys are helpful for girls as well. So the first place to start is with the strength of the parents' marriage, being mindful that little eyes are watching.

Another influence—especially if the daughter has brothers—is the family's attitude toward feminine things. One of the roots that can often lead to a wounded female psyche is the light in which women are portrayed. Diane Eller-Boyko, a psychotherapist and ex-lesbian, makes this clear:

> Our culture especially honors the masculine—strength, dominance, achievement, striving. That creates in many women a neurotic split from their authentic natures. The woman represses the inner hurt and pain, and starts to identify with the masculine. It is out of the unhealed places of the wounded feminine psyche that she becomes aggressive and loud.[5]

The importance of a healthy relationship with Mom is also vital. Mothers who are too self-absorbed, unwilling or incapable of nurturing, or detached will affect their daughters' developing gender identity negatively. The Nicolosis repeat the words of one therapist who bluntly summarized the problem relationships she came in contact with while working with women who struggled in this area:

The little girl who turns to homosexuality never has a chance to create herself. She is a creation of her mother, whose self-love she was meant to enhance....Mothers seemed to use their children as sometimes desperately needed, sometimes desperately repudiated extension of themselves.

But she's quick to point out the importance of Dad's role as well.

When these little girls tried to turn to their fathers, they did not fare much better. Preoccupied with their business deal, the men sporadically paid attention to their daughters, overstimulating them, and then appeared to forget that they were around....These fathers, when they took the time to react at all, responded to their daughters as persons who had to be made over in their own, masculine image.[6]

Parents need to assess their attitudes toward femininity and make sure that they're relating to their developing daughter in healthy, productive ways.

A safe environment is also essential for young girls as they develop a healthy gender identity. Few things are more damaging to young women than abuse—whether personally experienced or observed. You must protect your daughter from abusive situations at all costs. Seek professional help to work through abusive situations.

This is only a superficial look at prevention. You can find a deeper examination of the role of parental influence in *A Parent's Guide to Preventing Homosexuality* by the Nicolosis. Another excellent resource is *An Ounce of Prevention* by Don Schmierer.[7]

2

Answers for Families

As you might expect, the most heartfelt questions I receive are from those most deeply affected by the homosexuality of a loved one—their family members. Hearing the words "I am a homosexual" can be devastating for an unsuspecting parent, grandparent, spouse, sibling, or child. Such an admission will likely be just the beginning of an ongoing process that may take years to work through.

But there *is* hope. Change can happen. For some, the admission of homosexuality can bring a family closer together as they unite to help the gay family member through some very deep waters of change. But even when your loved one doesn't seek change, your understanding of the answers that follow can be immensely helpful.

6. We just found out our child is gay. Is it our fault? Did we do something wrong?

This is often the first question that comes to the mind of any parent who has just learned of their child's homosexuality. Your heart may be broken, and your mind will probably race back to review every milestone in the life of your child to see what could have possibly gone wrong. But take heart. The answer to this painful question will rid you of any false guilt and free you to respond in a helpful way.

When Joe Dallas, author and former president of Exodus International, teaches his class Top Ten Questions Loved Ones Ask, he begins by reciting a line from the movie *A River Runs Through It*. A Presbyterian minister reminisces about his renegade son who has died a tragic death:

> Each of us will at some point in our lives look upon a loved one and ask a question: We are willing to help, Lord, but what can we do? For it is true that we can seldom help those closest to us—either we don't

know what part of ourselves to give, or, more often than not, that part that we have to give is not wanted. And so it is those we live with and should know the best who often elude us. But we can still love them. We can love them completely without completely understanding.[1]

Surely you can relate to this father's feelings. You want nothing more than to find a way to help, and the first place you look is at your own fallibility.

You must remember that no person has the power to make another child of God *anything*. Homosexuality is not the result of one single factor. Many influences can contribute to the condition: the child's perception, parent's behavior, the environment (which is often beyond any parent's control), interactions with others, predisposing personality characteristics, and so on. While some familial contribution may have weakened the psyche of your child, making him or her more susceptible to same-sex attraction, each person is accountable for his or her responses to circumstances. No parent would ever willingly cause sexual struggles in any of their offspring. We live in an imperfect, fallen world, and we all make poor decisions that we alone are accountable for.

Think of your own life—of your vulnerability to a certain weakness. What "makes" you indulge? Surely not your parents, regardless of how imperfect they may have been. As you continue to read and learn, I pray you will be comforted by these truths: You are in no way directly responsible for your child's sin, and the life, death, and resurrection of our Lord Jesus Christ provides a way out of that sin.

For further information regarding situations loved ones face in this situation, please read *Someone I Love Is Gay* by Anita Worthen and Bob Davies.[2]

7. We've noticed a few behaviors in our son that are causing us some concern (such as an interest in women's clothing and identifying with heroines in cartoons). Are these things normal?

Although parents whose sons are showing signs of worrisome behaviors ask this question most often, anyone who works closely with children should consider it. Some definite warning signs can dramatically increase the child's chances of same-sex attraction. These should not be overlooked.

Joseph and Linda Nicolosi's book *A Parent's Guide to Preventing Homosexuality* answers this question clearly and succinctly.

> Certain signs of prehomosexuality are easy to recognize, and these signs usually come early in the child's life. Indicators of childhood [gender identity disorder] GID, described by the American Psychiatric Association (APA), are listed below. Clinicians are told to use the following five markers to help them determine whether a child has this disorder:
>
> 1. Repeatedly stated desire to be, or insistence that he or she is, the other sex.
> 2. In boys, preference for cross dressing, or simulating female attire. In girls, insistence on wearing only stereotypical masculine clothing.
> 3. Strong and persistent preference for cross-sexual roles in make-believe play, or persistent fantasies of being the other sex.
> 4. Intense desire to participate in the stereotypical games and pastimes of the other sex.
> 5. Strong preference for playmates of the other sex.
>
> The onset of most cross-gender behavior occurs during the preschool years, between the ages of two and four. Cross-dressing... is one of the first signs.
>
> Of course, for most gender-conflicted boys, the signs of early homosexual development will be more subtle—a reluctance to play with other boys, fear of rough-and-tumble play, shyness about being naked in the presence of other males (but not when in the presence of females), lack of comfort with and attachment to the father, and perhaps an over-attachment to the mother.[3]

Dr. Nicolosi goes on to clarify that parents must

> differentiate between games and obsessions if your child shows an interest in opposite-sex clothing and activities. You need not worry about rare occasions of cross-dressing. You should become

concerned, though, when your little boy continues doing so and, at the same time, begins to acquire some other alarming habits. He may start using his mother's makeup. He may avoid other boys in the neighborhood and their play activities, and prefer being with their sisters instead, regularly joining them in their play with dolls and dollhouses. Later, he may start speaking in a high-pitched voice. He may affect the exaggerated gestures and even the walk of a girl or become fascinated with long hair, earrings, and scarves. Feminine things may take on a special interest for him, even to the point of obsession. In fact, he may actually act more girlish than his own sister and mother.[4]

These warning signs must be addressed. Dr. Nicolosi highlights this importance by stating, "The odds are that, without intervention, a boy [with these obsessions] has a 75 percent chance of growing up homosexual, bisexual, or transgender."[5]

Dr. Nicolosi is also emphatic in saying that

a gender-nonconforming boy *can* be sensitive, kind, social, artistic, gentle—and heterosexual. He can be an artist, an actor, a dancer, a cook, a musician—and a heterosexual. These innate artistic skills are "who he is," part of the wonderful range of human abilities. No one should try to discourage those abilities and traits. With appropriate masculine affirmation and support, however, they can all be developed within the context of normal heterosexual manhood.[6]

Ironically, Nicolosi's warning signs are corroborated by two people who don't share Nicolosi's views: Simon LeVay, a pro-gay scientist whose efforts have included attempting to identify a portion of the brain that he believed to cause homosexuality, and Dean Hamer, another individual who is known for "finding" the "gay gene." (See question 95.) LeVay makes this observation:

When a gay man, for example, says he was born gay, he generally means that he felt different from other boys at the earliest age he can remember. Sometimes the difference involved sexual feelings, but more commonly it involved some kind of gender-nonconformist or "sex-atypical" traits—disliking rough-and-tumble play, for example, that were not explicitly sexual.[7]

Hamer seconds the motion with these words:

> Most sissies will grow up to be homosexuals, and most gay men were sissies as children....Despite the provocative and politically incorrect nature of that statement, it fits the evidence. In fact, it may be the most consistent, well-documented, and significant finding in the entire field of sexual-orientation research and perhaps in all of human psychology.[8]

Need you be concerned? Consider these comments logically, void of emotion—and if you're still troubled, seek counsel from a trained therapist. Be sure to find one who will not seek to affirm these behaviors in your child but instead help in devising a treatment plan that you can share with all potential caregivers involved in the child's life.

For further information on this issue, please read Dr. Nicolosi's book *A Parent's Guide to Preventing Homosexuality* in its entirety. If you feel the need to contact a trained expert, one who understands these issues and has expertise in reorientation therapy, contact the National Association for Research and Therapy of Homosexuality (NARTH) at (818) 789-4440 for a potential referral in your area.

8. I'm a single mother with two sons. I've heard that boys can be negatively affected by the loss of a father. Would another male role model help? What advice can you offer that would enable me to raise healthy sons?

Any man decidedly committed to investing in the life of a young child can have significant influence. However, the damage done by the loss or rejection (real or perceived) of a father figure can have a scarring effect that can last a lifetime. If your children are lacking a positive male role model, find someone either in your family or at church who will help to dull the ache of this missing influence.

Please rest assured that not every child who grows up without a father ends up struggling with homosexuality. Other factors come into play. And yes, you need to be aware of and do some things to help increase the probability of a healthy gender-identity formation. Take comfort in knowing that homosexuality can be prevented. But the fact still remains that for those dealing with homosexuality,

> in a large number of instances, no male role model existed during the early childhood developmental years in the home. Whether it be father, father substitute or older male sibling. The absence of male role models with whom to identify was even more characteristic of the most severely disturbed effeminate boys. In cases where the father or a father surrogate was present in the home, he was typically described as psychologically remote from the family.[9]

The upshot of all this? Not any substitute male will do. Make sure the man you select understands the importance of consistency, commitment, and affirmation. You sons can't afford another negative example of masculinity.

In their book *A Parent's Guide to Preventing Homosexuality,* Dr. Joseph Nicolosi and Linda Nicolosi suggest three ways a single mother can enhance healthy emotional and gender development in her sons.

1. *She can monitor the mother-son relationship.*

> Single mothers should be mindful not to develop an excessively close relationship with their sons. If a single mother has no emotionally secure relationships with a man, she may unconsciously seek to satisfy her emotional needs with her son, maintaining an unhealthy, overly intimate connection that may seemingly meet her own needs but that will not be in the best interest of her son.[10]

The authors go on to caution how this is especially true for boys more prone to a gender identity deficit. "The gender-fragile boy, in particular, is typically bright and very verbal. Such a boy seems to be able to read his mother well, and sensing his mother's codependency with him, he may learn to manipulate her emotions and consequently grow up as an undisciplined, overindulged, and (ultimately) immature and self-absorbed young man who is ill equipped to face the demands of the world."

2. She can encourage masculine identification.

> The single mother has to go the extra mile in affirming her son's masculinity. From day one, she has to make him feel that his maleness is different from her femaleness and that that difference is good, healthy, and a part of who he is.[11]

I've watched my wife invest in our sons' masculinity in a way that might be instructive for any mother. While my boys are outside playing—which for them often means dirt, mud, sand, and bugs—I've frequently heard my wife say, "Boys, I'm so glad that God has made you just the way you are! Mommy and most girls I know hate getting dirty, but you like it, and that's one thing that makes you so special." Their reaction is to stick their little chests out and look to Mommy for further affirmation.

Try to find similar ways to reinforce your child's gender identity creatively.

Single mothers also need to be very aware of how they speak about men or portray masculinity to their already vulnerable sons. "A single mother can respect and maintain the memory of the father in a positive way, even though the father may never return, thus promoting the positive image of the 'good father,'" Dr. and Mrs. Nicolosi note. "On the other hand, when men are often spoken of in a negative way in the home, a young boy may unconsciously adopt a feminine identity and effeminate mannerisms to make sure he remains safe from his mother's rejection."[12]

3. She can find a father figure.

As I already mentioned, finding a surrogate father figure can be beneficial. The Nicolosis mention one more detail worth noting:

> It is important that the single mother support the boy's masculine interests and that she encourage and endorse them. It is detrimental if the mother conveys the message that she and her son can "just

as well go it alone" because men are unnecessary elements within family life."[13]

So, take heed, and don't be overly protective—or anxious. Allow your son to be a boy, help him celebrate his masculinity, and take precautions to not overindulge him due to guilt feelings that can often manifest in overcompensation for his lack of a dad. Try to make decisions calmly, use common sense, and be mindful of the warning signs mentioned here. If you feel as if you need some outside help, please see the resources listed in chapter 12.

9. We see some things in our daughter that are causing us some concern about her sexual identity. Are we being overly sensitive, or do we need to seek some help?

Few people have studied the issue of gender identity more than Dr. Joseph and Linda Nicolosi, the authors of *A Parent's Guide to Preventing Homosexuality*. Dr. Nicolosi is a clinical psychologist and the current president of the National Association for Research and Therapy of Homosexuality (NARTH). The Nicolosis' succinct list of questions will help parents assess the possibility of unhealthy development in girls.

The following is a list of questions for parents who suspect that their daughter may be gender-confused. Reflect on the following questions, then discuss them with your spouse and, if possible, with a qualified therapist. This list will not fit all pre-lesbian girls, since the roots of lesbianism are more complex than those for male homosexuality, but they do provide an important starting point:

1. Is your daughter markedly gender-atypical?

2. Does she reject her sexual anatomy?

3. Does she go to her mother with questions? Does she ask her mother to do things with her? Does she show Mom her toys, games, and activities, or does she prefer to go to Dad? Does she have a warm, comfortable relationship with Mom? Does she enjoy doing "girl things" with her mother?

4. To what extent does your daughter interact and relate comfortably with other girls?

5. Does your daughter adamantly reject the possibility that she will grow up to be married and have children someday?

6. How early and how often have you observed any of the following behaviors?

—dressing like a boy and refusing any girls' clothes

—opposite-sex gestures and mannerisms, including voice inflection

—preferring opposite-sex toys and activities

—rejecting or having no interest in girls and their games

—insistence on using a boy's name

7. Does her father encourage the girl in developing her femininity?[14]

I hope these questions will help you evaluate your concerns. Remember that not all cross-gender interests need cause panic, so be careful not to humiliate your daughter because of an occasional episode. Watch for the frequency and the duration of such activities. Don't worry if she walks around the house in Daddy's shoes. But if she continues doing this month after month, insisting that you buy her boys' clothes, then you may need to look for some outside counsel or assistance. Reassure her as a young girl. Showing and telling her how you value her femininity will go a long way toward helping your little girl find her place in the world of women.

10. Our daughter just told us she's gay. What do we do first?

I'm glad you're taking the time to become informed before responding. The intense emotions that accompany an announcement like this can often cloud your responses as parents. Harsh actions rarely breed the kind of dialogue that's needed. Instead, they create distance in the relationship that can be almost impossible to overcome. Let me offer five practical things to do to direct your emotions in a more positive way.

1. *Take a deep breath—then listen and learn.*

The first thing to do, once you recover from the initial shock, is to locate as many pertinent resources as you can. (See chapter 12 for a complete guide to recommended resources.) Find books and other resources that address the development of homosexuality. Educating yourself on the contributing factors of same-sex attraction may be very enlightening. It may also be very painful.

Facing the factors that may have contributed to your child's struggle—whether peer ridicule, sexual abuse, or the most painful of all, your own involvement—can be more than some parents can take, especially when they've just gotten the news. If the pain becomes more than you can bear and you find yourself needing to set these books aside for a while, don't feel guilty.

But understanding the genesis of your child's homosexuality can do a lot of things for you—both good and bad: It can give you greater empathy, bring about (or eliminate) feelings of guilt, certify that "gut feeling" that made you uncomfortable about "that one relationship," or encourage dialogue about sexual abuse.

Whatever the particulars of your case, at some point you're going to have to face the reality of your child's struggle if you seek any resolution in your own heart and, more importantly, in the relationship with your child. If you need time to learn, assimilate, and process this information, that's fine—but don't use that as an excuse to avoid conversation. Nothing is more uncomfortable than walking around the "giant pink elephant" in the living room. Acknowledge your need for time to process this news, and when you're ready, invite the conversation. Remember that your child has feelings too and may need some feedback or reassurance from you. "If your child is experiencing same-sex attraction, feels shame and fear about that, and is concerned about whether you would reject them, listen to their fears," advise Mark Yarhouse and Lori Burkett in their book, *Sexual Identity: A Guide to Living in the Time Between the Times.* "Listen for their story, and provide your child with assurances of your love, followed by actions that clearly reinforce what you have verbally communicated."[15]

2. *Give yourself permission to grieve.*

I've already acknowledged the grief that often accompanies a child's disclosure of homosexuality, but I'm going to let Anita Worthen, one of my dearest friends and coauthor of the book *Someone I Love Is Gay*, add her important perspective. Anita isn't just speculating about what you're going through—she's been there, and she's well acquainted with the guilt that often paralyzes parents of gay children.

> Parents are prime candidates for guilt. To their anguish, a child has gone astray. Soon they are stuck in the "if only" syndrome: If only they had been a better parent...if only they had become a Christian earlier in life...if only they had lived their faith more consistently.... The list is endless. Thousands of condemning thoughts plague our minds when things derail. Suddenly we are filled with insights on how we could have (perhaps) prevented this latest tragedy.
>
> There are specific issues around which parents feel guilt. Let's look at the most common.
>
> *"I was an imperfect parent."* This is true. But *all* parents make mistakes. So welcome to the human race! You are no different from any other parent. And let's face the facts here: Some kids from the worst homes come out smelling like roses.
>
> All of us have read stories of abused or underprivileged children who have grown up to become famous surgeons, lawyers or pastors. Against all odds, these kids have survived and gone on to make huge successes of their lives.
>
> We also hear about the child from the "perfect" home who dropped out of school and got arrested for using illegal drugs. How is that person's mother coping?...
>
> Parents of homosexual children carry a lot of shame. Despite the huge gains that have been made in terms of pro-gay activism, the majority of people in our society still disapprove of homosexuality. And parents share the stigma of their child's sexual behavior. This is particularly true for parents who belong to conservative Christian churches....
>
> *"I caused my child's homosexuality."* This statement is totally false and is probably the biggest lie you will have to stand against.

No one person has the power to cause another's homosexuality. At worst, a parent-child relationship may be *one factor* in a whole group of complex influences.

So it's not fair to blame parents as *the* cause of their child's homosexuality. At the same time, some parents go to the other extreme and insist that family factors have absolutely nothing to do with their child's struggles. Actually, the truth lies somewhere in between, and the situation is different for every family.[16]

Someone I Love Is Gay is a must-read for anyone facing the acknowledgement of a loved one's homosexuality. On this topic of grieving, I highly recommend the chapter "The Grief Cycle: Surviving the Emotional Turmoil."

3. *Find some support.*

You aren't the only person in the world who has a gay loved one. You aren't the only one embarrassed by this. You aren't the only one hurting. If you don't believe me, maybe I can persuade you by sharing one parent's story.

After giving my testimony at a homosexuality conference, I was approached by a mother I will never forget. While struggling to maintain her composure, she told me, "Before I got here today, I didn't feel like I could go on. I've lived the last couple of days closed up in my bedroom. I've closed the blinds, I've turned off the phone. There was no way I could face the world. Last week my daughter told me she was gay." This must have been the first time this dear lady let herself say the words out loud, because her sobs became uncontrollable. When they subsided, the truth of her next words pierced my heart. "She's my only child…my only daughter. There may never be a wedding, I may never have grandchildren. I know things may never change, but just being here today amongst others that I know are hurting like me has given me the ability to go on."

You aren't suffering alone. If you behave as though you are, you have no one to blame but yourself. A very strong network of support is at your disposal. Focus on the Family can provide resources, counseling, and prayer. Exodus International can help you understand the root causes of homosexuality and offer hope and healing to those who want to overcome same-sex attraction—and their loved ones. And Parents and Friends of Ex-gays (P-FOX) can connect you with a support group near you.

You may feel ashamed. You may be afraid other people will find out. These feelings are hard to handle, but the weight of suffering alone is far more detrimental. One of the most important lessons I've learned through my healing process is that *healthy people ask for what they need.* You must admit your need, make yourself vulnerable, and ask for help. Whether you need a friend's shoulder to cry on, understanding from another parent who's been where you are, or just someone to bounce ideas off of, *ask for help.*

4. *Examine your expectations.*

We often live up to our parents' expectations, whether good or bad. In light of that, the only suggestion I have to offer regarding finding out about your child's homosexuality is to pray for the best and prepare for the worst. Parents rarely want their children to grow up to become homosexuals, and your greatest desire is probably for your child to leave the gay lifestyle. People have left homosexuality, but be wary of allowing your hope to become an expectation. Such expectations feel more like commands to your child, and those feelings will strain your relationship. In their book, *Sexual Identity,* Mark Yarhouse and Lori Burkett underscore this truth:

> With the recent ads from ex-gay ministries citing examples of people changing their sexual orientation, some parents may have the unrealistic expectations that their child can make a complete change in their sexual orientation. Sending this message to your child may set them up for feelings of failure and rejection, especially if they continue to invest time and financial and emotional resources in professional treatment or paraprofessional ministry to facilitate change. Even among those who are highly motivated to experience change, there are no easy answers or pat formulas to remove every vestige of same-sex attraction. Avoid blaming your child and using "if only" statements, such as "If you would only do what they tell you, you would get better," "If you didn't hang

around _____, you wouldn't have this problem," or "If you would only begin to wear makeup and fix yourself up."[17]

Some of those "if only" statements may contain a trace of truth, but expressing them can do far more damage than good. Don't allow your expectations to hinder God's gentle conviction from doing its work.

God's truth rings forth for each person: "I have set before you life and death, blessing and curses. Now choose life" (Deuteronomy 30:19). But you must soberly assess the fact that few who struggle with homosexuality ultimately choose life and blessing.

However, children who desire help in addressing their same-sex attractions and are blessed with the safe and honest support of family often experience accelerated progress.

5. Pray.

God's Word states that "the prayer of a righteous man is powerful and effective" (James 5:16). This is a truth that you as a parent must always stand on. Never cease to pray, regardless of how tiresome your burden may seem. I truly believe that I walk today in the forgiveness that I received because of the prayers of my family, especially those of my grandmother.

Still, this Scripture must be seen in light of the words just preceding it: "Confess your sins to each other and pray for each other so that you may be healed." Your loved one must confess his or her sin for healing to take place. If you see no apparent possibility for repentance on his or her part, then that's where your prayers can begin.

11. My 14-year-old has just "come out." He is attending the Gay-Straight Alliance at his high school, and he wants to date other boys. Should I force him to go to counseling?

I often receive calls from parents wanting me to meet with their son or daughter regarding their child's newfound "gayness." The first thing I try to help the parents understand is that unless their child wants to meet with me, our time together is going to be unproductive. However, I've yet to refuse to meet with any teen at least once. When a teenager is brought to me "kicking and screaming," I tell the parents and the child that forced counseling rarely works, and I help the parents to see that the best thing they can do is seek help and support for themselves.

Many factors are at play in the mind of any adolescent who has just "come out." And Dr. Joseph Nicolosi, who has worked with hundreds of young men, realizes the uphill battle boys this age can face. He reiterates that

> treatment before the early twenties has its particular difficulties. The teenager is experiencing his sexual drive at its most intense, and after years of secrecy, isolation, and alienation, most young men find the gay world powerfully alluring, with its romantic, sensual, outrageous, and embracing qualities. At the same time that libidinal drive is at its highest, personal identity is at its most fragile. At this time the adolescent wants to experiment. Although he may later have a change of heart, to propose a treatment requiring self-reflection, conviction, and self-denial is almost more than he can bear.[18]

One step that can still be effective is letting your son know that there is another option. The Lord promises that His truth will never return void (Isaiah 55:11 KJV), and with this promise behind me I am always willing to give my testimony, knowing that I'm planting seeds which may help him see that change is possible. For this reason, you may want to locate a local Exodus International ministry to have your son speak with an ex-gay man who can share the reality of his freedom from homosexuality.

Besides this, what are you as a parent to do? Reassert yourself as the parent. Over and over in the book of Proverbs, we see that children are called to obey and fathers are expected to teach (1:8; 2:1; 3:1; 4:1; 5:1; 7:1). You cannot compromise your beliefs or values and allow your dependent child to make decisions contrary to the moral standards of your home. Things will get rough, but you cannot allow immorality to go unaddressed. Therefore, you must not tolerate his attendance at any "gay affirmative" group or club. These groups will further condone his behavior, affirm his false identity, and work against any possibility of repentance.

Please never lose hope. While he might not be ready now, I've met with many boys who have come back to me years later, desiring to leave their unfulfilling gay life behind. Remember this:

> The average age for a homosexual client entering reparative therapy is early twenties or early thirties. Many other therapists have made the observation that this is the age group most receptive to treatment (Bieber 1962, Mayerson and Lief 1965, Rubenstein 1958). This is the time of young adulthood, when friends are getting married and family is exerting pressure to do likewise....Social pressure, however, is not the only impetus. This is a time when the natural desire to enter into an exclusive relationship is most intensely felt and when the choice must be made for either isolation or adult intimacy (Erickson 1958). One must now make a lifelong relational commitment, and one must know what gender that partner will be.[19]

So set your boundaries now and never cease praying for repentance. Though change may never occur, it's most likely in the twenties and thirties. Pray toward these windows of opportunity and take the time (which may seem to be longer than any parent could endure) to research, prepare, and locate support should your son make a decision to turn his life in God's direction.

There are some great resources for teens who need help, support, or just to "kick the tires." Exodus Youth (EY) and www.livehope.org[20] are two great resources geared toward your questioning teen.

I also recommend two great resources for any parent setting boundaries and offering tough, bold love. The first is called *Bound by Honor: Fostering a Great Relationship with Your Teen* by Gary Smalley and Dr. Greg Smalley.[21] The second is *Those Turbulent Teen Years: Hope for Parents* by Jeenie Gordon.[22]

12. My son just told me he is gay. He says he's finally accepted who he is and that he's never been happier. Can this really be true?

What we might think about your son's experience isn't what's at issue here. The important consideration—the only consideration, really—is how your son views this experience. Here's why:

Society has silenced any message of hope regarding change from homosexuality, and the church hasn't stepped boldly up to the plate either. So individuals with same-sex attractions have been left to fend for themselves. When the pain of denial, hiding, or repression becomes so heated the pot begins to boil and the top is blown right off, men and women "come out" and express a newfound "freedom" like never before.

I can say from experience that this move truly does make you feel as if you've finally stopped the façade and you are living true to yourself. So your son is actually being more honest with himself and those around him than ever before. He no doubt feels that he has found a community that understands him (which they do), accepts him (which they do), and doesn't judge him (which they don't). He's fulfilling the desires of his flesh and not having to hide his sexual desires. He may indeed feel happier than he has at any other time in his life.

The key for your son in the weeks and months to come is for him to realize it is not too late to turn back. This is where the church and loved ones like you come in. If he hears that change is possible, that he was not "made" this way, and that he is loved within godly boundaries even if his lifestyle choices don't change immediately, there is hope that when the feeling of relief wears off and the emptiness sets in, he will try to live his life in line with God's will.

In the meantime, I advise you to pray that he becomes as miserable as possible, as soon as possible, and that God will protect him through it.

13. We recently learned that my brother is gay. He wants to tell *everyone!* What should we do?

Frankly, you may not have much to say about this. He may be trying to embarrass you, especially if he has sensed for years that homosexuality was the taboo of all taboos in your home. The silent pain he has endured for years and the feelings of shame he's experienced at every flippant comment made about homosexuality have come to a boil. The result? He's ripped down the door of his "closet" and thrown it into the street for everyone to see.

Why would he do this? To take control of the situation (which feels very out of control—and more than likely is) and to feel empowered. If he can "strike the first blow," the "enemy" (that's you, in his eyes) may not be able to fight as hard. And this is what he expects. Leaving a situation in anger is much easier than facing the pain and heartache he is causing his family by making choices he knows they cannot and will not support.

When this gets difficult, take a deep breath and practice self-control. Don't do anything to fuel the situation. If you're at a loss for a way to respond, doing nothing is better than making the situation worse by adding gas to the blazing fire. His emotions are running high—as are yours. Take the time to regroup as a family (apart from him), seek support, and come back together with a game plan that will benefit all involved.

Most importantly, never stop fighting for him. Remember that the most effective weapon you have is prayer.

14. Our child came out to us 14 months ago. Most of our friends and church family do not know. We've asked him to stay silent. Is this right?

When family members become aware of a child's struggle with homosexuality, they are riddled with emotions such as guilt and shame. These emotions are often the fuel behind the family's efforts to live in silence and hide their pain or embarrassment. The energy this takes, however, is unproductive, unhealthy, and misguided.

I'm not suggesting a need to "shout it from the mountaintops," but by not seeking support, encouragement, and help from those around you, you'll soon begin to feel as though you are drowning in your feelings and emotions—all alone. Do yourself a favor and allow the body of Christ to minister to you, pray with you, and show you godly empathy by rejoicing with you when you rejoice and mourning with you when you mourn (Romans 12:15). If your church is not a safe place to seek this type of caring support, you must find it somewhere else.

Grant your child the courtesy of knowing whom you've told and when you've told them. This is especially true when he or she may come in contact with those you've confided in. When these individuals show him or her respect, kindness, and love, the impact will be powerful. No longer can your son or daughter say, "If they really knew my secret, they wouldn't treat me like this."

---

15. We are rebuilding our relationship with our son, but we never speak of his homosexuality. How should we bring it up—or should we?

My short answer: Yes. My longer answer: Yes, yes, yes, yes, yes!

Nothing is unhealthier than denial and avoidance. When everyone walks around the elephant in the middle of the living room, or people make a mad dash to turn off the television every time a gay-themed sitcom or commercial airs (and to do that these days would require daily replacement of the remote-control batteries!), you need to face up to your family's inherent weakness. You have spoken a message—explicitly or implicitly—that you must avoid uncomfortable subjects.

Silence in these situations could be construed by others as approval of your son's behavior. I once counseled a family whose youngest daughter did just that. "Mom and Dad take us to church every Sunday. They've always taught us right from wrong, so how can they support Dylan's homosexuality?" In reality, this young girl's parents were adamantly opposed to Dylan's homosexuality.

You are responsible as the leaders of the family to break the ice and the "silence" rule. Find resources that will help you address the crisis head-on. (Reading this book is a start in the right direction.) Then call a family meeting—without your homosexual son if he doesn't live in your home—and open the dialogue, taking comfort in the fact that you've done your homework and can guide a productive discussion.

Let your gay son know that this meeting will be taking place. Reassure him that his absence is not rejection but meant to let the other family members be as honest as possible. Encourage your family with a plan that you believe will best ensure redemption and repentance. Allow all your family members to express their feelings. Validate their emotions, but redirect conclusions that you believe to be out of line. Let everyone know you have talked to your son, he's aware of this meeting, and any further family gatherings will include all members unless special situations arise.

If your child is still living at home, organize a similar meeting, but be prepared for it to unfold quite differently. Encourage openness and honesty, but make sure to protect everyone by dealing with snide or hurtful comments properly. On the other hand, don't allow silence. Draw the quiet family members out. Take the bull by the horns and address awkward situations, knowing that other family members are feeling uncomfortable too. This process will be hard and may feel very foreign, but you will soon begin to realize the freedom available to families who choose to live in the light (Ephesians 5:8).

16. How can I inform my parents that I have embraced my sexuality and am not ready to change? I tried the whole "change thing" for a while, but I'm just not ready. How do I let them know without hurting or offending them?

I understand your desire to not hurt or offend your family, but hiding the issue is prolonging the inevitable. You aren't doing your family any favors by not being honest with them. This is especially true if your parents' greatest hope is that you will leave homosexuality. If you are feeding into their hopes, please stop. Proverbs 13:12 says that "hope deferred makes the heart sick"—and you aren't doing anything but delaying the hope that for them may never come. You need to allow your family to grieve.

Imagine that you've just fallen overboard a large ship engulfed in a heavy fog. Your parents hear you yelling from the ship, "I'm over here, 50 feet off the starboard side!" They attempt to save you by tossing you a 50-foot lifeline, hoping you'll grab on and they can pull you to the safety of the deck. But in reality you are 100 feet from the port side, frolicking in the warmth of the tropical waters. Your parents are frantic—"Why can't we get this rope to him?" "Why can't we reach her?" In their panic, they decide to jump in, risking their own lives to locate you.

This isn't much different than what's going on in your home. You appear to be headed in the direction your parents wish for you, but you are actually nowhere near their hopes. They are diligently working for an outcome they believe you both desire. They're researching, asking for forgiveness, attending conferences, praying, and seeking counsel, but nothing seems to be changing. They're chasing a mirage that you're helping to perpetuate. You owe it to them to clarify the situation. They may continue doing many of the things they were doing before, but at least they will have the opportunity to adjust the length and the location of the lifeline they are trying to get to you. And you may prevent them from having a sick heart.

---

17. Whenever I'm around my son, I feel the need to minister to him regarding his poor choices. But I seem to be driving him away. What do you suggest?

First, let me say that I understand you love your child more than any other person and that your greatest desire for him is to follow Christ and live a fulfilling life. But "ministering" to him every time he's around is only going to drive a wedge between you and push him further away from any impact you're hoping to have with him. If he thinks that every time he comes to see you he's going to get a three-point sermon on the evils of homosexuality, he's eventually going to stop visiting altogether.

If I were a betting man, I'd bet money that your son already knows without a scintilla of uncertainty where you stand on homosexuality. If arguing about this is endangering your relationship with him, I would ask you to reconsider your definition of "ministering." Focus instead on nurturing the relationship. Show interest in his career, ask about his latest vacation, or simply enjoy your time with him over dinner. Don't make homosexuality the focus of every conversation you have.

In Paul's letter to the Romans, he put forth a challenge you might want to meditate on: "If it is possible, as far as it depends on you, live at peace with everyone" (Romans 12:18). If you alienate your son, where will he go when he, like the prodigal, comes to his senses? If home hasn't felt safe, loving, and accepting (not of his homosexuality but of *him*) then that's the last place he's going to want to return.

> **18. I feel the need to write my grandson, who recently announced his homosexuality, because he doesn't call or visit. I've sent devotionals, written out Bible passages, and tried to encourage him to change, assuring him of my love and encouraging him to keep in contact. I pray for him daily. Can I do anything more concrete?**

Yes, there is something concrete you can do: *Stop!* Your motives are obviously pure, but you are actually having the opposite effect than you hoped for: You are driving your grandson further away from you, and from the healing power of Jesus.

If your grandson knows you are a Christian or he has been raised in the church, he already knows what the Bible says about homosexuality. If he also knows that every time he hears from you or sees you he's going to hear about the "evils of homosexuality" or of "Eleanor's grandson who's changed," he's going to run fast and far.

I encourage you to do two things—one you've already alluded to. Never stop praying that the Holy Spirit will convict him and that he will realize the hope that the cross of Christ offers him. My second recommendation is much more difficult. Pick up the phone, call him, and ask for forgiveness. Assure him that your love for him will never stop but that your ineffective ways of expressing that love to him most certainly will. Then ask him how you might do a better job of showing your love for him. He'll probably suggest you simply accept his homosexuality. You cannot do that, given God's view of such behavior, but you surely can accept *him* and lay aside your need to prove to him the error of his ways.

I've offered you some tough counsel, so let me leave you with a little encouragement. Please never doubt that your grandson needs you. I know this is true because my fingers type out these words today—the words of a man who has walked away from homosexuality—in a large measure due to the prayers of my 99-year-old grandmother, who continues to lay me at the feet of her Savior daily. Thank you, Grammy Cross!

---

19. How should we respond to our son who wants to bring his live-in "significant other" to spend the weekend in our home? We've been asking them to stay in a motel, but that has just led to our son not visiting at all.

This is a question often asked by families with a loved one who has proclaimed his or her homosexuality. A child's first couple of visits home with a same-sex partner can be a jolting experience for everybody, one that will require all the wisdom you and your other family members can muster.

Consider the parable of the prodigal son (Luke 15). When the prodigal "came to his senses," he went home. He wouldn't have done that unless he thought it would be safe—that someone would be there to joyfully welcome him. Many homosexuals don't believe they have welcoming homes to run to, and in fact, many of them don't. Here's the dilemma: Your child's gay friends are not going to encourage righteousness, so where will he see authenticity that contrasts with the counterfeit life he's living? At home.

That's why the first thing to do is to talk the situation over as a family. Are all family members aware of the situation? If they're not, do they need to be? Have those who should know had a chance to share their feelings about the potential visit? The bottom line is that regardless of the decision you make, it must be a *family decision*.

Once the family makes a decision, all family members must present a united front. If you decide to let your son and his partner stay overnight in your home, the family members who are uncomfortable with that decision should seriously consider whether they want to take part in the gathering. Conflicting messages from family members, especially family members who profess to be Christians, can drive a wedge between you and your son at the very time you're trying to demonstrate your love for him.

When my family faced this very question during my years in homosexuality, they joyfully welcomed me home for holidays and other visits. As a matter of fact, I could come home anytime I wanted—with or without my partner. However, I was asked to maintain the moral standards of their homes at all times: I was not allowed to sleep in the same bedroom as my boyfriend or show physical affection to him in front of my niece and nephews. My family made sure I knew this was a decision based on *their morals*, not *my homosexuality*. They would have asked me to do the same if I had brought home a woman I was dating but not married to.

It was easy to respect that decision, and I felt respected by their explanation of it. And I wasn't the only one impacted by the love my family showed me. One of my partners later decided to leave homosexuality and pursue holiness because of the unconditional love my family showed him. Here's a tough question: Would your family be ready to love, nurture, and accept your child's partner if he or she left homosexuality—*and your child didn't?*

Let me leave you with this: Tolerance is a two-way street, and it's perfectly fine for you to ask your son and his partner to extend to you the same tolerance they expect from you—until you have had sufficient time to process and pray through his request.

20. We've decided to allow our daughter and her partner to come for family visits. We have young children, and a couple of younger nieces and nephews might be present. What should we tell them?

God directs every parent to protect, nurture, encourage, and educate children about things that are right, wrong, just, fair, healthy, and sinful. A visit from a same-sex sister or aunt and her partner can be an incredible opportunity, a truly teachable moment for a child. Just think of all the different facets of God's character that you can demonstrate when you approach this opportunity with prayerful and insightful consideration.

But remember that you can't make that decision for other people's children. You must either include your siblings and other loved ones in the decision-making process or at least tell them of your plans so they can decide whether they want to expose their sons and daughters to a potentially awkward situation.

Many parents will decide that allowing their children to be around such a situation is too dangerous. In fact, concern about how kids will be affected is the number one reason gay loved ones aren't allowed to visit home. But parents also need to be aware that refusing to address the topic with their children at all might also be dangerous. Families faced with a loved one's homosexuality are often thrown into disarray and emotional turmoil. Children raised in these environments are often very perceptive and inquisitive, especially when they sense tension, confusion, or discomfort from those that they love. Avoiding their questions or concerns, or promising to answer them later and never getting around to it, can allow children to develop inaccurate ideas about sex and sexuality and can squelch their budding sense of discernment.

Parents who do agree to let their young children experience such a visit should explain the situation to them well in advance, and even then they may take some time to be ready to be in the presence of the gay loved one and her partner. This process will require diligence; parents should not allow their discomfort, or the discomfort of their child when dealing with this issue, to overshadow the need for continued education.

A few good resources can help parents discuss this issue with their children. For kids in grades three to five, I recommend *Mommy, Why Are They Holding Hands?* by Deborah Phrihoda. This book sensitively deals with the issue of homosexuality by telling a story of a little girl named Sarah and the questions she asks her family. It "systematically builds layer upon layer to assist you in preparing a complete, solid, biblical basis for formulating your beliefs and passing them on to your children."[23]

If your children are older, another excellent resource is *Celebrating God's Design* by Don Schmierer. This book is "a unique new curriculum series that takes a balanced and biblical look at important youth issues including gender confusion, tolerance and challenging family dynamics."[24]

My wife and I had an experience at Christmastime that illustrates some of the principles I've been discussing. We had been teaching our elder son, Bennett, about the dangers of smoking. When we gathered with our extended family, Bennett came to my wife and said, "Mommy, why does Aunt Tracye smoke?" This provided a perfect opportunity for us to show him that Mommy and Daddy love Aunt Tracye but aren't happy that she smokes. We compared her smoking to the things he might do that we've asked him not to. We don't want him to do those things, just like God doesn't want Aunt Tracye to smoke—it's hurting her body, and God loves her enough to tell her, "Don't do that."

Bennett's question wasn't about homosexuality, but if it had been, we would have explained God's truth on the subject to him in a similar fashion. If children ask, don't be afraid to sit with them and show them what the Bible says about homosexuality. Show them that it's not God's original intention for mankind and that God wishes their loved one was behaving differently, but He still loves them enough to have given His own life for them.

Dr. James Dobson, one of America's leading authorities on raising children, suggests that regarding sex education, "The best approach is one that begins casually and naturally in early childhood and extends through the years, according to a policy of openness, frankness, and honesty. Only parents can provide this lifetime training—being there when the questions arise and the desire for information is evidenced."[25] But he warns that parents must be careful. "One of the most common mistakes made by parents and many overzealous educators is teaching too much too soon....Furthermore, it is unwise to place the youngster on an informational timetable that will result in full awareness too early in life."[26] He continues by providing a helpful guideline.

> Generally speaking, children should be given the information they need at a particular age....Admittedly, this ideal timetable can be turned upside down by exposure to precocious friends, racy videos, or unwise adults. When that occurs, you have to cope with the fallout as best as possible. It is regrettable that we expose our vulnerable children to far too much of the wrong kind of sexuality.[27]

Dr. Dobson continues by suggesting the time when this type of education is often too late. "You should plan to end your formal instructional program about the time your son or daughter enters puberty (the time of rapid sexual development in early adolescence). Puberty usually begins between ten and thirteen for girls and between eleven and fourteen for boys. Once they enter this developmental period, they are typically embarrassed by discussions of sex with their parents."[28] But if issues of sexuality arise, please don't leave them unaddressed. Embarrassing or not, you need to make sure that your children understand a biblical definition of sexuality, especially as it pertains to sexuality outside of His plan.

For further help with talking to your developing child, read *Preparing for Adolescence* by Dr. James Dobson. It provides a wealth of helpful advice and information.[29]

21. We are expecting an invitation to my cousin's "wedding" or "commitment ceremony" next July. We are the only Christians in the family, and I sense "all eyes are on us." Can you suggest a very loving response? I feel attending would be showing support for the union. Are we wrong for not wanting to attend?

In today's cultural climate—with traditional marriage under siege from gay activists intent on redefining this institution as something other than the union of one man and one woman—the answer for any Christian should be "No, thank you." That's not to say, however, that the decision is easy to carry out. Many people I've talked to have experienced great heartache when faced with what feels like a choice between pleasing the Lord and accepting a loved one.

The triune God instituted marriage when He created man and woman, in His image, to be complementary to one another. Jesus showed His blessing on marriage when He performed His first miracle at a wedding. Marriage is a sacred relationship and a symbol of man's relationship to God. We should not support attempts to subvert the sanctity of that union.

However, simply declining the invitation is not enough. If you want to build on the relationship between you, your family member (or friend), and his or her partner, discuss the matter with them. Invite them for coffee or a meal and let them know your absence at their ceremony is not intended to create a rift between you (though it potentially can). Explain that your decision is based on principle, not a judgment on them as individuals. Help them understand the true definition of tolerance—"sympathy for beliefs or practices differing from or conflicting with one's own"[30]—and ask them to extend that to you as well.

Family and friends may judge your actions as unloving, but they have accepted a morally relative belief system with no absolutes. If you were to adhere to society's definition of tolerance, you would end up tolerating everything and ultimately standing for nothing. As representatives of Christ and His truth, we must be willing to sometimes appear intolerant if we hope to remain principled.

22. How do I talk my husband out of his belief that he is homosexual?

Your question has no magic answer, no single argument or line of logic that has the power to change his mind.

As a matter of fact, if his "coming out" is relatively recent, your chance of reaching him may be virtually nil—at least for now (and barring God's miraculous intervention). I'm sure you've heard some people from the gay community talk about the "freedom" they feel—

how "coming out" has filled them with a sense of power or elation and given them a new life. This new experience can feel invigorating when one has lived in a permanent state of denial. Many a man has erroneously married, some even being counseled to do so, thinking that a "good woman" will take care of his "condition." Marrying is potentially the worst thing a man or woman struggling with sexual identity can do. Denying the severity of a homosexual struggle by attempting to "cover" it through marriage can be damaging for everyone involved.

So when your husband grew tired of living what felt to him to have been a lie, he probably kicked the door of the closet down and came out with a vengeance. In the midst of this turmoil, you desperately reach for something to do. You might need to stop trying—for now. Lest we forget the power of sin, Scripture reminds us that sin is pleasurable for a short time (Hebrews 11:25). And sometimes nothing can stop his pursuit of this newfound pleasure.

An analogy might help. Let's say that an elephant that had been captured has just escaped. In an attempt to recapture the escapee, the zookeeper steps in front of the animal. What happens next, in all probability, is that the zookeeper, not the elephant, will get hurt. Similarly, trying to stop your loved one at this stage of the game is often futile—and you might be putting yourself in harm's way emotionally.

Often, the best thing to do in a situation like this is to seek some godly counsel for yourself, focusing especially on setting boundaries. While your husband "runs wild," pray continually that he becomes tired, convicted, and restored.

I highly recommend that you read *Boundaries* by Dr. Henry Cloud and Dr. John Townsend.[31]

23. My spouse just left me for a homosexual relationship. *Help!*

Words cannot express how distressing this situation can be. Finding out that a son or daughter is struggling with homosexuality is tough, but many parents in that situation have one another for comfort, understanding, and support. When husbands or wives "come out," however, the heterosexual spouse has lost the one person he or she would most hope to turn to.

Feelings of isolation, betrayal, and grief are absolutely to be expected—and absolutely too weighty for anyone to carry alone. If your spouse has sworn you to secrecy or you're trying to avoid embarrassment or shame, you must realize that wrestling with this by yourself is not an option. You must seek support. Your spouse would be selfish to make you promise confidentiality, and the secrecy could be very unhealthy for you. You need to revisit this promise with your spouse; let him or her know you need a sounding board—the compassion of another in whom you can confide.

For Wives

Once the pain of silence becomes greater than the impending fear of embarrassment, a wife may turn to her mother, a sister, or a close female friend. These relatives and friends can offer vital support, but any woman must be prayerful about the advice of those with a superficial understanding of this issue. Ill-advised, emotionally charged advice can damage an already raw or shaky foundation. Comments like "How can you stay with him?" or "You need to get as far away as fast as you can" don't mirror God's character or your commitment to the vows you made before Him and your spouse.

So a woman in this situation should prayerfully consider who would be best to confide in. Close friends and relatives may seem the most obvious choices, but those closest to you are not always the best. Besides, your husband may not be able to bear knowing that those closest to you now perceive him as "the enemy." This tension may distance him from some of his dearest relationships. If, however, you do confide in someone that is a mutual friend or relation, your husband has a right to know. Nothing can be more damaging than having to constantly wonder who knows what at social gatherings or family get-togethers.

For Husbands

A husband whose wife has admitted to having a homosexual struggle is likely to react in one or both of these ways: He may try to avoid the situation, and he may try to "fix it."

The wound for a man who now feels as though he's not been good enough for his wife can be devastating. He may seek affirmation in his vocation or in the arms of another woman. But his masculinity is not what's being challenged. It's his attention to his wife's feminine needs. A man must not allow his masculine strivings to prejudice his actions. Being more attentive to her sexually will not win her back. Instead, a man can woo his wife with appropriate emotive responses that take into consideration her feminine makeup. He must not allow his pride to keep him from seeking knowledgeable support. A healthy third-party perspective can bring a fresh breeze to what can feel like a suffocating reality.

Men, don't be fooled into believing that if your wife's relationship with another woman hasn't become physical, it isn't destructive. She may never commit sexual adultery, but her emotional infidelity can wreak havoc on your marriage.

Is Separation Okay?

Whether you're the husband or the wife of someone who is acting out homosexually, the inevitable question of commitment comes into play: *Should I stay or should I go?* This decision should never be based on your emotions. Only assess this option with prayerful, godly counsel.

I counseled one woman who asked this question, and after much prayer and deliberation I asked her, "Betty, are you able to influence him spiritually? You know him better than anyone else—his weaknesses, his strengths, his vulnerabilities, and his fears. God will show you how to minister to him—and how to love him in a way others may never be able to. As painful as this may be, God sees your pain and will give you the strength and ability to love and forgive him. Can you do that?"

Another motivating factor may be your children. God hates divorce (Malachi 2:16). He allows it under certain circumstances, but it's never His intention. His very nature exemplifies reconciliation and forgiveness, and He showed that on the cross. He hates divorce not only because of how it will affect you and your husband but also for the damage it can do to your children. You must take them into consideration. In fact, they may be the sole reason you seek to forgive, for knowing how much they love you both and how devastating a divorce could be.

However, you are not being noble if you are subjecting yourself to emotional, physical, sexual, or spiritual abuse. We are not to become doormats in the name of Christianity. Godly humility is far different from humiliation.

Can separation ever be a viable consideration? Yes, but always with the godly intention of reconciliation. This step must never be considered lightly. It's a serious measure and requires the help and support of a pastor, counselor, or marriage therapist whose ministry or practice is aligned with sound biblical teaching.

In their book *Someone I Love Is Gay*, Anita Worthen and Bob Davies give a helpful list of symptoms that may indicate that separation is an option to consider:

1. The gay spouse is spending a lot of unaccountable time away from the family.

2. The gay spouse appears to have given up trying to solve the homosexual problem. One lesbian wife flaunted her "special friendship" with another woman to her husband and refused to heed his pleas to separate.

3. The gay spouse (especially in the case of a husband) shows a constant disregard for his partner's physical and sexual health. Both men and women can bring incurable diseases into the marriage from another sexual partner. For example, the husband can infect his wife with HIV, which is fatal.

4. The gay spouse blames his or her partner for all the problems occurring in the marriage and refuses rational discussion.

5. The gay spouse is engaging in other destructive behavior, such as heavy drinking or illegal drug usage.

6. The gay spouse exhibits a pattern of habitual deception. "I hated the lying more than his running around," said one wife. "I began to doubt my discernment. I would confront my husband and he'd retort, 'How could you think such a thing about me?'" Later, his

wife discovered that her suspicions were correct. Her husband was not ready to change his ways.[32]

For further guidance in this difficult time, I recommend a great book by Dr. James Dobson titled *Love Must Be Tough*.[33]

24. To what extent should a homosexual father, living with another man, be involved in the lives of his children?

Several considerations apply in this situation. The first is that children need their dad. The pain of his absence can far outweigh the pain of his lifestyle. Remember that "homosexuality is not 'caught' from a gay parent. In fact, an affectionate father decreases a boy's vulnerability to homosexual temptation."[34]

Still, an openly homosexual father's presence in the life of his children must be carefully evaluated.

The best place to go for that evaluation is to the kids themselves. Openly and frequently address their father's homosexuality. How are they feeling? Are they overwhelmed? Are Daddy's actions making them uncomfortable? To get truthful answers to these questions, notice what they are saying when they aren't talking about it. If they are acting up or acting out in inappropriate ways, or if they have an obviously hard time being around their father and his new partner, then they probably need to be shielded from him—at least in certain situations and for a time. If the children are in danger for any reason, or if they are being exposed to graphic, inappropriate behaviors, their mother or another responsible adult may have to turn to the court system—with appropriate documentation.

If you determine that the children shouldn't spend unsupervised time with their father, explain the situation to him forthrightly as a non-negotiable reality. If he refuses to accept it—remember that some men believe that children's feelings aren't as important as "learning tolerance." Don't fall for that lie. One of the characteristics of many homosexual men is narcissism, and the children's father may be no different.

Talk with your children about God's truth and sexuality. Be careful not to talk negatively about the children's father as a man. He may be exhibiting some terrible behaviors, but dogging him isn't going to help. Focus the discussion on what God says about homosexuality and sin, and identify potential dangers that can arise from these trying circumstances. "Any ungodly influence can hinder a child's development. And some children with a gay parent experience periods of doubt about their own sexual identity."[35] Don't trust that your children aren't thinking these thoughts just because they've never uttered them. Allow for no confusion—make a conscious effort to teach them the truth of this issue.

No child comes out of such a situation without some scars and bruises, but I've met a number of incredible kids who have emerged from similar circumstances with wonderful testimonies about the sufficiency and healing power of their heavenly Father.

3

Answers for Friends

Most individuals who walk away from homosexuality do so holding the hand of a godly friend. Those with the best outcomes often have a loving and supportive family, but a friend is usually the initial catalyst the Lord uses to draw someone to the possibility of change. Unfortunately, some friends cater to or endorse another's homosexuality out of a false sense of friendship. On the other hand, few things are more effective than people who learn how to be "a friend [who] loves at all times" (Proverbs 17:17) while not being afraid to uphold God's truth that "better is open rebuke than hidden love" (Proverbs 27:5). They show their gay friends that "wounds from a friend can be trusted" (Proverbs 27:6).

To be that kind of friend, you don't need to be an expert on homosexuality. The following answers will help prepare you for the obstacles ahead and equip you to overcome them.

25. I have a hunch someone I know is struggling with homosexuality. How do I approach him about this without pushing him away?

This is one of the most difficult quandaries to be in whether you're a youth worker who suspects the struggle of one of your students, a coworker worried about a fellow employee, or the family member of someone exhibiting some troubling signs. Rest assured, though, that you can approach this situation in a way that will breed open dialogue and the opportunity for further ministry.

First, let's talk about what you *shouldn't* do: Just walk up to the person in question and blurt out, "Hey, I think you're gay. Am I right?" As ridiculous as this may sound, some people—even well-intentioned people—believe this to be their only viable option. Let me assure you, it isn't. The damage done by this approach can be irreparable. Think of the pain you can cause—especially if your suspicions prove untrue.

The best way to approach the situation is to first realize that you don't have to know the answer to this question today—or tomorrow, for that matter. A few weeks isn't going to make your friend or coworker or loved one any more or any less homosexual, if he or she is indeed struggling with same-sex attraction in the first place. In fact, you'd be wise to begin addressing the matter by educating yourself about factors that can contribute to homosexuality.

Even a superficial understanding of influences that can lead to homosexuality will give you a nonthreatening place to begin your investigation (praying all the while that your motives are pure for researching this information in the first place). Homosexuality is a manifestation of deeper issues in someone's life. Your goal should not be to expose someone's homosexuality but to unearth and minister to the underlying problems.

In his book, *You Don't Have to Be Gay*,[1] Jeff Konrad offers an enlightening visual aid of an iceberg that illustrates this. (See page 67.)

As you can see, many hidden issues can contribute to a struggle with homosexuality. If you suspect your acquaintance is flirting with homosexuality, start by exploring these issues.

Vulnerability on your part will breed vulnerability in your friend. Strengthen the trust needed in any relationship when discussing such intimate issues. Once the relationship is secure, you can address the behaviors that caused you to assume homosexuality as a problem.

If you are a youth pastor who wants to approach a youth, you could begin by saying, "Gary, I've noticed when you are at youth group you always seem to be with the girls. Have the guys done something to make you feel unwelcome or uncomfortable?" Another tack might be, "Gary, when you talk to me about your family, you light up when you talk about your mom—always making sure I understand how much you 'can't stand' your dad. Have you ever thought about how this negative relationship with your dad affects your life?" You've

HOMOSEXUAL BEHAVIOR
(*Symptom* of underlying deficiencies)

- Envy
- Misinterpretation and eroticization of homo-emotional needs into homosexual desires

---

- Feelings of masculine inadequacy
- Gender confusion
- Need for recognition of masculinity, identification, same-sex approval

---

Other unfulfilled homo-emotional needs:
- Sufficient male bonding with peers
- Male gender identification and affirmation of gender role
- Same-sex acceptance and approval
- Same-sex nonsexual love

- Insecurity in gender role
- Isolation/separation from male peers (physically and/or emotionally)

- Defensive detachment from father-figure who may be inefficient, hostile, or even absent
- Lack of proper male role model
- In most cases, insufficient bonding with the father and unfulfilled same-sex love need

---

- Feelings of being hurt, unloved and/or rejected: Even if love is offered, the boy has unconsciously blocked it from being received

---

- Overly-sensitive disposition
- Incident(s) boy interprets as intentionally hurtful
- Absent, inefficient, or hostile father/father-figure: Not necessarily how the father was, but more importantly, how the boy perceived his father's behavior as signifying a lack of love.

mentioned a few warning signs in a way that extends concern and enhances the possibility of further dialogue—possibly even a subsequent admission of homosexuality.

Here's another example. As you've come to know your coworker, she confides in you that years earlier she was the victim of sexual abuse. You may approach her this way: "Thank you for sharing with me, Marla. I'm sure that wasn't easy. I want to assure you I'll be praying for you. But I was wondering, if you don't mind me asking, have you ever thought about how this might have affected you?" You may uncover homosexual inclinations, but more importantly, you are ministering to the core of the problem.

The most important thing to remember is this: Those of us who have helped men and women face their struggles rarely find homosexuality itself to be the focus of our conversation. As with any sin issue, we must look beyond someone's behaviors and minister to the wounds that have prompted them. Fixating on homosexuality is like trying to cure the symptoms—not the sickness.

26. I often feel hesitant to minister to my gay friends. I'm afraid that I'm going to condone what they're doing and grieve the Holy Spirit. Is doing nothing better than crossing the line?

This question spotlights the number one reason Christians don't reach out to gay friends or loved ones. But there's another way to look at it: What if, by doing nothing, you're ignoring the Holy Spirit's prompting and ultimately grieving Him anyway?

So let me answer this question with a question: Are you willing to be used? And before you respond, ask yourself another one: In reaching out to my friend or loved one, am I ministering to their humanity or supporting their homosexuality?

Consider this scenario as you ponder your answers. Someone you work with, the woman in the cubicle next to yours, is an "out" lesbian. You know this because she's talked openly at lunch and in other social settings about her partner. One day, you hear her crying in her cubicle. You ask her what's wrong, and she says her girlfriend just left her for another woman. She is devastated, and your first impulse is to comfort her.

And that's exactly what you should do. Having compassion for a friend who happens to be a lesbian does not mean you are condoning her lesbianism, just as having compassion for a friend who is an alcoholic does not mean you are supporting his alcoholism.

This is a perfect opportunity to minister to her humanity. If she knows you are a Christian and has overheard you praying for others, what would be wrong with asking if you could pray for her? But this is where you must stay true to your beliefs. You aren't going to pray something like, "Lord, please bring Jill's girlfriend back to her and comfort her in her pain." Instead, you might pray, "Lord, I'm asking that you would comfort my friend Jill. Her heart is hurting, and I know that matters to You. Please show her how much You desire to comfort her with Your presence. And please show me how I might be able to help her through this time of pain and loneliness."

If, after responding to a situation like this, you feel a gentle nudge of conviction from the Holy Spirit that you might have compromised your conviction, remember that we have a Father who proclaimed forgiveness loud and clear through His Son. You might make a mistake, but God is bigger than any blunder you may commit.

27. The lesbian couple next door has adopted a child and invited me to attend a "celebration of life" event at their home. What should I do?

This invitation is most often received by people with friends in the gay community as a invitation to "celebrate life." Unlike "weddings" or "commitment ceremonies," these are events that Christians should jump at the chance to attend. Nothing could agree more with our foundational belief in the sanctity of human life. "So God created man in His own image; in the image of God He created him; male and female He created them" (Genesis 1:27). All life is sacred and deserves to be celebrated.

Such an event offers incredible potential for ministry. Take it from me, the father of two young boys, when I say that the quickest way to win any parent's heart is to express love, appreciation, and respect for their children.

28. I know lots of gay people. How do I introduce them to Christ?

Don't think of it as "introducing a gay person to Christ." Why should ministry to a gay person be approached any differently from ministry to anyone else? Friendship evangelism should never be conditioned on an individual's difference. Chicken soup for a sick friend is still chicken soup for a sick friend.

The best place to start is with prayer. Ask the Lord to reveal to you His heart for your friend. Remember, "while we were still sinners, Christ died for us" (Romans 5:8). Jesus didn't need you to stop sinning before He accepted you. Christ wants each of us to come to a saving knowledge of Him first and foremost. We must never forget that Christ doesn't want your friend's *homosexuality* anymore than He wants our gossip or anger or pride. He wants your friend's *heart* every bit as much as he wants your heart.

Also, remember that introducing someone to Christ isn't the end of your calling. The Lord directs us to "go and make disciples of all nations, baptizing them in the name of the Father and of the Son and of the Holy Spirit, and teaching them to obey everything I have commanded you" (Matthew 28:19). Continue to invest in these relationships. Pray with your homosexual friends, read God's Word with them, and disciple them. And be sure to remember all the while that you aren't the Holy Spirit. You might feel led to immediately introduce them to passages of Scripture dealing with homosexuality, but Leviticus 18 and Romans 1 have rarely been effectively used as introductory tools of discipleship. As with any new convert, introduce your friends to the Gospel of John. Trust the Holy Spirit to make them aware of His truth as you help them get established in their relationship with their newly found Savior, Lord, and Friend.

> **29. I've known John 3:16 since I was a little boy, and I desperately want to share that truth with all I come in contact with. However, when I attempt to share this with others from the gay community, my efforts seem to fall flat. Am I missing something? What should I be aware of when reaching out to the gay community?**

While closely related to the previous question, this question lacks the inherent prejudice and instead humbly acknowledges potential stumbling blocks this mission field might present. And more importantly, it appears to desire to reach out through understanding and love.

Sadly, that is somewhat rare. The Christian community spends $20 billion each year on the work of missions.[2] The majority of that is spent on reaching other cultures for Christ. Committed missionaries give up their comforts, spend hours learning the nuances of their target group in hopes of not offending, and often learn the native tongue of those the Lord has laid on their heart. Yet how much effort, energy, discomfort, or money does the church spend on reaching the gay community—an often forgotten mission field?

When reaching out to the gay community, we must avoid behaviors that would keep our gay friends away from the open arms of their Savior. When gays are convinced that Christians embrace hateful, bigoted, intolerant, or homophobic thoughts, we have to acknowledge that part of the reason may be that we don't exemplify love in a way the gay community can receive.

Consider the most widely used phrase within Christian circles regarding the issue of homosexuality—"love the sinner and hate the sin." Those of us sitting in the pews can comprehend this, but those we are attempting to reach often don't have the cognitive or spiritual framework to appreciate this phrase. That's because many in the gay community don't separate themselves from their actions; they refer to themselves as homosexuals, equating who they *are* with what they *do*. So the moment we utter the second verb in the phrase above, they've written us off as possessing none of the first verb.

Consider this explanation from a pro-gay writer:

What an odd word choice "hate" is. I mean, why not, "Love the sinner, be worried about the sin"? Why not, "Love the sinner, heal the sin"? It raises a question many of us don't understand: Why do so many Christians love the word "hate"?...Yes, "Love the sinner, hate the sin" is a catchy phrase, yes it neatly cleaves the doer from the deed, but the word choice reveals more about the person throwing that blade than the one knifed by it.[3]

That writer doesn't understand God's call to "hate evil, love good" (Amos 5:15). But then, how could he? We can't expect him to understand spiritual perspectives without a frame of reference. We can't ignore how this phrase has hurt him and many others.

And as Joe Dallas, author and past president of Exodus International, so aptly states, "If we use words as strong as love and hate, the burden of proof is on us to show evidence of those strong emotions. If we're going to say we *hate* something, we need evidence. If we're going to say we *love*, we need evidence of that."[4] Joe goes on and humorously draws his listeners to a stark reality: "Now, I think we have the 'hate' part down!"[5] But in all seriousness, we each must remember that we will be called to account for how we have handled the precious lives of each person the Lord died to redeem.

So, what does all this add up to? There *are* certain nuances that you must be aware of when reaching out in love to someone who is homosexual. The key things to remember are that each person you encounter might not understand your terminology, and we can't expect redeemed behavior or understanding from the unredeemed.

The Lord often gives us discernment—which many experience as a "gut feeling." This discernment is one of the most underutilized tools we have for dealing with situations that require us to step out into uncomfortable territory. If you believe that you've made a comment or extended a gesture that has caused offense, ask about it. This will show that you value people and their feelings, that you are interested in understanding, and that you are humble enough to ask for forgiveness. From that the seeds of friendship can spring.

30. I work with a girl who is very "out" about her homosexuality. I've noticed she's much more offensive around me than she is with other coworkers. What is this about? What should I do?

One of the most common factors that leads individuals to struggle with homosexuality is a feeling of rejection. This deep feeling can become a filter through which people observe their surroundings. This is probably the case with your coworker—especially if she knows of your faith and belief in Christ.

Because you are hopefully just as "out" about your Christianity as she is about her lesbianism, she can presume your position on homosexuality. Fearing rejection from you (especially if this has been her experience with other Christians), she becomes intentionally offensive to protect herself. She goes on the offensive because she is really feeling very defensive. If she can cause you to reject her by her offending you first, she maintains control and feels empowered.

The loving thing to do in response is to directly but gently confront her, pointing out that she doesn't seem to act the same with you as with other coworkers. Acknowledge the offense forthrightly, but assure her that the relationship is important to you and that you are committed to it. A great way to express this may be as simple as saying, "I feel like there are times you say things to intentionally offend me, but I want to let you know I'm in this relationship for the long haul. There isn't going to be anything you are going to do that will push me away. So let's just stop that game—all right?"

But don't just leave it there. Conclude the conversation by inviting her to tell you how you may have offended her unknowingly. This will show her how much you value her. And if she takes you up on it, be humble and ask for forgiveness.

31. A man in my church is struggling with homosexuality. I really want to extend a hand of friendship to him but feel uncomfortable around gay men. What should I do? I'm just an average Joe.

Well, Joe, let me start off by telling you a story. After living 12 years in the gay community and struggling with homosexual feelings for more than 17 years, I approached my wedding day (three years into my healing process) with fear and trepidation. Two weeks before I was to be married, I shared my deepest fear with a group of godly men I was in relationship with—none of whom had ever struggled with homosexual feelings or temptations. Through tears I explained to them how I was dreading my wedding night. I remember saying, "I'm scared to death. I know I'm going to have to perform sexually, and I don't know what to do. What if I don't know how to please her? Maybe I really am still gay."

I was absolutely mortified—and then one of the men I was sharing this with—an average Joe—began to laugh. As you can imagine, this didn't sit well with me. But before I was able to tear his head off (in Christian love, of course), he apologized: "Mike, I'm not laughing at you—I'm laughing with you. You know my story—I've never struggled with homosexuality, and I was a virgin when I got married. You need to know that your feelings are natural. I had many of these same questions and fears. Your problem is the whole 'gay filter.' These inadequacies are normal—you have to stop attributing them to the fact that you used to be gay."

The freedom I experienced in that moment—with that "straight" man—was a turning point in my life. Not only did I stop filtering all my problems through the lens of having been gay, but that day I became part of the club—I realized I really was a man and that many of my fears, anxieties, and temptations are just like those of every man.

I wish you could understand the significance of this moment in my life. Did these guys understand homosexuality? Not really. Did they know the turmoil of having inappropriate desires for other men? Absolutely not! And yet I am still experiencing the impact they had on my life. The power of their commitment to me as just another man of God changed my life. You can do the same for other people—without having to completely understand their situations.

Just being willing to get to know this brother in Christ—as uncomfortable as it may be for you at first—could mean a world of difference to him.

Let's start with the basics. Most men who struggle with homosexuality have attempted to fill an unmet emotional need for same-gender bonding inappropriately through sex. Thus, just the simple fact that you show him value and acceptance is a tremendous start. And just like my friend in the story above, you need to be honest about your struggles, fears, and temptations. Even if they are different from his, he will learn how to implement principles of accountability, forgiveness, and grace as they are exemplified in your walk. Commit to praying with and for him, and invite him to do the same as you share your areas of needed support. Show him that he can be as helpful to you as you are being to him.

As difficult as this may be, you may have to talk about some things that are uncomfortable for you, issues not customarily bandied about within the four walls of any church: homosexuality, masturbation, and sexual fantasy. But remember, there are zones of propriety even for these topics. One helpful rule of thumb is to make sure that each of you use clinical terms for sexual activities, body parts, and the like. This can help to minimize any potential these slang terms might have to conjure up mental images or inappropriate associations.

What to do when conversations get off track or become too much for you? Anita Worthen and Bob Davies give some great advice in their book *Someone I Love Is Gay:*

> You will also have to be honest in letting him know how much specific detail you can handle about his current struggles. For example, if knowing his attractions to a mutual friend is too burdensome for you, he needs to know that. He can keep you abreast of his struggles without giving specific names. He needs to know your limits in other areas too, so that he does not cause you to sin by stirring up sexual fantasies in your own mind.[6]

They continue by pointing out that

> you may be surprised to discover how many current or past struggles in your life match those of your friend. His homosexuality is not really a sexual problem—it is merely the surface symptom of deeper root issues which need healing. The roots of

homosexuality are mainly emotional, and center on issues like envy...rejection...loneliness...and deception.[7]

Worthen and Davies conclude by affirming the power you can have in the life of a friend who struggles with homosexuality.

Do any of these sound familiar [speaking of the roots of homo-sexuality]? Of course they do—many of these feelings and thoughts plague all of us to varying degrees. So you can share with your friend that these issues are not "gay," they are universal. And you can share how God has helped you deal with comparable struggles in your own life.[8]

Without a doubt, you risk a lot when you establish a godly rela-tionship with an acquaintance who struggles with homosexuality. Your reputation and your comfort are just two of the many things that may be challenged as you walk with this brother in Christ. But rejoice in the fact that your efforts are putting a smile on the face of the One who truly matters—Jesus, who risked it all to bring you to His side.

32. One of my closest friends just told me she struggles with homosexuality. I know enough about this to understand that she needs other women to help her. As a man, how can I help?

You are absolutely on target in your understanding of her need to build healthy, nonsexual, emotionally balanced relationships with other women. But this doesn't mean you can't play a role as well. As you seek to affirm her femininity (not just her appearance) by showing her respect and extending her dignity, you can be crucial in helping her combat her distorted view of men.

Her negative view of men may come from a history of abuse at the hands of men. Worthen and Davies believe it's important to remind men in your situation that

the vast majority of women dealing with lesbianism have been sex-ually abused. Often they have a fear and even hatred of men because of deep emotional wounding. Your friend may have many fears lurking behind her friendly façade. Give her time to establish trust in your relationship. For example, one woman declined a ride home after Bible study because she would be alone with a man she didn't know well...Respect her boundaries and don't get offended if she says "no" to what you consider a kind offer.[9]

You may feel affirmed by her camaraderie. But be sure to maintain a healthy relationship. Being "best buds" may not be best at all. Sharing a game of pool and a six-pack of beer may not fulfill her need for acceptance of her femininity. And most importantly of all, take a long look at your motives:

> Beware of premature romantic involvement if your friend is just beginning the process of overcoming her lesbian background. Sometimes a woman will become emotionally entangled with a male friend who seems "safe." If you see this occurring, don't pull away totally but seek to establish healthy boundaries in the relationship. You may want to become accountable to a mature Christian friend.[10]

Pray for your friend and encourage her toward healthy relationships with mature Christian women. At the same time, allow the Holy Spirit to show you when He desires to use you. Be careful to not push your way into her life until He leads you there. You may only damage the situation further if you become just another man with poor boundaries.

33. What is a mentor's role when helping women who struggle with same-sex attraction?

[The entire response to this question is by Mona Riley. Mona's husband, Mike, was our pastor when my wife and I were working with Love in Action, a ministry to men and women leaving the gay life. Mona has spent years mentoring women—many of whom have struggled with lesbianism.]

From the time she was old enough to know anything, my daughter wanted to ride horses. I tried to get her interested in a little play kitchen; she gave it to her cousin Hannah. I showered her with dolls at birthdays and Christmas; they lived in their boxes. But when I took her to the stable and helped her find ways to work for riding time, I found the key that opened her joy. Now, many years later, she has completely surpassed my meager skills as a rider. We both look back with gratitude on the choice I made as a parent. I tried to encourage my daughter in many ways, but when I found the thing that she was called to, my efforts were successful.

This little example points out what mentoring is *not*. Mentoring should never be an attempt to create something in another person that isn't there and was never meant to be there. Rather, it should always be the nurturing of what God has already planted in a life.

Too often, so-called mentoring is really social repatterning. A woman may be very butch, so we encourage her to become more domestic, bake brownies, plant violas, or press them and make pretty cards. But these aren't the things that make us women. I'm a woman because God created me a woman. Our womanhood is going to look very different and unique in each of us.

By beginning with the positive (what God has created), we rely upon God to show the steps a woman must take to realize His plan for her life. Both the mentor and the protégé become willing to do the hard work of finding the woman and nurturing her, always recognizing that God knows her and will help us find her. And we do have to find her because along the way, growing up, she may have gotten lost. Seeking her out takes courage.

I believe the most valuable task of the mentor is to encourage with a mixture of affirmation and battle cry. As a mentor, I have a huge bank account of confidence built by watching God work in other lives, and I am able to invest some of it in someone who has too little. In the business world, mentors share some of their power and knowledge with their protégés. In the ministering world, we share our courage and faith.

An easy trap for both the mentor and protégé to fall into is to rely too heavily on the relationship and what the mentor supplies. As I've indicated, the mentoring relationship is intended to augment what God is doing. We must remember that God is at work. Too eagerly, we begin trusting in the mentor's bank account—her ability to encourage the protégé—rather than both parties looking to God for confidence.

The primary danger in this is for one or both parties to become emotionally dependent upon the other. The protégé enjoys the attention and affirmation she is getting. The mentor is very aware of being needed. Those feelings can easily cloud the purpose of the relationship.

In other words, this should not be a deep personal friendship. Neither party should be getting her needs for relationship met through mentoring. If that happens, one of the best values of the relationship is gone: The mentor has lost her objectivity. Both must remember that true change is frightening. If the mentor becomes emotionally involved, she can't dispassionately encourage the protégé. She's reduced to shouldering the burden of the transition process rather than allowing the protégé to struggle with God's help through the stages of growth.

The mentoring process is intended to build a true love relationship between the protégé and God rather than between the protégé and the mentor. The mentor's purpose is to continually point the protégé to the source of healing and encourage her to seek the Healer. Upon occasion, the mentor will be more active in walking beside the protégé through problems, but this should always happen less and less frequently.

Is the help a mentor brings worth the dangers? Most definitely, as long as we realize the drawbacks and recognize two things. First, change doesn't happen overnight. Where two or more are committed to Christ and to growth, it will happen. The mentor is a witness of this in the lives of others and can remind the protégé when she loses her bearings.

Second, healing tends to start with internal concepts and work outward. The mentor has seen transformation before and can share a measure of faith in this process that the protégé may not have. When you're in the middle of something, you may be too close to it to see that change is happening. You may need a nudge here and there to keep going.

The mentoring relationship can provide that nudge. Mentors don't know everything and can't have all the answers. Rather, they make themselves available and affirm the protégé by spending time with her and speaking into her life. Additionally, although the mentor is not a surrogate parent, she can nurture those attributes in the protégé that should have been encouraged by her parents. When this is done in submission to the authority of Christ and with appropriate affirmation and objectivity, true ministry occurs.

---

34. I'm a female hairstylist who works with several gay men at a salon. I am a Christian and want to show these men God's love, but sometimes I let them "be one of the girls" to show them I accept them. Is this wrong? What kind of influence can I have on them?

This is the most common pairing found in gay or ex-gay circles—the gay man and the heterosexual female friend. This bonding is in fact the premise of one of the most popular sitcoms of the day, *Will & Grace*. The easy acceptance gay men find in women is often due to one of the common issues of males who struggle with homosexuality: rejection by or feelings of inadequacy with other men.

A woman often makes two common mistakes in relating to a gay male friend. First, she may adopt an "I'm going to straighten him out regardless of what it takes" attitude, erroneously believing she is the one person who can rescue him from destruction. Her maternal instincts kick in, and she is committed to seeing him through. The problem is that her inappropriate single-mindedness frequently keeps him from the thing that most promotes his healing—healthy relationships with heterosexual males. Worthen and Davies bring this point home with their advice: "Encourage his friendships with other men. This is one of the most important things you can do. Often, gay men have felt separated from other men as they grow up; they fear other men and feel insecure around them."[11]

The second common mistake women make with gay male friends is continuing to allow them to unhealthily identify with feminine attitudes and behaviors. I remember when a well-intended Christian friend of mine asked me to help her shop for her dress for an upcoming event she would be attending. Like many gay or ex-gay men, I have an eye for fashion (which, for the record, is an asset in my marriage!). But a day of shopping at the mall with my closest girl friend doesn't exactly propel me in the right direction. She even expected me to join her in the dressing room, helping her zip up and tuck in. Would she ask this of any other man? Of course not. By asking it of me—even though she may consider me "safe"—she was unwittingly fostering the very identity struggles that had plagued me since childhood.

Perhaps most importantly, women in such close relationships with gay men need to be honest about their intentions. "Too often," Worthen and Davies write, "women in these types of relationships begin to become romantically inclined toward the man. They begin to hope that this platonic relationship could develop into a romance. Unless the man has had considerable time to move forward in his healing process, such a hope will only lead to hurt and disappointment." You need to guard your heart against this. As Worthen and Davies add, "Typically, the ex-gay man will 'turn tail and run' when he senses even a hint of romantic interest on your part. The relationship will quickly become strained and probably break apart."[12]

So set healthy boundaries that don't allow a male homosexual friend to be "one of the girls." Guide him toward appropriate relationships with godly men. Pray for him, show interest in his new friendships with men, and encourage him when he feels like giving up or is fearful of these newfound interactions.

35. I know many gay men, and they all seem to remember feeling gay very early. Two of them have told me they were certainly born that way and that they knew they were gay as young as five years old. How can I deny their feelings?

First, understand that this is hardly a unique experience. "Most gay men and lesbian women have their own opinions about why they are homosexual," Simon LeVay says in his book *Queer Science: The Use and Abuse of Research into Homosexuality.* "Although there are exceptions, gay men in the United States today generally tend to claim that they were 'born gay'. Ninety percent of gay men surveyed by *The Advocate* (a gay magazine) in 1994 claimed to have been born gay."[13]

Why do so many homosexuals believe this? Maybe my personal experience will be instructive. I didn't understand much about homosexuality except that I thought I "was" and that most people "weren't." Because I knew this wasn't something that was accepted by most people, I thought soliciting advice on the subject from Christians wasn't an option—especially since I interpreted the attitude at my church to be that there was a hotter place in hell for gays and lesbians. I surely wasn't going to approach my parents. I decided to look for help at school.

As a 16-year-old sophomore in high school who needed some clarity, I went to see a counselor. I sat with her and shared that I thought I was gay. She assured me that if I had felt this way for years, then this must have been the way God made me. If I desired to "live a healthy, productive life," I was going to have to accept who I was— including my homosexuality. A weight seemed to fall from my shoulders. At last, something that made sense: I was born gay! Why hadn't I thought of this before? It all became so clear. I had felt different for years—all the way back to kindergarten. Now everything was coming together.

Does the fact that I (and many others) can recall feeling "different" as young as age five mean we really were "gay"? Of course not. Who at the age of five even knows heterosexual strivings and functioning exist (unless one has been sexually abused)? Our feelings certainly were real, but our interpretation of them was not. Some of us had gender-identity deficits as early as we can remember, but that doesn't mean we were homosexual. Most people who continue to embrace this notion are guilty of interpreting their earliest feelings through the lens of their adult homosexual identity.

The thinking works like this: If I'm gay now, then those feelings I had at age five were gay too. This deductive reasoning is flawed. Those feelings we had at age five were not gay but were very real feelings of longing, difference, inadequacy, or lack of belonging. They were not signs that we were homosexual.

This reality is corroborated by gay researcher Simon LeVay:

Should one take these assertions seriously? Not entirely, of course. No one even remembers being born, let alone being born gay or straight. When a gay man, for example, says he was born gay, he generally means that he felt different from other boys at the earliest age he can remember. Sometimes the difference involved sexual feelings, but more commonly it involved some kind of gender-nonconformist or "sex-atypical" traits—disliking rough-and-tumble play, for example—that were not explicitly sexual. These differences, which have been verified in a number of ways, suggest that sexual orientation is influenced by factors operating very early in life.[14]

So, to answer your question more directly, you can't deny the validity of your gay friends' feelings, but you can challenge their interpretation of them. Base that challenge on your understanding of the roots of male homosexuality. Help your friends see the influence their environment and their relationships with parents and peers had on their feelings. Believing in a "born gay" theory is easy and convenient, but it lacks personal responsibility and gives many a false sense of righteousness.

For more insight on the "born gay" theories, refer to the questions and answers in chapter 11.

4

Answers for the Church

SALT, LIGHT, WISDOM, HEALING, OBEDIENCE, AND BALANCE characterize effective bodies of believers. However, many churches have settled for blandness, darkness, ignorance, hatred, rebellion, and inequity instead, particularly where overt sins such as homosexuality are concerned. No church is without flaws, but churches must show their members how to walk as closely as possible in the sandals of the One who is perfect. Many concerns, fears, and questions must be addressed in churches wishing to reach out healing hands toward homosexuals. I'm hoping you'll find in this chapter the resources you need to reach people who may seem to be beyond God's reach, and that God will use your arms to draw and hold them closer to Himself.

36. I'm a pastor. How do I lead our church to effectively love homosexuals?

Start by informing your leadership of your desire to become a church that represents the fullness of Christ's ministry. When the road gets bumpy—which it will—you will need their support.

Once you set the course, the next step is to educate your staff.* After that, start scouring your congregation for people with a heart for this type of ministry, and do everything in your power to get them trained and spiritually prepared for the unveiling of this effort. Don't proceed without this preparation. Nothing is more damaging than opening the wounds of those affected by homosexuality, be it those

---

* See chapter 12 for some suggested resources. After your church leadership has absorbed the information, put these materials in your church library and let the congregation know about them.

directly affected or their family members, and then leaving them with nothing to cleanse or bandage their hurts.

Next, begin to educate your congregation regarding God's truth as it pertains to this issue. Be careful to focus on the balance of truth and grace. This will accomplish two very important things: Your congregation will know that your stance is unwavering regarding the issue of sin, and they will find hope in Christ for those affected by homosexuality.

Another important step is to encourage the teachers of your teen and adult Sunday school classes to lead discussions or lessons regarding the issue of homosexuality so that the church comes to understand that your leaders share your commitment. Make sure the tone of these lessons or discussions is in line with the tone you're establishing in your church.

You will also want to connect with a worthy ex-gay ministry in your area and get to know its leaders so that your endorsement of them is rooted in trust. Place their contact information in the bulletin or church newsletter. Those involved in Exodus International have a strong calling to educate the church regarding this issue.

And lastly, a powerful ex-gay testimony from the pulpit will grant credibility to the promise of hope that can be found in the power of Jesus Christ.

37. How can we help someone who has tried to overcome homosexuality and failed—especially since she has been hurt by the response of churches and other Christians?

At the 1995 Exodus International conference in San Diego, a pastor walked to the podium, leaned against it as if he were talking to friends, and uttered some of the most powerful words I've ever heard: "On behalf of Christian leaders and pastors, as well as any calling themselves Christians across this country, who have been guilty of showing a lack of attention to your dilemma and dismissed you as unimportant, for any of the unbalanced messages we've spoken that have hurt you and for ways we've offended you without even knowing it, I ask for your forgiveness—I truly am sorry."

Had this man ever done anything to offend me? No. In fact, I'd never even heard of him before the conference. Yet his message ministered to me in a way that freed me to receive and begin to trust the very community I desperately needed—the body of Christ. And I wasn't the only one touched. You could hear sobs through the auditorium from those who desperately needed this message.

What did this man do that was so profound? He stood in the gap as an example of a Christian offering hope—hope that others were out there like him and that someone had noticed our pain. He was treating us like Jesus had treated him: "Surely he took up our infirmities and carried our sorrows" (Isaiah 53:4).

That's what you and anybody else who wants to reach into the life of someone struggling with homosexuality need to do too. Validate your friend's pain and be a true ambassador of Christ. That's what she needs to begin to experience the freedom that is available to her in a deep, abiding relationship with Jesus Christ.

38. I understand that multiple contributing factors are involved in homosexuality, including environment, biology, and family. Is a spiritual component included as well?

All the factors you mentioned (and others) can contribute to the development of homosexual attraction, but we dare not overlook the spiritual influences that contribute to homosexuality. Scripture specifically says that "our struggle is not against flesh and blood, but against the rulers, against the authorities, against the powers of this dark world and against the spiritual forces of evil in the heavenly realms" (Ephesians 6:12).

Demonic spiritual influences find fertile soil when environmental, biological, and familial situations go awry. The powers of darkness can much more easily seduce those who are spiritually vulnerable. Children raised in healthy homes are going to be far less susceptible to same-sex temptations—and a host of other temptations, for that matter—when their needs are being met and sustained legitimately. This doesn't mean that negative spiritual forces cease to tempt in strong

Christian families, but one whose needs are being legitimately met will more easily resist any counterfeit.

We must never forget the power of prayer, Scripture, fellowship, and the other aids to a healthy Christian walk. The voice of the Shepherd must predominate.

Just as we need to recognize and address the spiritual component of the homosexual's struggle, we must not dismiss the other, more earthly influences. I've seen this done in some Christian circles among sincere, well-meaning brothers and sisters who believe that "the power of the Spirit" is all that's needed. This is biblical truth, of course, but to think that praying against the "demon of homosexuality" is all one must do is shortsighted. After all, God chooses to manifest His power in myriad ways in our struggles with any sin—alcoholism, drug addiction, sexual addiction, anger, envy, or gossip. And in most of these cases, the road to recovery is a process played out not only through prayer and the revelatory power of the Holy Spirit but also through godly counseling, one-on-one accountability, and forgiveness.

39. The Christian community has many different approaches to handling homosexuality. How can I evaluate whether my church is handling it appropriately?

In their book, *Unwanted Harvest*, Mona Riley and Brad Sargent help by defining six potential responses to homosexuality for the body of Christ.[1] These definitions will help you assess your congregation's approach.

The Permissive Church

Mona starts by clarifying that "the job of churches is to bring men and women to life in Jesus Christ." She characterizes the permissive church as one that "does not have a strong message of that hope. When Christ is presented there, He is not God, but rather a more human friend who has, through extraordinary sacrifice, obtained in the minds of men a special place of quasi-deity. He is not God enough to obey nor man enough to disrespect. His teachings are only teachings."[2]

Mona describes this church as one that

> will most likely have some of the best programs for people with AIDS, which is admirable. They may sponsor events, incorporating other segments of the community, whose only link is the human need they benefit....Paradoxically, though this church offers help to men and women who want to continue in sexual sin, they provide no comfort for those who seek help in overcoming homosexuality....In brief, the permissive church is heavy on compassion but woefully short on truth.

The Rebellious Church

Mona describes this type of congregation as one that "will have openly gay members. These members may even be very demonstrative in public and at services. They may be politically active and use the church to promote their agenda."

This church is marked by members and leaders who "use all parts of the Bible that keep them comfortable, but explain away anything that conflicts with their opinions." This church may seem similar to the permissive church, but Mona illuminates their stark divergence in the handling of God's Word:

> While the permissive church tends to ignore the teachings of Scripture, the rebellious church openly defies the Word of God.... Ultimately, then this church rewrites the Bible to fit the beliefs of the congregation. In their view, people are more important than God; therefore, God could not have meant the things written in His Word....[The rebellious church] does not want truth. It wants autonomy—self-defined authority—instead....They live according to their own law, shaking their fists at both God and anyone else who oppose them.

The Judgmental Church

Mona defines the third type of church as judgmental. It

> errs on the side of truth without compassion....[and sidesteps] the entire message of the gospel. They have somehow forgotten that although people are hopelessly mired in sin and fail to keep God's Law, God's ever-present love and compassion have made a path for

forgiveness through the death of His Son, Jesus Christ....For this reason people justifiably call the judgmental church hypocritical. Judgmental Christians only rescue the perishing if they can ensure their life preservers will come back clean and in good repair.

The Uncommitted Church

[The uncommitted church] neither helps gays and lesbians out of their sin nor teaches a message that would convict them of sin. It says, "We don't know, so we can't get involved."...[Unfortunately,] men and women in this church have a false sense of security. They fail to realize they have neither truth nor compassion. The leaders are misleading by default; that is, they fail to offer the clear guidance and direction the Lord expects from leaders for His church.

The Ignorant Church

The ignorant church simply does not know the truth of God. They may believe that homosexual involvement is wrong and that people who want out should be able to be helped. They just do not know how to help. [These churches]can only detract from the kingdom of God.... [and] need to search God's Word and pray until the Lord shows them His truth and His will.

The Healing Church

And lastly, the most effective church is described as one whose

members believe in the infallibility and authority of Scripture. Homosexual acting out is sin, and this church knows it. But they also know that for homosexual involvement—as for any sin— there is a complete and sure cure in the blood of Jesus Christ. And so this church balances biblical truth about homosexuality with the compassion of God for homosexual people as revealed through both His Word and His Son.

But more than just knowing the truth, they put their money where their mouths are and act upon the truth that they proclaim.

Its leaders commit to using their gifts to assist men and women overcoming homosexuality, just as they use their gifts to help anyone else with life-dominating sins....Their actions exemplify the fullness of God's Word; an important aspect of the healing church will be the presence of church discipline. If and when people exhibit a true lack of desire to repent…this church will have leadership able to discipline them.…Ultimately, the healing church works because its leaders and members are committed to reaching out as individuals with mercy, grace, support, and the sometimes-hard-to-hear truth.

40. How can we love active gays who attend our church services but prevent them from being in leadership roles, such as a Sunday school teacher, youth pastor, or choir member?

A phenomenal little resource written by Joe Dallas entitled *How Should We Respond?* is part of the Love Won Out booklet series by Focus on the Family. This easy read includes a jewel of a story about a pastor who has been successful at balancing this very concern you bring up:

> There was a pastor back East who developed a real burden for AIDS patients. On his own, this middle-aged, former member of the Moral Majority (so we're talking conservative) just felt a desire to do something for persons with AIDS. He started going to hospitals and visiting AIDS patients—many of them young homosexual men who were dying. And he went in to talk to them, to get to know them, read to them, pray with them and preach if they would allow it. If not, he would just be there as a man who cared about them.
>
> Pretty soon the local gay radio station found out what he was doing. They called him up and said, "Hey, pastor, we hear you're out there ministering to AIDS patients. Where do you stand on homosexuality?" He said, "Oh, I believe it's sin." They said, "Well, we don't like that, but we like you. Would you be willing to come on our radio show?" And so, soon after that, this middle-aged conservative pastor found himself across the microphone from a gay radio host doing a show, talking about his ministry to AIDS

patients. When the show ended, he gave out the name of his church and the location.

Soon, gay people started showing up at his church—not necessarily to repent. Sometimes in pairs. Just coming to hear what this man had to say who had been so loving and gentle and open on the radio program. And the congregation got nervous. They said, "Pastor, the homosexuals are coming! They are coming down the aisles by twos! What are we going to do?" He said, "Well, I guess they can take a seat next to the idolaters and the gossips and the fornicators and the whoremongers. Make room."

Then he said from the pulpit, "When I teach on sexual ethics, I will teach that anything short of heterosexual, monogamous marriage is wrong. If you are openly homosexual and practicing that sin and unrepentant, you cannot hold a position in this church. I cannot legitimize your relationship in that sense. I will not spare when I am teaching the Word of God, but if you're lesbian or gay and you came here, we're so glad to have you. Welcome. We want you to hear the gospel and we want to be your friend."[3]

---

41. I'm involved in youth work in my local community and at church. What can I do to create a positive and safe environment where at-risk kids will feel welcome and we can deal with issues of sexuality in a healthy way?

In his book *An Ounce of Prevention*, Don Schmierer suggests 12 "positive action steps" that can be taken by those who deeply desire to make a difference in the lives of youth who struggle with gender identity.[4] Let's take a look at them:

1. *Do everything in light of God's Word and God's love.*

Schmierer suggests that the perfect place to start would be "a group lesson on biblical views of homosexual behavior, including facts and falsehoods surrounding the subject, and a forthright discussion addressing the stigma attached to the issue..."[5] This discussion will help ensure that students understand that in God's commodity there is no "wiggle-room" regarding the issue of healthy sexuality.

"There is a remarkable amount of fear associated with this subject, especially among adolescent males," Schmierer explains. "It is a topic that inspires relentless ridicule, locker room humor, and unapologetic prejudice....Christian love is the ultimate goal. And teaching young people to love the 'unlovable' is a key life lesson."

And, God forbid, if you as a leader have engaged in any inappropriate joking at the expense of others, make a public confession and commit to creating a no-tolerance zone for bullying and teasing.

2. Always be inclusive.

To create an inviting environment—one free from situations which could further isolate any child—care providers (such as youth pastors and teachers) should attempt to foster an atmosphere of inclusion.

One way to do this, Schmierer suggests, is by avoiding situations where students might be ostracized or indirectly rejected like being chosen last when teams for any activity are elected.

3. Introduce positive role models.

In today's society, when androgyny, promiscuity, and other forms of immorality are portrayed as the latest rage, kids have a strong need for positive role models who display godly characteristics. Therefore, any planned exposure to healthy same-gender heterosexual role models will "contribute to a healthy socialization process."

4. Reinforce true sexual identity.

Schmierer suggests that "affirmation of the whole person, his or her accomplishments, appearances, and sexually appropriate behavior can rebuild the broken places in a young person's heart and soul." Look for opportunities to do this yourself and educate those who work in the youth department to do so as well.

5. Find a way to address abuse.

"Seek, if possible, to identify molestation/abuse issues, and find godly counsel for him/her," Schmierer says. "Be sure any counselors involved have a biblical and informed view of homosexuality, not assuming it to be 'genetically predetermined.'"

6. *Note possible hormonal problems.*

Schmierer points out that "sometimes extreme cross-gender behavior is the result of hormonal imbalances and can be successfully treated by a qualified physician." While these situations are extremely rare, they can be very real and successfully treated. However, treatment alone won't "cure" a student's potential for later homosexual problems. Sexual identity formation is the accumulation of multiple factors—some of them biological, some of them environmental.

"If you suspect this may be the case," Schmierer advises, "try to raise the issue with the young person's parents and suggest a medical evaluation," as uncomfortable as this may be.

7. *Communicate!*

Create a safe environment in which people can freely and appropriately discuss issues that might be uncomfortable. "Listen carefully and be informed enough to answer questions that arise."

8. *Applaud every positive effort.*

If you see any warning signs of a gender identity deficit, be careful to acknowledge healthy movement in the desired direction in order to breed interest and investment in such behaviors. Schmierer reminds us that many at-risk children are attempting to fill a legitimate unmet emotional need, and therefore, "this young person is emerging from a deception—make sure the truth is reaffirmed often and enthusiastically" so that he or she can find true fulfillment and will not settle for a counterfeit.

9. *Teach the Bible.*

God's truth regarding sexuality isn't the only area requiring clarity and instruction. "Both the youth group and each individual young person should be well taught about Christian principles regarding homosexuality, chastity, forgiveness, thought control, and being 'transformed by the renewing of your mind.'"

10. *Confront carefully, if at all.*

"If confrontation is to be made, do so with wisdom, discretion, and prayer," Schmierer says. "And whatever you do, don't accuse!" Few things are so deeply damaging to a child already at risk than being falsely labeled.

11. *Encourage openness.*

"Allow emotional release, and don't be surprised by an intense outpouring of feelings and fears," Schmierer suggests. "If a professional counselor seems appropriate, find a way to make this possible."

On the other hand, he points out some limits. "This does not mean, by the way, that you should be subjected to an endless recital of problems or an airing of 'dirty laundry.' A 'talk show' approach can cause a person's wrong behavior to become the center of attention and can perversely reward bad actions."

12. *Prepare for honest disclosure.*

Schmierer notes that some students may raise issues or identify homosexually as they come to trust you. If so, be preemptive—find resources and referrals to help them and their families grapple with the issue. Do not take this to mean that "fixing" the situation is your responsibility. Quite the contrary. Your role is to express your concern and your desire to stay involved while helping the young person and his or her family find long-term, professional help from someone versed in gender-identity disorders.

By following these 12 guidelines, you will help students experience positive peer and social interaction. And they will find great solace and healing—especially those with fragile gender identity—when they can express their concerns, give voice to their pain, and experience unconditional love and acceptance.

---

42. Most outreach seems to happen at churches. Have you experienced successful outreach to homosexuals on their own turf?

We who are involved in the ex-gay movement have been elated to see an increase in the number of churches that are becoming havens of truth and grace. Still, such efforts are not enough. We must be willing to extend ourselves even further by stepping way out of our comfort zones and attempting to reach those who avoid or disdain the very things we stand for. Let's face it—the gay community isn't breaking down our doors seeking our support. To help them, we need to break down our walls and meet them the way Jesus meets us—where we are.

This requires wisdom and discernment. "Gay turf" is not always conducive to the types of relationships and commitment needed for someone to surrender his life to Christ and sustain his walk with the Lord. Many well-meaning Christians, for instance, attend gay-pride parades and similar homosexuality-affirming events, hoping to reach the lost for Christ. But such celebrations are rarely favorable for evangelism. In fact, those attending usually react to Christian outreach efforts with disgust.

My suggestion is to focus your outreach efforts by investing in the life of a gay individual in a neutral setting. After all, neither extreme—church turf or gay turf—is where the harvest is going to produce the most bounty. Neutrality is optimal, and once someone's heart has learned to trust, the church will hopefully become the place where he or she is restored, discipled, encouraged, nurtured, and above all else, *loved*.

43. When does 1 Corinthians 5 apply to an immoral relationship between Christians in the church?

In 1991, I entered Love In Action, an Exodus International residential program that helps men and women overcome unwanted homosexuality. Since this Exodus program was closely associated with Church of the Open Door in San Rafael, California, that was my church during my involvement in this program. After six months, just as I had begun to trust the church leadership, my pastor stood before his congregation to announce that one of its members was being "disfellowshipped." This individual (a woman whose struggle happened to be homosexuality) was no longer considered a part of this congregation and was no longer able to associate with its members at any depth.

I couldn't believe my ears! *Jesus would never do that,* I thought. How could these men who seemed so loving and balanced do this to another person? Over the next few weeks I allowed my anger to boil. Finally I decided to find out for myself what this was all about (and confront my pastor for being so harsh).

When I got to see Pastor Mike a few days later, I wasted no time setting him straight.

"Pastor Mike," I began, having a hard time with the words because I couldn't understand how he could even call himself a pastor. "I need you to explain how you could be so cruel. How could you ask someone to leave your church?"

Pastor Mike started by validating my feelings. "I'm sure this is hard for you, but please let me explain. Mike, do you believe that all Scripture is to be followed?"

"Of course I do," I shot back.

He began to read, "It is actually reported that there is sexual immorality among you, and of a kind that does not occur even among pagans: A man has his father's wife. And you are proud! Shouldn't you rather have been filled with grief and have put out of your fellowship the man who did this?…Hand this man over to Satan, so that the sinful nature may be destroyed and his spirit saved on the day of the Lord.… Don't you know that a little yeast works through the whole batch of dough? Get rid of the old yeast that you may be a new batch without yeast—as you really are. For Christ, our Passover lamb, has been sacrificed. Therefore, let us keep the Festival, not with the old yeast, the yeast of malice and wickedness, but with bread without yeast, the bread of sincerity and truth. I have written you in my letter not to associate with sexually immoral people—not at all meaning the people of this world who are immoral, or the greedy and swindlers, or idolaters. In that case you would have to leave this world. But now I am writing you that you must not associate with anyone who calls himself a brother but is sexually immoral or greedy, an idolater or a slanderer, a drunkard or a swindler. With such a man do not even eat."

I couldn't believe what I was hearing. Was that really in God's Word? My anger broke as my pastor shared with me through moist eyes just how difficult but right this was—not only for him, but for our congregation and, more importantly, for the sister who was asked to leave. Pastor Mike spent the next couple of hours explaining this process to me, staying true to God's Word each step of the way.

When I realized this question was going to be one I needed to include in this book, I called "my pastor" (he'll always be "my pastor") and asked him to answer this one for me.

So, it's my privilege to introduce you to Pastor Mike Riley:

> Over the many years that I have been a pastor, few moments have been more painful than when we, as leaders, found it necessary to remove someone from our church fellowship. Removing someone from church fellowship becomes necessary when an individual willfully, decidedly, and without remorse or willingness to change, chooses to live a lifestyle or cling to a behavior that violates God's standard for our lives according to the Bible.
>
> We find the primary example of this process in Paul's first letter to the Corinthians where he rebukes the church for allowing a man who is sexually involved with his father's wife to remain in fellowship.
>
> Paul makes clear in this passage that the purpose in removing someone from church fellowship is twofold. First, that offenders will come to their senses, realize the error of their ways, and be willing to change and receive whatever help they may need in the process. Second, that the church will not be affected by the individual's ungodly behavior. Here Paul uses the example of a little yeast growing through a batch of dough. The point is that if a double standard is allowed to exist, it will eventually weaken the resolve or desire of others to maintain God's design or standard for their lives.
>
> Regarding the process of removing someone from church fellowship, a few things need to be underlined. First, God does not play favorites. In other words, we are not allowed to pamper one sin and discipline another. We are not allowed to discriminate. Second, God's discipline is always redemptive. Its purpose is always to heal and restore. Removing someone from church fellowship should never be vindictive, self-righteous, or punitive. Third, as the father received the prodigal son who had come to his

senses, the church must always be eager and willing to receive the wayward but repentant individual back into fellowship with arms wide open. And fourth, may God's love and grace dominate the situation. Be patient and give the individual every opportunity to agree with God before action is taken.[6]

I can't leave this answer without letting you know that during my four years of attendance at the Church of the Open Door, two more individuals were asked to leave. The amazing thing about the conclusion of these situations was that each one of these three people ultimately repented and were restored and welcomed back into this family that lived out God's truth. This church leadership exemplified grace and truth for those who were straying, to the glory of their Savior.

5

Answers for Men

Naturalism reduces people to animals. I can only imagine the stench this leaves in God's nostrils. He shed His precious blood for us, but few people sense their true worth and value. Is it any wonder so many men adopt homosexual identities in search of meaning, relationship, and love? The true nature of a man is found in his likeness to Almighty God. Healing for all men is available in this recognition and truth. Living as a true son of God and walking in a desire to please the heavenly Father will bring the peace, freedom, and assurance all men strive to know. The heavenly Father desires to show each of us the protective barriers He's set in place to protect us from harm. May these answers set you on the right path to finding the one True Man you need. "Blessed is the man who listens to me, watching daily at my doors, waiting at my doorway. For whoever finds me finds life" (Proverbs 8:34).

44. How does homosexuality occur in men?

As you will learn in chapter 11, no proof exists of a genetic cause for homosexuality. Many developmental issues can lead a man to assume a homosexual orientation. When considering these issues, try not to ascribe too much significance to any one. A combination of factors makes up each homosexual man's unique struggle.

- sexual violation or experimentation with men or boys
- incest or molestation
- exposure to pornography
- negative spiritual influences

- media influences
- personality and temperament
- negative body image
- peer labeling, harassment, or alienation
- fear of or an inability to relate to the opposite sex
- dysfunctional family relationships

This last factor is perhaps the most common, especially the relationship between a boy and his father. Let's explore why that is.

A child's first significant bond is formed with Mom. "In the initial stage of life, the child receives foundational security from the one closest—namely, his mother. The infant acutely senses the emotional atmosphere from such cues as voice tone. Touch is also an important source of information for infants."[1] A young boy forms "basic trust" from his early interaction with his mother, and this will help him succeed in the developmental stages to follow.

Between the ages of 18 months to five years, a boy needs to receive gender affirmation both verbally and physically. His perception of his sexual identity will come from the primary people in his life—his parents.

Beginning at around 18 months, a boy begins to discern the difference between male and female. He will notice he is different from his mother and his body is like his father's. Dad, in turn, becomes more significant, and the boy wants to reach out to him, to connect with him. This is what Dr. Joseph Nicolosi calls the "separation individuation phase."[2]

This process logically leads to healthy gender identity—if the boy's interaction with his father is healthy.

> If the father is warm and receptive, then the son can make this transition. He can dis-identify with the mother and connect with the father to fulfill his natural masculine strivings and establish a secure sense of gender identity. But if the father is cold, distant, disinterested, critical or rejecting—according to the boy's perception—the boy will experience a hurt or rejection, which is what we call a "narcissistic hurt."[3]

This narcissistic hurt often leads a young boy to detach himself from what he views as the futility of trying to form a masculine bond—and the pain associated with the rejection he feels from his father. These experiences can often lead to further problems when the boy reaches the next stage of masculine development—identification with same-sex peers. If the boy lacks confidence as a male, his relationships with other boys will seem foreign, uncomfortable, and forced. He is likely to avoid such interactions in one of two ways: He will either isolate himself, finding safety and security in solitude, or he will gravitate toward female friends.

At the onset of puberty, boys struggling through such feelings of rejection and isolation may sexualize their unmet emotional needs. Unlike boys who develop heterosexually, however, their fascination is not directed toward that which is different—girls. Instead,

> the pre-homosexual has already been disconnected from his father, friends and his sexuality by this point in his life. His own masculinity is a mystery to him. It's like the teen boy who, due to masculine inadequacies, is most drawn to females to feel comfortable, safe and unthreatened. The world of boys and men is completely foreign. Getting there feels like crossing a great canyon. So while heterosexuals find females intriguing and in possession of something they do not have, so it is that pre-homosexual boys find members of the same sex intriguing.[4]

This transition occurs during what Nicolosi calls the "erotic transactional phase." He also states that "homosexual behavior is really a symbolic attempt to become familiar with their own bodies through other male bodies."[5]

> Even though homosexuality is becoming more socially acceptable and even promoted as an attractive and preferable way of life...most boys in junior high and high school do not want to be gay. Most hope what they feel is a "passing phase." Many keep their confusing desires to themselves. Christians are told to simply "pray about it." Some try dating the opposite sex to remedy their desires. But none of this helps those who are struggling because their feelings and attractions are not being explained to them. They are left

confused, and many will come to their own conclusion that they must be homosexual. The words, "homo, queer and fag" sting just as badly as they did when they first heard them. With an even lower self-esteem, they plunge ahead to their futures, trying to accept that they must be gay and, as such might as well fulfill the desire and act out in homosexual behavior....

The last step in the development of a homosexual identity usually comes in the years after high school, when all kinds of options become available. Leaving the constraints and influences of home and church, a young man will often discover a world eager to usher him into the homosexual community. With the availability of gay bars, gyms, beaches, even the Internet, numerous opportunities beckon a confused young man to be sought out or to seek out relationships with men.[6]

Add to these developmental mile markers any of the other contributing factors mentioned above—not to mention the misguided messages about homosexuality advanced by the media and reinforced by our culture—and it's no wonder we are seeing more and more boys dealing with gender issues at younger and younger ages. Psychologist Dr. Uriel Meshoulam reiterates this truth: "All too often I see people in therapy, sexually conflicted and confused, have their plight compounded by social pressures....Well-intentioned affirming messages, such as 'be true to your real self,' imply a fixed, 'true' and probably inborn sexual orientation."[7]

So we must see each boy or man as God would see him—holding personal worth, value, and difference, created in God's image and needing to come back to this reality in hopes of overcoming these deficits.

45. What impact does childhood sexual experimentation have on boys?

Childhood sexual experimentation is much more common for boys than for girls. The three main things to consider with boys are the age at which the experimentation took place, the duration of the experimentation, and the type of behavior.

Young boys often play games like "I'll show you mine if you show me yours" with little to no negative effect later in life. Boys commonly have this type of curiosity. This is why being exposed to their fathers' or older brothers' nudity in healthy ways is good for boys. If however the male body is always hidden and holds an inordinate amount of mystery, a young boy may find his curiosity piqued and thus begin to eroticize it.

These behaviors in a young prepubescent boy tend to have little lasting impact. Do address these activities, but the number one rule is to make sure that you don't shame or humiliate the boy in the process. If the young man in question engages in this type of activity during or after puberty, the ramifications can be much more severe. This natural curiosity can become a fixation that turns into a full-fledged homosexual attraction.

Little boys normally respond to their curiosity through nonsexual comparison, but some boys can become enamored with this activity and engage in it for months or even years, learning an inappropriate way of relating. Many men I've talked to, both heterosexual and homosexual, remember a stage of curiosity that culminated in "looking" or "showing." These behaviors fall into the "normal" stage for curious young boys. But if this curiosity becomes a fixation, then these boys are often left with an urge to continue the behavior. Such continued sexual experimentation can very easily become a sort of playful habit, which then becomes a stronghold that causes relational problems later if left unattended. If these behaviors have occurred, don't be dismissive. Address them and take as many precautions as possible to keep them from happening again.

Lastly, consider the type of experimentation the boy has tried. If it was more serious than the I'll-show-you-mine-if-you-show-me-yours game—if it involved oral or anal sex—then that merits much more concern. Many boys who have engaged in these more serious behaviors experience one of two main consequences. Some boys attempt to "regain" the masculinity they believe they lost through this type of behavior. In doing so, they become womanizers or attempt to

prove their masculinity whenever possible. Other boys who are insecure in their gender identity often find that this activity offers a connection to their peers that seems to meet a legitimate need for
closeness and relationship. Any sexual pleasure the young boy experiences strengthens this connection. In turn, homosexual relations
become a mainstay for fulfilling his unmet homo-emotional needs and
result in a homosexual problem.

46. If homosexuality isn't genetic, why do so many gay men have feminine mannerisms such as "lispy" speech and effeminate postures and movements?

The most direct answer to this question is to point to the words "so
many." If homosexuality were genetic, wouldn't *all* gay men manifest
these traits?

A more instructive answer, though, comes from revisiting the root
cause of homosexuality in males. Think of a young boy who has been
raised in a home with no positive male role model. His father may be
absent because of divorce or death, or the son may feel emotionally
starved due to the lack of emotional availability from his dad. A
deterministic reaction can take place as a young boy tries to integrate
into his father's (or other men's) world but gives up after his attempts
are frustrated time and time again. This frustration may manifest in
"acting out" behaviors with a goal of gaining him the male attention
he is looking for.

Within the unhealthy family system these displays of protest are
ignored and in some cases punished. This teaches the boy a lesson
that direct protest gets him nowhere—in fact, it may make things
worse. When parents do not respond to the boy's protests, he
eventually lapses into helplessness and surrenders the struggle.
The lesson learned from the failed protest is that he has no alternative but to retreat to mother....As protection against future
hurt, he defensively detaches from father (Moberly, 1983). This final
self-protective stance is subjectively experienced as "never again"

(Schechter, 1987). It says, "I reject you and what you represent—namely, your masculinity."[8]

This is the source of effeminate mannerisms for some men. Think about the young boy who wants nothing to do with masculinity. He begins to model his life after those whom he feels comfortable around—women. When you really look at it, this is no different from some people speaking with a "suthn' drawwwl" or a "Neuw Yauwk" accent. We begin to walk, talk, and express ourselves like those who surround us, especially those we desire to emulate. These mannerisms are taken on or *learned*—the classic "nurture" scenario in the old "nature vs. nurture" debate.

One of my dearest friends is Alan Chambers, executive director of Exodus International. Listen carefully as he remembers how he intentionally embraced the hallmarks of femininity out of his fear of "all things men":

> Growing up, I had the equivalent of June Cleaver for a mom—but mine wasn't an actress playing a part. My mom cooked three delicious and nutritious meals a day, made sure our home was the cleanest in town, that our clothes were always fresh and ironed (even our T-shirts), and you could tell that she loved her role, her family and her life. Mom was a member of the PTA, a frequent chaperone on field trips, a favorite carpool mom and even my elementary school's crossing guard. She nursed wounds, tucked me in at night and never failed to express in word and deed how much she treasured and loved her family. My mom was my best friend and my hero.
>
> As a child I saw my dad as a mystery. He was gone a lot on business trips, uninvolved in our daily lives and activities, and when he was around he was the resident disciplinarian—a very strict one. Mom didn't let much pass by the radar, but her discipline was full of patience, life lessons and some spankings that were always followed by consolation. Dad, on the other hand, was quick to anger, his bark and bite left me fearful of getting in trouble with him. He was neither fun nor consistent like Mom.
>
> From the earliest age, I remember preferring my mom over my dad. I wanted to look like her, act like her and grow up to be just

like her. By the time I was 6, my favorite thing to do with friends was play house, and I always wanted to be the mom or the sister. Around that age I also remember copying my mother's habits. For instance, at meals, when she took a bite, I took a bite; when she wiped her mouth with a napkin, I wiped my mouth with my napkin. I walked like her, talked like her and desperately wanted others to see the striking resemblance. She was the symbol in my life of all that was good, and I thought there was no better goal than to be just like my mom.

I remember my mom trying to help me become more boyish. She enrolled me in T-ball and baseball; she asked my brother to teach me to throw a ball and even tried to help me run more like a boy. On the other hand, my dad scolded me for acting like a sissy, boys at school teased me, and other men in my family just thought I was weird. I couldn't relate to being a boy; all I knew about being one was what I learned from Mom.

It's no wonder why I was effeminate for much of my school-age years. Was I born genetically pre-disposed to effeminacy? No. I was simply living out what was modeled to me and behaving like the person I most respected.[9]

Alan's story is repeated more frequently than you might suspect. Many men I have counseled remember many of these same feelings, actions, and fears. Understanding their experiences helps us comprehend the genesis of effeminate mannerisms of many gay men.

47. Why does male homosexuality often include promiscuity?

One of the most illusive promises of the gay community is that of a monogamous long-term relationship. "While lesbian partnerships generally are of longer duration than male relationships,"[10] the probability still remains next to nil for men seeking lifelong fidelity.

The most significant work on this subject was done by a gay male couple themselves: David McWhirter and Andrew Mattison, a psychiatrist and psychologist, respectively. In their book, *The Male Couple,* they studied 156 couples whose relationships had lasted from one to 37 years.[11] What did they find? That all the couples whose relationships had lasted more than five years incorporated some provision for outside sexual activity.[12] Let me repeat: Not a single couple living together more than five years was able to sustain a monogamous relationship.

So why does this occur? In his book *Reparative Therapy of Male Homosexuality,* Dr. Nicolosi summarizes a number of the explanations for gay promiscuity.

> Many researchers believe that the more closeted a gay man, the more likely he is to engage in anonymous sexual activity. Some researchers blame gay promiscuity on the lack of the restraining influence of woman. It has also been suggested that the cause of infidelity is due in part to the gay culture, with its built-in sexual opportunity structure.[13]

But the most prevalent reason for the promiscuity of male homosexuals comes from the gay community itself: Gays often cite the lack of cultural support from society as the culprit. Nicolosi summarizes their argument: "There are few successful role models for gay couples to learn from, particularly since their heterosexual parents could not serve as examples. It is said that as the gay life-style gains visibility and social acceptance, homosexual couples will stay together longer."[14]

Will this prove to be true? If so, then we should be able to see long-term monogamy increasing in those areas of the world that tout tolerance of homosexuality as their norm. Amsterdam has always been notorious for its acceptance of homosexuality. As a matter of fact, the Netherlands is arguably the most gay-friendly country on earth, as the author of a recent study conducted there confirms: "The Dutch social climate toward homosexuality has long been and remains considerably more tolerant" than other countries.[15] Even more telling is that the Netherlands was one of the first countries to legalize same-sex marriage.

So we should be able to deduce that same-sex relationships in the Netherlands are reflecting full-fledged monogamy, right? Wrong. A study released in 2003 found that the average duration of "steady" homosexual male partnerships was "0.75–2.25 years."[16] What's more, those in the study who identified themselves as being in a "steady" relationship were also found to average eight casual partners a year in addition to their significant other.[17]

As this evidence shows, this notion of "open relationships" in which gay couples tolerate or even idealize cheating is not one sensationalized by "right-wing, anti-gay conservatives." It is an idea glorified and celebrated within pro-homosexual circles. Consider this boast from homosexual writer Michelangelo Signorile, who notes that "rather than being transformed by the institution of marriage, gay men—some of whom have raised the concept of the 'open relationship' to an art form—could simply transform the institution itself, making it more sexually open, even influencing their heterosexual counterparts."[18] And homosexual author Andrew Sullivan, in his book *Virtually Normal*, boasts that homosexual relationships might even be superior to heterosexual marriage because of the homosexuals' capacity to understand the need for "outside relationships."[19]

So here's the bottom line: No matter how accepting any community or society becomes, promiscuity within the gay community is still going to be the norm. As Dr. Nicolosi explains it: "In the face of these repeated findings on infidelity, some counselors advise the homosexual to develop a monogamous relationship. However, a true understanding of the cause of homosexuality—the symbolic seeking of one's own maleness—explains the naivete of such counsel."[20]

---

48. I have been trying to change my life and get out of homosexuality, but I still deal with a lot of temptation and attraction to other men. How do I deal with thoughts when I see someone I think is attractive (which, right now, seems to be a daily occurrence)?

Understanding the root of your attraction to other men is of the utmost importance. This "daily occurrence" is based on two things. The first can be traced to one of the most common root issues in the lives of men struggling with same-sex attractions. Those roots are deeply embedded in the fertile soil of envy.

If you're a man who struggles with same-sex attraction, let's do a little experiment. Take out a piece of paper and write down all the things you don't like about yourself, such as "I'm too fat," "I'm not buff," "I'm not confident around men," or "my hair's too curly." Set that paper aside when you're done.

Now take another piece of paper and think of the men you find attractive. (Understand that I'm not giving you license to lust.) Assess their attractiveness critically: What specifically are you drawn to? Write those things down. When you've done this, compare those two pieces of paper. I would venture to say that most of the things you find as weaknesses in yourself are the opposites of the things you find attractive in other men. So what's going on here?

Many observers see this as a sort of subconscious cannibalism—an extreme kind of envy. Maybe my own experience can help you more fully understand this phenomenon.

I have skinny legs. Since you can't see them, let me illustrate: When I wrap my thumb and middle finger around my ankle, they actually *touch*. So, without any further humiliation, what do you think I was drawn to in men? You've got it—muscular legs.

Understanding this component of my struggle has freed me up tremendously. I've had to come to grips with this weakness in myself (skinny legs) and realize that no attention from another man, no matter how big his legs are, is going to make mine any bigger. I'm able to speak against the lie of the attraction and move on. This same power is available to you. Think through and assess your attractions. You'll find that they are based in envy and that giving in to the temptation is leaving you with the same outcome—coming up short in the area that sent you looking for affirmation in the first place.

Alcoholics Anonymous calls this insanity—doing the same thing over and over but expecting a different outcome. You know the outcome will be the same. You'll still feel negative about whatever you haven't accepted in yourself, and the sexual act will leave you feeling worse—shameful, embarrassed, and unfulfilled.

The second factor that seems to be fueling your attractions has to do with your focus. Try another experiment. Listen to me now: Don't think of the number eight. Don't think about it. Careful...don't think about the number eight!

What are you thinking about right now? That's right—the number eight. While attempting to overcome your homosexual fantasies and attractions, you are far more aware of them, even as you tune into your desire to be successful. So the very thing you are trying not to think about is all you can think about.

This is why accountability is so important in the beginning stages of your healing process. You are trying to give up something that used to dominate your thoughts and may still be doing so.

Have faith. Examine your attractions for what they are really all about. And when you find yourself tempted, assess your mental state as well.

Jeff Konrad, my best friend and the author of *You Don't Have to Be Gay*[21] (which, by the way, was a by-product of his commitment to helping me find freedom) would remind me to H.A.L.T.

In the midst of temptation he would ask me these questions: "Are you Hungry? Are you Angry? Are you Lonely? Are you Tired?"

He understood how important taking care of myself was, especially in the midst of the difficulty of overcoming sexual temptations. Try this yourself: Take care of yourself, ask for help, learn to understand your desires, and give yourself a break. No one can think about this stuff all day, every day. When you find yourself growing weary of the battle, you might need to refocus. "Fix [your] eyes on Jesus, the author and per-fector of [your] faith, who for the joy set before him endured the cross, scorning its shame, and sat down at the right hand of the throne of God. Consider him who endured such opposition...so that you will not grow weary and lose heart" (Hebrews 12:2-3).

49. I'm an ex-gay man, and I'm interested in dating. Do I need to tell any potential girlfriends about my past, and if so, when?

The place to begin answering this question predates you. In fact, it predates your father's father's father's father's father's father's father. It takes us all the way back to the story of Adam and Eve's fall to temptation, where we encounter God's curses for their disobedience.

To Adam, God said, "Cursed is the ground because of you; through painful toil you will eat of it all the days of your life" (Genesis 3:17). To Eve, he said, "I will greatly increase your pains in childbearing." But Eve's punishment doesn't stop with increased pain in childbirth. God continued by saying, "Your desire will be for your husband, and he will rule over you" (Genesis 3:16).

This desire often shows up in relationships in the common complaint that women never seem to have enough of their man. Some might say, "I just wish he would share more of his heart with me" or "I just can't seem to get enough of him." Women have been wired to respond emotionally to a man who extends himself to them. In light of this, men must be careful to steward this desire and are called to protect this weakness in women. So you, as the man, are responsible for guarding her heart.

That's the context for the answer to your question. The best way to address your former homosexuality is to let the woman you are dating know about it before offering any physical expression of love—even before you hold her hand. You see, in God's design, He has created men very differently than women. These differences, if not understood, can lead to confusion.

Let me give you an example. Holding hands with a woman may cause a physiological or sexual response in you, but to her it can often mean something quite different. When you engage her physically, she processes your action *emotionally.* To you, holding hands is fun. In her mind, she has picked out the wedding dress, chosen the bridesmaids, and decided on the colors. As the man in the relationship—the protector—you must allow her the opportunity to engage her heart with disclosure of what a relationship with you might hold. Marriage is difficult to begin with, and starting one with a lack of honesty is only going to make matters worse. Disclosure at a later point, especially after marriage, can be very hard for any woman to process.

50. Why do some men turn to homosexuality after being married?

Most men who leave the commitment of a marriage for a homosexual relationship do so when faced with unresolved same-sex attractions. Unlike women, most homosexual men had these feelings long before they recited their vows—and they have felt forced to hide or deny their feelings in hopes that they will disappear. When some courageous men have sought support from Christian friends or the church, many have been erroneously counseled to find a good, loving woman. Unfortunately, many of them have taken this absolutely awful advice.

The problem is that after years of denying these feelings, this unresolved sexual attraction explodes. That's why men must enter into marriage with a woman to *complement* their masculinity, not *fix* it. Entering marriage with unresolved same-sex attractions is one of the surest ways of preventing any man from experiencing the closeness and intimacy he longs for and needs from his wife. Only after working to overcome these attractions through a healthy, godly process should any man enter the sanctity of marriage.

6

Answers for Women

NOTHING IS MORE BEAUTIFUL, FEMININE, OR PURE than a woman who has realized her true identity as a daughter of the King. Some families, our culture, and sadly, a number of our churches and denominations often support a feminine ideal that conflicts with God's design. This can hurt vulnerable women, leading some to adopt counterfeit homosexual identities. Christ's treatment of women in the Scriptures—whether it was His mother, the woman at the well, or the woman caught in adultery—shows how much He loves, respects, and wants to protect them. We should follow His example and help every woman to reflect His likeness and image. To help accomplish this, I've sought the expertise of women who have tremendous wisdom and experience working alongside their sisters in Christ. "Many women do noble things, but you surpass them all. Charm is deceptive, and beauty is fleeting; but a woman who fears the LORD is to be praised" (Proverbs 31:29-30).

51. How does homosexuality occur in women?

Until recently, the majority of research done on homosexuality has reflected an overemphasis on men. Etiological similarities do exist between male and female homosexuality, but the important differences must never be ignored.

In Anne Paulk's tremendously helpful book, *Restoring Sexual Identity,* she identifies and explains many of the contributing factors that can lead a young woman to adopt a lesbian identity. "Many influences are implicated in the development of same-sex attraction," she notes, citing "childhood trauma, including incidents of sexual abuse, gender role rejection, atypical childhood play patterns, damaged mother-daughter relationships, unhealthy father-daughter relationships and personality temperament."[1]

To answer this question, I want to summarize Anne's research and allow her—the expert in this area—to explain her findings. They come from an exhaustive survey of women from all walks of life, but primarily from those who have dealt with or were currently dealing with lesbianism. Anne tabulated and synthesized the findings of this two-year study in her book.

Let's take a brief look at each factor Paulk suggests can be a potential contributor to any woman's struggle.

Childhood Trauma

Few who have invested in the noble task of helping people over-come same-sex attractions can deny the prevalence of childhood trauma in the lives of women who struggle. Those who are painfully aware of another's experience of childhood abuse—be it verbal, phys-ical, or sexual—can't deny the toll this takes on the gender development of young girls.

"An astounding 90 percent" of those women in her study, Anne says, "experienced some form of abuse themselves." She then notes that "the three most common forms of abuse experienced before the age of 18 by these women were emotional (almost 70 percent), sexual (more than 60 percent), and verbal abuse (more than half of the women)."[2]

After further detailing these grievous statistics, Paulk points to the bleak impact these experiences can have in contributing to same-sex attraction in women. She quotes Dr. Stanton Jones, who says that "experience of sexual abuse as a child…more than tripled the likelihood of later reporting homosexual orientation."[3]

Any type of abuse is going to wreak havoc on the healthy devel-opment of any child. The exploitation of anything feminine can cause a growing girl to be repulsed by her very gender. Paulk concurs: "Childhood abuse or witnessing abuse can lead a girl to reject her own female self early on."[4]

But Paulk also points out that abuse also harms girls who aren't direct victims of abuse. Even being a bystander can negatively affect young girls. "More than 60 percent witnessed some form of abuse against a family member."[5]

Gender Role Rejection

Paulk explains gender role rejection as "a deliberate, almost constant, and somewhat inflexible adoption of male interests and attributes by a female child."[6]

George Rekers, one of the foremost experts on childhood and adolescent sexual problems, suggests that...

> "Tomboyish" behavior in girls is far more prevalent and much more likely to be merely a transient phase than is "sissyish" or "effeminate" behavior in boys[7] (Rekers & Mead, 1980). Normal girls who prefer masculine activities during childhood are typically secure in their basic female identity, and developmentally they usually adopt many feminine interests in adolescence (Brown, 1956; Saghir & Robins, 1973). In contrast to normal girls, the "tomboyism" of gender-disturbed girls typically persists into and throughout the adolescent years and is more likely to result in conditions of adulthood...homosexuality.[8]

The upshot? Don't be too dismayed if your daughter shows some signs of tomboyish behaviors. Yes, pay appropriate attention, but tomboyish behaviors alone are not a precursor to complete gender role rejection. Paulk does suggest, however, that concern is appropriate when these behaviors become "more than just a tomboy image" and tied to "not identifying themselves with their female role model—mother."[9]

Atypical Childhood Play Patterns

In their article "Childhood Sex-Typed Behavior and Sexual Orientation," J. Michael Bailey and Kenneth J. Zucker found that "for both men and women, research has firmly established that homosexual subjects recall substantially more cross-sex-typed behavior in childhood than do heterosexual subjects."[10]

Paulk further clarifies the dangers of this phenomenon while cautioning that atypical play patterns need not lead parents into a pandemic of panic.

> Early childhood behavior, such as an avoidance of typical female games and activities, a preference of male playmates over

female ones, and an unwillingness or rejection of typical female interests in a routine or hard and fast way can be significant. These should be seen as indicators of how a girl sees and accepts herself as a female in childhood.

Keep in mind, though, that the research that Dr. Rekers has reviewed over many years shows that brief episodes into opposite gender stereotypical play is part of learning how to be a little girl. Also, this alone does not predispose a female to homosexual attraction later in life.[11]

Damaged Mother-Daughter Relationships

The wounds that spring from a breakdown in this relationship can start very early. Paulk sets the stage like this:

In the earliest phase, from birth to two and a half years, the baby girl attaches to her primary caregiver through learning that her mother is trustworthy and reliable....Through this process, the baby girl comes to associate closely with her mother. As you might imagine, neglect on the part of the mother or primary caregiver can wreak havoc on this desired outcome. Instead of learning that she's safe and her caregiver is trustworthy, the baby girl may instead get the message that her mother (or other) is not reliable. Therefore, she may decide to not identify with or trust her mother.[12]

Mothers who are not emotionally healthy, Paulk adds, tend to put their needs ahead of those of their developing daughters. "Or perhaps the mother isn't emotionally available for her daughter. Emotional abandonment is terrifying to a young child."[13]

Paulk concludes her summary of mother-daughter relationships by quoting from Dr. Elaine Siegel's survey of women claiming same-sex attractions. "The daughters recalled in great detail how they had often been emotionally abandoned and how hard they had tried to please their mothers. Of course, they blamed themselves entirely for the failure."[14]

Unhealthy Father-Daughter Relationships

In normal development, little girls first become secure in their relationships with Mom, and the next venture is into the loving arms of Daddy.

The father is meant to reflect back to the daughter her worth as a female, through appreciation and adoration. Unfortunately, some fathers are not safe or emotionally available to encourage this joy of "girlhood" within the daughter. If the father is abusive to his wife, if he is somehow threatened by his daughter's femininity, or if he is abusive toward his daughter, she is less likely to enjoy her femaleness. If the father is hostile, abusive, or emotionally unavailable to his daughter, he communicates a bad feeling about being a woman to the daughter.[15]

And that can lead to a gender identity disorder (GID) that burns into an inferno of same-sex attraction.

Personality Temperament

Each child is born with a God-given personality. Parents often expect little girls to be soft, sweet, and compliant, and when they aren't, some parents don't know what to do. Their daughters sometimes feel wounded and rejected.[16] If the girl's personality is easily damaged, later vulnerabilities to lesbianism are heightened.

Female homosexuality is driven by nonsexual, emotional, and relational deficits that are usually—but not exclusively—based on one or more of the [preceeding] preconditioning factors...please keep in mind that homosexuality is complex and a combination of factors work together to create this condition. It is too simplistic to attribute undue significance to any single aspect. Each preconditioning factor listed here, as well as others not discussed, can destroy a girl's healthy perception of what it means to be female and often, ultimately lead to a same-sex attraction.[17]

52. Can you help me to understand lesbianism? It seems so complex—much more so than male homosexuality.

While doing research for this book, I ran across a great article, "Understanding the Lesbian Client," that helps to explain the "distinct characteristics of female homosexual relationships."[18] Its author,

Andria L. Sigler-Smalz, has worked with many people struggling with gender-identity issues, both male and female.

The author begins by clarifying that no two women's experiences are going to share identical etiology. But some common struggles are found in the lives of women who have identified themselves as lesbian—struggles that are not characteristic of male homosexuals.

The following is an extensive and insightful excerpt from her article that will help to clarify the complex dynamics often associated with lesbianism that differ from male homosexuality:

> The first—reflecting a basic difference between men and women—is that sex and sexual attraction are not necessarily key components of lesbian relationships. In many instances, the role of sex is minor and occasionally, non-existent. Instead, the physical activity more highly valued is holding and affection. In the case where sex is a critical component, it is because of the emotional intimacy that it symbolizes....For the female homosexual, "emotional attraction" plays a more critical role than does sexual attraction....
>
> Next, within these relationships there appears to be a capacity for particularly strong attachment. However, a closer look reveals behaviors that indicate a fragile relational bond ridden with fear and anxiety. Core conflicts are evidenced in recurrent themes related to identity formation. For example, we see fears of abandonment and/or engulfment, struggles involving power (or powerlessness) and control, and desires to merge with another person to obtain a sense of security and significance....
>
> Female relationships lean toward social exclusivity rather than inclusivity and it is not unusual for a lesbian couple to increasingly reduce contact with family members and previous friends. This gradual withdrawal serves to ensure control, and protects against separateness and perceived threats to their fragile bond....
>
> It is not uncommon for lesbian lovers to have a "can't live, if living is without you" kind of feeling toward each other. A client once said to me, "I don't know how I would live without her. Before she came into my life, I was so empty. Now she is my life."[19]

Understanding a woman's core needs will better equip those seeking to help a lesbian loved one to see how she is using counterfeit solutions to fill her legitimate needs. As these needs are met through real unconditional love and acceptance, her desire to fulfill them through same-sex dysfunction will dissipate and make room for the Lover of her soul to take His rightful place as her all in all.

53. I have noticed that many lesbians look manly and unfeminine. Why is this?

[Another of my dear friends is Melissa Fryrear. I have the privilege of working alongside Melissa at Focus on the Family. One of her favorite things to do is to testify about the mighty work the Lord has done in her life. He's allowed her true inner beauty to be manifested in her outer appearance as well. The healing the Lord has done is visible. Trust me—I've seen the pictures! Her story of God's healing power follows.]

I was standing in a food cafeteria line with my mother. Nineteen years old at the time, I was home from college for the Christmas holiday. My mother and I had been running errands all day and had stopped for a quick bite to eat. The food server took my mother's order and then he turned to me and said, "Sir, what would you like?" When I answered in my high-pitched voice, he quickly realized I was a young woman and not a man. Neither my mother nor I was amused by the situation. She was embarrassed that her only daughter looked like a man, and though I took pleasure in not being affirmed as a woman, I felt painfully responsible for my mother's embarrassment.

That was not the first time I had been mistaken for a man, and it would not be the last. In my ten years living as a lesbian, I was mistaken for a man more often than I was recognized as a woman. Outwardly, I looked very masculine. I wore either men's clothing or androgynous clothing. My favorite "uniform" was a pair of men's jeans and an oversized button-down shirt. My hair was styled short, my fingernails were cut to the tips of my fingers, and I considered makeup a taboo. I even wore men's cologne. I was deliberate to eradicate any remote traces of femininity from my appearance. I was also not the exception. Anne Paulk, former lesbian and author of the book *Restoring Sexual Identity: Hope for Women Who Struggle with Same-Sex Attraction,* surveyed 265 women overcoming lesbianism. In her study she found that 87 percent of the women identified themselves as tomboys in childhood, 61 percent were mistaken for a boy at some time as a child, and nearly 90 percent felt ambivalence to or great dislike for being a girl.[20]

The majority of gay women appear masculine for several reasons. I wore my "false masculinity" as a type of suit of armor to protect myself. Having been sexually violated by a man, I did not want to be noticed by men, much less thought attractive by them. That, I thought, was a liability. Dressing like a man also made me feel strong and empowered—the opposite of a victim. I also esteemed masculinity over femininity. I hated being a woman and seethed disdain for anything related to womanhood. I knew I was not a man, although I wished I was, so dressing like one fed that inner wish.

Curiously enough, I also thought lesbian women might find me more physically appealing if I looked like a man. Of course the huge majority of women (96 to 98 percent) *are* attracted to men, and rightly so. From that I surmised if I looked like a man, perhaps I would be appealing to women. The logic was anything but logical. Gay women are not attracted to men; they are attracted to other women. But I was trying to satisfy a false masculine ideal. Looking like a man and being in a relationship with a woman made me feel that way.

Today, I celebrate my femininity and my womanhood. I have not been mistaken for a man in years! My "uniform" now consists of skirts, blouses, and high-heeled shoes. I like my hair long, and make-up makes me feel pretty. These externals, though, do not make me a woman. Some of the most feminine women I know do not wear makeup and are more comfortable wearing slacks. For me, my outward appearance is simply a reflection of how I now feel in my heart. God made me a woman, and that is good!

54. Sometimes when I am emotionally drawn to a woman, I experience sexual temptation. How do I deal with these thoughts?

[For this answer, I went straight to one of the foremost authorities on women's gender issues—Janelle Hallman. Janelle is a licensed professional counselor who has ministered to hundreds of women struggling with same-sex attraction. Her response, as you'll see, is full of grace, truth, and goodness—three traits she exudes in all that she does.]

Enjoying another woman is not sinful. A basic sense of attraction is a necessary part of any healthy friendship. Unfortunately, sometimes these natural feelings of affection can become confused with sexual desire—especially if you have already opened the door to sexual thoughts or behaviors with women.

You can do many things to begin to separate your God-given longings for relationship from your sexual feelings. First, remember that you are much more than your sexual temptations. You are a woman designed by God to desire, want, and even need friendship and intimacy with other women. The emotional draw to another woman is part of your God-given design. Learn to know and accept this part of yourself. I suspect that deep in your heart you even desire purity and integrity in your relationships. Stand against the shame that may tell you otherwise.

As a counselor, I notice that women with a lesbian past often avoid pursuing their desire to get to know another woman for fear of becoming emotionally dependent or sexually involved. These women often believe that they are dangerous because of the powerful pull of sexual temptation. Unfortunately, this avoidance only adds to their deep loneliness and neediness, making them all the more vulnerable to an inappropriate relationship down the road. Avoidance is not a solution. You may struggle for a season as you learn how to separate your God-given desire for friendship from your sexual desire, but remember that the former is truer of your heart.

Second, ask yourself why you are drawn to this particular woman. Perhaps you like the way she relates to other people. Maybe you find her beautiful and feminine. You may sense her strength and character. You may begin to realize that you wish you could be like her. Take time to explore what you see this woman possessing (such as character, relational style, or physical appearance) that you might believe you lack. You can never take traits from another person and make them your own, but you can, with God's help, work to discover and develop your own special and unique traits and character qualities.

A third thing you can do is to explore, hypothetically, what you think you might experience or gain through physical or sexual involvement with this other woman. This is *not* an invitation to fantasize but to dig a bit deeper into your heart. When my clients take this step, they are always surprised to discover that they don't really care at all about sex, but they desperately want to feel loved, accepted, and cherished. Whenever we can separate these core longings from the superficial desires of sex or losing ourselves in another, we can then begin to find healthy and God-honoring ways to fulfill those longings. Sexual or emotionally dependent relationships end up simply being a counterfeit of the true love for which we seek.

A fourth step is to seek wise counsel. Talk about your readiness to sustain a healthy, upright friendship with this woman. Honest friends with discernment will serve you well. They may advise you to not pursue this relationship, sensing that the other woman may also struggle with similar dependencies and confusions. It may not be possible at this point in your journey to avoid slipping back into old, unhealthy ways of relating. Both you and the other woman are worthy of love and respect in its purest form. Guarding your own heart—and perhaps hers—is a profound way of offering love to yourself and to her. If the strong sexual desires for her remain, you may need to find a professional counselor who will help you process the deeper needs or beliefs beneath the temptations.

On the other hand, your accountability partner may encourage you to actually spend *more* time with the woman in an effort to get to know her true personhood. This may be frightening to you, so take one step at a time. With the support of trusted friends, reach out to the woman you are drawn to with the attitude that you have something to offer her. Often my clients are shocked by the idea that they might be the ones to bless another instead of always receiving a blessing.

You are a daughter of the King, made in the image of a gloriously good God, called to walk with others as a co-heir and sister in Christ. With this truth on your side, you may enter confidently into the relationships God has for you and discover that you can be a wonderful friend.

(For further information about Janelle and her wisdom regarding women's issues, visit www.JanelleHallman.com.)

55. Why do some women turn to lesbianism after being married?

Generally speaking, women rarely abandon their husbands because of unresolved same-sex attractions.

Still, women who have never engaged in or even thought about emotional or sexual attraction to another woman can find themselves on this unfamiliar terrain when their marriages become emotionally unfulfilling.

This lack of emotional satisfaction causes them to look outward to "someone who can understand." Women need someone to emote with, talk with, and feel safe with. Many husbands, out of a lack of understanding—or worse yet, a lack of caring—force their wives to fend for themselves.

If her husband isn't meeting his wife's needs, she will find another woman (or often another man) she believes will. If the other woman is insecure, unsupported, unhealthy, and unaffirmed in her own femininity, this can make for a tragic situation.

More and more women (even within the church) are finding themselves involved in inappropriate emotional relationships that may become sexual. While many of these relationships never cross the boundary of sexual impropriety, the damage is still palpable. Any woman who forsakes her husband (whether through his fault or not) to get her emotional needs met inappropriately is still responsible for her choices and will reap the harvest of shame, guilt, and further distance from her husband.

For more information regarding the damage of relationships defined as emotionally dependent, please read Lori Rentzels' pamphlet, *Emotional Dependency.*[21]

56. How is it that sexual abuse can lead both women and men to homosexuality? Wouldn't abused men be more likely to turn to heterosexuality?

Your question is a logical one. A little discussion of how males and females customarily respond to sexual abuse may help you better grasp this apparent contradiction.

Even though abuse is emotionally traumatizing for boys, it also can often be physically enjoyable. When boys are molested, many experience physical sensation that is pleasurable. Most women, on the other hand, describe the experience as aggressive, violative, traumatic, or painful.

Girls who have been abused often fear men and masculinity. Thus the women turn to other women out of a fear of men, and boys who embrace homosexuality often do so out of a search for the "pleasure" they experienced. Abuse damages gender-identity formation in both sexes.

Answers for Those Desiring Change

THE ROAD OUT OF HOMOSEXUALITY IS LONG and often arduous, but the rewards are great. Many who have walked the road before you will tell that this is a struggle they wouldn't wish on anyone, but they've grown thankful in the midst of it because of what it's taught them. It's given them everything they value in their lives—family, friends, fellowship with other believers, and most importantly, a dependence on and relationship with Christ that they never would have developed without this struggle. Life without temptation exists for no one this side of heaven, but a life of victory here and now is possible for all. You can become the man or woman of God He has always intended for you to be. And the ultimate reward is reflected in His promise to you that "he who overcomes will...be dressed in white. I will never blot out his name from the book of life, but will acknowledge his name before my Father and his angels" (Revelation 3:5).

57. Can a homosexual really change?

If you believe in an all-powerful God, the obvious answer to this question is the loudest possible "Yes!" First Corinthians 6 spells this out gloriously when it proclaims that true freedom for homosexuals can be found in that one four-letter, life-giving word found in the first phrase of verse 11: "and that is what some of you *were*." After listing a number of vices that focus our need for Christ's forgiveness, Paul proclaims this truth for all mankind—regardless of what sin has beset them—that true change is possible through the provision of Christ.

But things aren't so cut-and-dried for the men and women who have prayed for years for this same God to take away their unwanted homosexuality—and still find themselves losing the battle against their desires.

For people like that—and I used to be one of them—the divine potential for change seems little more than a silly pipe dream. They are the ones who must first see the love of Jesus through their friends and loved ones. That is the only way they will ever be able to trust in the redemptive power of Jesus.

And what of those who don't struggle with homosexuality themselves but have simply bought into the gay activists' agenda? How do we convince them that change is possible? A good place to start is with science, where the most recent findings supporting God's promise for freedom have come from one of the most unlikely voices— Dr. Robert Spitzer. You might have heard his name before: He was, in fact, the architect of the movement within the psychiatric community to stop classifying homosexuality as a disorder (see question 98). Dr. Spitzer says, "In 1973, I opposed the prevailing orthodoxy in my profession by leading the effort to remove homosexuality from the official list of psychiatric disorders. For this, liberals and the gay community respected me."[1]

But in 2001, he lost that respect when he issued a new study that sought to prove whether men and women struggling with unwanted homosexuality could effectively alter their orientation. What he found echoed the results of much earlier research by Irving Bieber, who concluded that "the therapeutic results of our study provided reason for an optimistic outlook. Many homosexuals became exclusively heterosexual....Although this change may be more easily accomplished by some than others, in our judgment, a heterosexual shift is a possibility for all homosexuals who are strongly motivated to change."[2]

Spitzer phrased it this way: He found "many made substantial changes in sexual arousal and fantasy—and not merely behavior." Sadly, those findings left him facing the wrath of those gay activists whose cause he still overwhelmingly supports:

> Now, in 2001, I find myself challenging a new orthodoxy. This challenge has caused me to be perceived as an enemy of the gay community, and of many in the psychiatric and academic communities.

The assumption I am now challenging is this: that every desire for change in sexual orientation is always the result of societal pressures and never the product of a rational, self-directed goal. This new orthodoxy claims that it is impossible for an individual who was predominantly homosexual for many years to change his sexual orientation—not only in his sexual behavior, but also in his attractions and fantasies—and to enjoy heterosexuality. Many professionals go so far as to hold that it is unethical for a mental-health professional, if requested, to attempt such psychotherapy.[3]

So is there hope for change? Yes, but whether a homosexual desiring change seeks his or her answer in the reality of unbiased psychological study—like Spitzer's—or in the undeniable truth of the Bible found in 1 Corinthians, that person must be highly motivated and "hold unswervingly to the hope [we] profess, for he who promised is faithful" (Hebrews 10:23).

58. How does a person struggling with homosexuality become heterosexual?

No "one size fits all" method exists for transformation. The process is as varied as the people who engage in it. Yet some common dynamics do mark the path to overcoming same-sex attraction and embracing a heterosexual identity.

As I've mentioned in some of my answers to other questions in this book, a host of root causes can contribute to any individual's adoption of a homosexual orientation, including the formation of a gender-identity disorder (GID) in early childhood, peer ridicule, a lack of same-sex bonding and identification with peers, a skewed relationship with either mother or father, and sexual abuse. For effective change to happen, these roots must be discovered, ripped up, and replaced—a process often best done through either personal counseling or involvement in an Exodus International or similar ministry. Personal study and reflection is necessary, but it is not usually sufficient alone. A homosexual seeking change needs support, and part of that support can come through a good local church. Those who integrate and invest in a church tend to be propelled in their process.

If change is your goal, you will find that you have a lot to offer the body of Christ. The Lord has gifted you, and He wants and encourages you to give back to Him and those He loves. Don't for a minute play into the hand of Satan by believing that your case is "different" or that you have nullified yourself from being of value in the kingdom of God here on earth through your previous life. "God's gifts and his call are irrevocable" (Romans 11:29).

Once you recognize the contributing factors at work in your own struggle with same-sex attraction, a game plan for how best to address them is crucial. But before you take this step, find a group of three to five same-sex individuals in whom you can confide and ask for assistance, prayer, and accountability. Facing the factors that lead to homosexuality can bring up old hurts and you'll need friends to support you on this journey.

The contributing factors add up to this: You have sexualized unmet emotional needs. So the healing process includes finding appropriate ways to meet these legitimate needs through healthy activities and relationships. As you do so, you will notice the longing for inappropriate activities and relationships melts away.

Early in my healing, I remember uncovering the painful reminder that I never felt accepted by the other boys growing up. I wasn't comfortable in their realm. So through the encouragement of Jeff Konrad, my best friend and author of *You Don't Have to Be Gay,* I ran *toward* my fears. I found myself, with no small amount of trepidation, approaching situations that years earlier would have petrified me. They still were scary, but I walked away from these situations feeling confident, secure, and better about myself in the world of men. After conquering one of these fears, I noticed that weeks would go by without sexual temptation with little to no effort on my part. What was going on here? The answer is that I was now getting my needs met appropriately instead of seeking solace from a sexual experience.

Any gay man or woman who wants to change must realize this process isn't going to be easy. Scripture encourages us to count the cost of any commitment (Luke 14:28). The key to this process may take years, so be patient.

You can't be expected to work through everything tomorrow. As a matter of fact, almost 20 years later, I'm still finding aspects of my life that the Lord wants to redeem as He continues to mold me into the man He intends me to be.

To explore the healing process in greater depth, please read *Coming Out of Homosexuality* by Bob Davies and Lori Rentzel, published by InterVarsity Press.

---

59. I've just started researching the change process. What program do you find to be the most successful?

This is a common question for those who have recently made the decision to leave homosexuality. The problem, however, is that there is no one "generic" answer because the available programs, methods, and techniques are as varied as the individuals seeking their support. Mark Yarhouse and Lori Burkett concur with this observation in their book, *Sexual Identity:*

> No one approach works for everyone, and not everyone will be helped by a particular approach. Contrary to popular belief, there are no systematic hoops to jump through to achieve "healing" from homosexuality. Each person is unique. As different as fingerprints, we each bring in humble petition to the throne of grace a multitude of interconnected experiences and actions that impact every area of our lives. The struggle with same-sex attraction will be similar in some ways, yet markedly different for each individual, as will the working toward your specific life goals.[4]

Consider two things before you explore your options: First, you must have an unwavering commitment to the process regardless of how painful, arduous, or long it is. Second, you must understand that no method, process, or technique is more important than a heart that is obedient and submitted to God.

But various types of support are available. Some, called "drop-in" groups, demand very little commitment other than showing up when you want to. Another type of group, known as a "committed" group, is much more regulated. It often involves an interview process, some financial investment, and a strong commitment to attendance and study. These groups often last for a specific length of time—usually no longer than six months—and require your attendance at the majority of the meetings. Such a group will only really work if you are willing to accept strict behavioral guidelines and are ready to face your pain, secrets, and doubts in the presence of others.

If neither of these options would work well for you at this time, you might choose to explore one-on-one therapy. But remember, not just any therapist will do. Many well-meaning counselors are not well versed in the complex issues that govern sexual identity. You'll need to do a fair amount of research here: How many people with homosexual struggles have these counselors helped? What do they believe about homosexuality, its origins, the change process, and recovery? If a given therapist's tenets don't line up with God's Word, move on.

Other options include programs that offer residential support—both long- and short-term. Be sure to investigate the admittance requirements, program guidelines, and curricula.

Something to keep in mind in all of the research you do is that similar kinds of groups can have differences in approach. Some programs approach homosexuality from a clinical standpoint, while others take a much more spiritual approach. Please remember that neither of these is better than the other. But the group you decide to become a part of—regardless of its means, technique, or style—must never conflict with biblical teaching and truth.

60. I've just made the decision to leave homosexuality. What do I need to know? What have you seen in the lives of those who are successful?

Make no mistake about it—leaving homosexuality is not easy. Many gay men and women do *start* the healing process, only to drop out when the going gets tough. I remember sitting at my first Exodus International conference in the summer of 1990 in San Antonio. It was one of the lowest points in my life. I had just left the only community I had known for 12 years, I missed my gay friends terribly, and I didn't seem to be making any progress in abstaining from homosexual activity. I prayed that here, at this conference, I would find some practical tools that would help me in my struggle, or at the very least, a flashlight to help me navigate the darkness. I left with something more important, something God knew I needed—hope!

Years later I had the opportunity to speak at an Exodus International conference. While praying about what I should teach, the Lord reminded me of what I had so desperately wanted at the beginning of my process. So, wanting something tangible—something that would help me to evaluate my status and progress—I came up with an idea. I would share with the attendees at the 2002 Exodus International conference the top five characteristics of those who find lasting freedom from homosexuality.[5]

I based my five characteristics not only on my own experience but on the advice of experts like Bob Davies, director emeritus of Exodus International and author of several books on the topic; Frank Worthen, author and one of the founding fathers of Exodus International; his wife, Anita, author of *Someone I Love Is Gay*; Sy Rogers, past Exodus International board president and nationally known speaker; Jeff Konrad, author of *You Don't Have to Be Gay* and the man whose unconditional love helped me out of homosexuality; and Anne Paulk, author of one of the only resources for women on this topic, *Restoring Sexual Identity*.

Here's what we all identified as the five most common characteristics of those who succeed at permanently leaving homosexuality.

1. *A Right Motivation*

The hallmark of this quality is a "no matter what" type of devotion to leaving the gay lifestyle. You must be desperate for change. The author of the devotional *Thoughts from the Diary of a Desperate Man* put it like this: "Christianity is a religion of rescue, designed for the desperate. Just as an awareness of one's depravity is essential for holiness, so too a feeling of desperation, manifested in perpetual brokenness and dependence, is the heart of the believer's life in Christ."[6] Mark 5:24-29 illustrates this trait clearly in the story of a desperate woman who had been sick for a number of years:

> A large crowd followed and pressed around him. And a woman was there who had been subject to bleeding for twelve years. She had suffered a great deal under the care of many doctors and had spent all she had, yet instead of getting better she grew worse. When she heard about Jesus, she came up behind him in the crowd and touched his cloak, because she thought, "If I just touch his clothes, I will be healed." Immediately her bleeding stopped and she felt in her body that she was freed from her suffering.

Think she was desperate for healing? Look at what she endured. She was more than likely anemic from the loss of blood, which was probably menstrual in nature. And by the way, in those days a woman with such an ailment would certainly have been considered unclean, unwelcome in public, and undoubtedly the object of much open scorn. Yet she persevered. She went toward Jesus with a desperation that caused Him to notice. She touched His garment and she was healed.

Have you realized your desperation? Are you only looking toward Jesus, or do you have your eyes turned toward the familiarity of your sin? Are you willing to endure public ridicule from the gay community? These are just a few of the questions to ask yourself regarding your motivation.

2. A New Goal

The only true goal that sustains the type of perseverance needed for this journey is summed up in one word—*obedience*. If you focus on obtaining heterosexuality, not achieving obedience, your chances of failure are enormous. That's because the opposite of homosexuality is not heterosexuality—it's *holiness*. And when we strive toward holiness in a quest to become more Christlike, the desires of the flesh fall away and we begin to obtain freedom like never before. A freedom that for *some* will include heterosexual desires.

If you feel as if you're stifled in your relationship with Christ and you just can't seem to be obedient, remember what Jane Boyer, a past Exodus International board member and national speaker on this topic, says: "God will never reveal more truth about Himself until you have obeyed what you already know."[7]

Are you being obedient? Is your goal to achieve holiness or heterosexuality?

3. *Changed Relationships*

The person who is successfully dealing with his or her homosexuality has a strong commitment to healthy relationships—especially in the area of open, honest, and strong accountability. James 5:16 tells us, "Confess your sins to each other and pray for each other so that you may be healed." True healing is found in confession and bringing our weaknesses into the light, regardless of how ashamed or scared we might feel. Remember, our God is a God who forgives sin when we confess it. He doesn't condemn us for it.

4. *A Commitment to Action*

Are you running toward your fears or are you sitting and waiting for someone to serve you your healing on a silver platter? Are you reading books, memorizing Scripture, actively seeking support? Second Peter 1:3-11 has some practical advice for those who are motivated for success:

> His divine power has given us *everything* we need for life and godliness through our knowledge of him who called us by his own glory and goodness. Through these he has given us his very great and precious promises, so that through them you may *participate* [not take or receive] in the divine nature and escape the corruption in the world caused by evil desires. For this reason, *make every effort* to add to your faith goodness; and to goodness, knowledge; and to knowledge, self-control; and to self-control, perseverance; and to perseverance, godliness; and to godliness, brotherly kindness; and to brotherly kindness, love. For if you possess these qualities in increasing measure, they will keep you from being ineffective and unproductive in your knowledge of our

Lord Jesus Christ. But if anyone does not have them, he is near-sighted and blind, and has forgotten that he has been cleansed from his past sins. Therefore, my brothers, *be all the more eager* to make your calling and election sure. *For if you do these things, you will never fall,* and you will receive a rich welcome into the eternal kingdom of our Lord and Savior Jesus Christ (emphasis added).

Do you want to be successful? There's the recipe.

5. *A Different Passion*

Success in overcoming homosexuality—or any sinful lifestyle for that matter—is almost impossible to sustain unless your heart's passion is to know Christ and do what pleases Him. Second Timothy 2:3-4 explains such passion this way: "Endure hardship with us like a good soldier of Christ Jesus. No one serving as a soldier gets involved in civilian affairs—he wants to please his commanding officer."

Consider this admittedly offbeat example: Back in the late 1970s, the Palestinian Liberation Organization (PLO) orchestrated numerous hijackings, attempting acts of terror much like those of the al Qaeda network of today. During one of these hijackings, a passenger was able to engage one of the terrorists in a very telling conversation, filled with questions designed to remind him of the ramifications of his actions should he be caught:

"Don't you know that the police are going to come?"

"Don't you know that you will be caught?"

"Don't you know that you could be killed?"

"Aren't you afraid to die?"

The hijacker's response was very telling: *"I died the moment I joined the PLO."*

That, my friend, is *passion*—used incorrectly, but passion just the same. Oh, that you and I would follow Christ with such passion.

Examine your life in light of these five characteristics. Don't feel defeated if you come up lacking, but pray and ask the Lord to reveal to you His direction. Then wait, listen, and be faithful.

61. What about trained professionals? Have therapists favorable to change found some factors that increase the likelihood of a positive outcome?

Some factors definitely increase the likelihood of success for someone attempting to leave homosexuality. These factors have been the subject of much research and debate, but they will increase anyone's chances of leaving homosexuality behind.

By far the most significant factor in predicting a positive outcome has to do with one's motivation. Studies have shown a strong correlation between an individual's unwavering motivation and his or her outcome. Even Dr. Robert Spitzer, the man behind the efforts in the psychiatric community to remove homosexuality from the list of psychological disorders, has since found this favorable relationship to be a strong indicator of success.[8]

Few professionals in this area have as much expertise as Dr. Joseph Nicolosi. He's worked with over 1000 men and is the president of the National Association for the Research and Treatment of Homosexuality (NARTH). Since I have personal experience but not clinical experience, I'll let Dr. Nicolosi speak about the factors that foster successful outcomes.

> Other indicators of favorable prognosis are lack of indulgence in self-pity, a positive sense of self, and the ego-strength to tolerate stress and frustration. Heterosexual fantasies and dreams are also strongly favorable. Also the stronger the family relationships the client has, the better the prognosis....
>
> Traditional values and the sense of oneself as a member of heterosexual society are also strongly supportive in providing a framework from which to reflect on the homosexual experience....Other factors in treatment success are the ability to resist impulsive behaviors and to postpone gratification, the ability to set goals, and the capacity to reflect upon, verbalize, and learn from past experiences....
>
> Men who have been less sexually active have better prognoses. Considering the habit-forming nature of sexual behavior, the

more homosexually active the client is, the more difficult the course of treatment....

Two final qualities that are of the utmost value—second only to motivation to change—are *patience* with oneself and an *acceptance* of the ongoing nature of the struggle.[9]

So, whether you want to change or are rooting for someone else's success, these are great qualities to commit to prayer. Ask the Lord to strengthen these traits in you, your friend, or your loved one. Hold fast to the promise of Christ that He will never give you more than you can handle and will always provide a way of escape should negative opportunities arise (1 Corinthians 10:13).

62. Is the issue of masturbation something that I need to be concerned with?

It's common for those who have found comfort or fulfillment of their unresolved identity issues by engaging in same-sex sexual relationships to continue to have a strong urge to masturbate long after their homosexual relationships have ended. Many continue to engage in this behavior while questioning if it's wrong. Although the Bible is not specific regarding whether this behavior is sinful, there are two important thoughts to consider.

The first pertains to whether masturbation is right or wrong for the Christian. For the majority of people that engage in this behavior—whether homosexual or heterosexual—it usually is accompanied by an active fantasy life. Jesus minces no words regarding the reality of sin in our thought life. "I tell you that anyone who looks at [another] lustfully has already committed adultery with [him or her] in [his] heart" (Matthew 5:28). So, the first concern we should have is the presence of the lustful fantasies that accompany masturbation.

Secondly, consider whether masturbation furthers your healing. Many believe that since they are no longer engaging in sexual behavior with another person, they are decreasing their desires or addiction. Just the opposite is true. You see, your body and mind don't know the difference between an orgasm brought on by a physical encounter with another or masturbation accompanied by sexual fantasy. The result? You are continuing to strengthen these unhealthy desires and behaviors and reinforcing the addiction. Besides, masturbation is often used as a coping mechanism, a form of comfort, when you feel out of sorts or are leery of facing feelings you'd prefer to avoid. But the healing process includes learning to deal with these feelings forthrightly and finding healthier ways to cope. This is where true freedom comes from—not being bound to inappropriate behaviors but fulfilling healthy desires with genuine relationships—relationships that have the ability to reach places in your heart you never thought possible.

63. Will my struggle ever completely go away?

This question is one that plagues many people who are overcoming a homosexual struggle. A person's level of motivation does help to predict his or her success, but effort is not always the answer.

In their book, *Sexual Identity,* Mark Yarhouse and Lori Burkett write:

> It is important to understand that effort does not always predict success when it comes to a change of orientation. Many people try for years and invest emotionally and financially in a change program only to continue to experience same-sex attraction at least occasionally. They are often hurt when they come across Christians who tell them that they just haven't tried hard enough, or that they just don't have enough faith that God will heal them....Although we believe that God can intervene in a person's life and miraculously act to change any concern, including a person's unwanted sexual orientation, in most cases God does not intervene in this way. As with most other besetting conditions, God can bring healing, but He often chooses not to. In each specific case we don't know why God allows a person to live with any one of a number of conditions, but we do know that God promises not to abandon us in our struggles.[10]

This is true in my case. While temptations still occasionally come my way, I liken them to a pesky fly. They pass my way and bother me for a minute, I shoo them away, and then they're gone. I must frequently remind myself of the truth that I am a new creation in Christ (2 Corinthians 5:17) in the spiritual realm—but in the physical one, I will continue to deal with temptation. However, this does not negate the fact that I live in complete victory.

None of us, this side of heaven, is completely free from temptation. That's why Jesus offers Himself with the words, "Come to me, all you who are weary and burdened, and I will give you rest" (Matthew 11:28). And in doing so, He also promises to be faithful. "He will not let you be tempted beyond what you can bear. But when you are tempted, he will also provide a way out so that you can stand up under it" (1 Corinthians 10:13).

64. What would you suggest to a person who is religious (Muslim, Buddhist, or Hindu) but not a Christian and who is interested in leaving homosexuality?

Leaving homosexuality isn't something only Christians can accomplish. People of many faith backgrounds seek to overcome homosexuality when they're unable to reconcile their same-sex attraction with their religious beliefs. Not every religion, though, is as well-suited as Christianity to help men and women accomplish this. Some religions don't believe change is possible. And in some faiths, death can be the punishment for confessing one's homosexuality.

Religious faith is not a prerequisite for pursuing change. Prominent medical and mental health professionals have been helping people overcome unwanted homosexuality and recover heterosexual identities since the 1930s.[11] And many respected clinicians confirm the possibility of change from a psychological perspective.

- The National Institute of Mental Health states that over 50 percent of homosexually oriented (or acting) individuals who present themselves for treatment can be helped to become heterosexual.[12]

- According to Dr. Charles Socarides, once a professor at Albert Einstein College of Medicine, "There is at present sufficient evidence that in a majority of cases homosexuality can be successfully treated by psychoanalysis."[13]

- World-renowned sexologists William Masters and Virginia Johnson reported evidence of a 71.6 percent success rate for patients leaving homosexuality after a follow-up study of six years.[14]

But the most impressive summary of documented recovery from homosexuality was compiled and illustrated in Dr. Jeffrey Satinover's book, *Homosexuality and the Politics of Truth*. Dr. Satinover tabulated the success rates of several researchers, highlighting their methodology and the percentage of successes per number of clients treated.

He noted that "the composite of these results gives an overall success rate of over 50 percent—where success is defined as 'considerable' to 'complete' change."[15]

So, what would I tell a person who is interested in leaving homosexuality and whose faith is different from mine or who has no faith at all? Trusting in Jesus Christ is what worked for me and many others, but in any circumstance there is hope for change!

65. When am I, someone who has struggled with homosexuality, healthy enough to help another?

I appreciate your heart to "comfort those in any trouble with the comfort [you yourself] have received from God" (2 Corinthians 1:4). However, I would be remiss if I didn't temper that sentiment with a little caution. You are going to be able to bring someone who struggles only as far as you have already brought yourself. Therefore, you have to honestly assess your progress. What are your weaknesses? Your temptations? What issues need further attention?

Helping others will spotlight the areas in your life that still need further healing. Not that this is a negative, but without the security of strong accountability, this may become hazardous. Proceeding with accountability allows you the safety valve of pulling back should you find your desire to help is stronger than your resolve.

One of the safest ways to test your readiness is by helping others in a group situation. This allows you to share the responsibility, allowing you to help but still be able to bounce your concerns, struggles, and other issues off someone else. Remember, "many advisers make victory sure" (Proverbs 11:14).

I would rarely encourage someone to help another one-to-one—especially in this area of struggle. If you believe God is calling you to do this, however, public settings are highly recommended. Those who, like you, are able to get over their own introspection and give back to others tend to accelerate in their own process. May the Lord richly bless your efforts!

8

Answering Theology

THE THEOLOGICAL DEBATE OVER what God's Word says about homosexuality is a fairly new phenomenon. Postmodern society has trampled the truth at the expense of His creation, trading true freedom for the lies of this world. There is no shortage of opposition to God's plumb line regarding sexuality. I hope these answers will help you to spot a few ways some people are trading His life-giving truth for the lies that bring darkness, doubt, and death.

66. I have a friend who believes it's all right to be gay because Christ never mentions anything specifically about homosexuality in the Gospels. What is your response to this?

This line of thinking assumes that if Jesus doesn't explicitly forbid a behavior, it must be perfectly okay. But Jesus doesn't say anything in the Bible about environmental concerns, animal rights, or the neglect of the elderly. Does that mean He blesses decimating the rain forest, torturing kittens, and taking a baseball bat to Grandma?

If we base our standards only on the spoken words of Christ as found in the Scriptures, numerous moral issues are up for debate, including spousal abuse and pedophilia among them. But God gave us the entirety of Scripture from which we are to ground our faith and align our beliefs with His.

67. Which Scripture passages about homosexuality do I need to be familiar with?

There are six main passages regarding homosexuality that any Christian should be familiar with. The first three are found in the

Old Testament, beginning with Genesis 19. That's where we read the story of God pouring His judgment out on Sodom and Gomorrah. Although homosexual acts occurred in the story of the destruction of these cities, Christians must be careful not to assign what befell Sodom and Gomorrah solely to these acts. God's Word is clear regarding the reason for their destruction—their complete depravity, of which homosexuality was a part.

The next direct references to homosexuality can be found in two almost identical verses in Leviticus. The first is in chapter 18: "Do not lie with a man as one lies with a woman; that is detestable" (verse 22). And the second, in chapter 20, says: "If a man lies with a man as one lies with a woman, both of them have done what is detestable. They must be put to death; their blood will be on their own heads" (verse 13).

The truth of the sinfulness of homosexual activity remains the same, but thankfully, the punishment doesn't have to. The birth, death, and resurrection of our Savior provide another option for those who believe on His name.

The next passage often quoted in relation to this issue, the first from the New Testament, is Romans 1:24-27:

> Therefore God gave them over in the sinful desires of their hearts to sexual impurity for the degrading of their bodies with one another. They exchanged the truth of God for a lie, and worshiped and served created things rather than the Creator—who is forever praised. Amen. Because of this, God gave them over to shameful lusts. Even their women exchanged natural relations for unnatural ones. In the same way the men also abandoned natural relations with women and were inflamed with lust for one another. Men committed indecent acts with other men, and received in themselves the due penalty for their perversion.

One in-depth work dedicated to addressing the Bible's treatment of homosexuality is Robert Gagnon's *The Bible and Homosexual Practice*. In this resource, Gagnon explores this passage in Romans.

> With good reason, Romans 1:24-27 is commonly seen as the central text for the issue of homosexual conduct on which Christians must base their moral doctrine. This is true for several

reasons. It is the most substantial and explicit discussion of the issue in the Bible. It is located in the New Testament. It makes an explicit statement not only about same-sex intercourse among men but also about lesbianism. And it occurs within a substantial corpus of material from a single writer, which allows the interpreter to properly contextualize the writer's stance on homosexuality. Romans 1:24-27 is also the most difficult test for proponents of homosexual behavior to overturn.[1]

First Corinthians 6:9-11 is the passage used most frequently to encourage those struggling in this area or to refute the arguments of those who don't believe change is possible. In verses 9 and 10, Paul— through the divine inspiration of the Holy Spirit—levels the playing field regarding sin: "Do you not know that the wicked will not inherit the kingdom of God? Do not be deceived: Neither the sexually immoral nor idolaters nor adulterers nor male prostitutes nor homosexual offenders nor thieves nor the greedy nor drunkards nor slanderers nor swindlers will inherit the kingdom of God." Few who read this list believe it to be an exhaustive summary of what can keep someone from inheriting God's kingdom. The far more relevant truth of these verses is that no one is going to enter His kingdom but by a saving knowledge of Jesus Christ. Paul seems to be saying, "Look, folks, we all have something in our lives that has the ability to keep us from living in Christ's fullness as we pass from this life into the next." Homosexuality is neither the greatest nor the least—it's just another sin that can keep anyone from experiencing God's best. But repentance and salvation exist for all: "And that is what some of you were. But you were washed, you were sanctified, you were justified in the name of the Lord Jesus Christ and by the Spirit of our God (verse 11).

And the last of the six passages most frequently used in theological discussions about homosexuality can be found in 1 Timothy 1:8-10:

> We know that the law is good if one uses it properly. We also know that law is made not for the righteous but for lawbreakers and rebels, the ungodly and sinful, the unholy and irreligious; for those who kill their fathers or mothers, for murderers, for adulterers and perverts (*arsenokoitai*), for slave traders and liars and

perjurers—and for whatever else is contrary to the glorious gospel of the blessed God, which he entrusted to me.

The New International Version does not directly translate it as so, but the word *arsenokoitai* in Greek means *males who take other males to bed*. It means homosexuals.[2]

The bottom line for all Bible-believing Christians is that the Bible leaves no wiggle room regarding the issue of homosexuality. Scripture is clear that homosexuality is against God's original intent for mankind. More simply stated, it's sin.

68. Our pastor says that all homosexuals are going to hell. Is that true?

Does your pastor also believe all alcoholics are going to hell? How about all gossips? All liars? Salvation isn't dependent on some sort of sliding scale of whose sins are more serious. Each of us must believe in, acknowledge, and submit to the lordship of Jesus Christ. If brokenness is the criterion for keeping one out of heaven, I know of no one who qualifies. Man's salvation is not dependent on *our* actions but on *our belief* in His.

Many people believe in Christ—gay and straight alike—who have not yet been convicted about or enlightened to God's full truth regarding particular moral issues, temptations, or sins. That's why Jesus issued the command to "go and make disciples of all the nations, baptizing them in the name of the Father and of the Son and of the Holy Spirit, *teaching them to obey everything I have commanded you*." The revelation of God's best often must be taught.

Once someone comes to know the truth and continues to live in open rebellion, though, their love for God must be questioned. This is not my truth but His: "If you love me, you will obey what I command" (John 14:15). God calls us to judge no man's salvation but instead to trumpet His best for mankind in the hope that others will experience true freedom and live in His fullness, which can only be found through following Christ and obeying His commands.

Sadly, Christians don't always follow this example. How do we know that? Because while there are no churches targeted specifically for drug addicts, no churches for post-abortive women, no churches for adulterers, there *are* churches whose congregations are largely active gays and lesbians. An example is the network of Metropolitan Community Churches. This can only be because there *are* homosexuals who desire to love Jesus, who have not felt welcome in the congregations that have forgiven the sins of the drug abuser and the abortion survivor and the repentant adulterer. So sadly, these gays and lesbians have sought church homes in compromising denominations all too willing to ignore or distort God's intention for sexuality in an effort to appear more accepting and inviting.

Paul nailed this phenomenon in his second letter to Timothy: "For the time will come when men will not put up with sound doctrine. Instead, to suit their own desires, they will gather around them a great number of teachers to say what their itching ears want to hear. They will turn their ears away from truth and turn aside to myths" (2 Timothy 4:3-4). Those in these congregations preach a belief that thwarts Scripture in a few areas of sexuality and idolatry, in the mistaken hope that they can live lives pleasing to Him without abandoning their sin.

69. Where do some churches get the idea that there is no redemption for homosexuals?

The notion held by some churches that God won't redeem homosexuals finds its basis in Romans 1. Many editions of the NIV have a heading before verse 18 that reads, *God's Wrath Against Mankind*. The verses following this heading tell the truth of God's wrath that was revealed due to man's "godlessness and wickedness" (Romans 1:18). It continues by explaining that God's truth has been made plain, and man has rejected it by worshiping the creation rather than Him and thus, "their thinking became futile and their foolish hearts were darkened" (Romans 1:21). But the verses that are cited as proof texts of God's complete "wrath" on homosexuals read like this: "Therefore *God gave them over* in the sinful desires of their hearts to sexual impurity for the degrading of their bodies with one another.... Because of this, *God gave them over* to shameful lusts. Even their women exchanged natural relations for unnatural ones" (Romans 1:24,26, emphasis added).

Some people believe these are four eternally damning words: "*God gave them over.*" Their eisegesis (reading one's own ideas into God's Word) goes like this: "If God gave them over, then they don't have the capacity for redemption because God won't contradict Himself by changing His mind and offering salvation." Stated another way, they think that once you jump off the cliff of homosexuality, you have no hope of anything except hitting the bottom.

These people miss two truths. The first nonnegotiable to any Christian's faith is the truth of *Christ's complete work of salvation on the cross.* And the second truth is that homosexuality is just one of many sins listed in 1 Corinthians 6:9-10.

Thank the Lord for 1 Corinthians 6:11: "And that is what some of you *were.* But you were washed, you were sanctified, you were justified in the name of the Lord Jesus Christ and by the Spirit of our God." AMEN!

If you are an overcomer attempting to leave homosexuality and you find yourself doubting your salvation, stop looking at what others say, ignore the "science," pay no attention to the voices of the media and the gay community that say it isn't possible. God's Word says it, Jesus died for it—and that settles it!

70. My gay friend says that God destroyed Sodom and Gomorrah for inhospitality, not homosexuality. Is this true?

Those who profess a pro-gay Christian ideology have long used this argument—and twisted Scripture in the process. At issue is the meaning of *yada,* a Hebrew word in Genesis 19:5: "They called to Lot, 'Where are the men who came to you tonight? Bring them out to us that we can [*yada*] them.'"

Yada has two meanings. One is simply "to know, be acquainted with"; the other is "to know in a carnal sense."[3] Gays seeking biblical approval of their homosexuality choose the former meaning, even though in doing so they ignore the clear context of the passage.

Are we really to believe that "all the men from every part of the city of Sodom—both young and old" (Genesis 19:4)—broke the ancient code of hospitality by surrounding Lot's house and demanding that he send his angelic guests out so that they could "get acquainted with" them? The following verses make such an interpretation dubious at best: "Lot went outside to meet them and shut the door behind him and said, 'No, my friends. Don't do this wicked thing. Look, I have two daughters who have never slept with a man. Let me bring them out to you, and you can do what you like with them."

Why would Lot do such a despicable thing—offer his daughters who had never *yada-ed* a man—unless these men had sexual intentions? They weren't simply coming to check if Lot's guests were intruders—they wanted to sodomize them.

One last note on this subject: Jude 7 says that "in a similar way, Sodom and Gomorrah and the surrounding towns gave themselves up to sexual immorality and perversion." This clear and descriptive language does not refer to inhospitality, but plainly denotes homosexual activity.

71. If homosexuality is no worse than other sin, why did God destroy two cities for it and call it an abomination?

Several verses in Scripture refer to the destruction of Sodom and Gomorrah without isolating homosexuality as the sole reason. Some don't even mention homosexuality when discussing Sodom and Gomorrah's unabashed unrighteousness.

- "And among the prophets of Jerusalem I have seen something horrible: They commit adultery and live a lie. They strengthen the hands of evildoers, so that no one turns from his wickedness. They are all like Sodom to me; the people of Jerusalem are like Gomorrah" (Jeremiah 23:14).

- "Now this was the sin of your sister Sodom: She and her daughters were arrogant, overfed and unconcerned; they did not help the poor and needy. They were haughty and did detestable things before me. Therefore I did away with them as you have seen" (Ezekiel 16:49-50).

Other Scriptures, without a direct mention of homosexuality, obviously include these cities' acceptance of sexual perversions as a reason for their destruction.

- "In a similar way, Sodom and Gomorrah and the surrounding towns gave themselves up to sexual immorality and perversion. They served as an example of those who suffer the punishment of eternal fire" (Jude 7; see also 2 Peter 2:7).

What are we left to conclude? Grievous evils were commonplace in Sodom and Gomorrah. God's wrath was poured out on them for all of those evils, not for any individual one.

And that leads us to God's description of homosexuality as an abomination. Leviticus 18:22 is clear: "Thou shalt not lie with mankind, as with womankind: it is abomination" (KJV). Yet to distort this truth as a means of painting homosexuals as more "fallen" than anyone else is as unconscionable as gay activists' attempts to twist Scripture to sanctify their behavior.

After all, homosexuality is hardly the only thing referred to as an abomination in Scripture: covetousness (Deuteronomy 7:25), idolatry (Deuteronomy 12:31), and dishonest dealings (Deuteronomy 25:16) are just a few of the others. And don't forget, "There are six things the LORD *hates*, seven that are *detestable* (*abomination* in KJV) to him: haughty eyes, a lying tongue, hands that shed innocent blood, a heart that devises wicked schemes, feet that are quick to rush into evil, a false witness who pours out lies and a man who stirs up dissension among brothers" (Proverbs 6:16-19). Those who pride themselves on being more righteous than those involved in homosexuality must humbly realize that God hates our haughty hearts just as much as He hates every other sin.

We all need a Savior as much as homosexuals do: "All have sinned and fallen short of the glory of God" (Romans 3:23). Without Christ's work on the cross, we all would be following Sodom and Gomorrah down the wide path to eternal destruction.

---

72. A gay pastor I met said the Levitical regulation against homosexuality has more to do with idolatry than homosexuality and, in fact, no longer applies to our society. How do I respond to that?

Such comments are hardly uncommon among gay and pro-gay clergy. They most often include statements such as "Why do fundamentalist Christians quote the Old Testament on homosexuality and then ignore the commands that prohibit eating shellfish or wearing clothing of mixed fibers? How can you ignore some laws and adhere to others, especially regarding homosexuality?"

Let me address the latter argument first, since it's one I'm most often confronted with while being interviewed by gay activists or advocates with a superficial understanding of the Bible. In fact, I was once asked to respond to a section of a book called *The Lord Is My Shepherd and He Knows I'm Gay* by Troy Perry, a pro-gay minister, in which he recounts an exchange he had with a Christian woman:

> She said, "Young man, do you know what the Book of Leviticus says?"
>
> I told her, "I sure do! It says that it's a sin for a woman to wear a red dress, for a man to wear a cotton shirt and woolen pants at the same time, for anyone to eat shrimp, oysters, or lobster—or your steak too rare."
>
> She said, "That's not what I mean."
>
> I said, "I know that's not what you mean, honey, but you forgot all those other dreadful sins, too, that are in the same book of the Bible."[4]

To understand how to respond to an attack like Perry's, we first have to take a closer look at the book of Leviticus. Chapters 18–20 are known as the Holiness Code and include a set of commands given to the people of Israel for injunctions of personal and familial conduct. As Joe Dallas says in his fine book *A Strong Delusion*:

A commonsense approach to the Bible shows that certain ceremonial and dietary laws in the Old Testament, such as those quoted by Perry, aren't necessary to follow today. Christians are not, thankfully, under the Mosaic Law (Galatians 3:17-25). But the biblical commandments against homosexual conduct do not appear in the same sections as the dietary and ceremonial laws; in Leviticus…they appear alongside other sexual sins forbidden in both the Old and New Testaments.[5]

As for the claim by pro-gay theologians that the Levitical laws have much more to do with idolatry than homosexuality, the logic behind this view is that homosexuality isn't the true problem—it's only sinful when practiced as part of any idol worship. They suggest that God never condemned homosexuality per se, only the sort associated with idolatry. But this argument falls apart when you consider that adultery and incest are mentioned alongside homosexuality in these passages. Are we to conclude, then, that cheating on your wife and raping your daughter are perfectly all right—so long as they aren't undertaken in the context of idol worship?

The truth is that all these behaviors are outside God's intent for the proper expression of sexuality; all are forbidden in both the Old and New Testaments. Any Christian seeking to honestly engage the gay community with this truth would be wise to read *A Strong Delusion*. But if you are confronted with pro-gay theology before you've had a chance to look more deeply into the issue, don't try to silence your "opponents." Thank them for bringing this apparent discrepancy to your attention. Assure them of your desire to investigate, seek counsel, or research this issue so that you can meet again to discuss it.

73. I've heard that some gay-affirmative churches teach that Jonathan and David were gay. Where do they get this?

This deluded notion, like all attempts to pervert Scripture to justify homosexuality, is based on a few misinterpreted verses. The story of Jonathan and David spans several chapters within the two books of 1 and 2 Samuel. The two men meet shortly after David slays Goliath, when Saul (Jonathan's father) honors David by bringing him into his own house (1 Samuel 18:2). This was one of the highest forms of acceptance from Saul, who was the ruler of the land. Jonathan and David became as close as brothers, and "Jonathan loved him as his own soul" (1 Samuel 18:1 KJV).

People who would "prove" David and Jonathan's homosexual relationship point to two incidents. The first begins with David's growing favor in the eyes of the people, which so incenses Saul he begins to threaten David's life. Through this trying time, Saul berated his son Jonathan for maintaining a relationship with this "traitor," a conversation Jonathan shared with David, prompting David's decision to flee for his life. In 1 Samuel 20:41, the two friends say goodbye: "David...bowed down before Jonathan three times (which speaks of Jonathan's authority as the son of the king)....Then they kissed each other and wept together—but David wept the most."

Those inclined to affirm homosexuality believe this kiss to be sexual in nature. In fact, just the opposite is true, according to scholars: "There is nothing inherently homosexual about two men kissing each other in ancient Near Eastern society. These were not erotic kisses but kisses of sorrow that conveyed the deep emotional pain of a committed friendship and alliance cleft by circumstances beyond their control."[6]

Secondly, David's own words in eulogizing Jonathan years later have been misconstrued as proof of the friends' homosexuality: "I grieve for you, Jonathan my brother; you were very dear to me. Your love for me was wonderful, more wonderful than that of women" (2 Samuel 1:26). The heartfelt depth of their relationship far "surpassed anything David had ever known from a committed erotic relationship with a woman."[7]

But scholarly insight from the likes of author Robert Gagnon, however helpful, isn't really necessary to disprove the gay apologists' point. We are, after all, talking about David—a man's whose Achilles heel was his desire and insatiable lust for women. Remember, he's the same guy who had numerous concubines and wives and still couldn't be fulfilled, so he took another man's wife—Bathsheba—and killed her husband to cover his transgression. That doesn't sound much like most gay men I've met.

And besides, since when have the Scriptures ever shied away from direct expressions of inappropriate sexual relationships? If God intended for this relationship to be an endorsement of homosexuality (which would contradict His nature and the rest of the Bible), the Bible would have stated something like this: "And Jonathan knew David" or "and Jonathan lay with David." Never is the Bible unclear where sexual relationships were obvious.

The only way around the true meaning of these passages—the dearest and purest of relationship between two men—is to sacrifice God's truth on the altar of self-deception.

9

Answering Culture

Will & Grace, Queer Eye for the Straight Guy, the ordination of gay clergy, the fight to redefine marriage, teaching homosexuality in the classroom...who could deny that our culture is awash with messages that breed confusion about God's true meaning for sexuality and relationships? Society's moral compass is far from reading true north these days, and lives are being shattered as a result. What's the cost for those who find themselves off course in relation to identity and sexuality? Pleasure for a season, but torment in the long run. These answers will help you understand where society is veering off course and how you might be able, through prayer and educated responses, to dispel the darkness—a darkness that can never overcome a righteous life that is shining bright.

74. I've heard that my city has one of the highest populations of homosexuals. Is this true?

As I traveled the country, I'm often approached by people thanking me for bringing a message of hope to their community. The conversation usually goes like this: "Thank you so much for coming to our city; we really needed this message. I hear that our city has the second-highest population of gays and lesbians in the country. Do you know if that's true?" The odd thing is that every city seems to claim this title. Perhaps this is a result of the gay lobby's attempts to present itself as more prevalent than it really is.

So let's set the record straight once and for all. The U.S. Census data for 2000 shows that urban areas tend to draw most of the same-sex couples. Roughly 45 percent of same-sex couples live in 15 major metropolitan areas. Men favor downtown living—gay men tend to concentrate in gay-friendly downtown neighborhoods and urban cores. Gay women, on the other hand, prefer to cluster in smaller metro areas and suburbs.[1]

Top Ten U.S. Metro Areas for Homosexuals[2]

Women	Men
Santa Fe, NM	San Francisco/Oakland, CA
Burlington, VT	Miami/Ft. Lauderdale, FL
Portland, ME	Santa Fe, NM
Springfield, MA	Atlanta, GA
San Francisco/Oakland, CA	San Diego, CA
Corvallis, OR	Orlando, FL
Madison, WI	Los Angeles, CA
Albuquerque, NM	Seattle, WA
Eugene, OR	Austin, TX
Iowa City, IA	Portland, ME

75. There seems to be a prevailing message in our culture that homosexuality isn't different from heterosexuality. How do we contest this assertion?

The first thing to understand is the underlying message behind a statement such as "Homosexuality is just as natural, healthy, and desirable as heterosexuality."

This couldn't be further from the truth.

Homosexuality is *not* desirable—just ask anyone who considers himself or herself homosexual. Many wish for another option. But the media, some members of the scientific community, and the gay political movement have done their best to silence those voices who say that change is possible. Thus, those who accept their homosexuality often do so by default, not believing they have any other choice.

To see that homosexuality is not natural, one need only to look at the biology of the body—especially the genitalia of men and women—to recognize the truth. In fact, not even everyone in the gay community buys into the "natural" argument. Lesbian activist Camille Paglia, for instance, has this to say: "Homosexuality is not 'normal.' On the contrary it is a challenge to the norm....Nature exists whether academics like it or not. And in nature, procreation is the single relentless rule. That is the norm. Our sexual bodies were designed for reproduction."[3]

Let's also consider the healthiness of homosexuality when compared to heterosexuality. The gay community and its supporters would have you believe homosexuality is as healthy as heterosexuality. In their book *Human Sexuality*, Masters, Johnson, and Kolodny suggest "there is no evidence of higher rates of emotional instability or psychiatric illness among homosexuals than among heterosexuals."[4] This statement couldn't be further from the truth.

Quantitative and qualitative research proves just the opposite, even in cases where researchers set out to prove that homosexuality and heterosexuality were equally healthy. Stanton Jones and Mark Yarhouse exposed two studies that claimed homosexuality to be normal by finding flaws in their sampling from the start. "After volunteering, subjects were further screened and excluded on the basis of prior psychiatric hospitalization. Interestingly, 14% of the male homosexual sample and 7% of the female homosexual sample were excluded from the study because of prior psychiatric hospitalizations, yet none of the heterosexuals who volunteered (the control group sample) were excluded on that basis."[5]

So what do the studies say? Pathology (unhealthy ways of coping) is far more common in homosexuals than in heterosexuals.

More Smoking

For men: One gay man sums up the truth when he says, "The most reliable figures available suggest that nearly 40% of us do. This is almost double the rate of straight men."[6]

For women: One national survey on lesbians found that "among the sample as a whole, there were a distressingly high prevalence of life events and behaviors related to mental health problems." Just one of the many that were listed was that "almost one-third used tobacco on a daily basis."[7]

Greater Incidence of Alcohol Abuse

For men: A study in *Family Planning Perspective* found that homosexual males were at a significant risk for alcohol abuse: "Among men, by far the most important risk group consisted of homosexual and bisexual men, who were more than nine times as likely as heterosexual men to have a history of problem drinking."[8]

For women: The *Journal of Consulting and Clinical Psychologists* found some notable differences in the amount and frequency of alcohol consumption by lesbian women and that of their heterosexual counterparts. They also reported that homosexual women were more frequently involved in both heavy and binge drinking than heterosexual women (7 percent compared to 2.7 percent and 19.4 percent compared to 11.7 percent respectively).[9]

More Domestic Violence

For women: In an article entitled "Intimate Violence in Lesbian Relationships," Guat Yong Lie and Sabrina Gentlewarrier reported that among the 1099 lesbians surveyed, "slightly more than half of the women reported that they had been abused by a female lover/partner. The most frequently indicated forms of abuse were verbal/emotional/psychological abuse and combined physical-psychological abuse."[10]

For men: Authors David Island and Patrick Letellier found increased levels of domestic violence among gay men. In their book, *Men Who Beat the Men Who Love Them*, they reported that "the incidence of domestic violence among gay men is nearly double that in the heterosexual population."[11]

More Mental Illness

Dr. Dean Byrd is alarmed by the repression of this truth. "What is particularly disturbing is the lack of attention paid by the media to the research evidence reported in the *Archives of General Psychiatry* which concluded that gay, lesbian and bisexual people were at higher risk for mental illness, specifically, suicidality, major depression and anxiety disorder."[12]

More Promiscuity

For men: In their classic study, *Homosexualities: A Study of Diversity Among Men and Women*, Bell and Weinberg found that 43 percent of white male homosexuals had sex with 500 or more partners, with 28 percent having 1000 or more sex partners—numbers that far exceed that of the heterosexual community.[13]

For women: The promiscuity numbers for lesbians are nowhere near those found among male homosexuals, in part because far less research exists regarding women's issues and homosexuality. But there are some studies that, if juxtaposed, speak to the heightened promiscuity of women who have sex with women. One study found that 7 percent of white women and 11 percent of black women had six to ten same-sex partners within the prior year of the study.[14] Another study found that among heterosexual women, fewer than 1 percent had had six or more partners in the previous year.[15]

When the focus shifts to the number of partners in a lifetime, like numbers are found. One study found that 13 percent of white lesbian women and 19 percent of black lesbian women had between 25 and 99 partners in their lifetime.[16] Compare this to a study done on heterosexual women, which found that only 3 percent had 20 or more male partners in their lifetime.[17]

This is only a brief survey of the many differences between homosexuality and heterosexuality, but the conclusion is undeniable: The biblical truth that all people are created in God's image must never be extended to a belief in the equality of the behaviors of all people.

76. If God is love, then what's wrong with a man loving a man or a woman loving a woman?

Nothing is wrong with a man loving another man or a woman loving another woman, but a sexual expression of that love is strictly prohibited.

Scripture teaches that "God is love" (1 John 4:16). But that teaching cannot be twisted to support behavior that contradicts other verses that establish God's boundaries for emotional and sexual intimacy. Jesus couldn't have made this any clearer: "Haven't you read...that at the beginning the Creator 'made them male and female,' and said, 'For this reason a man will leave his father and mother and be united to his wife, and the two will become one flesh'? So they are no longer two, but one" (Matthew 19:4-6).

God *is* love, absolutely. But true love has boundaries that protect, guide, and show concern for its recipients. I desperately love my sons, but I'm not going to allow them to indulge in behaviors that I know to be harmful. Some people see such indulgence as "tolerance," but that's not the Lord's view at all. As the apostle Paul says, "For the time will come when men will not put up with sound doctrine. Instead, to suit their own desires, they will gather around them a great number of teachers to say what their itching ears want to hear. They will turn their ears away from truth and turn aside to myths" (2 Timothy 4:3-4).

---

77. Why should we Christians be so against gay marriage? It's not going to hurt our commitments to one another.

This mind-set permeates society and is also influencing the church's attitude. In an article entitled "Will Same-Sex Marriage Hurt Your Family?" Glenn T. Stanton, my friend and coworker at Focus on the Family, outlines the problem with this line of thinking with five simple points.

Number one is the fact that we have little respect for or understanding of the institution of marriage.

> Same-sex marriage proponents believe that marriage is simply a loving relationship between people that provides access to legal and health benefits. Same-sex unions turn marriage into an emotional relationship that is flexible enough to include any grouping of loving adults.... The truth is: Marriage is and has always been much more than this."

Glenn's second point focuses on the influence of marriage on society.

> Marriage exists as much for society as it does for the couple. Every society throughout the world—at all times in history until now—has held that marriage is designed to be a permanent relationship between men and women that serves the good of all. Monogamous marriage encourages men to control their sexual and aggressive energy and commit to family life. Marriage also gives

one faithful, caring husband to a woman, protecting her from becoming a thing to be collected and used by other men. Marriage is the best way to make sure that all children grow up with the benefit of a mother and father. Same-sex marriage says none of these matter, but these factors are exactly why every society has found marriage necessary.[18]

Third, Glenn points to marriage's ability to meet the needs of all involved.

Rarely have the social sciences come to a surer conclusion than on the question of how heterosexual marriage benefits men, women and children. When men and women marry, they live longer lives. They enjoy higher levels of physical and mental health. They are less likely to suffer from substance abuse. Husbands and wives are less likely to abuse each other sexually or physically. Married people miss fewer days at work, hop from job to job less often, and save and invest more money....Likewise, children with a married mother and father...have less need to visit doctors for physical or emotional problems. They do markedly better in intellectual and educational development. They are more sympathetic toward others and less likely to be in trouble at school, home or with the police....Just as a male and female are needed to create new life, they are both needed to bring a young life to healthy maturity. It is uncompassionate to deny children mothers and fathers in order to fulfill adult desire.[19]

Glenn's fourth point has to do with the way in which "marriage affirms our masculinity and femininity." After God created Adam, He realized that "it is not good for the man to be alone." And so God created Eve, who "in her female uniqueness, completed Adam just as Adam completed Eve.... Same-sex unions deny the idea that any real, deep and necessary differences exist between the sexes.... Because male and female do matter, then same-sex unions are lacking something important."[20]

Lastly, showing support for "marriage between one man and one woman is not intolerant. If so, then nature itself would be intolerant. Marriage has not been 'imposed' by some religious institution or government power. It was established by God and is enforced by nature....The meaning of marriage is not something that each new generation is free to redefine."[21]

So, as you can see, giving way to gay activists intent on redefining marriage would have devastating effects on our culture, our children, our churches, and even on our own marriages.

---

78. I saw a story on TV about Rosie O'Donnell and other gays who are adopting kids. The children seemed to suffer no ill effects. What do I need to know about this when talking to others who support gay adoption?

Children in same-sex homes are a relatively new phenomenon, but a body of research collected over the past 40 years spells out the potential ramifications for children raised in homes without fathers. A notion permeating our society is that children aren't affected by being raised in homes with same-sex parents. This belief has not only been widely perpetuated through the media but is now finding its way into social-scientific journals and, even more disheartening, into the judicial system, which is basing many of its decisions on this assumption.

The unbiased research speaks for itself. A recent ad called "When It Comes to Raising Kids, Same-Sex Marriage Isn't the Same" did a great job of spelling this out. Surveys are showing that the majority of children in same-sex homes are living with women. The authors' meta-analysis of the research concluded that children raised in these homes are more likely than other kids to experience a number of negative outcomes:

- poorer physical health
- poorer emotional health
- increased risks of suffering physical abuse
- poorer school performance
- lower self-confidence
- less compassion for others

- less respect for women
- higher rates of criminal behavior
- higher rates of sexual experimentation
- earlier onset of sexual experimentation[22]

Dr. David Popenoe, who has spent a lifetime examining the research supporting the necessity of fathers, makes this conclusion:

> We should disavow the notion that "mommies can make good daddies," just as we should disavow the popular notion of radical feminists that "daddies can make good mommies."... The two sexes are different to the core, and each is necessary—culturally and biologically—for the optimal development of a human being.[23]

We must be willing to speak on behalf of those who will be negatively affected by this—risking at times being labeled "intolerant"—to protect the most innocent of victims: today's children.

79. Don't kids just need a set of parents to love them—either same-sex parents or a man and a woman?

Our politically correct society has opened this door so far that the children's best interests have become an afterthought. Mounds of research document the harm that is done to children who are raised without a loving, married mother and father. "The most loving mother in the world cannot teach a little boy how to be a man. Likewise, the most loving man cannot teach a little girl how to be a woman. A gay man cannot teach a little girl how to be a woman. A gay man cannot teach his son how to love and care for a woman. A lesbian cannot teach her daughter how to love a man or know what to look for in a good husband."[24]

Same-sex parents will inevitably give a child an incomplete understanding of and appreciation for the differences in gender.

An e-mail from a good friend of mine, Brenda Gilman, brought this truth home to me. While catching me up on her life she shared this story:

While working at an on-campus elementary school at the University of Memphis, I encountered a child in my class of three- and four-year-olds that had two mothers. The women wore "wedding" rings and shared the same last name. One was the child's biological mother, but the child called them both Mommy. One morning, while dropping off their child, I greeted them as I did every morning and asked how they were. They replied, "Fine, but we have sure learned some new words this week." I replied, "Oh?" (rather shocked by the unpleased tone of her voice). She said, "Yes—'Power Rangers' and 'Daddy.'" We certainly don't talk about either of those things in our house, so he must have learned them here!" I was unsure what to say, so I said nothing. But I wondered how this child was not supposed to learn those words, especially "Daddy," in a public setting where every other child in the classroom talks about his or her Daddy or rides with Daddy to school.

Consider this observation from a pamphlet called *Is Marriage in Jeopardy?* by Focus on the Family: "Is love enough to help two gay dads guide their daughter through her first menstrual cycle?" This question shines the light of truth on the situation. The pamphlet goes on by answering, "Like a mom, they cannot comfort her by sharing their first experience. Little boys and girls need the loving daily influence of both male and female parents to become who they are meant to be."[25]

80. How do I respond to supporters of gay adoption when they ask me, "Isn't it better for a child to grow up with two loving same-sex parents than to live in an abusive home or be bounced around in foster care?"

In *Is Marriage in Jeopardy?* Glenn Stanton addresses the problems that pro-gay legislation poses to children through the redefinition of marriage:

You're comparing the worst of one situation (abusive hetero-sexual parenting) with the best of another (loving same-sex parenting). That's apples and oranges.

Actually, research reveals that child abuse is at its lowest when children live with both biological parents compared with higher rates for children who live with at least one nonbiological parent or caregiver. Same-sex parenting situations make it impossible for a child to live with both biological parents, thus increasing their risk of abuse.

Those who want homosexual marriage are not asking to take the children living in the most difficult situations, so it's intellectually dishonest to preface the argument with that claim. They are asking for the same thing all parents desire: healthy, happy children they can call their own. So let us dispense with the idea that same-sex couples will serve some high social good by only taking children in the most difficult situations. They have never asked for this.[26]

When debating any of these arguments, we must never forget the children whose healthy development is at stake.

81. I attended a youth pastors' meeting in my city, and many of us discussed a growing trend of girls confessing lesbian activity among their friends. Can you help us understand what's going on here?

You may have thought that the latest youth trends are cell phones, low-cut jeans, and tattoos, but don't be fooled! One of the hottest fads among teen girls today is known as "bisexual chic."

Just turn on your TV and you'll see it. Britney Spears and Madonna's infamous kiss at the 2003 MTV Video Music Awards. Episodes of *Friends* in which Joey encourages Monica and Rachel to make out for his viewing pleasure. Reality dating shows like *The 5th Wheel* and *ElimiDATE* featuring same-sex hook-ups among young women. Even your favorite sporting event isn't immune—beer commercials show a group of guys watching two women "catfight" in a public fountain. And television isn't the only advocate of this new craze. Teen magazines, music, and even clothiers like Abercrombie & Fitch promote this idea with a frenzy.

And it's catching on in cities all across the country. Consider these recent headlines: "South Florida Teen Girls Discovering 'Bisexual Chic' Trend."[27] "Partway Gay? For Some Teen Girls, Sexual Preference Is A Shifting Concept."[28] "Teen Girls Practice Sexual Equivocation."[29] Yet even more provocative are what these articles are saying. Here's an example:

> A group of teenagers is gathered at a party. Music's playing; smuggled booze is flowing. Two girls grin sheepishly at each other as a crowd goads them on. Finally, the teens relent, rewarding their audience with some mouth-on-mouth action. It's not an unusual scene, according to South Florida high school students, who say the newest trend for teen girls isn't wearing the latest designer jeans or driving a cool car, but declaring themselves to be bisexual.[30]

Another story says this: "A group of girls at a private school in Northwest Washington charge boys $10 to watch the girls make out in front of them. At one school dance earlier last year, a chaperon had to break up a group of guys circled around two girls kissing."[31]

A fun and harmless trend, or another of a host of pressures facing today's young girls? While the fallout from this phenomenon hasn't yet been realized, it isn't too hard to extrapolate that girls might experience emotional, sexual, physical, or social wounds that could affect them the rest of their lives. Parents, pastors, and youth workers must begin to impart to young girls a positive, cherished, and valued view of femininity.

For more information, contact Exodus International to order the CD *The Glory of Gender* by Janelle Hallman.

82. I've been accused of being a homophobe. How do I respond to this accusation?

Today's morally relative culture sends a message that anyone holding to absolute truth is backward, unenlightened, or old-fashioned. This "anything goes" mentality has caused many people to hold back when they have an opportunity to stand up for the truth of Scripture. Few people dare speak the truth unless they are with those who wholeheartedly agree. No one enjoys being labeled.

Gay activists are swaying the masses with false information and marginalizing any who oppose them. Marginalization can lead to vilification, which can lead to criminalization, which can end in true persecution.

Let's take a closer look at these stages:

People who would create an intimidating environment begin by identifying their opponents. Those from the gay community, for instance, don't have to look too far to find a large group that disagrees with many of the tenets of their belief system. The Christian community fits this bill just fine.

Once the opposing group has been defined, the next step is to begin to marginalize them. With the help of the media, the gay community has succeeded in portraying the "Christian right" as largely buffoonish, unrealistic, and out of touch.

But mere marginalization isn't enough. Christians are vilified with labels like "homophobic," "hate-monger," and "intolerant."

Once a group has been vilified as a real and present danger, criminalization of its actions and speech is likely. It's already happening in Canada, where gay activists are quickly moving to get "hate speech" laws passed that will prohibit pastors from describing homosexuality as a sin from the pulpit.

America is only a little behind Canada. We are in the vilification stage, quickly approaching the criminalization phase. If and when "hate crimes" and "hate speech" legislation is passed, we will quickly be ushered into criminalization, and persecution will soon follow.

Two additional points are necessary. First, Christians living in the United States need to be very careful about claims of true persecution. We can appear disingenuous when our cries of maltreatment—though they may be real—are considered alongside those of other Christians around the world who find their very lives in jeopardy simply for worshiping God.

The second point is that we can either help gay activists marginalize us or challenge their efforts. Think of the man who pickets abortion clinics, dressed in a three-piece suit, shouting at the young girl faced with the reality of an unplanned pregnancy. Is he standing for God's truth? He's got the letter of God's law correct, but he's missed the Lord's mercy by a mile. The baby will never be saved until the mother's heart is won. The same is true when you find yourself debating homosexuality. Always seek to love your accuser with more than just words. Minister to him or her with a love that is difficult to deny, a love that endures the mockery of society while holding tightly to the truth.

Is this easy? Of course not. But Jesus never promised our lives would be easy. In fact, He promised just the opposite: "If anyone would come after me, he must deny himself and take up his cross and follow me" (Matthew 16:24).

For further encouragement, please read *Why You Can't Stay Silent* by Tom Minnery.[32]

83. AIDS doesn't seem to be in the news as much as it used to be. Have we gotten a handle on it?

I'll let Dr. Harold Jaffe of the U.S. Centers for Disease Control and Prevention (CDC) take the first shot at this question. "The AIDS epidemic in the United States is far from over. HIV diagnoses among men who have sex with men surged 7.1 percent last year, according to data collected by the CDC from 25 states that have longstanding HIV reporting. New diagnoses in this high-risk group have increased 17.7 percent since 1999."[33]

Another article, "HIV Study Shows 4.4% Infection Rate For Young Gay Men," appeared in *The Wall Street Journal* (Friday, June 1, 2001) and had this to say: "A survey by the Centers for Disease Control and Prevention in Atlanta found an annual incidence of HIV, the virus that causes AIDS, of 4.4% among young gay men in six large cities. 'That means that for every 100 young gay men who aren't infected at the beginning of the year, four become HIV infected by the end of the year,' said Linda Valleroy, the CDC epidemiologist who headed the survey. She said the incidence is reminiscent of rates for gay men in the 1980's, the early years of the epidemic."[34]

Even scarier is the rate of infection for young gay African-American men. "Thirty percent of young gay black men are infected with the AIDS virus, according to a study of six large cities in the United States....The study, conducted by the Centers for Disease Control and Prevention from 1998 through 2000 in Baltimore, Dallas, Los Angeles, Miami, New York and Seattle, found that gay black men in their 20's had the highest HIV rate of any group in that age range."[35] The *Boston Globe* took this statistic and gave it some perspective. "Three in 10 young black men...may be HIV positive. If this community were a nation, only Botswana would have a higher infection rate."[36]

How can all this be happening with the prevalence of the "safe sex" message? The problem is that many young gay men are incorrectly assuming AIDS is curable. One possibility for this misunderstanding is that "because new drug treatments allow people with AIDS to live longer, officials said, younger gay men haven't seen friends die from the disease and may not take prevention as seriously as older gays."[37]

While it's true that AIDS is a universal disease and that many countries around the world are being devastated by this horrible epidemic (which for Christians should be seen as an opportunity to minister and give), we can't ignore the fact that 70 percent of new HIV infections each year occur among [gay] men.[38]

---

84. I'm a therapist in the public sector and a Christian. How would you suggest I encourage a homosexual or lesbian to reevaluate his or her lifestyle?

The hypocrisy that exists within the mental health profession is laughable. Many therapists—who should be the most committed to helping their patients pursue mental, social, and emotional health—choose political correctness over the ethics of their profession. More therapists should be willing to explore the truth with their clients.

An abundance of research points to the increase of pathology involved in homosexuality. (See question 75.) That should motivate treatment, and that treatment should address the root causes or contributing factors that ultimately led to the person's adoption of a homosexual problem.

Manipulating or changing the self-directed goal of any client is unethical. But you are being the truest to your profession when you address head-on your clients' deep-seated, unhealthy coping mechanisms. When clients see that their attractions are not based in genetics but rather on the developmental, environmental, and familial circumstances of their lives, they realize that living homosexually is not their only option.

Early in the counseling process with a patient who struggles with homosexuality, you will rarely if ever deal directly with the issue of homosexuality. Intentional confrontation of the deeper issues will surely reveal truths that cannot go unnoticed. As the individual you're seeking to help gets to the very core of his or her issues—whether it be fear, insecurity, isolation, self-esteem, sexual abuse, etc.—the counterfeit nature of homosexuality is all but certain to surface. The dissatisfaction with homosexuality will inevitably override emotional sexual desires if he or she is honestly seeking to become healthy.

When the legitimate needs of anyone's life are identified and met appropriately, the drive to fulfill them inappropriately is sure to lose its hold and the pursuit of true freedom from all detrimental coping mechanisms is sure to follow.

Answering the Gay Community and Agenda

SAME-SEX MARRIAGE, GAY RIGHTS, breaking down the notion of gender, lowering the age of consent, "tolerance," and "diversity." Not everyone who embraces a gay identity wants to see these things happen, but a small contingent of power brokers within the gay community will stop at nothing to make their dreams a stark reality for society. Gay activists base their rhetoric on "agenda" rather than true purposed reasoning, and most people won't realize what they're dealing with until it's far too late. But God's truth can still prevail in the lives of individuals struggling to free themselves from the lie of homosexuality. In fact, that truth can liberate entire cultures.

85. I listen to a lot of Christian talk radio, and I've heard the term "gay agenda" frequently. What's it really all about?

Unfortunately, the reason people use the term "gay agenda" so often is because it's shorthand for a complex, multifaceted movement. It doesn't have a simple explanation.

I learned this not long after I started at Focus on the Family. I was looking for some understanding and clarification regarding the gamut of issues related to homosexuality because I knew I'd get questions like this. After weeks of research, I found an article that encapsulates better than anything else I've ever seen the core goals of the gay movement. It's called "The Overhauling of Straight America."

The piece, written by gay men Marshall Kirk and Erastus Pill and first published in *Guide Magazine* in 1987, is a step-by-step guide to bringing about complete cultural change on the issue of homosexuality. "The first order of business is desensitization of the American public concerning gays and gay rights," Kirk and Pill write.

At least in the beginning, we are seeking public desensitization and nothing more. We do not need and cannot expect a full "appreciation" or "understanding" of homosexuality from the average American. You can forget trying to persuade the masses that homosexuality is a good thing. But if only you can get them to think that it is just another thing, with a shrug of their shoulders, then your battle for legal and social rights is virtually won.

And how did they foresee accomplishing this goal? They called for "a large-scale media campaign" to facilitate success on six essential fronts crucial to turning "straight America" on its head.

1. *Talk about gays and gayness as loudly and as often as possible.*

The idea is to normalize homosexual behavior by making discussions and examples of it commonplace. As that begins to happen, the theory goes, even those who would initially oppose homosexuality as offensive will eventually fail to be threatened by it or to even think much about it. It will simply become accepted as a routine, benign part of life. Key to pulling this off, the authors note, is the willingness of the media to play the role of gay advocate by providing "a gateway into the private world of straights, through which a Trojan horse might be passed."

Goal number one has been accomplished—as is evident in the acceptance of homosexuality in popular culture.

2. *Portray gays as victims, not as aggressive challengers.*

The notion here is that even heterosexuals who don't approve of the gay lifestyle will stand up for homosexuals if they perceive them to be oppressed and mistreated. Gays are supposedly "victims of fate," born that way and often brutalized by "homophobes" and discriminated against by society.

What is so astonishing about this, all these years later, is how this plan has been carried out with nary a hitch, manipulating the masses in just the way the authors hoped.

3. *Give protectors a just cause.*

The goal here is to get the masses focused not on homosexuality but on homosexuals. "Our campaign should not demand direct support for homosexual practices," Kirk and Pill write, "but should instead take anti-discrimination as its theme." The authors seek to manipulate heterosexuals into feeling compelled to protect the "poor" homosexuals.

4. *Make gays look good.*

The strategy here mimics the old song: Accentuate the positive. This takes on two forms: creating the impression in the minds of mainstream America that gays are everywhere and represent Everyman, and taking every opportunity to reveal the homosexuality (or alleged homosexuality) of respected historical figures from Shakespeare to Michelangelo. "In no time," the authors note, "a skillful and clever media campaign could have the gay community looking like the veritable fairy godmother to Western Civilization."

5. *Make the victimizers look bad.*

Making gays look good, though, is only half the battle. The other half is to marginalize those who believe homosexuality to be anything but God's best for mankind. This strategy has two main objectives. "First, we seek to replace the mainstream's self-righteous pride about its homophobia with shame and guilt. Second, we intend to make the antigays look so nasty that average Americans will want to dissociate themselves from such types."

Just one look at how gay activists have painted those who oppose their push for same-sex marriage shows how this technique from Kirk and Pill's playbook has been followed.

6. *Solicit funds: The buck stops here.*

The stated intent here is clear: Ask people who believe in the message and support this endeavor to put their money where their mouth is. "There are 10–15 million primarily homosexual adults in this country: if each one of them donated just two dollars to the campaign, its war chest would actually rival that of its most vocal enemies. And because those gays not supporting families usually have more discretionary income than average, they could afford to contribute much more."[1]

Now I'm hoping that you can plainly see that the "gay agenda" is more than a plan—it's a very real, well-organized, and vitriolic attempt to bring to fruition the sociological changes that would help to usher in its supporters' desires.

86. Any agenda needs support to sustain its growth. Who are the major players fueling the gay agenda?

[I'd like to have Paul E. Rondeau weigh in on this question. Mr. Rondeau has been an international sales and marketing executive for over two decades. He also has distinctive degrees such as an M.A. in Management with specialization in persuasive communication from Regent University and a B.A. in Marketing Management from Concordia University. Currently, he is a doctoral student in communication studies with a focus in rhetoric and mass persuasion. His research on gay marketing strategies has been presented to the United Nations, cited before the U.S. Supreme Court, and translated into Swedish and German. He is currently Senior Vice President with a national public policy group in Washington, D.C. Sound like someone who's in the know about organizations and their ability to fuel an agenda? I thought so too. That's why I'm going to allow him to answer this question for you.]

The Human Rights Campaign (HRC), based in Washington, DC, is the largest national homosexual lobby in the nation. Claiming 400,000 members, HRC and the Human Rights Campaign Foundation report income over $16 million. Their activity descriptions are...to propose, support or oppose legislation and the defense of human or civil rights, respectively. Their website explains that HRC is a vigilant bipartisan "watch dog" dedicated to educate Congress. Some issues that they take on include: advocating for hate crime legislation, fighting HIV/AIDS, protecting our [homosexual] families, and working for better lesbian health. Along with lobbying, intense training of future GLBT [gay, lesbian, bisexual, and transgender] political activists is part of the mission.

The Gay and Lesbian Alliance Against Defamation (GLAAD) is the dominant media relations and watchdog lobby of the homosexual movement with income of $4,199,134. The GLAAD website proudly recounts that "in 1992, *Entertainment Weekly* named GLAAD as one of Hollywood's most powerful entities and the *Los Angeles Times* described the group as possibly the most successful organization *lobbying* the *media*." One illustration is that GLAAD takes credit for getting the *New York Times* to change their editorial policy in 1987 to use the word *gay*.

GLAAD claims that it not only reached industry insiders, but has also influenced millions through newspapers, magazines, motion pictures, television and visibility campaigns. Training homosexual organizations how to deal with the media is GLAAD's mission. It supports positive portrayals of GLBT issues or images in the media but attacks any negative press. They are particularly proud of their campaign to derail Dr. Laura Schlessinger's move to television.

The National Gay and Lesbian Task Force (NGLTF, previously the same NGTF involved in the APA effort) reports income in excess of $3.5 million. Whereas HRC has an emphasis in national government and GLAAD in media, NGTLF's additional focus is also at the community level. The organization's website describes the organization's work this way: "We're proud of our commitment to the linkages between *oppressions* based on race, class, gender, and sexual orientation…NGLTF is waging a campaign against anti-GLBT *hate* crimes, which will focus on coalition-building and legislative work in key states…[and ending] institutionalized *homophobia*."

Key strategies include *public education,* grass roots training for activist skills, monitoring and reporting on legislation and building coalitions for advocacy.

"To discover what a thing is 'called' according to some system is the essential step in knowing, and to say that all education is learning to name rightly…would assert an underlying truth." Lesbian author Patricia Nell Warren put it much more succinctly: "Whoever captures the kids owns the future."

Two highly effective organizations who specialize in the K-12 education channel of influence are Parents, Families, and Friends of Lesbians and Gays (PFLAG) and the Gay, Lesbian and Straight Education Alliance (GLSEN).

PFLAG, with income of just under $1.5 million, claims membership of over 76,000 with 425 local groups. PFLAG promotes the idea that *ignorance* of homosexuality has bred a climate of torment, fear and *hatred* in our schools. They allege that the average high school student hears twenty-five anti-homosexual slurs daily and that homosexual youth *may* account for 30% of all teen suicides. Through "support," they implore an *adverse* society, an *ill-informed public*, to help create a more healthy and respectful society.

GLSEN, with income exceeding $1.8 million states that their mission is to fight the *homophobia and heterosexism* that undermine *healthy* school climates. They work to *educate* teachers, students and the public at large on how these issues have similar adverse impacts as racism and sexism. They educate the educators on how to stop discrimination and harassment based on sexual orientation and to help GLBT teachers and students fight for their rights. Their resources include such training as Homophobia 101 and 102. The organization asserts that they have trained 400 school staffs around the country and that the first statewide Safe School for Gay and Lesbian Students sponsored by the Commonwealth of Massachusetts is a result of and modeled closely on their work.

The Lambda Legal Defense and Education Fund reports income over $10,000,000 and is the homosexual-specific equivalent of the American Civil Liberties Union (ACLU). The ACLU is also very active in gay rights and reports income of over $25 million.[2]

I hope you are realizing the power behind this planned effort to impose the agenda of the gay community through the strategic efforts of public policy organizations, media outlets, grassroots activism, heterosexual sympathizers, and educational institutions. Corporations, schools, private organizations, and churches are feeling the pressure to cave to the weight this lobby is imposing. The day may not be too far away when upholding from the pulpit God's truth regarding issues of sexuality will be considered illegal. All one has to do is travel north to see it happen. Most recently, a bill (C-250) to include sexual orientation in Canada's hate-propaganda law passed by a 141–110 margin in their House of Commons. "As WorldNet Daily reported, opponents fear if the bill becomes law, the Bible will be deemed 'hate literature' under the criminal code."[3] Are we going to stand by and allow God's truth to be deemed "hateful"? We must prepare ourselves and never cave to the fear of speaking His truth in love.

For further information regarding this issue, I suggest reading *The Homosexual Agenda* by Alan Sears and Craig Osten.[4]

87. I've heard that 10 percent of the population is homosexual. Is this true?

No. But we need to understand the origins of this myth. It can be traced back to *Sexual Behavior in the Human Male*, written in the 1940s by Alfred Kinsey. In it, Kinsey states that "10 percent of the males are more or less exclusively homosexual for at least three years between the ages of 16 and 55."[5] Years later, when the gay community began to mature, it grabbed onto this figure and began to propagate the idea with the media's help.

The 10 percent fraud was conceived by Kinsey's faulty research methodology. His findings were then extrapolated and taken completely out of his intended context. For example, he included in his study population a high percentage of prison inmates and known sex offenders—groups that engage in homosexual behavior much more frequently than men in general.[6] Fully 25 percent of his sample consisted of convicted criminals—a group that comprised less than 1 percent of the U.S. population in the 1940s.[7] That's like doing a study on the percentage of Americans who like coffee—and taking your sample from the lobby of the local Starbucks.

The 10 percent myth continues to be bandied about by the media, even though some members of the gay community have admitted outright they used it fraudulently for social and political gain. Bruce Voeller is one such individual. He admits he

> campaigned with gay groups and in the media across the country for the Kinsey-based [10 percent] finding that "We are everywhere." This slogan became a National Gay Task Force leitmotif. And the issues derived from the implications of the Kinsey data became key parts of the national political, educational and legislative programs during my years at New York's Gay Activist Alliance and the National Gay Task Force. And after years of our educating those who inform the public and make its laws, the concept that 10 percent of the population is gay has become generally accepted "fact."[8]

Tom Stoddard, a former member of the Lambda Legal Defense Fund (a pro-gay legal organization) says, "We used the figure…to create an impression of our numerousness."[9] And Jill Harris, a member of the pro-gay group known as AIDS Coalition to Unleash Power (ACT-UP) says this about the "one-in-ten" myth:

> I think people probably always did know that it was inflated. But it's a really nice number that you could say, "one-in-ten," and it's a really good way to get people to visualize that we are here.[10]

88. If 10 percent of the population isn't gay, then what is the correct statistic?

The gay community and many of its sympathizers continue to spread the 10 percent myth, but the truth does occasionally come out. In a 62-page friend of the court brief filed by various pro-gay groups with the U.S. Supreme Court in the Texas sodomy case known as *Lawrence v. Texas,* a footnote buried on page 16 admitted that "the most widely accepted study of sexual practices in the United States is the National Health and Social Life Survey (NHSLS). The NHSLS found that 2.8% of the male, and 1.4% of the female, population identify themselves as gay, lesbian, or bisexual."[11]

Still, even while admitting these truthful numbers, gay activists can't help but exaggerate by adding that "this amounts to nearly 4 million openly gay men and 2 million women who identify as lesbian."[12] This number was obviously arrived at by multiplying the percentages of gays and lesbians by the total number of people in the U.S. But that overall number includes 60 million Americans who are under 14—of which 40 million are under 9.[13] To count them among the percentage of gays and lesbians is laughable.

Further insight into the accurate numbers of homosexuals in America can be found in an article titled "The Homosexual Numbers" in *Newsweek* magazine. It stated that "most recent studies place gays and lesbians at somewhere between 1 and 6 percent of the population."[14] A month later, in a surprising twist, both *Newsweek* and *Time* highlighted a study by the Alan Guttmacher Institute regarding the true percentage of gays and lesbians. *Newsweek* reported that "of the [3321 American] men surveyed, only 2.3 percent reported any homosexual contacts in the last 10 years, and only half of those—or just over 1 percent of the total—said they were exclusively gay in that period."[15] And *Time* called "the study, one of the most thorough reports on male sexual behavior ever."[16]

Even the researcher whose work was misinterpreted to give rise to the 10 percent myth—Alfred Kinsey—never actually promoted that number as the truth. Instead, he reported a statistic that is much closer to the truth: Only 4 percent of the males studied were exclusively homosexual throughout their lives, after the onset of adolescence.[17] Even with his flawed methodology and stilted sampling, Kinsey was only able to find 4 percent!

89. How has the 10 percent statistic become so widespread? Why is it so important to the gay community, and why have they worked so hard to get society to believe it's true?

A simple maxim will answer this question: If you tell a lie long enough and loud enough, people will eventually believe it. And as you can see from the proclamations of the gay activists in the answer to question 87, the promulgation of this lie is founded much more on an agenda than in fact. And still, the 10 percent figure is found everywhere: on television, in periodicals, and especially in academia.

Schools indoctrinate students across the country with this false statistic. They teach it as fact. A friend who is finishing her master's degree in counseling showed me what the text for her class had to say regarding homosexuality: "At least 10% of the population in the United States is composed of gays, lesbians and bisexuals."[18] And colleges and universities aren't the only place this statistic is taught as fact and left unchallenged. As a matter of fact, "Project 10," the first pro-gay curriculum to be implemented in public schools in California, takes its very name from the 10 percent fallacy.

That takes care of the "how" part of this question. As for the "why," consider homosexual activist Bruce Voeller's admission that he preached the 10 percent figure for years to convince the public and politicians that "we are everywhere"—clearly an effort to make homosexuality appear to be a legitimate lifestyle. (See question 87.) And don't think for a minute Voeller was the only one singing this tune or that inflating their numbers is the sole motivation behind the repetition of the lie.[19]

Gay activists also use the 10 percent figure to tie their quest for "equality" to the civil rights struggles of African-Americans, who not so coincidentally comprise about 13 percent of the population.[20] The goal here is to establish themselves as a minority group in need of equal protection and rights. Star Parker, a self-proclaimed "black activist, deeply committed to the principles of freedom and equality under the law" has eloquently noted:

> The gay front would like to be viewed as the latest chapter of the civil rights movement. According to their reasoning, gays are America's newest oppressed minority, seeking fairness, justice, and the right to pursue happiness in the same manner as other social groups in the country. Homosexuals today feel they are fighting the same battle that blacks fought 40 years ago. But, in fact, the gay movement is the civil rights movement turned on its head.[21]

If the gay community and its proponents can get the general public to buy into the notion that they are an abused, neglected, and forgotten minority, then people desiring to see justice prevail will surely come alongside this noble cause. But the gay community is far from powerless. It doesn't take someone whose IQ scores are in the top 10 percent of the nation to see the change this segment of the population has been able to effect on society as a whole through its 10 percent lie.

90. A friend of mine thinks that Christians are hateful when we don't think homosexuals should be granted equal protection or "civil rights" status. How should I respond?

This question shows the success of homosexual activists to ride on the coattails of the 1964 Civil Rights Act, which was implemented to grant minority class status to those in our country who were not being treated equitably. Larry Burtoft, author of *Setting the Record*

Straight, sums up the movement to tie the resistance homosexuals have felt toward their message to the discrimination experienced by blacks and others:

> Is such an analogy justified? Have homosexuals been the object of prejudice and discrimination *in the same way* as racial minorities and women? Do they really need more protection than what they now legally possess?
>
> If in asking this question, we mean something like, "Have homosexuals been the object of scorn, derision, ridicule and moral condemnation?" or "Have homosexuals been criminally abused and injured, as well as socially ostracized?"—then the answer must obviously be "yes." But if we mean, "Have they been legally discriminated against in the same way as African-Americans or women, so that additional civil rights laws protecting them are necessary?"—the answer is decidedly "no."[22]

Another way to consider this issue is to look at the criteria the U.S. Supreme Court established for groups to qualify for protection under the Civil Rights Act.

Criterion #1: A history of discrimination evidenced by lack of ability to obtain economic mean income, adequate education, cultural opportunity, or access to the political process.

It's all-too-painfully easy to see the reality of discrimination against African-Americans in this regard, but there has never been any noteworthy proof afforded the courts of this same discrimination being experienced by the gay community. Consider these findings:

- Factoring in comparative household sizes, gays average an annual individual income of $36,800, compared with $12,287 for average Americans and a mere $3,041 for disadvantaged African-Americans. This means that homosexuals, on average, make more than 300 percent more than the typical straight American and 1200 percent more than a disadvantaged African-American.

- More than three times as many gays as average Americans are college graduates (59.6 percent vs. 18.0 percent; gays average 15.7 years of education vs. 12.7 for average Americans)—dwarfing achievements of truly disadvantaged African-Americans and Hispanics. More than three times as many gays as average Americans hold professional or managerial positions (49.0 percent vs. 15.9 percent), making gays outrageously more advantaged than true minorities in the job market.

• 65.8 percent of gays are overseas travelers, more than four times the percentage (14.0 percent) of average Americans. More than 13 times as many gays as average Americans (26.5 percent vs. 1.9 percent) are frequent flyers.[23]

Criterion #2: Prospective suspect classes should, "averaged" as entire classes, clearly demonstrate political powerlessness.

The power of the gay lobby is impossible to miss. Public schools, federal, state, and local legislation, our country's military, the media, many mainline church denominations, as well as national organizations and corporations have all seemingly felt the push of this powerful force—a record of success made all the more remarkable by the fact that the overall population has far fewer homosexuals than there are concentrations of any other politically aware "minority" group. It's ludicrous, to say the least, for anyone to argue that this criterion applies to gays.

Criterion #3: Specially protected classes must exhibit obvious, immutable, or distinguishing characteristics, like race, color, gender, or national origin, that define them as a discrete group.

Though the gay lobby has attempted to convince the "powers that be" that homosexuality is indeed immutable, they have been unable to do so. On the other hand, there is ample proof that homosexuality is changeable, a fact to which large numbers of former homosexuals can bear witness. As Burtoft notes,

> Given the fact that the Supreme Court has refused to grant protected class status for the mentally ill and the retarded, or even the elderly, the characteristics of which can all be considered as "natural," it should hardly come as a surprise that they have overwhelmingly denied this status to homosexuals. Thus, homosexuals fail the third criterion of a special class.[24]

What does all this add up to? By the guidelines of the highest court in the land, homosexuals are not eligible for the legal protections that have been extended via the 1964 Civil Rights Act. That's helpful information to have the next time a friend accuses you of "hateful" judgment, allowing you to point out the injustice of any community attempting to make a mockery of efforts to grant fair and impartial treatment under the law to those who have truly been discriminated against.

91. I've read that the suicide rate among gay teens is high. Is this true?

The gay community would have you believe that 30 percent of all teen suicides are linked to kids struggling with their homosexuality in an intolerant, homophobic society. This myth was born in a 1989 paper entitled, "Gay Male and Lesbian Youth Suicide," the work of a federal task force headed by a gay man, Paul Gibson.[25] This paper was later published in the *Health and Human Services Journal,* lending it the specter of credibility. But Dr. Louis Sullivan, the Secretary for Health and Human Services (HHS) at the time, denounced the paper as flawed:

> The views expressed in the paper entitled "Gay Male and Lesbian Youth Suicide" do not in any way represent my personal beliefs or the policy of this Department.[26]

This paper is full of erroneous information and statistical outcomes. The first that's worth mentioning is Gibson's use of the "10 percent of the populace is homosexual" myth in calculating his findings. We all know that to use a skewed or inaccurate number in an equation will produce a false conclusion—especially when the number used is almost 10 times greater than that which any accurate surveys have presented (see question 88). The second glaring problem is his use of a "finding" that was published in a 1985 edition of a gay newspaper, the *Washington Blade,* which suggested that 3000 gay youth commit suicide each year.[27] The problem with this number is that it exceeded the total number of suicides by *all* teens that year by more than a thousand.

What makes all of this particularly galling is that these statistics are promoted time and time again by homosexual activists with nary a challenge. School boards, curriculum committees, teachers, and parents—all of whom care about children—falsely assume these numbers to be correct and base educational decisions on this and similar erroneous information. Statistics like these further the pro-gay agenda to paint gays as victims and heterosexuals as mean-spirited, intolerant bigots (see question 85).

For an in-depth look at problems with this study, please see "The Gay Youth Suicide Myth" by Peter LaBarbera which was published in the *Journal of Human Sexuality*.[28]

92. What's wrong with school-based programs that provide safety and support for kids struggling with their sexual identity?

One of the greatest threats facing children today is homosexuality education. Often under the guise of "safe school" curricula, schools force onto children inappropriate, inaccurate lesson plans reeking of the pro-gay agenda.

Of course, schools should become safer so that all children can learn. But isolating and bringing in an erroneous curriculum to support gender-confused children is the worst possible solution. Why? When those poor children walk into the counseling office for help, they are going to be offered one option for support: An organization or counselor who will help them "become comfortable with their homosexuality."

Consider this: One of the most popular offerings for schools looking to provide a "safe" place for kids comes from an organization known as the Gay, Lesbian, Straight Education Network (GLSEN). This group encourages schools to create clubs known as Gay/Straight Alliances (GSAs), designed to help "educate" and "support" all kids who need information regarding the issue of homosexuality. While GLSEN representatives attempt to include the straight kids to support and protect the gay students, their goal is the desensitization of all youth regarding issues of homosexuality. Few heterosexual students are comfortable in most of those clubs, and those who are experiencing same-sex attractions wind up being further isolated from the rest of their peers, pigeonholed into a club that ends up being little more than a haven for gay youth.

Such clubs, curricula, and "tolerance" trainings mislead the youth, faculty, and staff who must attend (as well as those who show up voluntarily). We all know that any decision is only as good as the information with which that decision is made. With the help of GLSEN and other pro-gay "safe schools" programs, more and more youth will erroneously decide that homosexuality is their only option and find solace with adults that encourage experimentation and identification with the homosexual community.

For more information regarding the dangers of pro-gay curricula, call Focus on the Family at 1-800-A-FAMILY and request *Teaching Captivity?*[29]

93. What are ex-gays going to say if scientists ever find a genetic link to homosexuality?

The person who asks this question is more than likely coming at the issue from a "born gay" perspective. And as daunting as it may seem—especially to those who have chosen to leave homosexuality—its power is annulled by an even greater one: God's truth.

The path of someone considering freedom from homosexuality must never be swayed by the findings of science but instead be led by the voice of the Scientist—the One who created all things.

Still, for the sake of argument, let's hypothesize about a day when an indisputable biological link is found. It wouldn't be the first dangerous or destructive behavior tied to genetics: violence, alcoholism, and depression are just a few that may have such roots. But does genetic predisposition mandate a behavior? The best answer I've heard to that question comes from Dr. Jeffrey Satinover in his book *Homosexuality and the Politics of Truth:*

An obvious example of this principle is basketball. No genes exist that code for becoming a basketball player. But some genes code for height and the elements of athleticism, such as quick reflexes, favorable bone structure, height-to-weight ratio, muscle strength and refresh rate, metabolism and energy efficiency, and so on.... Someone born with a favorable (for basketball) combination of height and athleticism is in no way genetically programmed or forced to become a basketball player.[30]

And even the loudest proponents of the "born gay" theory can't deny the role that one's environment and experience play in predicating certain behaviors. Dean Hamer (the "gay gene" guy) had this to say: "We knew also that genes were only part of the answer. We assumed the environment also played a role in sexual orientation, as it does in most if not all behaviors."[31]

The bottom line for anyone claiming a faith based on Scripture is that even if a genetic cause for homosexuality is discovered, God's Word still makes no provision for homosexual behavior. Joe Dallas, author and former president of Exodus International, hammers the final nail into this casket when he points out that "immoral behavior cannot be legitimized by a quick baptism in the gene pool."[32]

94. I heard a gay activist say that ex-gay organizations like Exodus International don't record statistics related to the number of people who have successfully come out of homosexuality. Is this true?

[This is a favorite attack from those in the gay community who want to discredit the truth that change is possible. Don't believe it. In fact, take a moment to listen to what Alan Chambers, executive director of Exodus International—the largest organization known to help those who struggle with unwanted same-sex attractions and their loved ones—has to say on this subject:]

Exodus International was founded in 1976 in response to a great need. At that time, those leading the individual ministries that established Exodus were simply grateful to have found freedom from their own battles with homosexuality and to be sharing that hope with others seeking it. There was little thought given to statistics, record keeping, and documentation. There was also little time.

Additionally, Exodus' beginnings were humble. Though more than a dozen ministries were included in Exodus in those first few years, Exodus itself was little more than a post office box and a desk drawer, with a volunteer director who spent one afternoon each week overseeing this new endeavor. As the need became apparent for a staff, an office, and formal policies, the focus was on the overwhelmingly positive response to the message that freedom from homosexuality was possible.

Since its inception, Exodus has continued with great momentum. We have literally never gone a day without dozens and sometimes hundreds of people calling for help. Today we receive over 125,000 calls and e-mails annually from men, women, youth, families, friends, educators, and clergy seeking biblical answers on the complex issues surrounding homosexuality.

Our critics claim we don't have proof that change is possible, but the truth is that Exodus and its member ministries have records and contact with tens of thousands of men and women who have found freedom from homosexuality. In addition, the national organizations with which we partner or affiliate, like NARTH, JONAH and Courage, have similar records and contacts.

In 1999, Exodus embarked upon a five-year study, headed by Dr. Stanton Jones at Wheaton College, tracking the lives of approximately 100 individuals who identified themselves as having gone through the change or reorientation process when the study began. In late 2004, the initial research results will be in—and whether all research subjects make it or simply one person makes it, the results will be published.* Dr. Jones and his team will then invite those same individuals to participate in a five-year follow-up study so that we can produce a ten-year study in 2009.

God uses all things for His glory and purposes. I believe that science and psychology are two extremely important areas that can help

---

* The results of the study will be posted at the Exodus International website www.exodus-international.org.

us explain the homosexual phenomenon. However, the spiritual controls the physical, and to place all of our bets on science and psychology, or even to give them more credence than the divine, is a common mistake. We are all genetically, physically, and spiritually flawed people; we are all susceptible to falling, and to look to some other source for healing is to miss God's supreme answer—Jesus. All of that to say, statistics, research, and information are extremely valuable and important, but if we believe what the Bible states in 2 Timothy 3:16, that all Scripture is God-breathed, then we know that our ultimate authority specifically calls homosexuality sin in Leviticus, Romans, and 1 Corinthians. But we also know that God never condemns sin without giving hope, as He did regarding this issue in the writings of Paul in 1 Corinthians 6:11, where Paul states about people, including homosexuals, "And that is what some of you were. But you were washed, you were sanctified, you were justified in the name of the Lord Jesus Christ and by the Spirit of our God."

Statistics may be comforting or discouraging. However, I exhort you to always live by what you know more than how you feel. If you know Christ, you know that change from anything is possible. And, like Chuck Swindoll says often, right is still right even if no one is doing it, and wrong is still wrong even if everyone is doing it.

11

Answering Science

Gay genes, lengths of certain fingers, gay behavior in fruit flies and other animals, inner ear measurements....there has been no shortage of attempts to prove a genetic link to homosexuality. But neither is there any shortage of problems with those studies that claim to have found such a link. The plain truth of the matter is that a complex combination of factors contribute to the adoption of a homosexual orientation—factors that are rarely exact from one individual to the next.

In this chapter, we'll consider and offer refutation for some of the most prevalent scientific myths surrounding homosexuality.

95. I've heard a number of studies quoted that support the "born gay" theory. Are these studies accurate? If not, why?

The majority of these studies are so far-fetched that few people give them much credence, except those who turn to the popular media for their "truth." But, as Proverbs 18:17 says, "The first to present his case seems right, till another comes forward and questions him." With that in mind, let's consider the validity of these studies.

Simon LeVay and the INAH-3

Neuroanatomic (or brain structure) research hoping to secure a biological determinant to homosexuality seemed to reach its zenith in 1991 when Simon LeVay published "A Difference in Hypothalamic Structure Between Heterosexual and Homosexual Men" in the respected journal *Science.*[1] He studied the brains of 41 corpses, including 6 women, 19 homosexual men, and 16 men presumed to be heterosexual. LeVay examined a portion of the hypothalamus (INAH-3), which is a small segment of the brain structure. He reported that the INAH-3 was more than twice as large in the heterosexual men as in the women and twice as large in heterosexual men as in the homosexual ones. What did LeVay deduce from all of this? That "sexual orientation has a biological substrate" because if the brains of homosexual men were closer in size to the brains of women than the brains of heterosexual men, then of course gay men must be more biologically like women.[2]

Even the simplest analysis of LeVay's methodology quickly uncovers numerous methodological errors. LeVay himself admits that his most glaring problem is that all 19 of the subjects identified as homosexual had died from AIDS complications.[3] Is it possible, then, that the size difference in their hypothalamuses was caused by their illness rather than their homosexuality?

In fact, that's exactly what Dr. William Byne suggested. He found that LeVay did not "adequately address the fact that at the time of death virtually all men with AIDS have decreased testosterone levels as the result of the disease itself or the side effects of particular treatments. Thus, it is possible that the effects on the size of the INAH-3 that he attributed to sexual orientation were actually caused by the hormonal abnormalities associated with AIDS."[4]

But we don't have to take anyone else's word for what LeVay's research doesn't prove; he's already spoken quite clearly on the subject. "I did not prove that homosexuality is genetic, or find a genetic cause for being gay," he admitted. "I didn't show that gay men are born that way, the most common mistake people make in interpreting my work. Nor did I locate a gay center in the brain." Even more emphatically, LeVay states that, "time and again I have been described as someone who 'proved that homosexuality is genetic'...I did not."[5]

The Bailey and Pillard Twin Studies

Another widely cited "proof" of homosexuality's genetic link is often attributed to the Bailey and Pillard twin studies. This research was conducted using pairs of brothers—identical twins, nonidentical twins, biological brothers, and adopted brothers—at least one of whom was gay. Here are the results:

- 52% of the time, both identical twins were homosexual
- 22% of the time, both nonidentical or fraternal twins were homosexual
- 9.2% of the time, both non-twin brothers were homosexual
- 10.5% of the time, both adoptive brothers were homosexual[6]

Those statistics seem to point to a genetic link—don't they? Not to N.E. Whitehead, Ph.D.:

> Identical twins have identical genes. If homosexuality was a biological condition produced inescapably by the genes (e.g. eye color), then if one identical twin was homosexual, in 100% of the cases his brother would be too....Genes are responsible for an indirect influence, but on average, they do not force people into homosexuality. This conclusion has been well known in the scientific community for a few decades but has not reached the general public. Indeed, the public increasingly believes the opposite.[7]

In the same vein, if homosexuality were to truly have genetic links, the group that should show the least amount of homosexual conformity would be the brothers with completely unrelated genes—the adoptive sets. Yet this isn't the case.

Dean Hamer and the X Chromosome

The last study that has advanced the "born gay" theory was released in 1993 and touched off a national media storm, including a *Time* magazine cover story called "Born Gay: Science Finds a Genetic Link"[8] What was all the hubbub about? Author Steven Rose remembers:

> Back in 1993 a euphoric press release announced the publication in America's leading scientific journal, *Science*, of a paper reporting the discovery of a "gay gene." Hamer, the senior author both of that paper and *Living with Our Genes*...works at the U.S. government's National Cancer Institute, but the relevance of his genetic study of 40 pairs of gay brothers to cancer research is obscure. What Hamer and his colleagues actually reported was relatively modest; that these 40 gay siblings shared a common genetic marker, a region of their X-chromosome, inherited from their mother, called Xq28. No actual gene has been discovered,

merely a genetic association, and what, if anything, such a gene might have to do with the brothers' sexual orientation was equally unclear. But this didn't prevent the press release labeling the discovery as "the gay gene" and speculating on its ethical consequences. Gay men wore T-shirts thanking Mom for Xq28.[9]

Hamer had indeed claimed that homosexuality could be linked to findings on the X chromosome. He found that out of 40 pairs of homosexual brothers, 33 (83 percent) received the same sequence on five genetic markers.[10] Like the two previous studies, anyone willing or needing to accept a genetic link to homosexuality would rejoice in these findings.

But scientists—men and women concerned with facts, not emotion or lifestyle advocacy—had a much different reaction. Whitehead pointed out the study lacked a control group from the general population, noting that if the same sequence from the X chromosome that appeared in the homosexual men also appears in the general population of heterosexual men, then the gene is insignificant. Hamer also did not test the heterosexual brothers of the homosexual men to see if they had the gene, but some of the data from those heterosexual brothers did indicate they had the identical gene sequence. Another conspicuous flaw in Hamer's study is that seven of the pairs of homosexuals did not have the needed gene sequence at all.[11]

Perhaps most telling, though, are Hamer's own words about his study: "The pedigree study failed to produce what we originally hoped to find: simple Mendelian inheritance. In fact, we never found a single family in which homosexuality was distributed in the obvious sort of pattern."[12]

The simplest amount of questioning on the part of one seeking truth regarding these studies inevitably produces the same fruit: *no evidence of a genetic link to homosexuality.*

96. Should we believe the theory that suggests that prenatal hormonal imbalances can influence an individual's gender-identity formation?

Hormonal imbalances can certainly affect the development of any fetus, but the stretch that's needed to support a *direct* causation between these imbalances and homosexual orientation requires the flexibility of a gymnast.

To be sure, such imbalances could affect the growing individual by either masculinizing or feminizing his or her physical features, which in turn could lead someone to feelings of inadequacy or spur ridicule and teasing if the effects are obvious to their peers. As Dr. Jeffrey Satinover notes:

> The boy (for example) who one day may go on to struggle with homosexuality is born with certain features that are somewhat more common among homosexuals than in the population at large. Some of these traits might be inherited (genetic), while others might have been caused by the "intrauterine environment" (hormones). What this means is that a youngster without these traits will be somewhat less likely to become homosexual later than someone with them.[13]

But this doesn't come close to meaning that homosexuality is predetermined at birth, any more than alcoholism or "rageaholism" is a forgone conclusion in individuals who were born with a proclivity toward drinking or anger. Homosexuality is a much more complex issue than simply the outcome of an unbalanced prenatal environment.

Further evidence of this can be found in studying hormonal differences that become prevalent after birth: Despite many studies that have attempted to find a direct hormonal cause for homosexuality, no scientist has yet succeeded in doing so. A few of the human studies have reported hormonal differences between homosexual and heterosexual men, but little convincing evidence has been found. In addition, these studies are extremely lacking in consistency and replication of findings. It has been hypothesized by many that a deficit in androgens, such as testosterone, could be responsible for homosexual behavior. One scientist looked into this possibility and concluded, "A deficit of androgens in adult men diminishes the sensitivity and reactivity of the sexual apparatus, reduces lust and eventually produces physical impotence, but does not abolish heterosexual orientation."[14]

97. You said homosexuality isn't genetic but environmental. If this is true, then how can one boy struggle with homosexual feelings and his brother, raised in the same environment, emerge as completely heterosexual?

Homosexuality, as I've noted before, is far too complex to be solely genetic or solely attributable to environmental factors. Each child in each family is born with certain predisposing genetic characteristics that determine such things as whether he is going to have black hair, a big nose, long legs, or blue eyes.

Any two boys in any given family, even though they will be raised in the same environment, will likely possess very distinct personalities and temperaments. One son may be overly sensitive, shy, and emotionally fragile, while the other may be more stoic, confident, and secure. Each will respond differently to just about every emotional stimulus, such as teasing. One may run to his room in tears, and the other may strike back with a more cutting retort of his own.

The addition of these and myriad other variables, including the relationships each develop with their parents and other siblings, can lead one to struggle with homosexuality and the other to have no inkling of such struggles whatsoever.

98. From what I understand, most of the major medical and psychological associations don't see homosexuality as abnormal. Aren't you a bit behind the times with your belief that homosexuality is pathological?

This question can't be answered comprehensively unless we take a look at the history of how the medical and psychological communities have regarded homosexuality.

- The original *Diagnostic and Statistical Manual of Mental Disorders* (DSM)—the official reference manual used to diagnose mental disorders by professionals in America and throughout the world, published in 1952—categorized homosexuality as one of the "sociopathic personality disturbances."[15]

- The DSM became the DSM II in 1968 and relocated homosexuality from the list of sociopathic disorders and instead included it with other sexual deviations.[16]

- The 1973 version of this manual, the DSM III, made the most salient change of all when homosexuality was considered psychologically problematic only when an individual was dissatisfied with it—a state referred to as "ego-dystonic."[17]

- The DSM III R, an even later revision, completely omits any reference to homosexuality at all.

The 1973 revision made the biggest headlines. The December 16, 1973, edition of the *Washington Post* proclaimed, "Doctors Rule Homosexuals Not Abnormal." And on December 16, 1999, 26 years later, this same paper reran this very article with a new title—"Sick No More."

So, how did this come about? Is homosexuality psychologically normal? A look at the truth surrounding these changes in the DSM is quite illuminating. In their book *Homosexuality: The Use of Scientific Research in the Church's Moral Debate,* Stanton Jones and Mark Yarhouse bring much needed clarification to these questions.

> The removal of homosexuality from the DSM was in response to a majority vote of the APA (American Psychiatric Association). The original APA vote was called at a time of significant social change and was taken with unconventional speed that circumvented normal channels from consideration of the issues because of explicit threats from gay rights groups to disrupt APA conventions and research.[18]

But the task force set up to review the status of homosexuality was extremely biased. Not one single psychiatrist assigned to this panel believed homosexuality to be abnormal.[19] It's no surprise, then, that this group arrived at a decision that supported homosexuality as psychologically normal. Stanton and Yarhouse continue:

However, it appears that in contrast to the results of the vote, the majority of the APA membership continued to view homosexuality as a pathology. A survey four years after the vote found that 69% of psychiatrists regarded homosexuality as a "pathological adaptation." A much more recent survey suggests that the majority of psychiatrists around the world continue to view same-sex behavior as signaling mental illness.[20]

"The removal of homosexuality from the DSM does not conclusively decide the issue of the pathological status of homosexuality," the authors add. "There is no absolute standard of judging normality or abnormality." Furthermore, they suggest that there are "four empirical (or at least partially empirical) criteria…commonly used to define behavior patterns as abnormal:"[21]

- statistical infrequency
- personal distress
- maladaptiveness
- deviation from social norms

Let's take a closer look at each of these.

Statistical Infrequency

As we saw in question 88, the percentage of homosexuals in the world's population is as low as 1 to 3 percent. Stanton and Yarhouse write,

> Compare this percentage to the estimated lifetime incidence rates of some other major psychopathological disorders. In comparison, the prevalence of homosexuality is much less frequent than such common disorders as phobias (14.3%) and alcohol abuse and dependence (13.8%), about as frequent as some disorders that are less common, as is the case with panic (1.6%) and schizophrenia (1.5%), and much more frequent than somatization disorders (0.1%)….In comparison to these prevalence rates, homosexuality is not so common as to be eliminated as a possible pathology on frequency alone.[22]

Personal Distress

Stanton and Yarhouse note,

> Psychopathology is often accompanied by personal distress as is the case with depressive disorders and sexual dysfunctions. However, personal distress is not a necessary aspect of psychopathology. Some problems that we all recognize as pathological are also characterized by patterns of denial and minimization of distress, as is the case with some experiences of alcoholism and drug addiction.[23]

In fact, they add, as is the case with some alcoholics,

> with homosexuality the claim is often made that "there is no evidence of higher rates of emotional instability or psychiatric illness among homosexuals than among heterosexuals." This claim has been made so often that it has taken on the status of truth that "everybody knows"; however, the factual basis for this assertion is debatable.[24]

Maladaptiveness

"A behavior pattern or characteristic is 'adaptive' when it is constructive, helpful, healthy and contributes to the person moving in a valued direction," Stanton and Yarhouse write. Can homosexuality ever be seen as constructive, helpful, healthy, or the attainment of a desirable goal?

Psychologist Elizabeth Moberly answers that question this way:

> God did not create homosexuals as homosexuals, but as men and women who are intended to attain psychological maturity in their gender identity....The mistake of some homosexuals is to assume that the goal has already been reached, when in fact development has been checked and still requires completion.[25]

Deviation from Social Norms

Homosexuality does indeed violate societal norms, Stanton and Yarhouse argue. The problem is that the psychological community refuses to acknowledge this fact. Most mental health organizations and associations have instead suggested that societal norms must be altered toward full acceptance of homosexuality as a normal variant, as some of them have done in 2002, trying to convince themselves and the American public that sexual abuse perpetrated on children is not always harmful to them.[26]

For Christians seeking to defend their beliefs in the marketplace of ideas, though, it doesn't much matter how the American Psychiatric Association or any other professional association views or classifies homosexuality. God's truth, that homosexuality is a deviation from His intent for mankind, always must have the final say.

99. Isn't the prevalence of homosexuality in the animal world proof that it's normal?

Let me begin by challenging the use of the word "prevalence." Homosexual behavior can be found among animals, but to suggest it is so common and widespread to be "prevalent" is quite a stretch.

Let's examine this question from a few different angles. First, are we to presume that just because something exists it must be "normal"? Cerebral palsy, Down syndrome, muscular dystrophy—they all exist as part of the consequences of a fallen world. But we call them birth *defects*, not birth *normalities*, precisely because they represent deviations from the norm. And what is that norm? The human being functioning according to God's design.

Second, let's consider the reasons for this behavior in animals: Animal homosexuality is observed most frequently in those that have yet to reach a mature state, and it's manifest as playful, immature antics. But homosexual behavior can also be seen by animals attempting to prove their dominance. When one male mounts his male counterpart, it is an act of hierarchical aggression, not an expression of sexual lust or even sexual interest. For proof of this, just present a female in heat. The same-sex behavior is abandoned—quickly.

And lastly, this whole line of argument should be insulting to any human being. We are not animals. We are endowed with superior minds by the Creator of the universe, who (even more importantly) came to die for us, giving us inestimable value. To compare humans in any way to dogs or cats or cheetahs or zebras or orangutans or platypuses trivializes God's design. So the next time you're faced with this argument, you might think of responding with, "I bet you're glad your mom doesn't believe the same way you do. In the animal world, some mothers eat their young."

Answering Your Need

THANK YOU FOR CONSIDERING THIS BOOK worthy of your attention. I pray you've found it helpful and enlightening. Many of the resources found in this chapter and throughout the book were those that changed my life and set me on the course toward holiness. I pray they will do the same for your loved one or friend as you seek to implement their suggestions.

If you struggle personally with same-sex attraction, take it from me (and thousands of other people who've been set free)—true hope, identity, and freedom are available to you through the crucifixion, death, burial, and resurrection of the One who loves you as no other can or will. Come to Him, acknowledge Him, believe in Him, and live in Him. He came that you "may have life, and have it to the full" (John 10:10).

100. What support and resources are available for youths who are struggling with homosexuality?

Had you asked me this question five years ago, my answer would have been, "Not much." In fact, until just recently, far more resources were available to encourage teens and young adults to embrace their feelings of homosexuality.

But today, a growing system of support for young people struggling with same-sex attraction is available. A key player in the development of these resources is Exodus Youth, or EY, which "provides resources where you can find biblical answers to your questions, links to support groups, youth pastors and online encouragement." Their website is (www.exodusyouth.net). A CD-ROM known as *The Map* includes cutting-edge information including the stories of six youth (three guys and three girls) who have struggled to overcome homosexuality, answers to the toughest questions facing today's students, "a resource newsstand featuring books, videos, pamphlets, Websites, and organizations from around the country and a 20 lesson interactive curriculum. Each lesson is equipped with an audio introduction. The CD comes with a 50-page journal for you to write in as you walk through your journey." Check it out at (http://www.reachtruth.com/about.html).

But the resources don't stop there. You also should check out *Celebrating God's Design* by Don Schmierer, "a curriculum with a difference—allowing teenagers to talk, think, and pray about such perplexing issues as gender, tolerance, sexuality, friendship, and family challenges. This curriculum features a stimulating video introduction to each session; reproducible pages that don't require separate student workbooks; and three four-week modules that focus on actual stories, thought-provoking problems and biblical solutions."[1] Another valuable tool is *SOULutions: Relational Healing for the Next Generation* by Cathy Morrill. "*SOULutions* boldly tackles the sexual and relational issues teens and young adults face today. Topics covered include Our Identity in Christ, Dating, Promiscuity, Homosexuality, and Addiction."[2]

If you're looking for something more structured, like a formal program to attend, consider The River, "an intense 20-lesson healing/discipleship program for high school students and young adults (ages 16–25) seeking Jesus and His healing in their relationships, identity and sexuality. Groups generally meet weekly for 15–20 weeks" and are offered at different times and locations around the country.[3] Also look into Refuge, offered by a ministry called Love In Action based in Memphis, Tennessee. Refuge offers two options, a two-week or eight-week commitment that includes attendance by both the adolescent and their significant family members.[4]

Teens who are interested in a safe online forum where they can interact with other students who are struggling with same-sex attractions have a great resource available to them at www.livehope.org.

One of the best opportunities to interact with other peers facing these issues is offered at the annual Exodus International conference. In the past few years, many young men and women under the age of

25 have attended (students ages 13–16 are not permitted at this event without a parent).

More and more youth are finding truth and being offered a hopeful alternative in Christ.

101. What resources are available for people who struggle with homosexuality?

A number of organizations provide help specifically for those with unwanted same-sex attractions and for their loved ones.

Evangelical
Exodus International
PO Box 54119
Orlando FL 32854
Nationwide: (888) 264-0877; in Orlando: (407) 599-6872
www.exodus-international.org

Parents and Friends of Ex-Gays (P-FOX)
PO Box 561
Ft. Belvoir VA 22060
(703) 739-8220
www.pfox.org

Roman Catholic
Courage
St. John the Baptist Church
210 W 31ˢᵗ Street
NYC NY 10001
(212) 268-1010

Methodist
Transforming Congregations
PO Box 7146
Pendel PA 19047
(215) 752-9655
www.transformingcong.org

Presbyterian

One by One
PO Box 648
Pittsford NY 14534
(716) 568-6180
www.oneby1.org

Episcopal

Grace & Truth
Charismatic Episcopal Church
8057 Arlington Expressway
Jacksonville FL 32211
(904) 220-7474
email: *graceandtruth@iccec.org*

Jewish

JONAH
PO Box 313
Jersey City NJ 07303
(201) 433-3444

Mental Health

National Association for Research and Therapy of Homosexuality (NARTH)
16633 Ventura Blvd. #1340
Encino CA 91436
(818) 789-4440
www.narth.com

Many of the books on homosexuality are hard to find, even in Christian bookstores. However, Regeneration Books has virtually every resource ever written on this subject from a conservative perspective.

Regeneration Books
PO Box 9830
Baltimore MD 21284-9830
(410) 661-4337
www.regenbooks.org

Certain books are "must haves" for those affected by homosexuality. Listed below are a few I highly recommend:

For those who struggle with same-sex attractions
Coming Out of Homosexuality by Bob Davies and Lori Rentzel

For men who struggle with same-sex attractions
You Don't Have to Be Gay by Jeff Konrad
Desires in Conflict by Joe Dallas

For women who struggle with same-sex attractions
Restoring Sexual Identity by Anne Paulk

For loved ones of those dealing with same-sex attractions
Someone I Love Is Gay by Anita Worthen and Bob Davies

For parents who want to prevent homosexuality in their children
A Parent's Guide to Preventing Homosexuality by Dr. Joseph and Linda Nicolosi
An Ounce of Prevention by Don Schmierer

For those who find themselves facing those who promote pro-gay Christian beliefs
A Strong Delusion by Joe Dallas

A number of helpful websites offer further support
www.exodusyouth.net
www.freetobeme.com
www.livehope.org
www.peoplecanchange.com
www.pureintimacy.org
www.stonewallrevisited.com
www.citizenlink.org

Also, you can click on "Homosexuality and Gender" at www.focusonsocialissues.org.

A helpful one-day conference by Focus on the Family called Love Won Out educates and equips families, the church, and concerned citizens by balancing truth and love regarding this contentious issue of homosexuality. It has been touring the country since 1998 and helping thousands. Upcoming dates and locations are available at www.lovewonout.com.

Notes

Chapter 1: Answering the Basics

1. Joseph Nicolosi, *Reparative Therapy of Male Homosexuality* (Northvale, NJ: Jason Aronson Inc., 1997), p. xv.

2. Ibid., p. xvi.

3. Quoted in Nicolosi and Nicolosi, *A Parent's Guide to Preventing Homosexuality,* p. 151.

4. Ibid., pp. 152-53.

5. Ibid.

6. Ibid.

7. Don Schmierer, *An Ounce of Prevention* (Nashville, TN: Word Publishing, 1998).

Chaper 2: Answers for Families

1. *A River Runs Through It* (1992).

2. Anita Worthen and Bob Davies, *Someone I Love Is Gay* (Downers Grove, IL: InterVarsity Press, 2002).

3. Joseph Nicolosi and Linda Ames Nicolosi, *A Parent's Guide to Preventing Homosexuality* (Downers Grove, IL: InterVarsity Press, 2002), pp. 44-45. Copyright © by Joseph Nicolosi and Linda Ames Nicolosi. Used by permission of InterVarsity Press, P.O. Box 1400, Downers Grove, IL 60515, USA. www.ivpress.com

4. Ibid., p. 45.

5. Ibid., p. 21.

6. Ibid., p. 48.

7. Simon LeVay, *Queer Science* (Cambridge, MA: MIT Press, 1996), p. 6.

8. Dean Hamer and Peter Copeland, *The Science of Desire* (New York, NY: Simon and Schuster, 1994), p. 166.

9. George Rekers, ed., "Gender Identity Disorder," *The Journal of Human Sexuality,* 1996, p. 14.

10. Nicolosi and Nicolosi, *A Parent's Guide,* p. 75.

11. Ibid., pp. 75-76.

12. Ibid., p. 76.

13. Ibid., p. 76.

14. Ibid., pp. 162-63.

15. Mark Yarhouse and Lori Burkett, *Sexual Identity: A Guide to Living in the Time Between the Times* (Lanham, MD: University Press of America, Inc., 2003), p. 132.

16. Anita Worthen and Bob Davies, *Someone I Love Is Gay,* (Downers Grove, IL: Inter-Varsity Press, 2002), pp. 42-44. Copyright © 1996 by Anita Worthen and Bob Davies. Used by permission of InterVarsity Press, P.O. Box 1400, Downers Grove, IL 60515, USA. www.ivpress.com

17. Yarhouse and Burkett, *Sexual Identity,* pp. 134-35.

18. Joseph Nicolosi, *Reparative Therapy of Male Homosexuality* (Northvale, NJ: Jason Aronson Inc., 1997), pp. 164-65.

19. Ibid., p. 164.

20. www.exodusyouth.net; www.livehope.org

21. Gary Smalley and Dr. Greg Smalley, *Bound by Honor: Fostering a Great Relationship with Your Teen* (Wheaton, IL: Tyndale House Publishers, 1998).

22. Jeenie Gordon, *Those Turbulent Teen Years: Hope for Parents,* (Grand Rapids, MI: Chosen Books, 2000).

23. Deborah Phrihoda, *Mommy, Why Are They Holding Hands?* (Souderton, PA: Cutting Edge Publishing, 1996), p. 1.

24. Don Schmierer, *Celebrating God's Design* (Santa Ana, CA: Promise Publishing, 2000), back cover.

25. Dr. James Dobson, *Complete Marriage and Family Home Reference Guide* (Wheaton, IL: Tyndale House Publishers, 2000), p. 152.

26. Ibid., p. 153.

27. Ibid., pp. 153-54.

28. Ibid., p. 155.

29. Dr. James Dobson, *Preparing for Adolescence* (Ventura, CA: Gospel Light Publications).

30. *Merriam Webster's Collegiate Dictionary,* 10th ed.

31. Henry Cloud and John Townsend, *Boundaries* (Grand Rapids, MI: Zondervan Publishing House, 1992).

32. Worthen and Davies, *Someone I Love Is Gay,* p. 143.

33. Dr. James Dobson, *Love Must be Tough* (Nashville, TN: Word Books, 1983).

34. Nicolosi and Nicolosi, *A Parent's Guide to Preventing Homosexuality,* pp. 33-34.

35. Bob Davies, *When a Loved One Says, "I'm Gay."* A Love Won Out series booklet (Colorado Springs, CO: Focus on the Family, 2002), p. 23.

Chapter 3: Answers for Friends

1. Jeff Konrad, *You Don't Have to Be Gay* (Hilo, HI: Pacific Publishing House, 2000), p. 240.

2. International Bulletin of Missionary Research, vol. 28, no. 1, 2004, pp. 24-25.

3. http://www.washblade.com/print.cfm?content_id=1456

4. Joe Dallas, *How Should We Respond,* Love Won Out Series (Colorado Springs, CO: Focus on the Family, 1999), p. 10.

5. Joe Dallas, "How Should the Church Respond," plenary session at Focus on the Family's Love Won Out conference, Nashville, TN, February 7, 2004.

6. Anita Worthen and Bob Davies, *Someone I Love Is Gay,* (Downers Grove, IL: Inter-Varsity Press, 2002), p. 173. Copyright © 1996 by Anita Worthen and Bob Davies. Used by permission of InterVarsity Press, P.O. Box 1400, Downers Grove, IL 60515, USA. www.ivpress.com

7. Ibid., p. 174.

8. Ibid., p. 174.

9. Ibid., p. 175.

10. Ibid., p. 176.

11. Ibid., p. 177.

12. Ibid., p. 177.

13. Simon LeVay, *Queer Science* (Cambridge, MA: MIT Press, 1996), p. 6.

14. Ibid., p. 6.

Chapter 4: Answers for the Church

1. Mona Riley and Brad Sargent, *Unwanted Harvest* (Nashville, TN: Broadman & Holman Publishers, 1995), p. 60.

2. Ibid., p. 60. Until noted otherwise, the quotes that follow are from Riley and Sargent, *Unwanted Harvest,* pp. 60-67.

3. Joe Dallas, *How Should We Respond,* Love Won Out Series (Colorado Springs, CO: Focus on the Family, 1999), pp. 8-9.

4. Don Schmierer, *An Ounce of Prevention* (Nashville, TN: Word Publishers, 1998), p. 187.

5. Until noted otherwise, the quotes that follow are from Schmierer, *An Ounce of Prevention,* pp. 187-89.

6. Pastor Mike Riley is still a very close personal friend. When faced with this question I asked him to answer it, and what I included in my book comes from our personal correspondence.

Chapter 5: Answers for Men

1. *The Truth Comes Out: The Roots and Causes of Male Homosexuality,* Love Won Out booklet series, (Colorado Springs, CO: Focus on the Family, 2002), p. 15.

2. Ibid., p. 16.

3. Dr. Joseph Nicolosi, "The Condition of Male Homosexuality," plenary session at Focus on the Family's Love Won Out conference, Nashville, TN, February 7, 2004.

4. *The Truth Comes Out*, pp. 23-24.

5. Ibid., p. 47.

6. Ibid., pp. 47-48.

7. Uriel Meshoulam, Ph.D., "Is It OK To Tell A Teen, Be True To Your Real Self?" *Boston Globe*, February 28, 1999, C6.

8. Joseph Nicolosi, *Reparative Therapy of Male Homosexuality* (Northvale, NJ: Jason Aronson, Inc., 1997), p. 58.

9. Alan Chambers and I work very closely together on the Exodus board and are personal friends. Knowing that his personal story would help those who read this answer, I asked Alan to send me his take on his experience as a young boy. His answer came to me via personal correspondence.

10. Andria L. Sigler-Smalz, "Understanding the Lesbian Client," Located on NARTH website: http://www.narth.com/docs/understanding.html.

11. David McWhirter and Andrew Mattison, *The Male Couple* (Englewood Cliffs, NJ: Prentice-Hall, Inc., 1984), p. 207.

12. Ibid., p. 252-53.

13. Nicolosi, *Reparative Therapy of Male Homosexuality*, p. 140.

14. Ibid., p. 139.

15. Theo Sandfort, et al., "Same-sex Sexual Behavior and Psychiatric Disorders: Findings from the Netherlands Mental Health Survey and Incidence Study NEMESIS," *Archives of General Psychiatry* 58 (2001), pp. 85-91.

16. Maria Xiridou, Ronald Geskus, John De Wit, Roel Coutinho, and Mirjam Kretzschamar, "The Contribution of Steady and Casual Partnerships to the Incidence of HIV Infection Among Homosexual Men in Amsterdam," *AIDS* 17 (2003), p. 1032.

17. Ibid., p. 1032.

18. Michelangelo Signorile, "Bridal Wave," *OUT* magazine, December/January 1994, p. 32.

19. Andrew Sullivan, *Virtually Normal* (New York, NY: Vintage Books, 1996).

20. Nicolosi, *Reparative Therapy of Male Homosexuality*, p. 126.

21. Jeff Konrad, *You Don't Have to Be Gay* (Hilo, HI: Pacific Publishing House, 2000).

Chapter 6: Answers for Women

1. Anne Paulk, *Restoring Sexual Identity* (Eugene, OR: Harvest House Publishers, 2003), pp. 69-70.

2. Ibid., pp. 56-57.

3. Stanton L. Jones and Mark A. Yarhouse, *Homosexuality: The Use of Scientific Research in the Church's Moral Debate* (Downers Grove, IL: InterVarsity Press, 2000), p. 57. Copyright © 2000 by Stanton L. Jones and Mark A. Yarhouse. Used

by permission of InterVarsity Press, P.O. Box 1400, Downers Grove, IL 60515, USA. www.ivpress.com

4. Paulk, *Restoring Sexual Identity,* p. 59.

5. Ibid., p. 56.

6. Ibid., p. 60.

7. G. Rekers and S. Mead, "Female Sex-Role Deviance: Early Identification and Developmental Intervention," *Journal of Clinical Child Psychology,* 9 no. 3 (1980), pp. 199-203.

8. M.T. Saghir and E. Robins, *Male and Female Homosexuality: A Comprehensive Investigation* (Baltimore, MD: Williams & Wilkins, 1973).

9. Paulk, *Restoring Sexual Identity,* p. 61.

10. J. Michael Bailey and Kenneth J. Zucker, "Childhood Sex-Typed Behavior and Sexual Orientation: A Conceptual Analysis and Quantitative Review," *Developmental Psychology,* 31 (1995), p. 49.

11. Paulk, *Restoring Sexual Identity,* p. 64.

12. Ibid., p. 65.

13. Ibid., p. 67.

14. Elaine V. Siegel, *Female Homosexuality: Choice Without Volition, a Psychoanalytic Study* (Hillsdale, NJ: The Analytic Press, 1988), p. 219.

15. Paulk, *Restoring Sexual Identity,* pp. 67-68.

16. Bob Davies and Lori Rentzel, *Coming Out of Homosexuality: New Freedom for Men and Women* (Downers Grove: InterVarsity Press, 1993), p. 47.

17. *The Heart of the Matter: Roots and Causes of Female Homosexuality,* Love Won Out Series (Colorado Springs, CO: Focus on the Family, 2002), p. 11.

18. Andria L. Sigler-Smalz, "Understanding the Lesbian Client," found on NARTH's website at http://www.narth.com/docs/understanding.html.

19. Ibid.

20. Paulk, *Restoring Sexual Identity,* p. 248.

21. Lori Rentzel, *Emotional Dependency* (Downers Grove: InterVarsity Press, 1990).

Chapter 7: Answers for Those Desiring Change

1. Dr. Robert Spitzer, "Commentary: Psychiatry and Homosexuality," *Wall Street Journal,* May 23, 2001.

2. Irving Bieber, *Homosexuality: A Psychoanalytic Study* (New York, NY: Basic Books, 1962), pp. 318-19.

3. Spitzer, "Commentary: Psychiatry and Homosexuality," p. 7.

4. Mark Yarhouse and Lori Burkett, *Sexual Identity* (Lanham, MD: University Press of America, Inc., 2003), p. 43.

5. Mike Haley, "Enduring Freedom," General address to the Exodus International 2002 Conference.

6. Walter A. Henrichsen, *Thoughts from the Diary of a Desperate Man* (El Cajon, CA: Leadership Foundation), p. 2.

7. Jane Boyer, from her testimony at Focus on the Family. Love Won Out conference, Nashville, TN, February 7, 2004.

8. Robert Spitzer, *Archives of Sexual Behavior* 32, no. 5 (October 3002), pp. 403-17.

9. Joseph Nicolosi, *Reparative Therapy of Male Homosexuality,* (Northvale, NJ: Jason Aronson, Inc., 1997), pp. 163-64.

10. Yarhouse and Burkett, *Sexual Identity,* p. 39.

11. Wilhelm Stekel, "Is Homosexuality Curable?" *Psychology Review* 17 (1930), pp. 443-51.

12. Michael E. Cavanagh, *Make Your Tomorrow Better* (New York, NY: Paulist Press, 1980), p. 266.

13. Charles Socarides, *Homosexuality: Psychoanalytic Therapy* (New York, NY: Jason Aronson, Inc., 1978), p. 3.

14. William Masters and Virginia Johnson, *Homosexuality in Perspective* (Boston, MA: Little, Brown, 1979), pp. 402, 408.

15. Jeffrey Satinover, *Homosexuality and the Politics of Truth* (Grand Rapids, MI: Hamewith Books, 1996), p. 186.

Chapter 8: Answering Theology

1. Robert Gagnon, *The Bible and Homosexual Practice: Texts and Hermeneutics* (Nashville, TN: Abingdon Press, 2001), pp. 229-30.

2. Ibid., p. 332.

3. http://bible.crosswalk.com/Lexicons/Hebrew/heb.cgi?number=03045&version=kjv

4. Troy Perry, *The Lord Is My Shepherd and He Knows I'm Gay* (Los Angeles, CA: Nash Publishing, 1972), pp. 150-51.

5. Joe Dallas, *A Strong Delusion: Confronting the "Gay Christian" Movement* (Eugene, OR: Harvest House Publishers, 1996), p. 178.

6. Gagnon, *The Bible and Homosexual Practice,* p. 152.

7. Ibid., p. 153.

Chapter 9: Answering Culture

1. "Why Market to the Gay Community" U.S. Census 2000 data on same-sex households, analysis by Dr. Gary Gates, http://www.witeckcombs.com.

2. Ibid.

3. http://htomc.dns2go.com/text/PAGLIA.TXT

4. William Masters, Virginia Johnson, and Robert Kolodny, *Human Sexuality,* 4th ed. (Glenview, IL: Addison-Wesley Educational Publishers, 1991), p. 394.

5. Stanton L. Jones and Mark A. Yarhouse, *Homosexuality: The Use of Scientific Research in the Church's Moral Debate* (Downers Grove, IL: InterVarsity Press, 2000), p. 103. Copyright © 2000 by Stanton L. Jones and Mark A. Yarhouse. Used by permission of InterVarsity Press, P.O. Box 1400, Downers Grove, IL 60515, USA. www.ivpress.com

6. http://www.avi.org/men/node/view/70 taking this statistic from R.A. Royce and W. Winkelstein, "HIV infection, cigarette smoking and CD4 + T-lymphocyte counts: preliminary results from the San Francisco Men's Health Study," AIDS 1990; 4, pp. 327-33.

7. J. Bradford, et al., "National Lesbian Health Care Survey: Implications for Mental Health Care," *Journal of Consulting and Clinical Psychology* 62 (1994), p. 239, cited in *Health Implications Associated with Homosexuality,* p. 81.

8. Karen Paige Erickson, Karen F. Trocki, "Sex, Alcohol and Sexually Transmitted Diseases: A National Survey," *Family Planning Perspectives* 26 (December 1994), p. 261.

9. Peter Freiberg, "Study: Alcohol Use More Prevalent for Lesbians," *The Washington Blade,* January 12, 2001, p. 21.

10. Gwat Yong Lie and Sabrina Gentlewarrier, "Intimate Violence in Lesbian Relationships: Discussion of Survey Findings and Practice Implications," *Journal of Social Service Research* 15 (1991), pp. 41-59.

11. David Island and Patrick Letellier, *Men Who Beat the Men Who Love Them: Battered Gay Men and Domestic Violence* (New York, NY: Haworth Press, 1991), p. 14.

12. http://www.narth.com/docs/innate.html

13. A.P. Bell and M.S. Weinberg, *Homosexualities: A Study of Diversity Among Men and Women* (New York, NY: Simon and Schuster, 1978), pp. 308-09.

14. A.P. Bell, M.S. Weinberg, and S. Hammersmith, *Sexual Preference: Its Development in Men and Women* (Bloomington, IN: Indiana University Press, 1981).

15. Dolcini, et al., (Demographic Characteristics of Heterosexuals with Multiple Partners: The National AIDS Behavioral Surveys," *Family Planning Perspectives,* 25, no. 5 (1993), pp. 208-414.

16. Bell and Weinberg, *Homosexualities,* pp. 308-09. See also A.P. Bell, M.S. Weinberg, and S.K. Hammersmith, *Sexual Preference* (Bloomington, IN: Indiana University Press, 1981).

17. Turner, et al., "Sexual Behavior in the United States, 1930-1990: Trends and Methodological Problems," *Sexually Transmitted Diseases,* 22, no. 3 (1995), pp. 173-190.

18. Glenn T. Stanton, "Will Same-Sex Marriage Hurt Your Family," *Focus on the Family* magazine, Single-Parent Family Edition, February/March 2004, p. 18.

19. Ibid., p. 18.

20. Ibid., p. 19.

21. Ibid., p. 19.

22. "When It Comes to Raising Kids, Same-Sex Marriage Isn't the Same," paid advertisement, *Boston Globe,* January 23, 2004.

23. Ibid.

24. "Is Marriage in Jeopardy?" Focus on the Family. Available online at: http://family.org/cforum/fosi/marriage/FAQs/a0026916.cfm.

25. Ibid.

26. Ibid. Original text footnotes Catherine Malkin and Michael Lamb, "Child Maltreatment: A Test of the Sociobiological Theory," *Journal of Comparative Family Studies,* 25 (1994), pp. 121-133; David Popenoe, *Life Without Father,* (New York: The Free Press, 1996).

27. "South Florida Teen Girls Discovering 'Bisexual Chic' Trend," *Sun-Sentinel,* Tuesday, December 30, 2003.

28. "Partway Gay? For Some Teen Girls, Sexual Preference Is A Shifting Concept," *The Washington Post,* Sunday, January 4, 2004, p. D01.

29. "Teen Girls Practice Sexual Equivocation," *The Gazette,* Monday, January 12, 2004, p. Life 2.

30. "South Florida Teen Girls Discovering 'Bisexual Chic' Trend."

31. "Partway Gay? For Some Teen Girls, Sexual Preference Is A Shifting Concept."

32. Tom Minnery; *Why You Can't Stay Silent: A Biblical Mandate to Shape Our Curture* (Wheaton, IL: Tyndale House Publishing, Inc.).

33. "Cases of HIV Rise In 2 US Groups," *The New York Times,* Monday, July 28, 2003.

34. "HIV Study Shows 4.4% Infection Rate For Young Gay Men," *The Wall Street Journal,* Friday, June 1, 2001.

35. "Study In 6 Cities Finds H.I.V. In 30% Of Young Black Gays," *The New York Times,* Tuesday, February 6, 2001.

36 "Seeking A Haven From Isolation," *Boston Globe,* Sunday, March 11, 2001.

37. "HIV Study Shows 4.4% Infection Rate For Young Gay Men."

38. CDC HIV/AIDS Update, http://www.cdc.gov/nchstp/od/news/at-a-glance.pdf.

Chapter 10: Answering the Gay Community and Agenda

1. All quotes taken from Marshall Kirk and Erastus Pill, "The Overhauling of Straight America," *Guide Magazine,* November, 1987.

2. Paul Rondeau, "Selling Homosexuality to America," www.regent.edu/acad/schlaw/lawreview/articles/14_2Rondeau.PDF, p. 46. This footnoted article includes 29 internal footnotes in the brief excerpt appearing in this book. The full documentation for those footnotes can be found at the website listed. Mr. Rondeau can be reached at Rondeau@directway.com.

3. http://209.157.64.200/focus/f-news/k-sexualorientation/browse.

4. Alan Sears and Craig Osten, *The Homosexual Agenda: Exposing the Principal Threat to Religious Freedom Today* (Nashville, TN: Broadman and Holman Publishers, 2003).

5. Alfred Kinsey, Wardell Pomeroy, and Clyde Martin, *Sexual Behavior in the Human Male* (Philadelphia, PA: W.B. Saunders Company, 1948), p. 651.

6. Judith A. Reisman, Ph.D. and Edward W. Eichel, *Kinsey, Sex and Fraud: The Indoctrination of a People* (Lafayette, IN: Huntington House Publishers, 1990), p. 9.

7. Judith A. Reisman, Ph.D., *Kinsey: Crimes and Consequences the Red Queen and the Grand Scheme* (Granite Bay, CA: The Institute for Media Education, Inc., 1998), p. 52.

8. June Machover Reinisch, ed., *Homosexuality, Heterosexuality: Concepts of Sexual Orientation,* The Kinsey Institute Series (Oxford, UK: Oxford University Press, 1990), p. 35.

9. "The Homosexual Numbers," *The New American,* March 22, 1993, p. 37.

10. "Gay Rights, Special Rights," Jeremiah Films, Inc., 1993.

11. See footnote #42 on page 16 in the brief at www.hrc.org.

12. Ibid.

13. I was able to take the numbers on age groups found at www.census.gov. With the simplest of equations these numbers can be found.

14. "The Homosexual Numbers," p. 37.

15. "Sex in the Snoring '90's," *Newsweek,* April 26, 1993, p. 27.

16. "The Shrinking Ten Percent," *Time,* April 26, 1993, p. 27.

17. Kinsey, Pomeroy, and Martin, *Sexual Behavior in the Human Male,* p. 651.

18. Samuel Gladding, *Counseling: A Comprehensive Profession* 4th ed. (Englewood Cliffs, NJ: Prentice Hall, 2003), p. 101.

19. Bruce Voeller, "Some Uses and Abuses of the Kinsey Scale," *Homosexuality, Heterosexuality: Concepts of Sexual Orientation,* The Kinsey Institute Series, June Machover Reinisch, ed. (Oxford, UK: Oxford University Press, 1990), p. 35.

20. http://www.census.gov/prod/2001pubs/c2kbr01-5.pdf

21. Star Parker, "Gay Politics, Black Reality," Sunday, January 12, 2004 at http://www.townhall.com/columnists/GuestColumns/Parker20040112.shtml.

22. Larry Burtoft, *Setting the Record Straight: What Research Really Says About the Social Consequences of Homosexuality* (Colorado Springs, CO: Focus on the Family, 1994), p. 69.

23. Reported in "Overcoming A Deep-Rooted Reluctance, More Firms Advertise To Gay Community," *Wall Street Journal,* July 18, 1991. Findings by Simmons Market Research Bureau and the U.S. Census Bureau. See also "The Gay Nineties," *The Marketer,* September, 1990; and "Invisibility=Stagnation," *Quest,* February, 1992.

24. Burtoft, *Setting the Record Straight,* p. 71.

25. Paul Gibson, "Gay Male and Lesbian Youth Suicide," originally contained in "Report of the Secretary's Task Force on Youth Suicide," January 1989.

26. Dr. Louis W. Sullivan, M.D., Secretary of Health and Human Services, letter to Representative William E. Dannemeyer, October 1989.

27. F. Parris, "Some Die Young," *Washington Blade,* May 17, 1985.

28. Peter LaBarbera, "The Gay Youth Suicide Myth," *The Journal of Human Sexuality* (Carrollton, TX: Lewis and Stanley, 1996), pp. 65-72.

29. *Teaching Captivity? How the Pro-Gay Agenda is Affecting Our Schools…And How You Can Make a Difference:* A Love Won Out series booklet (Colorado Springs, CO: Focus on the Family, 2000).

30. Jeffrey Satinover, *Homosexuality and the Politics of Truth* (Grand Rapids, MI: Hamewith Books, 1996), p. 94.

31. Dean Hamer and Peter Copeland, *The Science of Desire* (New York, NY: Simon and Schuster, 1994), p. 82.

32. Joe Dallas, *A Strong Delusion* (Eugene, OR: Harvest House Publishers, 1996), p. 117.

Chapter 11: Answering Science

1. Simon LeVay, "A Difference in Hypothalamic Structure Between Heterosexual and Homosexual Men," *Science,* 1991 vol. 253, pp. 1034-7.

2. Ibid., p. 1037.

3. Simon LeVay, *Queer Science* (Cambridge, MA: MIT Press, 1996), pp. 143-45.

4. William Byne, "The Biological Evidence Challenged," *Scientific American,* May 1994, pp. 50-55.

5. Simon LeVay, *The Sexual Brain* (Cambridge, MA: MIT Press, 1993), p. 122.

6. J. Michael Bailey and Richard Pillard, "A Genetic Study of Male Sexual Orientation," *Archives of General Psychiatry,* vol. 48, 1991, pp. 1089-96.

7. Whitehead, N.E. "The Importance of Twin Studies" http://www.narth.com/docs/whitehead2.html

8. "Born Gay: Science Finds a Genetic Link" *Time* cover story July 26, 1993.

9. Steven Rose, "War of the Genes," *The Guardian: Saturday Review,* May 8, 1999, p. 8.

10. Dean Hamer, et al., "A Linkage Between DNA Markers on the X Chromosome and Male Sexual Orientation," *Science* 261, July 16, 1993, pp. 321-27.

11. Neil and Briar Whitehead, *My Genes Made Me Do It!* (Lafayette, LA: Huntington House Publishers, 1999), p. 141.

12. Dean Hamer and Peter Copeland, *The Science of Desire* (New York, NY: Simon and Schuster, 1994), p. 104.

13. http://www.leaderu.com/orgs/narth/1995papers/satinover.html.

14. D.J. West, *Homosexuality Re-examined* (Minneapolis, MN: University of Minnesota Press, 1977), p. 65.

15. The *Diagnostic and Statistical Manual of Mental Disorders,* published by the American Psychiatric Association, is the handbook used most often in diagnosing mental disorders in the United States and other countries.

16. DSM-II (1968).

17. DSM-III (1980).

18. Stanton L. Jones and Mark A. Yarhouse, *Homosexuality: The Use of Scientific Research in the Church's Moral Debate* (Downers Grove, IL: InterVarsity Press, 2000), p. 97. Copyright © 2000 by Stanton L. Jones and Mark A. Yarhouse. Used by permission of InterVarsity Press, P.O. Box 1400, Downers Grove, IL 60515, USA. www.ivpress.com

19. http://www.islam-online.net/english/Contemporary/2003/02/Article01.shtml#3.

20. Jones and Yarhouse, *Homosexuality,* pp. 97-98.

21. Ibid., p. 98.

22. Ibid., p. 101.

23. Ibid., pp. 101-2.

24. Ibid., p. 102.

25. Elizabeth R. Moberly, *Homosexuality: A New Christian Ethic* (Cambridge, UK: James Clarke and Co., 1983), p. 30.

26. Jones and Yarhouse, *Homosexuality,* p. 112.

Chapter 12: Answering Your Need

1. Don Schmierer, *Celebrating God's Design* (Santa Ana, CA: Promise Publishing, 2000). See also www.hisservants.net/books.htm.

2. Cathy Morrill, *SOULutions,* www.desertstream.org/resources/catalog.htm.

3. www.desertstream.org/programs/theriver.htm.

4. www.loveinaction.org/Programs/Refuge/Refuge.html.

Other Harvest House Books on Homosexuality

DESIRES IN CONFLICT
by *Joe Dallas*

For more than a decade, *Desires in Conflict* has been the definitive "must-read" for those who wonder "Can a homosexual change?" This new edition with updated information offers more compelling reasons why the answer is "yes!"

A STRONG DELUSION
by *Joe Dallas*

Author and counselor Joe Dallas, in a loving and biblical manner, spells out what pro-gay theology is and how to confront it, then examines the believer's personal response and the need for bold love and commitment.

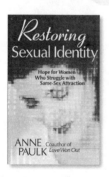

RESTORING SEXUAL IDENTITY
by *Anne Paulk*

Restoring Sexual Identity offers answers to the most commonly asked questions from both homosexuals desiring change and friends and relatives of women struggling with same-sex attraction.

HARVEST HOUSE
PUBLISHERS

When Homosexuality Hits Home

BY

JOE DALLAS

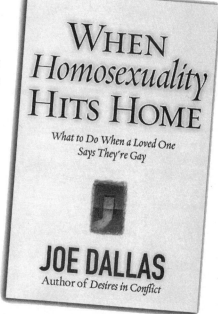

THE HEART-WRENCHING DECLARATION that a loved one is a homosexual is increasingly being heard in Christian households across America. How can this be? How can we respond?

Drawing from his own experience and from many years of helping families work through this perplexing and unexpected situation, Joe Dallas offers practical counsel on how to deal with the many conflicts and emotions parents, grandparents, brothers and sisters, or any family member will experience when learning of a loved one's homosexuality.

Important for these times, this book offers scriptural, compassionate advice to both struggling gays nad those who love them.

Joe Dallas, past president of Exodus International, lectures extensively at seminars and directs a biblical counseling practice in Tustin, California. He is the author of *Desires in Conflict* and *A Strong Delusion: Confronting the "Gay Christian" Movement.* His articles have been featured in *Christianity Today, Christian Research Journal,* and the *Journal of the Christian Association of Psychological Studies.*

Praise for Harper Sloan's Coming Home series!

- ★ -

Kiss My Boots

"The ending is quite smile inducing."

—*RT Book Reviews* (four stars)

"Harper Sloan hits it out of the park with *Kiss My Boots*. . . . This steamy novel is all about second chances and learning to trust again."

—*BookPage*

"Hot, sexy, and full of passion! A Western romance you'll love!"

—*Fresh Fiction*

Lost Rider

"Sloan . . . hits it out of the park with her first Coming Home contemporary western romance. . . . Maverick is a perfect hero: multilayered, complicated, deeply damaged, yet blooming with the new promise of love. Leighton is appealing and real, as are a strong supporting cast of characters whom readers will be glad to follow into sequels. **This absolutely spectacular effort catapults Sloan to the top of her genre.**"

—*Publishers Weekly* (starred review)

Cowboy Up

Also available from Harper Sloan and Pocket Books

Lost Rider

Kiss My Boots

Cowboy Up

THE COMING HOME SERIES, BOOK THREE

HARPER SLOAN

Pocket Books

New York   London   Toronto   Sydney   New Delhi

Pocket Books
An Imprint of Simon & Schuster, Inc.
1230 Avenue of the Americas
New York, NY 10020

This book is a work of fiction. Any references to historical events, real people, or real places are used fictitiously. Other names, characters, places, and events are products of the author's imagination, and any resemblance to actual events or places or persons, living or dead, is entirely coincidental.

First Pocket Books paperback edition January 2018

POCKET and colophon are registered trademarks of Simon & Schuster, Inc.

For information about special discounts for bulk purchases, please contact Simon & Schuster Special Sales at 1-866-506-1949 or business@simonandschuster.com.

The Simon & Schuster Speakers Bureau can bring authors to your live event. For more information or to book an event, contact the Simon & Schuster Speakers Bureau at 1-866-248-3049 or visit our website at www.simonspeakers.com.

Manufactured in the United States of America

10 9 8 7 6 5 4 3 2 1

ISBN 978-1-5011-5527-7
ISBN 978-1-5011-5528-4 (ebook)

To Lara Feldstein,
from book two to thirteen
Clay sends his love, darlin'.

1

CAROLINE

"Tin Man" by Miranda Lambert

— ★ —

The bright, speeding blaze of lightning shooting through and across the night sky illuminates the road ahead of me. The enormous boom of thunder that follows quickly on the heels of such a beautiful display makes me jump in my seat and grip the wheel tighter. Nothing but rain-soaked asphalt and darkness meet my gaze as I continue my drive. Normally, I would recognize the weather as an omen preluding my night's plans. A warning, perhaps, but one I won't be heeding. My mind is all over the place from my call earlier, and I just want to . . . escape, but, more importantly, I know I need a change.

"What am I doing?" I mumble into the emptiness around me.

No one answers. Of course no one does. I'm just talking to myself, like usual. Heavens me, if that's not a sign that I'm going insane, I don't know what is.

"That's what happens when you spend so much time closed off."

For the first time, the carefully constructed freedom that I've built for myself feels crippling. Or perhaps like it's caving in on me, the loneliness becoming too much. I've never been good at being alone, something I always knew, but I never realized how bad I was at it until now. I built my new life around just that, though, so like it or not, it's time to get over it. It could be worse, I remind myself. Shaking off the melancholy, I continue driving, knowing that when I reach my destination I'll be with people who care about me.

"Holy cow," I wheeze, gripping the wheel tighter when an even louder clap of thunder breaks the silence. I've always loved storms, but the sky's beautiful display is only amping up my already frazzled nerves, and I feel the unfortunately familiar burn of fear creeping up my spine before I can push it down.

I pull off the deserted back road and onto the shoulder, my headlights illuminating a sign announcing that I'm now leaving the town of Wire Creek. Beyond that is Pine Oak. It's a small town in northeast Texas, far enough from the big city for residents to be in their own little world. I grew up in Pine Oak, but after moving away just out of high school, I cut all ties and left some bad memories in my wake before returning to the area, opening up my dream bookstore, and calling Wire Creek my home.

I was close enough to feel the tug pulling me back toward Pine Oak every now and then, but far enough away that I wouldn't likely run into people who knew the old me.

My bookstore.

The Sequel.

It had been my second chance at happiness when I'd needed it the most—hence the name—and is something that I'm immensely proud of, even if being this close to Pine Oak brings back some bad memories I'd rather forget.

I have—or had, rather—a few friends in Pine Oak. It's not a stretch to think that they're still there—no one really ever leaves Pine Oak. I haven't seen or spoken to them in years though, so I think I've lost the right to call them friends. Actually, that right probably disappeared when I vanished without a word after graduation, and I'm not naive enough to think I'd be forgiven for that. But the stupid little hopeful cheerleader that pops into my mind every now and then likes to remind me that my girls from high school would welcome me back as though no time had passed, if I would just grow up and make my return to the area known. The fact that my mama's still there—not that it matters, since we don't speak anymore—is the driving force that has kept me at a distance, if I'm being honest. I don't need the memory of her to become a daily reality.

Not after everything that happened.

Never again.

"Get yourself together, Caroline. You're stronger than this," I mumble to the sign just outside my window.

I've *become* stronger than this. Logically, I know this, but still, old habits don't ever really die, do they?

I didn't survive the past twelve years to let fear keep me from living the life I've made. I promised myself that I'd take control of my life every day. It's time to stop making up reasons to stay closed off and not begin my new path of living. Impulsiveness might be something outside of my nature, but the only way I can think of to shake another call from *him* is to leap off the cliff of my comfort zone and *make* myself live.

I don't know why, after almost five years away, he started calling again. If it weren't for the memories long suppressed that hearing his voice brings back, I would thank him, though. It's because of that call that I was forced to really see my life, and what I saw, I didn't like.

Pushing *those* thoughts out of my mind, I turn the wheel to get back on the road and take the long way around Pine Oak's limits so I can get to the town on the other side—Law Bone. I could go home. I probably should, but I really don't want to be alone right now—something my mind knew immediately during that call, because I ran out into the storm the second I'd tossed my phone across the room. So I point my car to the one place I know without a shadow of a doubt will let me lose that feeling of being alone by finding safety in numbers but still remaining by myself at the same time.

- ★ -

Hazel's, the local honky-tonk, is just outside of Pine Oak—on the farthest opposite end of Wire Creek, inside Law Bone city limits. Okay, to call it a honky-tonk would be a stretch. It's a motorcycle bar that plays country music. It caters to a rough and rowdy crowd, but no one in there ever pays me a lick of mind. Of course, that's probably because one of my best friends is the owner, but even when he isn't there, I'm the last thing a man inside that place is looking for.

I'm shy by nature, an introverted book nerd who can handle fictional people a lot better than I can deal with real ones. I'm not a head turner. I never really gained the skills needed to make myself look anything but . . . well, plain. I tried. In high school, my best girlfriends always tried to teach me the ins and outs of being girly, but I was too interested in sticking my nose in a book and crushing on fictional cowboys to really retain any of it. I figured that, like in my books, the right man would love me for me and not for what the enhancements of makeup and fancy clothes could do.

I glance up at my reflection in the rearview as I pull into the lot and park, and fight off a cringe. I look sad, and that sadness makes me look much older than my nearly thirty years. My brown eyes don't shine with the mirth most women my age have dancing in theirs. Those are the carefree women who still believe they'll find a life partner to ride off into the sunset with. Just the thought makes me snort.

Where I always found my ordinary features and dull brown hair to be boring, I know the one thing I actually do have going for me is my figure. I've got the body of a dancer—thin and petite. It's my greatest attribute. I might not have all the curves most men seem to love, but I've been blessed with a body that requires minimum work to keep trim and firm.

There isn't anything about me that particularly screams, *Hey, look at me!* but I've been told men like my shape because it makes them feel like they were made to protect me—or so my good friend Luke always says.

"Speak of the devil," I mumble with a smile, seeing Luke standing under the awning outside of Hazel's front door, blowing a long stream of smoke from his mouth. The burning tip of his cigarette stands out in the darkness around him.

Luke Hazel, half of my best-friend duo, and twin brother to Lucy, is a dog, but at least he's an honest dog. Loyal to those he loves. Protective to the max. With his harmless flirting, he's also helped to give me back some of the confidence I lost over the years.

"Carrie," he drawls when I step out of my car and pull my cross-body purse over my head. I roll my eyes and cringe at the nickname he knows I hate.

"Lukie Dukie," I jest, tossing out the nickname that I know *he* hates, placing my hands on my hips and arching a brow at him.

Not even fazed, he kicks off the wall he'd been leaning against and walks my way. No, he struts. Because a simple walk wouldn't be good enough for this guy. He thinks he's God's gift to the females of the world. I laugh softly and fall into his arms for a hug when he reaches me.

"Not a good night to be here, sweetheart."

I push my hands against his abs and look up at him. "And what makes tonight different from all the other nights you say the same thing?"

"Rowdy, babe. Got some out-of-towners ridin' through lookin' for a good time. Not sure how they'll act when I pull the shotgun out if they try to get in your shorts."

I feel my nose twitch as I frown at him. "No one's gonna worry about me, Luke."

He shakes his head. "Not sure how many times I have to drill it in your head, babe, but every man in there is 'gonna worry about you.' "

"Don't be ridiculous, Luke. Even if you're right and I get some attention tonight, I've dealt with worse than some drunken bikers and you know it. And who says I wouldn't enjoy a little of their attention anyway?"

He frowns. "Yeah, Carrie, but that doesn't mean I want to put you through some bullshit just because I know you can handle it." His frown deepens, and I know the exact moment the rest of what I said registers. He doesn't call me on it, but he knows better than to ask if I'm ready for that kind of thing. "Told you, just like I tell Luce, this ain't a place to find a bedfellow."

I smile at the mention of Lucy. "You and I both know you're going to act like my babysitter the second I walk in there, so how about you stop acting like my big brother now and let me get a drink and forget about things for a while, hmm?"

His eyes narrow. "What you got to forget about, sweetheart?"

Too late, I realize my mistake. I haven't even talked to Lucy about the calls I've been getting, but with my emotions at the boiling point, my mind just slipped. Luke, the big macho protector that he's always been, isn't going to be happy without hearing what got me driving over to Hazel's on a Tuesday night either.

I sigh. "I promise, I'll fill you in later, but please, Luke, let me just forget about it all for a little while?"

He nods, but I can tell he isn't happy about giving in. One big, thickly muscled arm waves toward the door in a sweeping gesture for me to proceed. And even though he seems to be caving, I know a long talk will be coming. I just need to make sure I've had enough to drink so that I'm too intoxicated to deal with *that* chat tonight.

The heavy wall of smoke slams into me as we enter the bar. I always thought it was funny that Luke would go outside to have a cigarette when walking into Hazel's is probably the equivalent of smoking an entire pack of cigarettes in just one go. Most nonsmokers find the scent repugnant, but not me. I've always loved the smell of smoke—any kind of smoke—even if that is weird as hell.

An old Alan Jackson song booms through the air as we walk through the crowded bar. I feel the earlier tension slide off my body with each step and I know I made the right call in coming here. Luke grabs my arms, stopping me before I almost walk into a big, burly man, and pulls me to his side, securing me in place with an arm over my shoulders. I look up at him, smiling when I see his handsome face scowling down at me.

"What?" I mouth up at him, my smile growing.

He just shakes his head, continuing to guide me through the crowded room until we're at the very end of the U-shaped bar, closest to his office. He taps the shoulder of a man sitting down and, without a word, waves his hand in some sort of code that must say, *Get the hell up*, because the young cowboy doesn't even pause, sliding off the stool and disappearing into a darkened corner.

"You, sit." Luke pushes me toward the empty stool and crosses his arms with a glare at the men closest to the seat he demanded I take.

"You could say please, you know," I mumble under my breath, but I still follow his order.

"Could, but I won't."

"No surprise there, Lukie."

He bends down until his nose is touching mine. "Watch the 'Lukies' in here, *Carrie*."

"Whatever. How about a drink, Mr. Bartender?"

"Not joking, sweetheart. Don't want the men in here to think you're fair game."

"Look around, Luke. No one is worried about me." I don't know if that's actually true, but seeing as I've never been the type to turn a bar full of men's attention my way, I'm fairly confident in my assessment.

"Blind as a damn bat," he mutters loud enough for me to hear clearly over the noise, not backing away.

I open my mouth to give him a smart-ass retort but stop when I hear a deep, rumbling laugh to my side. I look over, not seeing much apart from the dark cowboy hat next to me. Its owner's face is concealed by shadows as he looks down at the golden-colored liquor in his glass. I can see a stubbled, very strong jaw though—the deliciously strong kind that's angled in such a way you could swear on a stack of Bibles on Sunday morning that someone carved it straight out of stone.

"Just please, stay here and out of trouble. You need to use the little girls' room, do it in my office. I can't run this place if I'm constantly worried about you."

"Got her, Luke," the stranger next to me mumbles loud enough to be heard over the music, still not looking up from his glass.

Luke flicks his gaze in my neighbor's direction, and even though there's no way he can see the man's face, he nods before pulling his attention away and back on me. "Be good, sweetheart."

He turns and stomps away.

"I'm always good!" I yell at his back, making the man next to me chuckle in such a low-pitched, manly way I almost feel like calling it a chuckle would be a sin. "What? I am," I defend.

"Sure you are, sugar." His deep, velvety smooth voice causes a wave of awareness to wash over me.

"Not that it matters, since I don't know you and all, but I'll have you know I'm the very definition of good. I wouldn't know how to be bad if it bit me in the butt."

He turns his head toward me. I'm unable to see his face, which is still hidden by the shadows, but I can feel his eyes on me. Their scrutiny is almost like a physical caress. "That so?" he rumbles after another few pounding heartbeats of silent study.

I nod mutely, wishing I had a drink to wash down the nervousness.

"How do you know Luke?" he continues.

"He and his sister are my best friends," I tell him without hesitation.

"Not your boyfriend?" he drawls.

"I— No. He's not my boyfriend," I answer, confused by his questioning.

"So what's a good girl like you doin' in a place like this?"

"Maybe I'm sick of being a good girl," I mumble, wishing I could see his eyes.

He continues to study me and I shift in my seat. Good

heavens, what kind of pull does this stranger have over me? I can't even look away, not that I want to, so I study him just as fiercely—even if I can't see his face, I can still see *him*. And what a mighty fine sight he is.

Dressed in the typical uniform of most cowboys around here, he's got his well-built frame in a navy-blue button-down shirt, tucked into jeans that I'm sure mold to his amazing-looking body perfectly when he's standing. Even in the dim light, I can see the dirty boots propped up on the step under the bar that keeps short legs like mine from dangling in the air. His hand wrapped around the tumbler is tanned, making me think he must work outside, but it's the long fingers that hold my focus as he uses them to slowly spin his glass against the bar top.

"Want to?"

Pulling my eyes from the strangely erotic sight of his hand, I look toward his shadowed face.

"Want to what?"

"Be bad, sugar."

Heat hot as fire washes over me with his words. Holy cow. My jaw works, but words elude me. I don't even know this man's name, let alone anything about him, and if my rusty knowledge of flirting is right, he just propositioned me. Why I find that as hot as I do, I'll never know, but before I even know what's happening, my brain finally figures out how to get the words past my shocked jaw.

"I think I do."

My eyes widen at the same time his hat dips, and then

he turns and holds up two fingers toward Luke farther down the bar. Call it male intuition, whatever kind of magic men have to know when another member of their brotherhood needs a drink, but Luke looks up the second the dark cowboy's fingers are in the air and nods. Not even a minute later, he's placing two glasses much like the one my mysterious companion just finished in front of us. Luke walks away without a word, clearly trusting this man if he's willing to let me drink with him *and* not give me a speech about drinking responsibly. When the chill of glass touches my knuckles, I look down.

"Somethin' tells me your mind might be ready to be bad, sugar, but your nerves aren't there yet. Goes down smooth, but sip it nonetheless."

My brain, still clearly under the dark cowboy's control, doesn't have a problem working now. My hand curls around the glass and I bring it to my lips, letting him control me without fighting it. He's not wrong—it goes down smooth as silk. At least, the first two sips do. Then I get a little confident and take a deep swallow, only to sputter my way through it.

"Sip," he calmly demands, leaning into me enough that I feel the heat of his body against my bare arms. "Want you feelin' calm when I show you how fun it is to be bad, not drunk."

"Who says I want to be bad with *you*?" I ask, taking a very small sip this time.

"Babe, you wanna be bad with me."

He's right, I do. "You seem confident." I look over the glass, trying to see through the shadows, but give up when I realize just how well he's cloaked.

He doesn't respond but instead takes a drink from his own glass.

"I don't even know you."

"Wouldn't make a difference if you did."

"You know, some people might actually think that you're actually just cocky and not confident."

"I'm old enough to go after what I want without playin' games. There ain't a thing cocky about that." *God*, his voice is pure sex.

"And what's that?"

"You'll find out," he promises darkly, playing the game despite his words.

"Cocky."

His deep laugh is low and gritty, almost as if it's a sound that normally doesn't come from him. For whatever reason, it makes me want to know everything I can about this man—this stranger.

We fall into a comfortable silence, but one that carries so much promise I can feel it building inside of me. Luke comes over to talk to me when he can, but it isn't often. My glass is never empty for long, but on Luke's fifth pass with the bottle of top-shelf whiskey, the dark cowboy places his hand over the top of my glass. I look over at him instead of Luke, to see him shaking his head.

"I got her, but how 'bout water and close out my tab?"

"You got it, Davis." Luke laughs, turning to grab me a bottle of water from the fridge behind him.

"Your name is Davis?" I ask the man next to me, weighing the sound of it.

He doesn't acknowledge me, waiting for Luke to come back with his credit card and his receipt to sign. He scribbles his signature and hands it back to Luke, dropping his feet to the wooden floor under us and stepping back. I follow his movements with my eyes, waiting to see what he'll do next, already anticipating the rush of disappointment when he leaves, knowing I'll likely never see him again. My jaw drops the second his hand comes out, palm up, in a gesture that clearly means he wants me to go with him. I look from his hand up to the darkness shadowing his face, wondering if I should actually be careless enough to go off with some stranger I don't know.

"You gonna give me shit about this?"

Confused, I look from that tanned hand with the long fingers back up at him, but I can tell by the tilt of his hat that he's speaking to someone behind me.

"Would it matter?" Luke laughs behind me and I turn to look at him.

"Not really. Only opinion that I care about is hers, but still askin'."

Luke shakes his head but still smiles. "Not her keeper, but I assure you if I had a problem with this shit I wouldn't have sat her next to you *and* continued to refill her glass." Luke looks down at me and gives me a wink. "Been a while, darlin', make sure he wraps it up."

I gasp and feel heat blossoming on my cheeks as Luke turns with a deep laugh and walks away. I'm going to kill him.

Heat blankets my back a second later and two strong hands clasp my hips. I feel him move until his breath is at my ear. "Let's go be bad, hmm?"

Am I going to do this? Go off with some man I don't know and sleep with him? Because I would be a fool to think this is anything else. Earlier I promised myself I was done living a ghost of a life and that I was going to find a way to be wild and free. I've never slept with someone I wasn't in a long-term relationship with. Oh, who am I kidding, I've only slept with one man. To say I'm in over my head here is an understatement. Lucy does it all the time. Hell, she keeps telling me I need a good rebound romp in the sheets. Screw it, I'll regret it if I don't at least jump in the saddle again, letting this man go without taking him for a ride.

I take a deep breath, lean back against the strong body behind me, and nod. "Yeah. Let's go . . . be bad."

My back vibrates with his laughter, and I shiver in his hold, my wide eyes meeting Luke's across the bar. He gives me a wink and smiles his ruggedly handsome, crooked smile, tipping his chin toward the door in silent confirmation that he has no problem with the stranger leading me away. Knowing that the dark cowboy has Luke's trust breaks the final restraint on my reservations. I turn, look up at my companion, and smile.

"Lead the way."

2

CAROLINE

"Bar at the End of the World" by Kenny Chesney

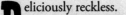

Deliciously reckless.

That's really the only way I can explain the feeling that's rushing through my body right now.

The darkness around us makes my other senses come to the forefront. The rasp of his five o'clock shadow against my sensitive skin as he kisses and licks his way down the column of my throat only makes my arousal spike to dangerous levels. Had we made it farther than even a foot into the motel room across from Hazel's, I would've turned on a light so I could finally see him, but now it's more fun to continue this ride with that unknown factor. He can be anyone I want him to be now. Or anyone I *don't* want him to be. For one night, I can take the pleasure my body hasn't had in years and live off the memories of it until I'm ready to give another man a chance. Hopefully I won't let another five years pass before that happens again.

I push my hands from his shoulders and palm his jaw as his stubble prickles against my fingers while my hands wander up to his hair. His hat falls to the floor with a thud and I know he's just as lost in me as I am in him, because he doesn't even make a move to pick it up. He lets out a deep grunt when I mold myself against his body, seeking some sort of friction. The next thing I know, my back is against the door and he's gripping my bottom. His mouth hits my jaw with a bite of his teeth, making a squeak of pleasure shoot up my throat, and his deep rumble of laughter reaches my ears as he presses me harder into the door with his hips. The heavy bulge of his erection against *that* spot makes me so desperate for him that I whimper in relief when his mouth *finally* closes over mine in a wet tangle of tongues.

I've never been kissed so thoroughly.

This is the kind of kiss that sets the bar for any that might follow.

The kind that shows you everything you've been missing and everything you never knew you wanted. I'm going to be comparing every kiss I ever have to my dark cowboy's, even though I know there's a good chance no one will ever compare. The sounds coming from my mouth, the ones being swallowed by his, are nothing short of needy. My hips move in tandem with the thrusts of his, and even though we're both fully clothed, I know it won't take much more of this for me to go off like the town's fireworks on the Fourth of July.

"Fuck, you taste just like apple pie," he whispers against my lips, breaking away with a gasp.

"Huh?"

"Goddamn, I love apple pie," he says before his mouth is back on mine, this time with a whole new kind of hunger deepening his kisses.

I'm held captive, enraptured. Then his hands move from my bottom to glide up my torso. He lifts his hard chest off mine and suddenly those delicious fingers are at my breasts. Even if I had big boobs his hands would dwarf them, I'm sure, but as it is he covers both with a firm grasp before adjusting his hold with a deft twist of the wrists. His mouth continues to feast on mine while his huge hands learn my body with slow movements. I tear my mouth from his with a breathy moan when he pushes my shirt up and slips his fingers into the cups of my bra to tweak my nipples.

"Oh, God," I moan when he does it again.

"I can't get enough of you," he rumbles.

"Please," I beg, not with the slightest clue as to what I'm begging for.

His hips dig even harder into mine as he leans back, supporting me against the door with that connection alone as he pulls my shirt off. The darkness makes me feel more confident than I normally would be, almost half naked with a man—no, a stranger.

"Yours too," I tell him as his fingers move to unclasp my bra. "I want to feel your skin on mine," I breathe, taking over the task so he'll hopefully give me what I want.

I fumble in my haste to feel more of this dangerous arousal he's creating in my body, but the second my bra is free and dangling toward the floor, his naked chest collides against mine, pushing me into the door with a force that sends the air rushing out of my lungs.

His mouth hits my collarbone at the same time his hands grasp my bottom, sliding me up the door until I feel the wet heat of his breath against my breast.

Then he stops.

"Wh-what are you doing?" I cry out, tugging him by his thick hair toward my aching breast. When he doesn't budge, I drop my head back with a thump hard enough to make my eyes water.

"Fuck, give me a second, darlin'," he rasps out, his heavy breath wafting against my flesh, causing my whole body to spark with another wave of need.

"Please, Davis," I whine.

He grunts, the sound of his name turning into a loud scream of pleasure when his mouth covers my nipple. Sucking deeply, he sends arousal shooting from every single nerve in my body. I've never in my life felt anything like it. One hand starts to caress and tease my other breast until I'm positive I'm going to come from this alone. My hips pump against his abs, and I wish I wasn't so short and that it was his crotch against mine, but with muscles like his, I'm thinking I still might be able to.

"More, need more."

He pops his mouth free, giving one more lick, then spins us and stomps away from the door. I'm so lost in him that when he drops me, I don't even think to panic. The hard mattress gives me enough of a bounce that when he follows on top of me we collide with dual grunts.

He's got me naked in a matter of seconds in a move so skillful I don't even realize I'm being undressed until a rush of cool air brushes against my wet core. I don't give myself a second to think about where he learned that; instead I push off the bed with my feet against the mattress and rut against his denim-covered erection. His groans mingle with mine, making me drunk with pleasure. The darkness around us, with not even the moon to cast some sort of light on us, only heightens the pleasure until I'm going out of my mind.

"I need you," I tell my dark cowboy.

"Fuck yes," he answers, but leaves me abruptly to stand.

I start to protest, until I hear his belt clang and the sound of his boots being toed off. "Light on or off, sweetness?" he rumbles.

"Off."

If he had an issue with my answer, he didn't verbalize it, instead he continues to undress.

"You taste like apple pie all over?" he oddly asks, when the sounds of him getting naked stop.

"What?"

"Never tasted anything better," he continues.

Lifting off the mattress with my elbows, I start to reach for him but stop the second he speaks again, and I know I'll spend the rest of my life swearing I saw the bright lights of heaven not even a moment later.

"Can't wait to find out if your pussy tastes as sweet as the rest of you."

Oh. My. "Heavens!" I scream when he grabs my hips and his mouth covers my sex. My eyes roll back in my head as I scream my throat raw, coming instantly with waves of intense pleasure that just keep getting more intense as his vibrating groans shoot against my core.

My toes curl, my fingers cramp as I fist the sheets, and I thrash my head from side to side with the roaring of my thundering heart matching the storm raging through my body.

He continues to drink from me. Sucking, nipping, licking, *devouring* me. The ragged sounds coming from me ring in my ears as I continue to come, begging him to never stop. All of this, without even knowing what the skillful man between my legs looks like, but knowing I will never forget him.

He gives me one long, slow lick from my clenching center to my oversensitive clit before releasing his hold on my hips and climbing up my body. Limply, I watch his shadow in the darkness move until something falls on my chest.

"You wanna be bad, sweetness, then let's be bad," he tells me against my mouth before kissing me. The taste of my arousal thick on his tongue makes me turn my head and deepen the kiss.

I could kiss this man for days and days.

He rolls us, my legs falling to straddle his hips as the hard length of his erection sits between my soaked lower lips. I start rocking my hips mindlessly, needing to be filled with him. He gives me free rein until his breathing is just as frantic as mine. Only then does he stall, his fingers digging into my thighs.

"Condom, get it on my cock and ride me until that sweet fucking pussy sucks me dry," he demands.

My hands shake as I search between our bodies for what he must've dropped on the mattress before rolling us. Finally finding it by my knee, I shift and grab his thickness gently. I give him a few pumps but stop when I realize just how big the man under me is. I look up and gasp, adding my other hand to better size him up. Holy shit, this will never fit inside of me.

"My cock will fit just fine inside of that sweet pussy."

"Shit," I hiss, giving him a squeeze with both hands. "You weren't supposed to hear that."

"Gathered that, sugar, but trust me when I say you're soaked and it'll fit just fine."

He's not wrong. I'm so wet I can feel the dampness

spreading across his thigh. I shift my hips, the friction making me pant loudly.

"Fuckin' hell. Get that shit on me so you can fuck me," he strains.

"What?" I sputter, freezing with both hands still fisting his huge erection. "You want me to . . ." I stop, unable to finish my thought.

"Say it, Carrie," he tells me, the nickname not bothering me as much coming from him. He must have heard Luke call me that and I don't correct him, using it as my own cloak. "Say you're going to fuck me. Tell me how you're going to ride my cock."

Oh my God, this man is going to be my undoing.

I squirm, but don't speak as the shyness I thought I'd lost comes roaring back. I start to drop him, but he must've realized I was losing my nerve. His hands shoot off my thighs and around each of my fists, closing around my hold roughly and pumping himself through our joined hold. A long and pained sound leaves him. He lifts up, one hand cupping my center, one long finger sinking into me and hooking inside my body as I scream.

"You feel this? Feel what your body wants? Or how fuckin' hard I am for you? I want you to use me, Carrie. I want you to ride me until I feel that wet pussy drippin' down my balls, and then I want to feel that sweetness of yours clamp down on me as you come. You'll keep ridin' me though, won't you, sweetness? You'll keep givin' me more because you want to know what bein' bad feels like.

And I'll give it to you just as soon as you give me what I want. Then I'm gonna flip you over until your ass is in the air and your ponytail is in my fist with my balls slapping against this soaked pussy until you come again. Fuck you so hard, darlin', you're gonna feel me for days. Then you're gonna get your sweet ass back against this mattress so I can put my knees at your sides and pump my cock until I come all over these fuckin' tits."

He slides his finger in and out of my body a few times, my core fluttering around him.

I'm ready to come again.

"Show me you wanna be bad," he says, his voice straining as his erection grows even harder between our hold.

I rip my hand away from his flesh and my mouth finds his as I search for the condom again. This time he's the one that finds it, but he pulls my hand from his neck and places the packet in my palm as I continue to roll my tongue against his. As I tear it open, my mouth leaves his and starts kissing every inch of his body while I fumble my way through putting a condom on. Then, thank the heavens above, I finish at the same time my mouth finds his nipple. I bite it, not even sure what's come over me, but I get a rush of power from the guttural noises spilling from him.

I scoot my knees until I feel him again between my legs, lifting up with my hands on his shoulders. "Put your cock inside of me," I pant against his mouth, shocked at the brazen words that left my own without thought.

"I thought you'd never ask, sugar," he grunts, one hand

leaving the breasts he'd been playing with to line himself up with my entrance. The second I feel his blunt tip, I let my body fall, taking every rock-hard inch of him at once.

The pleasure is blinding.

And I scream.

And scream.

And *scream*.

Every single time I go to lift myself off of him, I feel a strangled sound leave my mouth.

"Take it easy, darlin'. Fuckin' hell. Didn't think you would try to split yourself in two," he mumbles, kissing me sweetly while helping me rock my hips to get used to the size of him. It doesn't take long for those sweet kisses to turn desperate and my body to need more.

If he weren't such a large man, or maybe if I weren't such a small woman, I would have been able to ride him like he had wanted, but as it was, I couldn't even get myself halfway off his hardness before he realized I needed help. His hands clamp my hips and lift me all the way off before thrusting me down. We continue, both of us moving in a way that would make you think we'd been lovers for years. The sounds of my wetness fuel my desire as we swallow each other's moans.

"I'm going to . . ." I pant.

"Say it," he grunts when I stop speaking. "Tell me what you're gonna give me."

"I'm going to . . . God, Davis, I'm going to come!" I yell as I start to do just that.

He drops me, hard and heavy against him, and I start rocking my hips while my pleasure takes me to the brink of insanity. The whole time, he speaks soft words that I'm unable to understand through the force of my orgasm.

Then he proves he's a man of his word, because I come again on my hands and knees while he pulls my head back with a strong grip on my ponytail, his balls slapping against my hyper-sensitive flesh. Then and only then does he pull free of me, flip me onto my back, and climb up my body with his knees digging into the mattress next to my sides. I feel the tip of him touch my chest a few times as his furiously pumps himself; then the hot splash of his come hits my chest as he bellows out into the shadows around us. I hadn't even registered him removing the condom, so lost was I in delicious pleasure.

His body slackens when the last drop leaves him, giving me just enough of his weight but clearly not all of it since I can still breathe. I wiggle, the wetness on my breasts starting to roll toward my neck, and lift one hand up to swipe at it. I'm not sure what makes me lick my fingers clean, but when the salty taste of him bursts against my tongue, I moan loudly.

"Fuck." He hisses breathlessly. "Just came harder than I ever fuckin' have and I'm ready to take more from you. You too sore for my cock again?"

"Hmm?" I moan, still sucking the taste of him off my fingers.

"Doesn't matter, gonna fuck you again anyway."

And boy does he. By the time we finally fall asleep, he's taken me once in the shower and again in the bed before pulling me into his arms seconds before I pass out. The last thought that goes through my mind before drifting off is if this was how living wild and free feels, I am never going to stop.

Never.

3

CLAYTON

"Dirt on My Boots" by Jon Pardi

- ★ -

The overwhelming heat rushing through my body is enough to make me hate being a rancher during these hot-as-fuck summer months. The oppressing temperature assaults me the second I open my front door, the heat so stifling that it steals your breath straight from your damn lungs. The harder I work, the worse it gets, until I pray to whoever will listen for anything to filter some of these damn rays. Nothing changes the fact that shit needs to get done and I'm the one who needs to do it.

Trails of sweat drip down my back, slow tracks of fiery wetness that feel like they burn my skin on the way to my belted jeans. I drop the pitchfork I've been using to add straw to the horses' stalls and rip my shirt off, wiping my brow with it before placing my hat back on my soaked head as I toss the garment behind me and continue with my task.

Fucking Texas summers.

It feels like hell rises from the ground every day.

My days are all the same. I wake up, chug coffee, and work outside until well after the sun sets and the rest of the people in Pine Oak have set off for dinner with their families.

I'm alone, for all intents and purposes, and that feeling is even more pronounced on days when my brothers aren't around to distract me from my loneliness, which happens more frequently now that they're both married and living off the ranch.

But even if I wanted to find someone like Maverick and Quinn did, there's no place in my life for the responsibility of being the sole provider of someone else's happiness anymore. I'm at the tail end of my thirties, and it's too late for me to worry about finding someone I love.

No one can hurt me if I don't let them have the power to do it. Which means I'm better off alone.

"Fuckin' hell, old man, what's crawled up your ass and died?"

"Got shit to do, Mav," I tell my brother, not stopping in my shoveling.

"Looks like you need a break from that shit you gotta do, brother."

"Drew isn't here today. If I don't get this shit done, I'm

gonna be workin' all night. Tell me what you need so I can get this done."

"Leigh wants you to come to dinner tomorrow."

"Does she, now?"

"Says she doesn't see you enough, though I'm not sure why she fuckin' cares."

I bark out a laugh. "Jealous?"

"Fuck you," he retorts.

"Just saw her the other day when I stopped in at the PieHole. Why does she really want me to come to dinner?"

I hear my younger brother mumble something under his breath and smile despite the fact that I'm hot and exhausted, and my mind is in about a million other places. He continues to grumble—something he's always been mighty good at—as I finish placing the last few forkfuls of hay into the stall and turn to him. Even frustrated, I can see the contentment that his life now brings him written all over his face. I'm happy as fuck that he's got that. It hasn't been an easy road for him and his wife, Leighton, but they finally found their way back to each other. Took him almost dying, his rodeo career ending, and our father's death to do it, but it happened regardless, so if anyone deserves the full-to-bursting life he has with Leigh, it's my little brother.

"You didn't hear it from me, but she and Quinn want to corner you into comin' to their baby shower or some shit like that. Fuck if I know, Clay. I don't even want to be a part of it, but every time Leigh talks about the shower, her face does this thing that makes me want to give her anything in the damn world to keep it lookin' like that, so I'm here to make sure I keep gettin' those stars in her eyes and smiles on her lips. Even if it goes against everything to be beggin' my brother to come to a fuckin' baby shower."

I laugh, low and deep. "Admit you're just as over the fuckin' moon as she is and I'll be there." I don't need him to, but part of me loves to hear him talk about how thrilled he is that he's going to be a father. Even though I'm only three years older than him, I basically raised him and Quinn when our mama took off. I reckon this is as close to parental pride as I'll ever get, which is why I keep taking that pride whenever opportunities arrive.

He drops his brooding expression and gives me a smile that's usually only reserved for Leigh. "Shit, Clay. Can't even put it into words, but if that's what it means to feel like my heart is gonna explode daily, then yeah, I'm over the fuckin' moon. Scared outta my skull, too," he admits, his smile dimming a little.

"Why's that?"

"Did you know her mama had complications when she had Leigh? That's why they never had any more young'uns. She told me about how her mama almost died during childbirth and all I can think about is what I'll do if I lose Leigh."

No longer feeling the joy of his happiness, I prop the pitchfork against the stall, walk over to him, and clasp his shoulder in support. "Leighton's strong as hell and doctors are trained a lot better than they were thirty years ago, Mav. Don't let that ruin your excitement. She's gonna be just fine, and in the end you'll have a little piece of the two of you keepin' you up all night."

"I won't be able to move on if I lose her," he continues, completely ignoring my attempt at lightening the mood and I realize just how much this has been weighing on him.

"Maverick." I hiss through the thickness in my damn throat and pull my brother into my arms. His own come around me with bruising force.

"Can't talk to her about this shit, Clay. I don't want her worryin' about it when she should be focusin' on all the happy shit, but it's tearin' me apart just thinkin' about losing her."

"Fuck, brother."

Just like when we were younger and he was upset, he drops his forehead against my shoulder, and even though I'm no longer taller than him, he seems to shrink in my hold. It's then that I realize my baby brother—the badass ex–rodeo champion—is crumbling, his silent sobs only evident because of the choppy breaths coming from his lips.

"I could lose her."

"You won't."

"You don't know that," he bellows, ripping free from my arms and throwing his hands in the air. "Every day we get closer to the baby bein' born I feel like I'm losin' her. I can't turn it off."

Fucking hell.

I pull my phone out of my back pocket and move my thumb against the screen while he paces and mumbles in front of me, placing the device to my ear a second later.

"Hey," my sister sings through the phone.

"Tate around, darlin'?" Maverick stops in his tracks and looks over at me with a blank face. No hint of anger, the fear gripping him too deep for him to be mad that I'm bringing someone else into this and exposing his vulnerable fears to them.

"Yeah. Everything okay?"

"All's fine, Quinnie, just thought of somethin' I needed to ask him. Forgot the other day when I ran into him in town."

"Let me go grab him. We've been workin' on a junker he bought off Craigslist. Can you believe that? Only man in the world who would buy his wife a rust bucket as a gift."

"Sounds like the perfect gift if that wife is you," I tell her, forcing lightness into my tone while my eyes stay trained on Maverick.

"It is, isn't it." She sighs happily. "Here he is. Love you, big brother!"

"Love you back, darlin'."

I wait, hearing what sounds a helluva lot like them making out before he comes on the line.

"Hey. What's up, Clay?"

"Need you to come to the ranch, Tate. Keep that stupid smile on your face so Quinn doesn't think somethin' is wrong. Tell her I need help puttin' together a gift for the baby or some shit and come now. Got it?"

"Need me to bring any tools?" he plays along instantly.

"See you quick, Tate."

"Yeah, don't worry, I won't tell Quinn you're puttin' together a gift for her, man."

I hear Quinn make some girly as fuck noise as I disconnect the call and push the phone back into my pocket.

"You're gonna sit down and listen to what he has to say, Maverick. Then us three are gonna go inside and have some cold ones before you go home to your wife with a clear conscience. Got it?"

He grunts, doesn't speak but drops against the wall. He slides until his ass is on the ground and his head is hung low. The whole time my heart breaks knowing he's been carrying this load secretly until it became too much for him to keep buried. Work can wait for another day: right now, my brother needs me, and there's never been and never will be anything I won't do for the people I love.

I sit against the wall opposite him while we wait. Fifteen minutes later, Tate comes roaring down the driveway in the truck my sister restored for him almost a year ago. I'd sent him a text right after getting off the phone with him to let him know to find us in the old barn that we use for our personal horses. This one, while still nice, isn't top-of-the-line like the one we use to breed, and it lacks the air-conditioning system we put in the breeding stable a few years back. By the time Tate comes running in, I've finally gotten used to sitting in a puddle of my own sweat.

"Jesus Christ, Clay. Give me a fuckin' heart attack. What's going on?" he breathes, and I finally look away from Maverick. My sister's husband might not have been born and raised in Pine Oak, but all it took was one year back here and he shed every ounce of the city boy he'd become when he lived in Atlanta. Even if he still wears ball caps and not Stetsons, he looks like any other man that grew up here. 'Course, he would when Quinn's got his ass working on trucks, covered in dirt and grease.

"Maverick," I tell him, looking back at my little brother. He hasn't moved since I called Tate, who conveniently happens to be our town's lady doctor in addition being to our brother-in-law. If anyone knows the facts that can set Maverick's mind at ease, it's Tate. "Mav, want me to tell Tate or do you?"

He grunts, and I take that as him wanting me to fill Tate in, so I do. Each word that crosses my lips makes Tate look more and more sympathetic. His own wife, our sister, is due only a week after Leigh, so aside from Tate being one hell of a doctor, he can sympathize with Maverick on a level I couldn't begin to imagine.

"Jesus, man. That's some heavy shit."

"I'd die without her." Maverick finally looks up, his eyes pleading with the two of us.

"You wouldn't. Not because you'd move on, but because you'd have a reason to keep goin', but that's not gonna happen." Tate moves over to his side and starts spewing a bunch of medical knowledge that makes my ears bleed, but by the time he's done explaining to Maverick just how safe Leigh is, I finally see the tension leave my little brother's body. "Not only has medicine become more advanced, but we doctors are always thinkin' ten steps ahead, man. I promise you, Leighton and the baby are gonna be fine."

When the three of us are done talking, there isn't a sober one between us. Quinn came about an hour ago to pick up Tate, and Maverick just drove off with Leighton. Judging by him not being able to keep his hands off her when she showed up, I know I can go to bed tonight not worried about my baby brother.

The second their taillights disappear and the sounds of the night meet my ears, I feel the loneliness settle around me once again. Then I head back to the barn to finish the work I abandoned earlier this afternoon, but my mind is on my family and the apple pie I have waiting in the fridge, thanks to Leighton.

If I was a different man, maybe I'd do something about the deadweight of my solitude that's getting heavier and heavier to drag around. But I'm not, so I continue my work in silence before going to bed.

Alone.

4

CAROLINE

"I Could Use a Love Song" by Maren Morris

Dusting has become the bane of my existence. However, I do it with a smile because I love every second that I spend inside my bookstore. Even every second I spend outside of it, since my apartment is on top of The Sequel and the scent of books travels up the stairs and into my living space. There's no better smell on this earth than the pages of a book. Not one thing.

Well, maybe that of a certain dark cowboy . . .

I smile to myself. The memories of that night still hang with a delicious heaviness in my thoughts, even a month later. I always thought I wouldn't be able to detach the emotion from sex, but when I woke up alone the morning after that glorious night, all I could do was smile and take my well-used body home. I'd needed that night more than I thought. I needed to remember how to feel again without letting someone close. And it's been the memories from our night that have kept the loneliness I was drowning in at bay and a smile on my face. I think, in a way, my dark cowboy made it possible for me to not have any more lingering fear over the fact that my ex had started contacting me again.

"Thinkin' about that cowboy again?" Lucy sings with a smile, meeting me in the romance section toward the back of the store with her own duster.

"That obvious, huh?"

"Only on the days that end with *y*," she jokes.

"Yeah, yeah."

"You know, all you have to do is ask Luke. I bet he'd give you the stranger's name and you could enjoy another night of having your world rocked."

I laugh. "It was special, Luce, but I don't want to ruin what I got from him by tryin' to make it somethin' it isn't."

"And how do *you* know it couldn't be more?"

"How do you know it could?"

"Oooh, feisty."

The bell chimes, letting us know there's a customer, and Lucy takes off with a little skip, the smile still on her face. That girl is perpetually happy, and it doesn't take much to make her maniacally happy. She's been riding the same high as me for the past month, although she's been riding it for an entirely different reason. My best friend is just happy that I'm happy. For her, it's as simple as that. She's seen too many times when I wasn't close to that, been there for me since I met her at eighteen, and I know she'll be there for me until I die.

I hear her greet our newest customer and I continue dusting, moving through the romance books slowly as I study the spines. Romance is my favorite genre, the hopeless romantic in me still there despite everything my love life has been through, and I can't help it when my thoughts drift back to *him*. Our night together was the stuff fantasies are built from. There wasn't a single second of our coupling that gave me a hint to who he was. Even in the shower, we washed each other in darkness. He took me against the bathroom counter in darkness. We fumbled back to the bed in darkness. Even if a part of me wishes I knew who he was, I wasn't kidding when I told Lucy that I didn't want to cheapen the memory of our time together if he turns out to be less than the perfect man that I've created in my mind. It has nothing to do with what he might look like, but I'm afraid that if I were to find him and we had another chance at coming together, it'd never live up to the magic of that night.

So I'm almost completely content with never knowing.

Almost.

"Did you move the pregnancy books?" Lucy asks, popping her head around the shelf I was working on tidying up.

"Oh, sorry. I forgot to tell you. They're toward the front now, over by the self-help books. I didn't think it was right to have them all the way in the back *and* on the bottom shelf. Makin' it a little easier for the mamas-to-be and all, keepin' them up front."

"Gotcha!" she says, smile in place and pep in her damn step.

I shake my head and smirk.

"Holy shit! Leigh, it *is* her!"

I feel my jaw drop and quickly turn with a squeak. No way. I haven't heard that voice or that name in years.

"Quinn!" I exclaim, placing my duster on the shelf and rushing forward to pull her into a hug about the same time I notice her round belly. "Oh my goodness, congratulations, Quinn!"

She pulls away, smiling and rubbing her swollen and very pregnant belly. "Thank you. I can't believe it's you. I thought I recognized your voice."

"Caroline?!" I hear behind Quinn, and then Leighton James is pulling me into her arms, hugging me just as tight as I am her.

"Holy crap! You too!" I laugh, looking from belly to belly, my laughter growing. "I shouldn't be surprised you two would be pregnant together. There wasn't a thing y'all did without the other growin' up! How close are your due dates?"

They both beam, then, simultaneously, exclaim, "A week!"

"Of course it is," I say, laughing even harder at the fact that the two childhood best friends, both born within the same week, are pregnant with their babies due a week apart. "It sure is good to see you two."

"Have you been livin' in Wire Creek long?" Quinn asks, still stroking her belly. "I thought I heard you were in Houston. Or was it Dallas?" She looks at Leigh in question before focusing back on me.

I shake my head. "Austin, actually. I lived there after college but moved to Wire Creek a few years ago."

"Never thought I'd see the day. You hightailed it outta here so quick I think you still had your cap and gown on from graduation." Leighton laughs.

She isn't wrong: I took it off on the road out of town and tossed it out the window. "What can I say? I was young and foolish."

"Who was it you were datin' back then?"

I know Quinn probably means the question as one of those toss-away ones old friends ask when they haven't seen each other in over ten years, but if she only knew how deep it slices me. I take a deep breath and school my features. It's in the past: no sense in bringing the details up to two girls whom I haven't seen in too long—two girls who were my closest friends years ago.

"John Lewis," I tell her, pretty damn proud of myself for keeping my voice even.

"God, Leigh, you remember John?" Quinn laughs. "You probably would've dated him too, had you not been all in love with Maverick back then. Hell, half the girls in school were in love with John, Mr. Quarterback himself."

"He did have quite the following, didn't he?" Leigh agrees, looking at me like she can read between the lines.

"So, who are the lucky men?" I ask, pointing to their bellies and changing the subject.

"You'll never guess who that one finally landed," Quinn jokes, pointing toward Leigh.

"No!" I squeak with excitement, catching on immediately. "Maverick?"

Leighton's whole face lights up at the mention of Quinn's older brother. Last I heard, he was on the rodeo circuit, making a big name for himself in the sport. "Finally wrangled me a cowboy." She giggles.

"I'm so happy for you," I tell her honestly.

"It wasn't an easy road, but I love my grump."

"You always did, honey," Quinn says with a smile.

"And what about you, Quinn?"

"You remember Tate Montgomery?"

"The boy who used to spend his summers at his grandparents'? Sure I do. You two were practically joined at the hip. What did you do, get married right after the dust settled around me leavin' town?" I laugh, but my smile slips when she doesn't join in.

"Nah, took us a while and a lot of distance to realize where we belong, but we finally did. We got married last year. Shortly after I found out about this little one."

She points to her stomach with a smile that doesn't quite reach her eyes.

I sense a story that isn't full of hearts and flowers and, knowing it's time to steer the conversation away from that, I nod.

"Well, what brings you two into my bookstore?"

They both laugh. "Why am I not shocked that you'd end up owning a bookstore. We never could get you to put down those Fabio books you loved so much back in high school."

I giggle with Quinn. "Hey, he was a stud."

"We're lookin' for those baby books for daddies. You know, the ones that tell them what to expect when a tiny little demandin' human comes from their wife and life as they know it is changed forever. Tate, love him to death, seems to think he's fine because he's a lady doctor, but no amount of pullin' babies from other women's vaginas can prepare a man for the birth of his own child. Don't even get me started on my brother. Man can ride the meanest of bulls without breakin' a sweat, but you talk about his baby comin' soon and he starts gettin' pale as a ghost."

"She isn't wrong. My husband is hidin' it well, but I can tell he's nervous."

We continue to laugh as I show them where to look, catching up with small talk as they thumb through the selection, pulling a few out to purchase.

"Hey, you should come to the baby shower in a few weeks. We're doin' the whole joint thing, since the whole town is basically shuttin' down. You'd think the president was comin' to town the way they're all carryin' on."

"I'd love to," I tell them, surprising myself with just how much I want to be there.

They give me the info and we exchange numbers, promising to catch up soon. Seeing Quinn and Leighton only drives home just how much I've missed having them in my life. My fears haven't just kept me from moving on romantically—they've also kept me from people who I know, with no doubts, would do nothing but enrich my life. Now that we've been brought back together, I can't imagine my life without them in it again.

"You should stop by the PieHole, too," Leighton says. "You remember my mama's pies?"

"Boy, do I ever. Best thing I've ever put in my mouth!"

"That's what she said!" Lucy calls out from somewhere in the back of the store.

We all dissolve into laughter, and by the time Quinn and Leigh leave, I have a date to stop by the PieHole after I close up tonight. The memory of Leigh's mama's pies is so strong I swear I can taste them.

- ★ -

Four hours later, having finally closed The Sequel up, Lucy and I head over to Pine Oak, the excitement of seeing my old friends again bubbling in my belly like butterflies the whole way.

Lucy and I make small talk during the thirty-minute

drive, but the second we hit Main Street and pass my mama's salon, I stop talking. The windows are dark, so I know she isn't there, but the thought of running into her at Leighton's bakery makes me feel like I'm going to puke.

"Thinkin' about your mama?" Lucy asks knowingly.

"That obvious?"

"I understand your history, honey, but don't you think your mama would be happy to see you and forget about that stuff that kept y'all apart?"

I shake my head. "I think those kinda hurts are unmendable. I was a kid when I left, Luce, but she was a grown adult who turned her back on me when I came back beggin' for her help. Sometimes the hurt inflicted by others is just too great to move on from."

She hums in agreement and we pull into the parking spot directly next to Leigh's place. Lucy turns off her car and turns to look at me. "I hear you, Caroline, I do, but you're still holdin' on to that hurt, so maybe a little closure would be a good thing. Just think about it. Now that you have a reason to come into Pine Oak more, it's not like you can avoid her forever."

"Probably not, but that's a bridge I'll cross when it's time."

She gives me a look of understanding before nodding. "I'm here no matter what. Luke and me. Family isn't just those you're connected to by blood, you know."

"I do, sister from another mister," I joke.

For it being six at night, things are still pretty crowded

inside Leigh's place. An older woman behind the counter calls out a greeting when we step in, causing every head to turn in our direction. My cheeks heat and my shoulders pull in under the crowd's scrutiny. Lucy just plasters on her pageant smile and walks confidently in front of me. What I wouldn't give to have just an ounce of her conviction. I've been disgustingly shy my whole life, something that will never change if it hasn't yet. I look down at the ground while following Lucy's booted feet farther into the room. She's used to me being like this, so even if she wasn't a ball of happiness, she would've taken the lead.

"Hey you!" Quinn calls, and I look up to see her waving us toward a big table in the back. The man next to her with his arm around her chair looks just like the Tate I remember. On her other side sits the unmistakable Maverick Davis. He isn't smiling like Quinn's husband, but he doesn't look like the grumpy teenager I remember either. And finally, my eyes land on Leigh, curled into his side, her hand on top of his resting against her belly.

"Hey y'all. I'm Lucy Hazel!"

"Any relation to Luke Hazel?" Maverick rumbles, looking away from his wife's belly and at my best friend.

"Only the best twin brother a girl could ever have."

"Good man," he responds, looking back down to resume his study, his big palm moving around Leigh's belly a little.

"The best," Lucy agrees. She looks over at Tate. "Hi! You're the lady doctor. Taking new patients? Hate my gyno." She thrusts her hand out. Only she would think that asking a man when she first meets him if he can take a look at her vagina is acceptable.

"Uh, yeah. Call the office?" he responds, a little unsure, but he takes her hand anyway.

"Will do!"

"You're a happy one!" Quinn giggles.

"Life's too short to be anything but."

"Pull up a seat. Jana can get y'all whatever you want."

Taking a deep breath, I smell a certain sugary confection that makes me smile, memories of a whole other kind of high making my cheeks heat. "Got any apple pie?"

"Does she have apple pie? It's only always here since Clay can't get enough of the gross stuff," Quinn hoots. "Just missed my big brother, too. He got a call about a problem with one of his pregnant horses, so he had to head back to the ranch."

"All he does is work," Leigh adds.

"He's running the ranch now," Quinn tells me, and I know exactly how much weight that comment holds. Something even half the size of the Davis ranch would be hard work.

"That's got to be something. Does his wife help?"

Quinn looks at Lucy like she has two heads. Her question wasn't one that merits that kind of reaction, so I look over to make sure my best friend isn't picking her nose or something, but she's just smiling like normal.

"Clay's allergic to relationships. I don't think he's been

in one in at least four years, maybe longer. He got a little serious once with a total bitch, but thankfully that didn't last. Since then, nothin'."

"Relationships aren't for everyone," I mumble, thinking about my own issues with them, though I can't imagine someone like Clay would still be single. He was the most beautiful man I had ever seen when I was coming around with Quinn and Leigh.

I look up and meet Maverick's eyes across the table. He's studying me with such an intensity, I blush and look down. He's always been intense, but when he focuses on you like that, you would swear he can read your every thought.

The rest of the night continues, and before I know it the room around us has cleared out and Jana Fox, the gray-haired woman I saw when I entered, who I've learned is the PieHole's manager, has long since said her good-byes. I ate two slices of the best apple pie I've ever had in my life, and enjoyed one of the best evenings I've had in years.

God, I missed being home. More than I realized. Now, being near these people again, I can feel that pull stronger than ever.

5

CAROLINE

"Speak to a Girl" by Tim McGraw & Faith Hill

- ★ -

"**Y**ou stupid fuckin' bitch!"

I flinch, knowing what's coming before John grabs my biceps in a rough and painful grip.

He pulls me forward, my head snapping back. He's getting worse. The thought filters through my mind and I know, I know next time might be the time that he doesn't stop at just hitting me a little. It's been escalating over the years, but the past few he hasn't stopped at just the verbal abuse, manhandling me more and more roughly each time I do something that pissed him off until that doesn't even seem like enough for him. Even if it's just moving through our house, I never know what's going to set him off.

"I'm sorry, John!" I cry, holding my hands up in front of my face in case this is that time he doesn't stop.

"Fuckin' disgusting," he spits, giving me a shake before pushing me from him. I stumble but don't fall. *"I asked for a Bud and you bring me this cheap off-brand shit. Go to the store and get my fuckin' Bud or you'll find out what it's like to be sorry."*

I grab my keys and run to the car, my hands shaking the whole way. In the five years we've been in Austin, he's gotten worse and worse. Actually, the first couple years weren't bad. But when we turned twenty-one and he was able to get beer more often, things changed. The clerk at the twenty-four-hour mart doesn't even look at me while he rings up my purchase, handing me my change with a mumbled good night.

I spend the drive home thinking about just leaving. I could go. He's likely drunk off the very beer he turned his nose up at by now. There's nothing in the house I want. I long ago started carrying bigger purses so that all my important papers were always with me. My hands tighten on the wheel, the cross street that takes me back to our shack of a house just ahead. My foot pushes down on the accelerator at the same time that I decide to leave.

Then everything goes black and all I can smell is smoke.

I jolt up in bed; the memory of the crash so real I can still smell the smoke. It takes me a moment, but as soon as the fear from that dream clears from my mind, I realize my mistake. It wasn't the dream that had me smelling smoke. My whole loft apartment is filling with it. I jump from the bed, grab my phone, and call 911, rattling off my address before I even realize why it's filling the room so quickly.

My stomach drops.

"No!" I scream.

I grab my bag, rushing to the back stairway, and press my hand against the wood to check for heat, making sure the exit—the only one—is safe. I turn the handle, the smoke even thicker in the stairwell, but I run down as fast as I can without tumbling to my death. When I reach the bottom, and see the front of my bookstore in flames, I trip, falling hard to my knees. It takes me a few unsteady tries, but I get out the back door and run around the building to watch as the flames grow. I drop my purse and clutch my phone as I pray that the fire department is quick, watching the flames lick and dance closer to destroying everything I hold dear.

I don't realize I'm screaming and crying until I feel two strong arms pulling me from the ground.

"Shh, Carrie," Luke says with sympathy, and I turn to bury my face in his chest.

"How did you know?" I wail.

"Volunteering night," he answers, rubbing my back. I pull away long enough to see him wearing his fire gear, and it only makes me sob harder. "The boys will put the fire out, darlin'. It hasn't spread to the top yet, so let's think positive, 'kay?"

I shake my head against him and continue to cry, my

mind lost somewhere in the nightmare that woke me up and the one that was waiting for me.

"Holy shit! Caroline!" I lift my head off Luke's shoulder just in time for his sister to collide with us. He silently shifts his hold so that he has both of us as Lucy wraps her arms around us. The two of them create a Hazel family circle around me as I burst into another fit of tears. I have no idea how long we carry on—Luce and me—but he holds us strong the whole time, watching as his fellow volunteer firemen battle the fire inside my bookstore. By the time the all-clear is given, Lucy has moved to sit next to us on the curb across the street and Luke has shifted my body so I'm sitting across his lap, Lucy's hands grasping mine. I finally stopped crying shortly after the paramedics checked me over, but I can't help the deep depression that had settled into my bones watching my life go up in flames.

"It's gonna be okay, Carrie," Luke says again when I hiccup.

"It will be, Caroline. It will," Lucy agrees, tightening her grip on my hands.

"It's all gone." I continue to look at the charred remains of the front half of my store and feel my chin wobble.

"It's not, sweetheart," Luke tells me, trying to get my attention off the store with his hand on my chin, but I pull away from his grasp and continue staring. "We'll get you settled. Insurance will handle the damage, and the fire only got to your kitchen and bathroom. I'll get in there tomorrow and get out everything I can, and you can stay with me and Luce until they finish rebuilding."

I don't speak. I can't. The Sequel was so much more than just a store. It represented everything I had overcome. And now it's gone—even if just temporarily.

I don't remember Luke driving me back to his and Lucy's house across town, but by the time he pushed a pill into my mouth and poured a drink of water down my throat I'd already started crying again. I didn't even question him, trusting him without doubt. By the time I felt my lids getting heavier, Lucy was lying on one side of me and Luke on the other, all three of us stuffed in her double bed. I wasn't the only one who'd been scared tonight. I might've lost a part of The Sequel, but I can only imagine what my best friends thought when they didn't know whether I was hurt or not. I curl into Lucy's side and feel Luke's arms tighten around me.

You would never know that we hadn't known each other our whole lives, being as close as we are. I met Lucy when I was nineteen in school in Austin, and we instantly bonded over the fact that we'd grown up in neighboring towns. We shared a dorm for a month before John moved me into an apartment with him, but Lucy and I remained close. She decided to move back home with me after I opened up The Sequel in Wire Creek. She wasn't wrong the other night on the way to the PieHole when she told me some people share a bond as close as family without being related.

This, right here, is my family, and even though I'm heartbroken about the store, I still have them.

The rest will figure itself out.

I hope.

I finally stopped crying shortly before I fell asleep, but not once did my best friends let go of me all night.

6

CAROLINE

"Rich" by Maren Morris

- ★ -

Eight days later, the insurance adjuster had finally made it out to what was left of The Sequel. Luke wasn't saying much about what he'd heard about the investigation from his friends at the fire department, but I knew it was looking like someone had set fire to my store intentionally. I couldn't think of anyone who'd hold a grudge against me enough to try to kill me, something they'd clearly been hoping would be the outcome. Needless to say, Luke was being more protective than normal, and that was saying a lot. I honestly didn't mind one bit though.

It had taken five washes and a ton of fabric softener to get the scent of smoke out of my clothes, but at least it had finally come out. All of the furniture would have to be replaced, something the insurance adjuster would hopefully deal with. Everything inside of the store was ruined. If the fire didn't get it, the water did. All in all, it could've been so much worse. I was alive. I just had to pull myself from the ashes again.

"You hangin' in there?"

I look up at Luke, falling into his side when he offers his arm. "Yeah. Just sad to see it like this. Who would do this, Luke?"

"Don't know, sweetheart. Could be some dumb kid for all we know. They'll get it sorted, just have to trust the boys leadin' the investigation. You're safe and that's all that matters."

"It could've been worse," I agree, saying my earlier thoughts out loud for the first time, still looking on as the insurance man pokes around the bottom level of my building.

Luke shivers and I look up at him. "You're still breathin', so yeah, it coulda been a whole helluva lot worse."

"It's gonna take a while to rebuild, Luke. I don't want to keep imposing on you and Lucy."

"It's not imposin', Carrie, and you know it. Family isn't a burden. You'll stay until things are back up and runnin' here and not a minute earlier."

I nod but plan on finding a way to get out of their house before that. I know he doesn't see things my way, but all I've been is dependent on someone else my whole life until opening up The Sequel. I don't want to fall back on that just because I'm now homeless. I already talked to Sheila at the motel in Law Bone and she's worked out a deal to help me with a long-term-rent-type situation at the motel. I would've preferred to stay in Wire Creek, but we don't have a motel, so that was out. Pine Oak was definitely not an option. So, Law Bone it is. I'll find a way to break it to the Hazel duo in a few days.

"I'm goin' to head back to your house, if you don't mind stickin' around with this guy. It just . . . it's just seein' it like this. You know?"

Luke gives me a small, sad smile and nods. "Yeah. I'll be back to pick you up when he's finished and we can head over to Hazel's together."

After letting Dan, the older man checking things out, know that I'm leaving and that Luke is there for any questions he might have, I head back to Luke and Lucy's place to get a nap before heading over to Hazel's for the night.

Whether out of pity or a general need for someone, Luke asked me to work at Hazel's until things are back up and running at The Sequel. Since all he wanted me to do was act as his office manager of sorts, handling all the paperwork and orders he hates dealing with, I said yes. To be honest, it was something I jumped at in order to keep my mind occupied, more than anything. I'm good with numbers—actually, damn good with numbers—so handling his books was something I could do in my sleep.

It didn't hurt that, when I finished work for the night, I could get a drink while waiting for Luke to close up.

Lucy was only helping me out at the store on her off days at the hospital where she was a full-time registered nurse, so she isn't out of a job, thank God. However, now that I was working weird hours with Luke and sleeping during the day, I felt like I hadn't seen my best friend in weeks, not days.

I haven't been asleep for long when Luke gets back and lets me know it's time to head to Hazel's. I change out of my wrinkled sleep shirt and into some short shorts, a Hazel's tank top, and a new pair of sandals. The scent of the fire was too heavy on the old boots I'd normally wear and I had to toss them. Just another thing that was taken from me.

"You sure you're good to handle payroll?"

I smile at Luke as he drives. "Yeah, Luke. It's like asking if a genius can handle a color-by-numbers sheet."

He chuckles and shakes his head. "Sometimes I forget there's a feisty little smart-ass in that tiny body of yours, Carrie girl."

"Lukie Dukie, I'm just a big bag of mystery, you know."

He laughs under his breath, the radio playing some current pop country song. I look through the darkness and let my thoughts wander to my plans. I should've known Luke saw right through me earlier, though, and the second I start thinking about how I'm going to tell him and Lucy about leaving, he opens his mouth and I groan inwardly.

"I know you talked to Sheila about stayin' at the motel."

"I wasn't goin' to keep it from y'all," I tell him immediately.

"I know you weren't."

"I just didn't know how to tell y'all."

He clicks his tongue. "You could have just said it, sweetheart. Even though I meant what I said earlier, I understand your need to exercise your independence. You've come a long way this year and you deserve what you need to be happy."

"I need to prove to myself that I can keep survivin' on my own, Luke," I tell him, honestly. After all, that's the root of it.

"I know you do. If what you want is to stay in Sheila's motel until you rebuild, at least you'll be close to Hazel's and I can still make sure you're okay. I might not like it, and Luce is damn sure not gonna like it, but I understand where you're comin' from."

I twist the straps of my purse and mull over my words. "Can I . . . do you . . . will you still want me to work at the bar?"

Out of the corner of my eye, I see him turn my way, but I keep twisting the leather strap in my hand, not wanting to see his face if there's disappointment written on it. I almost jump out of my skin when his hand covers mine.

"Don't ask stupid questions, Carrie," he drawls in a

gruff tone. "You've got a job at Hazel's for as long as you want it. You know I hate that numbers shit, and you add a little brightness to that place. Family, yeah?"

"Yeah," I whisper, a lump forming in my throat.

"Yeah," he parrots, pulling into the parking lot of the bar and shutting his truck off.

I climb out of the cab, even though I know it drives him nuts when I don't wait for him to open my door, and follow him around the back to enter through the employee doorway. He'd normally just walk in the front, but since this is the easiest way for him to dump me in the office, I know he only does it so he can fool himself into thinking I don't see just how crazy things get here at night.

"Let me know if you need anything. Just shoot me a text and I'll come sort you out."

"Yes, Dad," I say sarcastically with a roll of my eyes.

A few hours later, I feel like I'm about to find out what it's like to have my eyes permanently crossed. Luke Hazel is a shit bookkeeper. Reading his handwriting was almost traumatic, but I finally sorted out his payroll and wrote the checks for all sixteen employees so he could come sign them later tonight. Having had enough of his office's four walls, I open the door and step into the smoke-filled air. My eyes roam around the room while I stand there and enjoy the music. It was so muffled by his office's heavy door that I could hardly hear it in there. I'm on my second glance around the room when I see him.

The shadowy stranger.

My dark cowboy.

I take a step forward before I realize what I'm doing, stopping instantly.

No way. As much as I want to, and boy do I *want to*, I know I'd be testing fate by giving in to another night with him, and I think fate has proven to be against me lately. I blindly reach for the knob behind me at the same time I see his back straighten and his head turn my way. I gasp when I feel his eyes on me. I could walk over there and offer him my body again, but instead I turn and rush back into Luke's office.

There's no place in my life for a man like my dark cowboy, as much as I wish otherwise. I'd love nothing more than to get lost in the feelings I know he can drown me in, but my life is crazy enough without adding more insanity to it.

Maybe another time—another place—but not now.

Not when everything feels so out of control.

This must be what it feels like to miss something so deeply you crave it . . . even if you never really had it to begin with.

7

CLAYTON

"Hometown Girl" by Josh Turner

- ★ -

"**A** little higher on the left," my sister says for the umpteenth time. I do what she wants and lift the banner up—again—to the left. "No, my left."

I turn on the ladder and look down at Quinn. "Your left is the same as my left, Quinnie."

"Oh, then the right."

Fighting the urge to roll my eyes, I adjust my hold and move the banner again. From my perch, the thing is right as rain, but no damn way am I arguing with my hormonal sister. Tried that once and I swear to all things holy, the devil came out of her body and tried to pull me down to the pits below.

"Quinn, you've got that thing so high, no one's gonna be able to see it!" Leigh calls from just outside the barn, coming into the large open area with one hand on her hip. "Why do you have Clay up there anyway; we decided the other night to put it above the door—outside."

"You've got to be shitting me," I mumble under my breath. I close my eyes, count to ten, then do it all over again because I'm still seconds away from blowing the top of my head off.

"Need some help?"

I look down, hoping that Maverick can tell without words just how close I am to wringing our little sister's neck, but keep my mouth shut out of fear that I'll lose my temper if I open it.

Control.

I don't just like it—I need it. Without it, I feel like I've lost the reins on everything around me.

Quinn and Leigh continue to bicker about the best place for the stupid-as-fuck banner while I continue to level Maverick with my seething gaze. His eyes dance, that lighthearted happiness that he developed in the past few years now pissing me off while I'm stuck up here.

"Come on down. I'll take care of it and you can go do whatever the fuck Tate's been doin' for twenty minutes with the fuckin' drinks."

I look over at my brother in-law and laugh when he steps away from the cart we pulled in here early this morning and looks at the drink table in confusion. Why so much shit is needed for a joint baby shower, I'll never know. Especially since this is something I never thought I'd experience personally, much less as an uncle.

"Why does he look so damn confused?" I ask Maverick, climbing down carefully and handing him both ends of the banner.

"Quinn said she wanted everything set out in the shape of fuckin' rattles. Can you believe that shit? Since when does she give a damn about all this stuff?"

"Since *she* and your wife have been planning what our baby showers would look like from age ten, Maverick Austin Davis-James."

I burst out in a loud bark of laughter at the sound of my baby brother's legal name. I understood his reasons for not wanting to keep our family name when he married Leighton, instead choosing to take hers, but hearing Quinn sass him with that mouthful never fails to crack me up. "You heard her, Mr. James." I laugh, slapping him on the shoulder before walking away to help Tate figure out how the hell a bunch of cans are supposed to look like baby rattles.

An hour later, I make myself a promise that the next time either one of them winds up pregnant, I'm moving to Alaska until the birth so I miss all this party shit. Or fuck, I'll just buy them all the stuff they need if it means I don't have to hang streamers, arrange food and drinks into shapes, and, worst of all, put a bunch of melted chocolate into diapers so they can play some fucked-up game of Sniff the Shit.

Thank God I'll never find myself in this position.

Shaking my head, I walk away from the last table I sprinkled a bunch of pink and blue confetti on, dusting my hands off on my jeans. The party isn't set to start for another hour, and I'm about to use every second to find a secluded, not fucking pastel corner in which to enjoy some silence. Maybe then I won't jump on the back of Dell, my palmetto, and hightail it back to the ranch.

Stepping out of the barn, I adjust my hat so the sun isn't so harsh on my eyes after being inside for so long. Sometimes I still can't believe the changes Maverick made to the old James property since he came back to Pine Oak. He's built himself one fine rodeo school: even from this distance, I can see some of his students out in the training arenas, working with their teachers despite the fact that it's Saturday. I come over here from time to time to watch Maverick in his element, beyond happy that he's been able to retain such a big part of his life after being forced to give up riding professionally.

"Somethin' else, isn't it?"

I nod, watching the boys in the distance instead of turning to look at the very man that was on my mind.

"Thank you for all the help today, big brother. How close were you to losin' your shit in there?"

"You don't want to know," I answer honestly.

Maverick grunts out a laugh.

"You doin' all right?" I ask, knowing fine and well he'll understand what I'm asking.

He kicks a rock off the cement drive we're standing on, and I give him the time he needs to mull over his words.

"Still weighs on me, Clay. I'd be lyin' if I said otherwise, but every time I feel our baby movin' in her belly, a little of that fear gets beat back. Never thought this was somethin' I would have. Not after all the shit I did to fuck it up back in the day. I love my wife bigger than life, but I love our baby somethin' even bigger. That pushes me through the dark thoughts."

I hum, looking away from the boys working damn hard to be the next best thing the rodeo ever saw, to look at Maverick.

"Somethin' else on your mind, brother?" I ask, frowning at his words.

"Shit, Clay," he says with a long exhale. "I keep thinkin', what if I'm just like the old man was?"

My jaw goes slack as I look at him in shock. "You fuckin' with me?"

He lifts his hat off his head, the wild, thick, black-as-night hair that all us Davis kids have not tamed in the least, even with the sweat wetting it from being under his black Stetson for hours. He runs his free hand through his hair, frowning at me the whole time.

"That man fucked with my head for so long, Clayton," he says solemnly. "What if I don't know how to be a good father to my child because of him?"

Grasping his shoulder, I turn him so we're face-to-face. "You hear me now, Maverick. Buford Davis was a shit father up until he was faced with his own mortality, but he is *not* us. You're gonna be the best father a kid could have. The fact that you're worried at all should tell you what you need to know. A man doesn't feel the fear of bein' a bad parent if he could even have an ounce of what it takes to not give a shit about them inside of him. You carin' about it at all means it could never happen. You get me?"

He swallows thickly but nods after a beat of silence.

"That kid's gonna be smothered with so much love it'll never know what life is like without it."

Maverick's eyes close and he drops his chin so I lose his gaze, but not before I saw what I said take root. My brother, while he might have been broken when he left, has become one hell of a man with the love of a good woman.

"What do you say we go find the whiskey Tate stashed behind the back of your big fancy-ass barn and toast the fact that I'm about the be the favorite uncle in this family?"

"Fat chance." He laughs after clearing his throat. "You aren't takin' top seat as uncle if I have a say in things."

We both laugh, but inside I feel my heart get big as fuck when Maverick gives me an unguarded, carefree smile. Those shadows normally pulling his scowls deep are nowhere to be found. Then we grab Tate and warm our bellies with some of the best liquor Texas ever did see.

- ★ -

I'll remember this day for the rest of my life.

If I survive it, that is.

I look over at the other men who were forced by their wives or girlfriends to attend, thanking the good Lord that I'm not the only one about to puke. Logically, I know it's just chocolate, but that doesn't mean shit when all your eyes see is a pile of brown goo inside a diaper.

"Come on, Clay!" Jana, Leighton's longtime bakery manager, hoots from the far corner. "Get that sniffer in there and hurry up before you lose this whole thing!"

Did I mention I'm on her team? She's been bellowing from the sidelines since the horn sounded and our time started. I'm down to my last two piles of shit to identify before I can get the fuck away from this insanity.

"If you don't get that snout into that diaper, you're gonna owe me an hour-long massage."

The prize.

Shoulda known she was frothing at the mouth for the gift card to some fancy spa in Austin. Seemed like every woman in town—because there's no doubt they're all here—is after that damn thing.

"I'll buy you your own dadgum massage if you'll pipe the hell down, Jana!" I yell over the laughter around us.

I look down at the diaper again and close my eyes before bringing it to my nose and sniffing.

Snickers.

Scribbling the word down, I move on and quickly repeat the process. I wisely keep my eyes shut so I don't fight my stomach to keep the whiskey I've consumed down.

"Done!" I bark, standing from my seat so swiftly, the old wooden chair topples over. I don't even look at the people cracking up at my discomfort. Stomping over to the two women who thought up this torture, I slap my paper on the table in front of them. "I'm not babysittin' until those rugrats are potty trained."

Quinn laughs her ass off. Leigh just smiles sweetly up at me.

I'm opening my mouth to tell them just how serious I am when Leigh looks over my shoulder, her smile growing. Then I hear a voice that's been haunting my dreams for almost two months now.

"Hey . . . uh, I'm sorry I'm late," the sweet-as-pie voice says from behind me.

Takes everything in me to not react when there's one hell of a war raging inside of me from just hearing that breathy apology. I clench my teeth so hard, my jaw hurts, but I don't turn.

"That's all right, honey. I know you've been going through a lot lately so I'm just happy you came out."

"She wouldn't have missed it," a new voice I don't recognize says.

"Lucy loves babies." My heart thunders in my chest when I hear her speak again.

Leighton stands and walks past me, I assume to greet the late guests. Quinn slaps my thigh and I look down at my sister.

"Get out of my way, you big giant."

Realizing I'm blocking her ability to heave out of her seat, I reach down and help her stand. She shoves me aside the second she's up with more strength than a tiny woman should have, and follows in Leigh's wake. I steady my breathing and turn. I should have known nothing I could do would matter. When I saw her across the smoke-filled bar the other night, I felt that like a punch in the gut. Now, seeing her this close is enough to have my cock going from zero to sixty. She doesn't notice me, or if she does, she isn't making it obvious. Her eyes flicker around the crowded barn, looking at what seems like everything and anything at once. If I thought it was hard to ignore this pull without being face-to-face, it's going to be next to impossible now. And I'm not even sure if I want to ignore it.

Fuck, I need to get out of here and figure out what the hell is going through my mind.

"You remember my big brother Clay right Caroline?"

I look away from the dark-haired beauty who has me licking my lips and praying for an apple pie to look at my sister. I know Luke called her Carrie that night, I heard it clear as day, and the name has stuck with me since. Just as the thought comes, I remember the name she was screaming in my ear that same night. Looks like we were both playing a damn game.

She looks up at me, her cheeks turning pink despite her olive skin. Her dark brown eyes search mine, but I don't see recognition. One dainty hand comes out, timidly, and she gives me a weak smile. What happened to the feisty woman who came on my cock so many times I felt the vise grip days after I snuck out of that hotel room?

"N-nice to meet you," she says softly.

Reaching out, I drag the tips of my fingers down hers and across her palm before engulfing her hand inside of mine. I know the exact moment she figures it out. Her plump lips part on a gasp and her hand spasms in mine.

"Pleasure," I rumble, my voice just as thick as my cock.

"Davis," she breathes.

"Yeah," Quinn chuckles, drawing the word out and looking at her like she's lost her mind. "My oldest brother, Clayton *Davis*, the family name and all."

My eyes stay on hers as the silence turns awkward for those watching. Putting her out of her misery, I regretfully release her hand and take a step back, tipping my chin down in a quick nod. "I'll leave you ladies to catch up."

Still looking at Carrie—no, Caroline—I raise a brow and hope to God she sees the promise in my gaze. This isn't over. Just touching her again was enough to make that thought clear as day to myself. No more denying this connection.

I might've been prepared to never give in to that again, but there isn't a force strong enough to keep us from colliding. And that's just what we're doing. I've felt that tug twice now in her presence as the connection between us pulled and pulled. We aren't going to ignore fate if she wants us to cross paths. I would have probably gone on my way without looking for this woman who's haunted my memories for two months, but I'm not a stupid man and I damn sure won't look a gift horse in the mouth now that this is proving to be inevitable.

We'll finish this later.

Caroline and me.

In private.

8

CAROLINE

"Flatliner" by Cole Swindell & Dierks Bentley

"**W**hat the hell was that?" Lucy hisses after Clayton *Davis* disappears through the open door that we had just entered a few minutes before.

I shake my head, not even sure where to begin explaining how I know the eldest Davis, and in front of his family no less.

There's no way.

Just my mind playing tricks.

I've been under so much stress lately it wouldn't be a stretch to think my mind conjured up the one person I haven't been able to stop thinking about. Between the sleep I've been losing since the fire, seeing that the motel I call home now has the thinnest walls, and the residual sadness I feel every time I handle more red tape from the insurance company dealing with The Sequel, I'm about as close to going insane as it gets. My life is up in the air—where my future had been is one big question mark, and now, on top of that, I'm hallucinating.

"You and Clay know each other?"

I blink at the question, not really sure which of the pregnant ladies in from of me asked, but hoping neither really expected me to answer. If what I felt when my hand touched his looked half as time-stopping as it felt, I wouldn't want to know the details if it was my brother or brother-in-law.

"That was intense," Lucy chimes in, not helping this situation in the least.

Even if that wasn't the same man, even in my naïveté I can recognize the connection that we felt. My palm tingles at the thought and I look toward the last place I saw him, oddly having to fight back the desire to run after him and demand answers.

Quinn steps into the path of my gaze and looks at me with fascinated shock, her green eyes as bright as gems, twinkling with mischief. "Jesus Jones. You and Clay?! I mean, you're beautiful, honey, so I don't doubt you turn heads, but he's just so . . . *Clay!*"

I sputter, shaking my head in denial so fast that I surely look like I'm impersonating a bobblehead doll. "No!" I exclaim, fidgeting with my purse strap as anxious, nervous energy starts to get the best of me. I can feel my hands grow clammy at the thought of being on display, and I have to fight to keep my back straight instead of hunching like I normally would when the spotlight is turned toward me.

"Oh my," Lucy gasps in a breathy tone. "She's lying."

I turn to my *ex*–best friend and continue shaking my head. *God, shut up, Luce.*

"She's lying so bad, I'm shocked her nose isn't a mile long," she keeps going with a laugh, sticking her bubble-gum-pink-tipped finger in front of my face, and I swear right then and there that her death will be slow and painful.

"This is better than pie." Leighton giggles happily.

"No, this is better than a '51 Ford ready for a complete rebuild," Quinn adds with a dreamy sigh.

"Or a sale at Target!" Lucy exclaims, clapping her hands and bouncing on the balls of her feet.

I drop my gaze, looking at my sandals as my face heats. It'd be pointless to continue denying what they just witnessed seeing, as I'm the worst liar in the whole state of Texas.

"You have to tell us everything," Quinn whispers, leaning into my side to push her shoulder into mine.

"Well, maybe not everything," Leigh snorts.

"Screw that, I want all the juicy details. He might be my brother, but he's been livin' like a monk since that stupid bitch he dated last and girlfriend, you'd think he was asexual the way those two *didn't* carry on in public. No sparks close to what we just saw between y'all." She waggles her perfectly sculpted brows.

"You might as well just tell her, Caroline." Leigh snickers. "You can't shock her easily. Trust me, I've tried."

Quinn continues nodding, her brows still going up and down suggestively. "Just wait until this one"—she points to Leigh—"starts tellin' you about the monster cock."

"Q!" Leighton gasps, but she smiles a second later, so she must not be offended. "Anyway, you gotta give us somethin', honey. The way he's always ridin' those horses, I bet he can work those hips like no one's business."

Oh my God. This isn't happening.

"Would you three shut up," I hiss, already seeing a few people listening in on our huddle. Thankfully, someone up there is on my side, because the girls stop the instant I ask them to.

"This isn't over," Leighton promises. "And, Caroline, you're goin' to need to get over that shyness of yours now that you're one of us."

One of them? What does that mean? Just because . . . no. A one-night stand doesn't mean I'm going to start coming to Sunday dinner. I haven't seen him in months. If he'd wanted more after that night, he wouldn't have disappeared before I woke up. I open my mouth to tell all three of the giddy women in front of me just that, but stop when a voice starts talking in a cheerful bellow.

"Who's ready for some presents!" Jana screams. I vaguely remember her from Leighton's bakery. Her question causes me to look up from the deep study I had been doing of the sandals Lucy made me wear today just in time to see her jump down from the chair she must have climbed up on to make her announcement. She pushes through the people between her and us in a rush before grabbing both pregnant women. I could kiss her for being the proverbial bell that is saving me.

"Those two aren't going to be satisfied with your terrible lyin', you know. Even if you really don't know him— which I know you do, no matter what you say—a blind old bat could've seen the sparks flyin' off the two of y'all," Lucy stage-whispers, drawing a few more eyes our way.

"That's what I'm afraid of."

A group of older women push between us on their way to get a better view of the presents being opened. I excuse myself and get out of their way. Only in a town as small and nosy as Pine Oak would a baby shower be an event that could rank right up there with Macy's Thanksgiving Day Parade. Well, the fact that two of the town darlings are the guests of honor doesn't hurt either. Oddly enough, I forgot how much I love the closeness the residents in Pine Oak appear to enjoy.

"Who was that anyway, Caro?" Luce says after we move to the back of the room.

I sigh, ignoring the fact that neither Hazel twin listens when I tell them how much I hate nicknames, and look around to make sure no one is listening. "*That* was the dark cowboy."

Her blue eyes all but bug out of her head and she

whips around to look in the opposite direction, blond curls fanning around her as she turns her gaze toward the doorway leading out of the barn. Well, at least I *think* this is a barn. On the outside that's exactly what it looks like, but once you step foot in here, it looks like some kind of western-style grand ballroom—complete with chandeliers made out of antlers.

What are the odds that I would run into him here? The dark cowboy I shared a faceless night of passion with couldn't have been a stranger passing through town? No. *My* dark cowboy—the very man that I've been using the memory of for two months now to keep me going whenever I start to get depressed about everything going wrong in my life; the man who showed me how powerful being with someone who cared about your pleasure was like; the one who ruined me for life—*he* was the same man I'd had a crush on for a whole year before I started dating John in high school and moved past the silly lust I thought I'd felt for the eldest Davis.

Davis.

Of course.

It makes sense, now that I'm not letting my hormones drive the show.

He never did correct me, nor did he confirm that actually was his name. I'd just taken what Luke said and assumed. Maybe I had subconsciously known it was him all along, using the illusion of anonymity to escape the unhappiness in my past that I had been overcoming since moving to Wire Creek. Nevertheless, I can't deny that my dark cowboy is, in fact, Clayton Davis and not some stranger anymore.

"Well." Lucy hisses, looking back at me and pulling me from my thoughts, "you should sneak out of here while they're distracted with the presents and find him."

I snort. "That is never going to happen."

"Why not?" she whispers harshly, drawing the attention of a few people standing near the back of the barn. I look up, meeting the steady emerald gaze of Maverick Davis and quickly look away from the intense curiosity I see in his eyes.

I take a step back, farther away from the crowd, and grab Lucy before leaning closer toward her to whisper softly, "Even if I was the brave kind of woman who'd run after a man, you know I'd clam up the second I catch up with him."

"What happened to the woman who went back to the motel with a man she didn't even know a thing about? Hmm? *She* was brave. *She* didn't clam up. She took the bull by the horns and enjoyed the hell outta that ride. That woman *is* you, Caroline. Don't pass up a chance like the very one in front of your face."

"What chance?" I sharply question. "I just happened to run into him here because this is his family, Luce, not because fate, the good Lord above, or Clayton Davis wanted me to find him again."

"Yeah? You think so? And how, pray tell, do you argue that this isn't one of your romance books comin' to life?" she continues like a dog with a bone. "I see all those dog-eared pages of yours, honey, and I know you believe in serendipitous moments just like this one. This is your fantasy in black-and-white comin' into full-color focus. Go get your hero."

"I'm not havin' this argument with you, and there isn't anything in the world that would get me to chase after that man."

I mean it, too. There isn't a damn thing the universe could throw at me that'd make me brave enough to go after a man like Clayton Davis. He's the epitome of perfection. Pair his good looks with just how well I know he can use *everything* he was blessed with, and you have the whole package—the whole package that a woman like me just doesn't know how to handle without looking like a fool.

He's been inside of me, for Pete's sake! I don't even think I could look him in the eye now. I can just see it, me staring up into those dark green eyes with drool dripping down my chin. There's no way I could hold a conversation with him in the light of day after I've had the part of him that makes my heart skip a beat just thinking about it touching the deepest parts of me.

I shift, my thoughts conjuring a throbbing between my legs. Lucy tries to get my attention again, but I ignore her, fighting the urge to grab my phone and google "how to move to the moon."

She pokes me in the ribs for the second time, and I finally pull my attention off the floor to look at her, ready to tell her to shut up if she starts on me again, but the words die on my lips when I see the expression on her face as she looks at something just over my right shoulder.

I pray my gut is wrong. That she just saw a spider or something. But I know there isn't anything my cheerful friend would look at like that except for the very person I feared would jump at the chance to confront me if she recognized me here today.

"Caroline?"

Well, damn. I close my eyes and try to prepare myself for seeing my mama for the first time since I was eighteen years old and ran away. I haven't heard that voice in almost five years either. Not since the last time I called the same telephone number that I learned in kindergarten and begged for the woman who should've loved me enough to save me, to help. She hadn't called me Caroline then, though; no, she had a new name for me by the time I had been broken enough to make that call. A whore. That's what I became to her.

My chin wobbles and my watery eyes shift away from Lucy's shocked face toward the open barn door, which taunts me with the promise of a quick exit. There's no question of staying or running now. Staying in here, away from the chance of running into Clay, means facing the woman who played a huge part in the nightmare I lived for years. Seeing her would bring back all the pain I had been healing from. Staying would be painful and I'm just not strong enough to deal with it. But going . . . going would bring me to the person that I've been dreaming of for weeks.

I would take Clayton Davis and door number one any day—even though that option scares me in a whole different way than the confrontation I'm escaping does. I never want to go back down the road the woman behind me represents again.

"Go," Lucy mouths, reading my mind. I nod and see her face soften with love before I run out of the barn. My legs pump furiously as I sprint toward the huge house in the distance and the safety I feel with each measured step away from the party calms me.

I keep churning my legs, my heart thundering as I cry silently for the girl who needed that woman so badly, blinking as the tears threaten to spill over.

When I come to the end of the rows of trucks and cars parked between the barn and the house, I suck in a painful burst of air when I realize I somehow completely missed a huge animal, which seems to have come out of nowhere. I slam into the horse with a painful jolt, my butt hitting the ground a moment later and my elbows digging painfully into the gravel a beat after that. The tears finally come and I make an embarrassing sound between a gasp and a wheeze as a sob bubbles free.

Some gravel hits my bare legs when the man atop the

horse that almost killed me jumps down. The water blurring my vision makes the sun look even brighter as he reaches my side. I look to my lap and push up to my elbows with a grunt of pain, avoiding looking at the man who witnessed my humiliation, but I don't need a visual to confirm just who is cursing low under his breath. I know from the awareness zipping across my skin alone who it is. How is it possible that, after only one night, my body is desperate for more of his touch?

Could this day be any more humiliating?

Probably not.

"You okay, sweetness?"

I squeeze my eyes closed at the endearment, curl my legs up, and press my forehead against my knees. I can't handle that word coming from him right now. Not when I'm vulnerably raw. Not when I've been hearing it in my head for weeks and weeks accompanied by the memory of his harsh breaths against my skin as he emptied himself inside of me.

"Please, just go," I beg, my tears coming even faster now.

"Caroline!"

At the sound of my mama's shrill voice in the distance, I whimper and try to make myself disappear by tightening my arms around my legs.

"What the hell?" he mutters.

The fear of ghosts past clawing closer, I look up and hiccup a sob before opening my mouth. "Get me out of here." I hold his worried eyes and beg him with everything in me to take me far away from here. Everything else that happened from the moment I slept with him up until the embarrassment I felt at coming face-to-face with him again vanishes.

It makes no sense logically, but once those frantic words leave my lips, I know he is the one person who can banish this feeling of uncontrollable desperation. I could rush back to Lucy and have her take me away from my mother instantly, but just looking into his worried eyes, I can feel the balm of calm that his nearness brings within me. I felt it during that night in the dark, and I feel it now—something inside me begging for him. He should be the last person I plead with to save me right now, but the second the words left my mouth, I felt with no doubt that he was the only one.

And, as if to prove that this really could get more humiliating, his hands go under my armpits, dislodging my hold, and pull me up off the ground as if I weigh nothing. Once he has me back on my feet, he bends and I see the top of his cowboy hat moments before he throws me up onto the back of the beast that took me down.

If I weren't seconds away from pure panic, I would catalog every moment that happened next to replay mentally for the rest of my life. It was a move straight out of the pages of a romance novel. Clayton Davis, cowboy in shining armor, heaves himself right up behind me and adjusts both of our bodies so that we fit on top of the horse together. I'm more in his lap than actually sharing the saddle with him, but with my butt pressed tight against his crotch and my thighs spread wide on top of his own, a whole new rush of feelings start inside me. One strong arm curls around my belly before I can even blink and he clicks his tongue. Suddenly we're blazing toward the fields behind the barn at lightning speed. I curl my hands around the arm holding me and pray I don't fall to my death as he guides the powerful horse away.

We burst through the field, not slowing in the least, and I have to force my nails out of the thick muscles of his forearm when it becomes clear I'm not in any danger of falling.

"Where," I choke on my words, clearing my throat. "Where are we going?" I call over my shoulder.

"Away." His one-word answer rumbles against my back, his arm tightens around my belly, and he continues to lead the horse with one hand holding the reins.

I look over the horse's head and almost throw up. "Please, Clayton! Stop!" I cry out as we get closer and closer to the fence line.

He immediately calls out a command and we slow before stopping completely just a few yards from the fence I was sure was about to kill us. I slump in his grasp, my position uncomfortable and borderline painful now that nothing is distracting me. He drops the leather reins and his hands move on my body, igniting fire in their path as they glide, now distracting me for a whole new reason.

Before I realize his intention, he's lifting my body and turning me in his strong arms as if I was a child.

I flail, thinking surely the horse is going to dislodge us both if he takes even a tiny step. Not wanting to fall, I loop my arms around his neck and hold on for dear life.

"You've got to stop tossin' me around like it's nothin'," I protest.

"Never been on a horse?" he asks, ignoring me and drawing my attention from the ground under us and to his handsome face. Without the darkness to hide in, I see him—really see him. Just as I'm sure he sees all of me. Every unremarkable bit of me.

That strong jaw that I had admired the night I found him as my barstool neighbor, the only part of him that I ever got a good look at, is proud in form and sprinkled with the same dusting of facial hair that I remember burned my sensitive skin as it rubbed against it.

My belly churns as I study the man who had, until now, been a faceless stranger. There isn't a flaw to be found. Perfect nose, full lips, and eyes brighter than a lush summer field right after the storm clouds clear and sun shines bright on the rain-soaked grass.

And those mesmerizing eyes are studying me just as fiercely as I am him.

"Thank you," I finally say, grateful that my mind wisely didn't blurt out how perfect I find him. "You're correct, I've never ridden before." Silence continues as his eyes probe mine. "Horses scare me," I explain, nervously trying to fill the void his mute perusal of me is creating.

The quiet ticks around us. I'm entranced as much by it as I am with the man holding me. That is, until the horse takes a step to the side and I turn into a mess of arms and legs as I attack my savior while basically trying to climb inside his body. His chest moves in what I hope is laughter, and he adjusts his grip on me while allowing me to settle. I somehow manage to turn myself completely within his strong arms and wrap all of my limbs around him like some kind of deranged spider monkey. I realize my mistake the second his hands settle on my butt and the heat of his hold radiates through my thin shorts.

I swear, I stop breathing right then and there.

I lift my chest back from his, that rush of heat on my bottom making me feel fearless and the shyness that normally hinders my every move in life falling to the wayside as I look into his eyes.

"I'm sorry," I gasp. "I'd get off you, but I'm terrified to move."

His lips tip at the corners in the tiniest of fractions and his eyes get warm.

"Not complaining," he rumbles softer than a man his size should ever be able to speak.

"If you could just help me get down and then maybe point me in the direction of where we came from, I'll get out of your hair. Or . . . off of your body, I guess."

He shakes his head. "That's not gonna happen, darlin',"

he answers, his tone leaving no room for me to disagree. Even if I wanted to, though, the expression on his face is enough to kill any complaint I might have voiced. I wasn't argumentative to begin with, but the second he stops talking and inches his face closer to mine, I'm held captive. "I like you lookin' at me like this a whole lot more than I like you doin' it with fear in your eyes. And I like this softness in your eyes a fuckin' helluva lot more than seein' you with tears, baby."

Oh. Wow.

"You want me to take you farther away from who-ever put those tears on your beautiful face? Or do you want me to bring you back to your friend so she can do it? Either way, Caroline, I'm not leavin' your side until I know you're okay."

Call me weak. Call me the very thing the woman I was running from had accused me of being years ago. But don't call me a coward anymore, because right now I'd do anything in the world if it means I get to keep having this man look at me like I'm the most important thing to him. Doesn't make a lick of sense, seeing as we don't really know each other—apart from in the biblical sense and all—but that doesn't seem to matter. My heart feels like I'm finally safe.

"Please don't take me back there," I whisper.

His head moves in one strong, sure nod. He takes one hand off my bottom as the other shifts so one huge palm is now directly between my cheeks, fingers spread wide to support me. I gasp, unable to keep from wiggling, when two of his fingers brush against the most sensitive area under my shorts-covered center. He doesn't bring attention to how close he is to my entrance; instead he holds my gaze, his face softening even more when a puff of air escapes my lips.

"Are you gonna be okay if I let Dell move again?"

"Dell?" I frown.

"My horse."

"Right." I look around us but jolt when I realize just how far off the ground we really are. Especially now that I'm not just on a horse, but even higher after I just used Clayton's body like some weird human pole.

"I won't let you fall," Clayton promises, his voice low and calming.

It could easily happen though.

"No, it couldn't."

My eyes widen when I realize I said that out loud, thankful he didn't realize I wasn't talking about the horse in the least.

"You're safe with me."

I take a slow, deep breath. "Don't let go of me," I tell my dark cowboy.

"Not sure that's gonna be possible, sweetness," he oddly answers, then makes a clicking sound. He doesn't look away from my eyes, not when we start moving at a slow walk. Not when we start to trot a little faster. He holds me captive while I trust not only him, but also the animal carrying us. I should be terrified at what his words make me feel. I shouldn't allow myself to think they mean something that should be impossible, but with my body plastered against his and his breath mingling with mine, I find myself melting into this man who is as much of a stranger as he was two months ago.

Only now that stranger has a face *and* a connection to my life through my friendship with his family. That means today won't be the last time we see each other, even if those seven words don't mean what my heart thinks they do. This isn't the end of Clayton and me.

9

CLAYTON

"Body like a Back Road" by Sam Hunt

— ★ —

I let Dell lead the way, knowing he'll take us back to the ranch eventually. I say a silent prayer that he does what he normally does when I let him take control during our rides and wander the long way through my property— enjoying the freedom of his hooves—because I'm not ready to let the woman in my arms go. I've never felt this connected to someone. I felt it the first time I had her in my arms, ignored it, but I won't make that mistake again. I'm sick of living a shadow of a life because I let my fucked-up past cloud my way toward some sort of normal future. Even if nothing comes of this, I'm going to try.

"I'd convinced myself what I felt that night was just the whiskey," I admit. I smile when her cheeks heat, my words hitting the bull's-eye.

Who would've thought a woman blushing could be so erotic? But with a vision of just how far that blush will spread, all I can wonder now is if her small tits turn pink with a blush when she comes—something I never got to see that night because of the darkness she seemed to need.

"Might've been," she whispers so softly I have to strain to hear her, and then she lays her head against my shoulder, relaxing just a bit in my hold. She probably doesn't even realize she's doing it, but that move right there shows me that she trusts me to lead.

"You make me feel like I'm comin' alive, sweetheart. I've got no words to explain it better than that, but what I know is there ain't no way on this green earth that it's the whiskey that is doin' the work. Wasn't the cause then and damn sure ain't now."

"Heat of the moment, maybe. An adrenaline rush," she weakly argues without conviction.

"I'm old enough to be able to control my cock in the heat of the moment. Even if I was feelin' some adrenaline, it wouldn't make me feel like I was out of control of my own body. You feel my heart poundin' in my chest now? You explain that as heat of the moment when the only time I feel calm is on the back of one of my horses."

She turns her head away, and as much as I love the feel of her relaxed in my arms, even when I know she's afraid of horses, I wish I could look into those rich chocolate eyes of hers—so dark that I could get lost in their depths—to try and figure out what's going on in that beautiful head of hers.

"Did you know who I was?" she asks, her mouth moving against my neck causing a chill to roll down my spine. My hand half on her ass and half on her pussy twitches violently with the sensation of it.

"No, I didn't. I knew you were a gorgeous woman who looked about as lost as I was feelin' when I walked into Hazel's that night. Knew exactly who you were back at Mav and Leigh's though."

"You wouldn't have tried to find me if we hadn't crossed paths today."

It isn't a question.

She's not wrong either. Something we both don't need me to verbalize, but I don't like her thinking I was just using her as some fuck toy either. We'd both been looking for something that night, but I don't make a habit of spending the night getting lost in a woman before vanishing, and I've felt bad about that since. My loneliness drove me to her, and it kept me from finding her after, but it won't keep me away from her now. There's a reason we crossed paths to begin with, I know that with absolute clarity.

"It's okay," she continues, a little softer. "I understand it better now."

I frown, seeing the roof of my house over the horizon. "Understand what, Caroline?"

"Why a man like you wouldn't have tried to find a woman like me."

"What the fuck does that mean?" I sharply ask, making her jump slightly.

She sighs. The sound holds notes of sadness, but she doesn't lift her head from my shoulder. Her lips continue to speak against my neck. "It's funny the things you remember. Those memories that you hadn't thought about in years comin' out of nowhere at the oddest times. I remember once, durin' one of the famous Davis boys' bonfires, somewhere around the time I turned eighteen, I was sittin' on the back of your sister's tailgate watchin' everyone let loose around me when I saw you with some tall Barbie doll–lookin' girl with the biggest boobs I had ever seen. The first thing I thought was how someone so thin could stand upright without topplin' over all the time. Stupidest thing to think about in that moment, but I did anyway. After that, though, I couldn't look away from y'all. Not even when you pushed her against Ronny Billings's truck and pulled her jean skirt up to her chest and started thrustin'. I kept watchin'. I don't even know why I'm rememberin' it so clearly now, but I was transfixed by you even then. Though I think that was also the same night I stopped walkin' around with my head in a cloud of fantasies."

Jesus Christ.

I don't remember a thing she's talking about, but I have no doubt it probably happened. I was careless with how I took my pleasure in years back. Those nights might've started out as a way for us to sneak beer in high school, but if she was eighteen when she saw me doing that, I was well past high school age and at that point, the bonfires had turned into an easy way for all the boys I grew up with to fuck young, tight, and eager-to-please pussy. I was no better than they were and I didn't stop being careless until I got burned by the wrong woman.

"I'm not the man I was back then," I defend myself, wanting her to believe my words more than I care to admit.

"I didn't say you were, Clayton." She takes a deep breath while I revel in the way her saying my full name makes me feel. "I was just explainin' why I know I'm not the type of woman a man like you would be goin' for. Well, I guess you might think I was that type of woman, since I gave myself to you just as easily as that girl did back then, but even if you did think that, you wouldn't have looked for me."

"Hey," I grunt with a harshness that even makes Dell pause slightly before continuing his lazy trot toward the stable.

"I wouldn't have looked for you either," she continues as if I hadn't spoken, unaware of the intense emotion she's igniting in me.

"Why's that?" I ask thickly.

"Because while I might *think* I'm not the kind of woman you want, I *know* I'm not the woman you need."

This girl. She can't be serious. Even if I didn't know deep in my bones she's worth the effort of trying to figure out her riddles, I'd still keep trying to get the answers if it meant I get to keep feeling like something I've been missing for a long damn time was just found.

"Oh, Linney, it's gonna be fun provin' you wrong." Her body jolts in my arms and I smile. "First things first, how about you tighten those sweet legs of yours around my body and hold on while I get us down from Dell. Then, if you don't have anywhere else you need me to take you, you let me start showin' you who I am now and not who you think I might be?"

"'Linney'?" she questions, one brow arched.

"Really, darlin', that's all you heard?"

"My name is Caroline."

"I know your name, Caroline Lynn Michaels."

Her eyes widen and she clears her throat. "Well, then you know Linney isn't it."

"I know you're sweet as pie when you're all heated. Anyway, I can get you that way. That woman isn't prim and proper Caroline. That woman is wild-as-hell Linney."

"I'm not sleepin' with you," she sputters after I get us down and hand Dell off to one of the stableboys, not an easy feat, but she hardly weighs anything, as tiny as she is. Her face gets red the second she realizes we aren't alone anymore and, with a squeak, drops her head back to my shoulder.

"Jorge doesn't speak English, sweetness, but even if he did, he's paid to work, not to worry about what kind of sleepin' is goin' on between his boss and the beautiful woman wrapped tightly around him." I mean to put her out of her misery, but I can't help but tease her a little. It's way too satisfying to see her embarrassment painting her cheeks.

She mumbles something against my skin, her position muffling her words so badly I can't understand her. Her legs loosen around me next, and I regretfully release my hold and help her stand. I look down at the top of her head, noticing for the first time just how tiny she is now that she isn't wearing boots. Not just her height, but her build too. Without her boots, I'm guessing she's got to be close to a foot shorter than my six foot three. Every delicate inch of her makes me want to do nothing but wrap my arms around her, protect and worship her until she makes me stop.

Not once in my life have I felt this way about a woman who wasn't my sister or Leigh. My family. If I feel this strong of a pull to Caroline without really knowing a thing about her besides us being compatible, I imagine it could swallow me whole when I finally do get to know her.

"Dinner, Caroline. Let me cook us some dinner tonight and we can get to know each other a little better. Then maybe you'll listen to why I wouldn't have gone lookin' for you and you can fill me in on why you wouldn't have done the same."

"I'm not sleepin' with you," she repeats.

"Didn't invite you to," I joke, bending down to her eye

level when she gasps. "But when I finally do get the privilege to have you again, there ain't gonna be any sleepin' then either, sweetness."

I press a swift kiss to her shocked lips before taking her hand and guiding her toward my house. The same house that makes me feel like I'm drowning in my solitude is looking a lot better now that I'm picturing her inside it with me.

- ★ -

I flip one of the two steaks on the cutting board and rub my own mixture of seasoning on the meat while Caroline shifts nervously on the barstool in front of me. She hasn't said much since we got inside. Every time I catch her looking at me, she ducks her head and blushes. It's cute as hell how shy she is. It's been thirty minutes of us playing this game while I prepare our dinner, and so far the only thing she's willingly asked me about is the ranch.

Safe topic, I reckon. Nothing that requires much input from her and not something that leaves the door open for me to press for more on her.

Not that I don't mind talking about how well the Davis ranch does breeding horses, especially if, by doing so, I make her more comfortable with me. But I'm not a patient man when it comes to something I want, and make no mistake, I want this woman.

"Tell me why you were runnin' back at the party," I ask her softly, continuing to handle the steaks. Hopefully by keeping my attention off her while I probe, I won't freak her out with the question that's been on the tip of my tongue since she collided with Dell and me.

She sucks in a harsh pull of air. The sound makes my hands freeze before I look up from my task to study her. She doesn't like attention, something I don't need to know her better to figure out, but with that pained sound, I want her to see the sincerity behind my asking so she can't doubt that I genuinely want to know what upset her. When she doesn't answer, I give her what I hope to hell is a reassuring expression of compassion before I turn and walk the four feet to the large farm-style sink to wash off my hands. I feel her stare follow me the whole time I clean my hands, dry them off, and walk back to the island. This time I stand next to the food I was prepping so I can press my hands down on the counter and wait. I keep my face calm, and I hope she senses she can trust me and open up.

"You aren't going to finish gettin' the food ready until I talk about what happened, are you?"

My lips twitch.

"I probably should just tell you all the ugly parts of me so you'll understand what a waste of time pursuing this would be. Save you from gettin' upset when you realize you're wastin' your time on someone broken," she mumbles.

"Darlin', you're not broken. You're still standin', which means you're just a little dinged up, maybe even a little bit bent, but you'd be hard-pressed to find someone who isn't."

She frowns a little, her eyes searching mine rapidly. "You really believe that?"

"Sure do. You aren't ever truly broken until you can no longer keep movin' forward and they're lowerin' you into the ground. It's what you call the ugly parts of someone that prove to others just how strong they really are."

I was expecting her to look away, but when I stop talking those dark eyes watch me with such intensity I almost feel like *I* should look away, but I hold her gaze and let her take whatever time she needs to weigh my words. To find the truth in them, even if she isn't ready to fully believe them. You don't change your beliefs at the drop of a hat, but all it takes is one moment of doubt that there could be another way for things to start coming into focus. I've seen bent. I've seen fractured. But if the people I know who've been both can find what they need to be happy and move on, so can this beautiful woman who has me wrapped in her spell.

"My mother was there," she finally says, as if that explains it.

I frown. "Who's your mama?"

"Misty Michaels."

Well, shit. I keep my face as clear as I can but inwardly cringe, curse, and kick shit—trying to keep the disgust I'm sure she was waiting to see from her. Well, sweetheart, that isn't gonna happen. There aren't many people's names I could hear and instantly want to curl my lips, but Misty Michaels is one of them. Regardless of what I think of Caroline's mama though, I damn sure won't condemn the woman in front of me just because the woman who birthed her has her nose so high in the air you'd think she could smell the angels passing gas. I could've taken one look at this girl, sweet and shy with just a little fire flickering inside of those brown eyes, and known she wasn't a thing like her mama.

"I take it y'all aren't close?"

She laughs humorlessly. "Well, let's see. . . . If your mama had called you a whore after you had just finished beggin' her to help you, would you continue to be close to her after?"

"My mama ran off because she enjoyed fuckin' cowboys and gettin' high more than she liked her kids, so no, darlin', I wouldn't expect you to be close to someone who doesn't deserve that privilege."

Her eyes go wide and her back jolts straight. I might not recall the younger version of her, but her mama was in Pine Oak long before I was born, so there isn't a chance Caroline hasn't heard at least some rumblings about my mama. There aren't secrets in this town. That doesn't mean I should've laid it out there like that, but I stopped giving my mama the power to upset me a long damn time ago, so the habit is impossible to break now.

"I'm sorry. About your mama," she says in a meek whisper, relaxing her back and looking down at her hands as she worries them on top of the island. "I remember Quinn missin' y'all's mama a whole lot when we were growin' up."

I nod, even though she can't see it. "She's made her peace where our mama's concerned, Caroline. You'll get there too when you're ready."

"Did you? Make your peace, I mean."

What a loaded question that is. "I accepted her place in my life a long time ago, but I was also older than my siblings when she left, so I didn't feel the sadness Quinn did or the hope that she could somehow become the mama she shoulda been, like Maverick did. I held my anger close to my chest, but I stopped allowin' her to hold those strings a few years ago. She played no part in makin' me the man I am now, and I can move on with my life knowin' I'll never abandon the people I love like she did."

"You . . . are y'all . . . is she in your life?"

I shake my head. "Maverick is the only one who keeps a small connection to her, but that's a story for another day."

"You haven't forgiven her," she muses, finally giving me those eyes again.

"No, but the difference is I've forgotten her."

She moves her head in the smallest of nods, shocking me when I expected her to argue the importance of forgiveness like my siblings do. I have a feeling that whatever her mama did to her, she doesn't feel the need to forgive either.

"She doesn't deserve my forgiveness, Caroline, but I didn't spend every Sunday with a sore ass because of the hard pews in church without learning why it's somethin' we should offer. It just isn't somethin' I can give her, so instead I've given her my disregard. I can move on with my life without lettin' what she did continue to fuck me up. We don't pick our parents, but we get to decide what to do with the life they gave us."

"I wish I could push it all aside that easily and that she didn't affect me still."

"What did she do to you back at the baby shower?"

She glances across the room toward the huge bay window behind the kitchen table that overlooks the back pasture, where a few of my horses are enjoying the freedom inside the fenced-in property, amid nothing but God's green earth and blue skies. There's nothing more beautiful than the land I've always been proud to call mine. Well . . . almost nothing.

"She said my name. That's it. She called my name and I didn't even need to see her—just the sound of her voice brought back all the things I never wish to remember again. All those memories I worked so hard to forget."

"Wanna talk about any of that?" I ask, knowing when it's wise to not push for more until she's ready to tell me, but wanting her to know I'll listen when she is.

"Maybe on our second date," she mumbles, more to herself than me. My smile grows when, after realizing what she said, her mouth snaps shut, her cheeks turn pink, and her eyes widen. Goddamn, she's one hell of a breath of fresh air. There isn't a part of her that isn't transparent, and after dealing with the kind of women who wear masks to get you, I find it incredibly alluring to know what I'll get with her.

"Fuck, you're cute," I tease sincerely, hoping to put her out of her misery. "Second date it is, Caroline Michaels." My smile grows and I shake my head with a laugh. I can't remember the last time I felt this lighthearted, especially considering that never happens when my mama was just in the forefront of my thoughts.

"How are you single?" she blurts in a rush, not looking the least bit shy now that her tongue is loosening up. Or maybe she's getting more comfortable with me, God willing, and no longer feels unsure about me wanting her here.

"Honestly?" She nods. "Spent a while screwed up because of my mama, but after I got past that, I was burned pretty damn bad and I haven't found a woman worth lettin' myself get vulnerable for again."

"That sounds like a doozy of a story."

"You want my ugly now? Or should I tell you about it on date three?"

She giggles softly at my teasing, but the sound still carries, hitting my ears and causing a rush of pleasure to burst through my body, knowing I made it happen. It's hard to believe she has such a hold on me, but there's no denying the powerful chemistry between us. Who knows if it's our bodies remembering each other or something deeper, but we're damn sure gonna find out.

"Who says there'll even be a date three?" she smarts off with a tiny smirk.

"Said I was still single because I haven't found one in the past . . . not that I haven't found someone since."

She sputters and I feel my cheeks get tight as my smile grows. She straightens in her seat before speaking. "I think I'll take that story now, if you don't mind, and then maybe we can figure out if date two and three are goin' to happen."

"Fair enough, darlin'."

I walk to the fridge and grab a beer, looking over my shoulder and holding the bottle up to silently ask if she'd like one as well. Her dark brown hair moves around her face like a sleek curtain when she gives a tiny nod. I reach in the fridge to grab another one before walking back to my spot. I keep my eyes on hers as I twist the top off, placing the open bottle between us for her to take. When she reaches for it, I keep my hand in her way long enough for hers to graze mine, wanting to know if I feel the sparking burn of awareness I felt back in Mav and Leigh's barn. She licks her lips at the same time that sensation lights a fire across my fingertips, and I know I'm not the only one who feels it. She takes a small sip before placing her bottle softly in front of her and folding her hands on top of each other to wait. I make quick work of opening my own before taking a deep pull.

It probably isn't wise to tell the woman I'm hoping to get to know better about my past relationships. Especially when the one she's asking about is the very reason I've sworn never to get close to a woman again. I probably would've kept living like I have been until the day I died, too, had I not run into Caroline today.

"Five or, hell, maybe closer to six years ago, I was datin' someone seriously enough that we had that discussion most couples have at some point about their future. She wanted my ring on her finger and didn't have any problems lettin' me know it. You can imagine it wasn't pleasant when she heard how I felt about gettin' hitched. I explained that I didn't want the same things she did and likely never would." I take another large swallow of beer, and she keeps staring at me with open interest.

"My future was here on the ranch. I had responsibilities bigger than she understood and plans to make this place somethin' different than my father had. My pops was still around then, and I hadn't taken full control yet. He wasn't the hard man he had been my whole life at that point, seein' as his health was gettin' worse, but he wasn't willin' to give up his control over the ranch. He didn't agree with my vision for things and I knew better than to argue with Buford Davis. But I knew one day I'd be in charge and until then, I was goin' to focus on makin' sure this place was the best it could be. On top of workin' from sunup to sundown, I was also still runnin' the books for the auto shop. My plate was full and my plans didn't include addin' a wife while I was spread so thin, and, to be honest, it was gonna take someone a lot different from her to change my views on marriage. I made clear that I wasn't gonna give her a ring anytime soon—if at all."

"But you stayed with her even though you couldn't see that for y'all's future?"

I nod. "I did. I'm not exactly proud of the fact, but despite how I felt about marryin' her, I was still immature enough to enjoy what she did give me. Not too long after that talk, she brought it up again, only this time she mentioned babies. I think she knew after that she was tryin' for somethin' I wasn't ever gonna give her."

"Marriage or babies?" Caroline asks, tilting her head slightly.

"Both, I reckon. I wasn't ignorant to the negatives of both in my life at that point. I hadn't ever had any good examples of relationships enough to see marriage as somethin' worth havin'. The second I found out how much she wanted babies, though, I knew we were drivin' on two separate roads that would never meet."

"Because you don't like kids?" she asks with a frown.

This is the most unconventional first-date conversation, I'm sure, but nothing about how I met this woman has been ordinary, so I shouldn't be surprised. And, if I'm honest with myself, she should know about my history with Jess before someone in town fills her in, especially if we're gonna continue exploring this thing between us. Seeing that I plan on continuing, I want her to hear it from me. There's no doubt, with her mama bein' who she is, that she'll find out sooner rather than later, and I want her knowing my side of it before the bullshit rumors hit.

"Long story short, I found her sittin' on the floor in my room one day not long after that with a pile of condoms in her lap and my bedside drawer wide open. Who knows how long she'd been pokin' holes in those condoms, somethin' I probably never would've known about if I hadn't come home to change the pants I tore open on some barbed wire. Lady Luck did me a favor. We had words. She tried to lie her way through the impossible until she changed tactics and broke down. Tried to explain herself and her actions, but how the hell can you justify that kind of shit? She went on and on with that bullshit until she finally dropped the act and got pissed instead. One second she was cryin' all over me, the next she was rantin' and ravin' about how she had been flushin' her pills for months, but when that didn't work—because I wouldn't ever fuck her bare—she started the condom shit. I don't think she ever cared enough about me to respect what I had told her I wanted, or maybe she didn't give a shit about me at all and only wanted what bein' a Davis gave her. She craved my name and the money that came with it more than she wanted my baby, but figured gettin' one was her ticket to try hookin' both those things at once."

"Wow," Caroline breathes the second I stop speaking. "That's some crazy stuff, but I'm sorry that happened to you. No one should force you to do somethin' you don't want to do."

And she just continues to shock me. I expected her to push me on why I had felt so strongly against marriage and children—that's what everyone else does when they find out why Jess and I split—but she heard my story and accepted my words with nothing but support and understanding. If this isn't just more proof she's someone worth . . . *more*, I don't know what is. If we come to be something more than two people exploring each other, I'll have to give her that, but it feels damn good to have her accept and support my feelings with no further explanation needed.

"We all have ugly in our past, sweetness. You just have to realize it was really life teachin' you a lesson. When you find something that finally proves all that ugly was worth survivin', it doesn't look so bad when you see what kinda reward you get in the end."

"You don't even know me," she gasps with wide eyes, correctly reading between the lines. I'd go through that bullshit again just to have one more taste of her. I have a feeling that after she lets those walls down and really lets me see her, I'm not going to feel any different.

"And you don't know me. What I do know, though, is how I feel when I'm around you. I know what you feel like when you're comin' undone. How you curl into my side when you're exhausted, your body trustin' me without thought. I know you hate your feet bein' under the covers while you're sleepin'. And that I've never felt like I was comin' and goin' at the same damn time and not been pissed I couldn't control the chaos of it." I walk around the island and brush my fingertips across her neck until I'm cupping her head delicately and tipping her face up to look at me. "One night of being bad with you, Caroline, and I felt more with you in the darkness than I've ever felt with anyone else in the light. We might not know every little thing that makes the other tick, but you can't deny our chemistry alone is enough to make explorin' the rest worth it. I feel the pull to you like some-one lassoed me around chest and yanked."

"Just because we're compatible in bed doesn't mean we'll be the same out of it." Her argument is weak, since she's staring up at me with hooded eyes and flushed cheeks that I know have nothing to do with her being embarrassed or shy. She feels it, that same yank right in the middle of the chest that is impossible to ignore any-more.

"How about we just figure out the rest together?"

"And I'm supposed to just . . . what? Trust a man I don't know blindly?"

"You know me, Linney. Your body already trusts me," I murmur as she jerks her head from my hold when she realizes she's been leaning into me. "You feel that trust. You know my family and you know more about my past than even they do."

She snorts, the sound cute as hell. "If we're being honest, then yeah, I reckon I do know you. I know what you feel like between my legs and in my mouth. Other than what you told me tonight, I don't know much more about you than how amazin' it feels when you fuck me."

I cough on the swallow I had just taken. I don't know what was more of a shock, what she said, or that she used the word *fuck*. I knew that feisty princess was in there.

"Well, aren't you a little whiskey in a teacup, darlin'? The most delicate thing you've ever held in your hand, but on the inside, there's a fire just waitin' to burn right through you. Tell me, Linney, tell me just how amazin' does it feel when I *fuck* you?"

"I don't know where that came from," she squeaks, a mixture of mortification and disbelief in those big round eyes. As the silence settles around us, she makes another tiny peep through her parted lips before looking away from me.

With a smile, I reach out with a gentle touch and take her fidgeting hands out of her lap and guide her to stand in front of me. She continues to give me the top of her head until finally, looking up with no encouragement from me other than the soft circles my thumbs are making on the top of each hand, she looks me straight in the eyes.

"I enjoy the hell out of seein' your skin turnin' pink because you say somethin' cute, Linney, so no more of that backpedalin' because you think I'm not gonna like it when you speak your mind and sass me." I bend, her eyes widening as I move. "Just so there's no mistake, I find it sexy as fuck when you speak freely."

She bites her lip while contemplating me. "I'm not used to bein' able to say what's on my mind, Clayton," she whispers, the way she says my name—my whole name—hitting me in the gut before makin' it roll with flutters. Jesus. "I never been with a man who allowed that."

Once it stops feeling like the ground under me is shaking and I mull her words over enough to read between the lines, the pieces start to click together. And when I start arranging the things I do know, I don't like what I see.

A small accepting frown tugs at her mouth and she nods, seeing understanding starting to bloom in me. "I don't want to talk about what I'm sure is goin' through your mind right now, but I can admit that you aren't the only one who feels the pull, and if you really want to keep gettin' to know each other, I promise I'll tell you everything you're wonderin' about another day. Might not be on date two, five, or even ten, but if things start becomin' more between us, I promise I'll give you all of my ugly."

Tucking a piece of her dark hair behind her ear, I nod. "You keep givin' me the fire that burns inside that teacup, I'm gonna be fine waitin' for you to be ready to give me more, darlin'."

She slowly leans into my hand, still hovering at the side of her face, and this time the move isn't something done subconsciously. "I don't understand the connection I have to you at all, but I like how you make me feel."

"And how's that?"

She shrugs and smiles a small, sweet-as-fuck smile that makes me fight the urge to wrap her up in my arms and never let go. What the hell is this woman doing to me? I might not have the answers to explain it, but when she opens her mouth to answer me, I vow right then and there that I'm not going to let my past be a reason to cloud my future anymore.

"Safe. You make me feel safe, Clayton Davis."

10

CAROLINE

"All on Me" by Devin Dawson

— ★ —

"What's the latest on the insurance stuff, Caro?" Lucy asks around a mouthful of fries.

"Yeah, Carrie, they seem to be takin' their sweet-ass time," Luke joins in, reaching across the table to nab one of my two pickles while he talks. I slap his hand away when he comes back for the other.

"Caroline," I scold, saying my name slowly while looking between the two of them. "We've been best dang friends since I shared a dorm with you, Lucy, but still years later, you two refuse to stop callin' me childish nicknames. Caroline. C-A-R-O-L-I-N-E. One is mature, elegant even, while those nicknames make me sound like a badly pronounced Spanish dish or a five-year-old."

Luke shrugs, lifting his hand to wave the pickle I

hadn't notice him successfully sneak while I was ranting away. I roll my eyes and reach for it, but he just laughs and pulls his hand farther away.

"That explains why you have a problem with callin' me a nickname a five-year-old would have, seein' as you're always actin' like one yourself, Luke."

Lucy giggles, and I narrow my eyes at her. "You—"

Her hand shoots up, interrupting me before I can go at her too. "Calm down, *Caroline*. You need to get out of that thundercloud you've been stuck in."

I grouse under my breath, but don't argue with what she said. Not because I don't want to—oddly, I do—but because she isn't wrong. Not only am I out-of-my-mind frustrated with the lack of progress with my insurance settlement, I'm a whole different kind of frustrated because of a certain tall, handsome, and dark cowboy of mine. And that's just what he is . . . *mine*. In the week since our awkward run-in at Quinn and Leighton's baby shower, he's made it impossible to doubt that.

I take another bite of my burger and think about Clayton. We haven't been able to find time to actually go on a date, but it hasn't stopped him from calling me whenever he has a chance, texting me when he doesn't, and making it known I'm not far from his thoughts. Every time his name pops up on my phone, I get a rush of happiness. I'm quickly becoming obsessed with those calls, but I miss the rush of being near him. I'm a giant mix of depressed happiness because I miss the man who is quickly ingraining himself in my life, but is too busy to do more than talk through a phone.

"She doesn't have anything to say to that, Luce, because she knows she's been bein' a little shit lately." Luke takes a bite of his burger before pointing it at me. "I figured she was just bein' pissy now that she found out how much work fixin' all my accounting was gonna be, but nope, she's flyin' through that mess like I didn't have two years' worth of shit in piles all around my office, so I've got no answers for you unless it's y'all's lady time."

"I'm right here, you know, you can stop talkin' about me like I'm not," I tell him with a frown.

Lucy thumps him over the head. "How many times do I have to tell you, Luke. Women don't all menstruate at the same time, so just because you can't miss when I'm on mine seein' as I live in the same house as you doesn't mean Caroline's cycle is at the same time."

He stops eating and looks deep in thought, like the mystery of a woman's uterus is some big secret he's just figuring out. His bad mood lightens up a little when he starts volleying his stare between Lucy and me before looking down in the general direction of our bellies and doing the same.

"So it's *not* your lady time then?" he finally questions, looking adorably confused now.

I glance around the tables closest to ours quickly, making sure no one heard him. "Would you shut your trap, Luke? I don't need all of Wire Creek knowin' about my time of the month. For your information, I'm in a bad mood because I got some bad news about the rebuild and I'm havin' a hard time shakin' myself from the funk that delay is puttin' me in." Not a lie. Also, not the whole truth.

"You're so on your lady time," he jests.

"I'm goin' to kill you slowly if you don't stop talkin' about me bein' on my period!" I hiss in a harsh whisper.

His face splits into a smug grin the same time someone clears their throat behind me. I glance over at Lucy in horror, hoping she'll help me disappear into thin air, but she's not paying me any attention. Just like her brother, she's now looking past me. Except, where Luke looks more curious than anything, Lucy is giving her best impression of that Snapchat filter that has the huge mouth—smiling so big and weird you'd swear she's in pain because of it.

"Linney."

My shoulders hunch and I close my eyes. I've never in my life liked my name shortened. However, the affection that I hear in the nickname Clayton gave me does nothing but fill me with happiness. It's something no one but him has ever called me—a short version of my middle name—and maybe because it's all his, I love it. But even with the rush of hearing him call out to me, his timing sucks. This can*not* be happening. Clayton's voice sounds behind me again, repeating the nickname he hasn't stopped calling me since last weekend. Even with the rush of pleasure I get from a nickname when it's coming from his lips, humiliation still chokes me at his embarrassing timing.

"Hey!" Luke exclaims, oblivious to the fact that I'm dying right in front of him, causing me to open my eyes to find him pointing at me. I see Clayton move to stand next to my side of the booth out of the corner of my eye, effectively blocking any chance I have at bolting. "How come *he* gets to call you something other than Caroline and we can't? You just met him and you've known me and Luce for close to a damn decade but won't let us."

I don't correct him. It wouldn't matter if I tried, because Luke wouldn't understand something I can hardly put my own thumb on. I haven't even told Lucy about the stupid brief crush I had on Clayton in high school, before I met my last boyfriend years ago. Having something special with Clayton Davis is beyond words. Never, not once, has anyone shortened my name and it not been like nails on a chalkboard, but the man who was my first crush many years ago lights something inside of me when I hear him rumble that nickname, and I'm in no hurry to lose this feeling. I'll be dammed if I'm going to explain that to Luke and Lucy, though. The secret is mine and Clayton's, no one else's.

Lucy elbows her brother and I decide now would be a good time to escape, but since I can't leave with the hulking cowboy blocking my way, I do the next best thing. I close my eyes and go with the good ol' theory that if I can't see them, they can't see me.

"What is she doing?" Luke questions.

I hear Lucy chuckle but keep my eyes closed. That is, until my body is moved by the solid weight of another person pushing his body into the booth next to me. I jolt, sucking in a shocked breath that does nothing but fill my lungs with a scent that is all man—outdoors, fresh air, and just a hint of soap. Before he pushes all the way into the booth, my eyes open and all I see is Clayton's smirking face, one side of his mouth tipped up and his eyes amused.

"Now what is she doing?" Luke stage-whispers to his sister.

"Reckon she's figuratively shittin' her britches, big brother," Lucy jokes, not even attempting to keep her voice low.

"Better than literally doin' it, but if that's the face she makes when she's takin' care of business, I think she needs to go get checked up at the doc. Somethin' ain't workin' right."

I whip my head around and gape at them. "Would you two *shut up*," I express venomously.

Luke holds up his hands in surrender. "What? All this could've been avoided if you'd just let the whole nickname thing go earlier. We wouldn't even be talkin' about your shit right now. It was you who started down this path, little one, don't get mad that I'm just tellin' you the truth."

"This did *not* start because of me. It started because

of your sick enjoyment of embarrassing me because, for whatever reason, you find the fact that I'm shy to be some sort of freak-show act for your entertainment purposes, Lucas Hazel."

"I do not," he defends instantly.

"Yeah, Luke, you really do," Lucy confirms with a nod.

"Hey!"

She shrugs. "Not maliciously, I know you're just tryin' to get her to come out of her shell. Caroline knows that too, but you take it too far sometimes."

"I'm sorry, Caroline," Luke mutters, and I can see written all over his face that he really does feel bad.

"It's okay, Luke." I lift my hand with the intention of grabbing his across the table, but I jump when it's hijacked by long tanned fingers that grab me with soft care. Then, with my mouth hanging open, I watch my wayward hand being lowered into Clayton's lap as he holds it gently with his. I blink at my captive hand, flex my fingers, and wonder how I actually forgot he had sat down. My skin tingles where he's touching it and I find my fingers curling tighter, loving the contrast of his suntanned hand against my pale one.

"Linney," he utters in his deliciously deep voice, bringing my gaze from our joined hands to his bright green eyes. "Thought you were havin' dinner at the ranch with me tonight?"

"What are you doin' over in Wire Creek?"

"Had to grab somethin' from the feed store that ours

in Pine Oak was out of. Saw you through the window," he answers, pointing out the window to the feed store across the street.

"Oh," I lamely breathe.

"So, are we not havin' dinner at the ranch tonight?"

"We are," I confirm with a frown.

He studies me and I take a moment to appreciate how handsome he looks with his thick, dark-as-night hair sticking in a million directions. I look around, half expecting the ever-present cowboy hat to jump out and bite me. "Where's your hat?"

"Granger, one of our newer horses, got spooked today," he answers with a shrug, as if the fact that a huge animal getting spooked isn't something that requires any more explanation. But seeing as I know nothing about horses, my imagination is running wild, something Clayton doesn't miss. He gives my hand a squeeze and leans a little closer. "Sweetness, you worried about me?"

I shove him with my shoulder lightly. "You'd be worried too if you were picturin' some huge beast tryin' to stomp you to death before eatin' what's left of you, Clayton Davis."

He tosses his head back and laughs, deep and loud, straight from the gut. His hilarity booms in my ears, the rich sound making me smile. I don't even care that everyone is looking in our direction, not when I get to see this guarded man be so carefree. He's one of those people who laugh with their whole torso, too. His shoulders jump, the corded muscles in his neck flex, and his whole body moves. I drink the sight of it in until he finally stops, untangling our fingers to wipe his eyes. I have a few seconds of disappointment that he let go before he's lifting his arm up and over my body to hook it around me. His fingers grasp my shoulder, and a moment later he pulls me into his side.

And I willingly scoot my hips to get myself as close as I can without urging.

"You're one helluva breath of fresh air, darlin'." His lips press lightly against my temple and the arm around me flexes. "I knocked my hat off because I was in the middle of dismountin' him at the same time he was tryin' to two-step, and my hat landed in a giant pile of manure. Didn't feel like goin' up to the house to grab another one when I had other places I needed to be in order to finish up my day."

"Oh." Well, now I feel a little ridiculous. "Do you need to go, then?"

His brows pull in as he frowns in confusion. "Go where?"

"You said you had other places you needed to be."

His eyes dance—I swear it looks like his dark green orbs have come to life and are swirling with lighter flecks of gold that I've never noticed before. If he keeps looking at me like that, I'm going to have a hard time ever giving this man up.

"No, darlin', I'm already there."

"Y'all together now?" Luke butts in, breaking the hold that Clayton's words have on me.

"Yes," my dark cowboy tells him, not looking away from me.

"We're explorin' things," I correct, looking over at Lucy as I see the expression on his face change slightly. She appears to be about to burst with excitement. When I look at Luke, his face is blank while he assesses Clayton. "What, Luke?" I probe, not sure I'm going to like what's on his mind.

This is why I hadn't told him about . . . whatever's between Clayton and me. I'm not sure what title to put on it, to be honest, and since Luke's been in my life for a long time I knew he'd expect something more than what I could articulate. He saw me at my worst, saw how hard I've worked to move on. He and Lucy are the only two people in the whole world who understand how big a deal it is that I'm taking this step with Clayton. But they're also the two people whose opinions matter most to me, and I'm not sure I could handle it if they didn't approve. Which is probably why, in the week since he first cooked me dinner at his house, I haven't told either of them that I agreed to see what's between the two of us. I couldn't even explain my feelings toward the man to myself, let alone verbalize them to anyone else.

I squirm under Luke's scrutiny as his stare bounces between us, the silence heavy except for the sound of my heartbeat thundering in my ears. What if he sees something in Clayton that I don't—or can't—something that could mean my judgment is still warped and I need to give Clayton up. Could I let go of a man who is quickly burrowing under my skin? Could I really just walk away if one or both of my closest friends don't like him?

No, I don't think I could.

Actually . . . I *know* I couldn't.

After what feels like hours, Luke shrugs, smirks, and then goes back to eating what can only be a cold burger now.

"What did *that* thing you just did with your face mean?" I snap, my period-driven hormones and my lack of patience colliding in a burst of sass.

"What're you talkin' about?"

I look at Lucy. "Why does he always do that? Make you think the worst, but not speak a dadgum word before some stupid *I know everything* smirk comes across his face. Then, still not sayin' a thing, continue on like nothing happened and you start questionin' your sanity?"

Her shoulder lifts, indicating she's just as clueless, and her lips twitch.

"It's the most annoying thing in the history of . . . *ever*, Lucas. I can tell you want to say somethin', so why don't ya stop actin' like I can't handle whatever it is and just spit it out, bucko!"

Clayton's chest moves in silent laughter that I ignore in favor of glaring at the man across from me. Lucy chokes on a loud cackle before covering her mouth with her hand. Luke, though, holds my very annoyed scowl.

"You sure you wanna hear it, Carrie?"

"Caroline, you big dummy."

He rolls his eyes and points to Clayton. "You let him call you Linney." He leans back and crosses his arms as if that statement holds all the answers.

I shrug, making the arm around my shoulders tighten the smallest bit. "So?"

I watch Luke's emotions change like someone flipped a switch inside him. One second he's serious as a heart attack, and the next he's smiling a toothy grin, his eyes crinkling at the corners. The change is so quick, had you not been watching him closely, you would've missed it.

"I think that right there about says it all for me, but since your lady time always makes you feel the need to pick fights with me, I'll clarify so you can stop lookin' for reasons to jump down my throat. You, sweet Caroline, hate when anyone calls you some shortened variation of your name. I know it's because your mama always had some different name for you growing up and it makes your remember that shit. When others do it, your nose always scrunches up, your eyes get all slitty until they almost look fuckin' closed, and your nostrils start floppin' around like they're gonna take flight and leave your face. You have never, not in all the years that I've known you, been able to hear someone shorten your name without losin' your mind. Which is why we always keep doin' it—

not just because we want to erase the negative things your mama did, but because it's funny as hell to watch sweet, shy, little Caroline Michaels get pissed off. But when Davis does it, you look like a stampede of kittens just ran up to your feet and promised you a life of fluffy cuddles."

"His name is Clayton. Not Davis," I stupidly say, clearly still looking for a fight.

"Name's still Davis, too."

"Don't think I've forgotten you made me think that was his first name, Luke."

He laughs. "Change the subject, fine. Means you know I'm right. And Caroline, it's not my fault you were callin' out his last name all because you didn't bother to properly introduce yourselves the night you met."

My face heats, and I know he's going to win if I keep trying to argue with him. What's the point? He isn't wrong. Not even a little. And all four people sitting in this booth know it.

I turn my head and look at the man holding me close, his face so near mine that his soft breath dances across my cheeks. My gaze falls to his mouth when he smiles and, having decided it's time for me to be brave enough to at least confirm what Luke just said, I open my mouth. "I like it when you call me Linney, Clayton. Luke, as frustrating as he is, isn't wrong, and you should know it means somethin' to me and that I'd like it if you didn't stop."

The left side of his mouth twitches twice before his full smile appears. "All right. And just so you know, I like the fuck out of you callin' me Clayton. No one calls me by my full name, but even if they did, I wouldn't like it half as much as I do when you're sayin' it in that sweet whisper. That's all yours, Linney."

He's halfway through his mini speech when my focus moves from his full lips to those green eyes that even a nun could get lost in. I blame those stupid, beautiful eyes for what I do next, because it's so out of character for me, it's the only way I can explain it. My back straightens, my head moves, and I press my lips to his in a soft, quick, but no less amazing kiss. He sucks in a sharp breath when my mouth connects to his, the hand resting on my shoulder flexes, and when I pull away, the soft look of happiness in those green depths shows me that I can trust the guy who chipped away a big piece of the armor that had been guarding my heart.

"Now that all that's out of the way, want to tell me why you're eatin' here when we made plans last night?" he asks softly, voice low and forehead resting against mine a second longer before lifting away, keeping his face close.

"Because I was hungry?"

"Darlin', it's four in the afternoon. Are you tellin' me you're still gonna be hungry for dinner after eatin' one of Big Tom's famous burgers?"

"Have *you* had a Big Tom burger?"

He nods, smiling a tiny smirk.

"Then I think you know why I'm eatin' one at four in

the afternoon. When someone says they're goin' to have one of the best burgers in Texas, you don't pass that up."

His eyes crinkle at the corners. "Are you still goin' to want dinner when I pick you up, or should we do somethin' else?"

At the mention of him picking me up, something real close to embarrassment starts to burn up my throat, which makes no dang sense. I certainly didn't set my store ablaze and in turn, make myself homeless—but that's just what I am, homeless. I shouldn't be ashamed of it, but even though I didn't intentionally keep it from him, I still feel badly about it.

"How about we just leave from here?" I offer lamely. "Save you the trouble of havin' to drive an hour from here to Law Bone, when we're both in Wire Creek." Of course, in my quest to save him some gas, I don't realize my mistake until it's too late.

"Uh-oh," Lucy whispers loudly with a giggle, clearly coming to the same conclusion.

"Why would I be drivin' out to Law Bone tonight to pick you up if you aren't helpin' out at Hazel's when you live here, darlin'?"

I hear Luke laugh, but I don't look away from Clayton. "I was goin' to tell you," I rush out, proud that I don't feel my cheeks getting red.

He lifts his head more and looks at me with one brow up, waiting for me to continue.

"You see, there was a tiny problem with my place. . . ." I

bite my lip and wince. "Okay, so maybe by tiny I mean real big, but that was before well, you, and I really didn't think to mention it last weekend when we were at your house after the shower and, to be honest, it kinda slipped my mind with the whole head-on-collision horse-crash thing and runnin' into my mama and well, *you*. . . ." I stop talking, thankful that my mouth finally just decided to snap shut when my brain wouldn't stop the flow of verbal diarrhea.

"She had a fire at her bookstore. She doesn't normally work at Hazel's—she only does that now because her place is gone. Tried to get her ass at Luce's and my place, but she's a stubborn one, our Carrie," Luke mumbles around a slice of pie I didn't even notice had arrived.

"Caroline," both Clayton and I tell him at the same time, breaking our staring contest in the process.

"Jesus Christ, not you too!" Luke grunts in annoyance.

I look back to Clayton just in time to see a mean-as-heck expression on his face, aimed at one of my best friends for something as simple as using a nickname that he now knows I don't like. I have no idea why that's so hot, but it makes my belly flutter in the most insane way.

"I really was goin' to tell you—it just didn't seem like the right time," I defend weakly.

Clayton looks down at the table and shakes his head, but I know he isn't *that* mad, because there's a slight tip to the side of his mouth. He mumbles something, but it's so low I can't hear him.

"What?"

He slants his head my way. "I said, you're lucky I find just about everything you do cute as fuck, Linney, because right now I want to pull you over my knee and tan your goddamn hide for thinkin' there wasn't a 'right time' just once during this whole week to fill me in. Talked to you every day and a few nights until you fell asleep. Tons of times in there you could've mentioned that you owned a bookstore, which you just so happened to live above; that it burned down; and that you don't really work at a place that makes me uneasy just thinkin' about you bein' in."

"Aww!" Lucy gushes. "Did you hear that Luke?"

"I'm sorry," I offer lamely, ignoring Luke's grumbles about me being safe at his bar.

Clayton nods and reaches out to pulls me back into his side before placing another kiss to my temple. That move would make my knees weak if I was standing.

"We can talk about it later, darlin'."

Lucy pretty much holds a one-woman conversation for the rest of our time at the diner. Luke leaves right after he finishes his pie when a pretty redhead walks in. He throws some cash on the table without saying a word and takes off toward the back of the diner in hot pursuit.

I spend my time listening to Lucy talk to Clayton, his deep voice rumbling against me when he answers, but I don't say much, not when all I can think about is what will happen later when Clayton and I talk.

I should've told him, he's right. I make light of it because if I don't, I'll break down in tears thinking that someone might've intentionally set that fire, and I don't want to ruin this evening.

Tonight is something I've been looking forward to. Not just because it'll be another milestone I reach. Ever since John, I haven't dated. Clayton's the first man I've wanted anything more from. Not only that, but it'll be my first date with someone who isn't a teenage boy. Well, my first planned date after the unexpected first one. And now, like it or not, I get to start it by telling him I'm homeless, technically jobless, and one hot mess.

Clayton's body shifts, his hard thigh brushing against my leg, pushing the skirt of my knee-length dress up my thigh a little. I shove it down quickly and smooth it out but freeze when I see his free hand reach down to adjust his crotch. Glancing up, I see his eyes trained on my legs, and a rush of excitement bursts through my body. I might not completely understand how someone like Clayton Davis could be into plain Caroline Michaels, but seeing him affected by something as simple as the six inches of skin above my knee does something to me. I feel empowered by his reaction. Maybe this is what normal people do when they're exploring things—this push and pull of powerful lust is exchanged between them—but I have never in my life experienced it.

Wanting to feel that rush again, I wiggle my bottom and curl my hands into the fabric of my dress, pulling it up a little. He stops talking the second I tug the hem higher; then he clears his throat and continues. I look back at his lap, disappointed that he didn't touch himself again, but no less determined. My hand doesn't even shake when I release my skirt and place it on his thigh. As my fingers inch closer to the bulge in his jeans, I don't feel a bit of shyness. The sense of freedom its absence inspires is overwhelming and I feel a rush of lust. I keep watching my hand as it creeps closer to the hardness pushing his denim up and almost come out of my skin when his hand drops on top of mine and yanks it to that very spot, his hips flexing as he grinds against my palm.

Oh, *wow*.

I press my thighs together and close my eyes. Memories of him moving just like that inside of me become overwhelming.

"What are you doin'?" Lucy questions, the sound of her voice shocking me like a bucket of cold water over my head.

I rip my hand from his hold, missing the hard heat against my palm instantly, and fiddle with my skirt before looking up at her. I'm not embarrassed or ashamed when she winks at me. No, I feel like I'm on top of the world—even if my best friend did just witness me rubbing my kinda-boyfriend's crotch shamelessly.

"You ready?" I ask Clayton, smiling at Lucy while I do so she knows I'm not ignoring the question she doesn't really need an answer to.

"Yeah, Linney. I'm more than ready."

It's been so long since I haven't been afraid that I

promise myself right there as we shuffle out of the booth with greasy food scenting the air that I'm going to give this little adventure everything I have and trust whatever is in store for us. Good or bad.

Because I have a feeling there isn't anything better in the world than being cared for by this man next to me.

11

CAROLINE

"Think a Little Less" by Michael Ray

- ★ -

"You'll text me later?" Lucy asks while hugging me good-bye outside the diner.

"Maybe tomorrow mornin', Luce." She shuffles her feet a little and makes a low noise of excitement in my ear. When she pulls away, she looks ready to burst with excitement, making me laugh softly. "Because it will be late, Lucy Hazel, not because I'll still be with Clayton." I whisper, hoping the man waiting just behind me doesn't hear.

Which of course he does, because that's how lucky I am.

"Try tomorrow afternoon, Lucy. And it will definitely be because she's still with me," he corrects, and I jerk around to gawk at him.

"Clayton!" I gasp.

"Linney, we both know you aren't goin' anywhere but to my bed tonight."

"But," I start, but close my mouth when I realize I really don't have an argument to offer. Turning back to Lucy, I shrug. "So, I'll talk to you at some unknown hour tomorrow, okay?"

She snorts and gives me a blinding smile before taking off to her car with a wave. I watch her get in and pull away before I turn to the man at my back. He's leaning against his truck with confidence. When I take a step toward him, he straightens but doesn't move aside from that, letting me set the pace. Still riding the high from inside the diner, I step toward him and wrap my arms around his middle and press my cheek to his chest, hugging him tight and smiling so big it hurts my face. His strong arms fold around me and his chin rests against the top of my head.

I'm just about to tell him how much I like feeling him against me, but when I start, my eyes light on the last person I ever thought I'd see again staring at us across the street, and the words die on my lips. I know Clayton notices the change in me because I jerk in his hold, but shockingly, the fear over seeing my old boyfriend doesn't last but a second. Not with Clayton holding me safe.

"You all right, darlin'?" he rumbles against my cheek, not letting me go.

I clear my throat, pull my eyes from the man across the street, and look up at Clayton with a smile. "I will be."

I can tell he wants to press, but for whatever reason he keeps his silence before kissing my forehead. He then opens the truck door for me and I climb in. I watch as he shuts the door and quickly scans the area around us. I don't look, not wanting to know if I really saw a blast from my past, but judging by the harsh lines that appear on Clayton's face, I don't think John was only a figment of my imagination.

The second he climbs into the driver's seat and jerks the truck into reverse, I know he saw John. The drive from the diner to Davis ranch isn't a terribly long one, but with the tension between us getting thicker, it feels like it's cross-country. The ride only makes me more uneasy, aware that I need to tell him about my past sooner than I wanted. I need to trust what's growing between us—that the strong connection we've felt from day one is worth taking a chance on. I need to start opening up.

"That was my ex," I whisper to the window, watching the pastures full of cattle pass by.

He lets out a rush of air, and I feel the energy around us get even thicker with tension.

"I was with him for a long time, Clayton." I speak slowly. "It . . . it wasn't good."

"When?"

I finally look over at him, confused by his one-word question. "When what?"

"When did he become your ex?"

"A few years ago, give or take some." I know exactly how long it's been. How long I've been afraid because of what he did to me in using my fear against me to make my normal, timid nature so much worse. Call me a coward, but I'm not going to go into the depressingly long length of time that it's been since I've been able to get to this place—to move on—if I don't have to.

His hands tighten on the wheel and a muscle jumps in his jaw, but he doesn't talk, and I have a feeling there's something more here. Something that I'm missing.

"John," I start, but stop immediately when Clayton starts cursing a violent streak, his nostrils puffing out like those of an enraged bull. Not wanting to be the reason he's mad, I slouch in my seat, unsure if I should continue. His hand leaves the wheel and reaches for mine, taking it in a firm grip and not letting go.

"Finish what you want to tell me, Linney. It's not you I'm pissed at."

"You know him well?"

A strangled laugh comes out of his mouth. "Yeah. I know John fuckin' Lewis pretty damn well."

"I don't have a good past where he's concerned. Are you sure you want to hear this?"

He pulls into the ranch's driveway, not answering me until we've parked close to the front of his beautiful home. He cuts the engine, gets out, and walks around the truck's hood to open my door. He unbuckles my seat belt and turns me with a gentle grip on my knees before opening my legs and stepping between them, dragging his palms up my thighs to rest under my skirt. I have to push the fog his touch puts in my mind away to focus, because only then does he speak.

"I know him, know him well enough to have a pretty good idea of what you're gonna tell me. I don't like it, but that isn't for you to worry about, darlin'. I don't want you ever feelin' like you need to keep somethin' from me because I won't like hearin' it. He's the ugly you talked about?"

I nod, my chin wobbling and drawing his attention immediately. His fingers tense, but he keeps going.

"I know you didn't want to talk about this yet. You promised to give it to me when we got serious, but darlin', I don't need more dates to tell you I'm already there. I'm not goin' anywhere because of the shit you went through in your life. No matter what you have to say to me, we're still gonna be explorin' us. I don't want to push you when you aren't ready, but Linney, there isn't a thing I wouldn't do to keep you in my life."

God, this man. How is it possible that we've only just started when I feel like my soul was made for his? I shift to get closer and drop my forehead to his chest, feeling his strong heartbeat. His thumbs rub my thighs, soothing and reassuring me.

Trust him.

The thought rushes through my mind and I suck in a breath, lift my head, and give him my ugly.

"I left Pine Oak when I was eighteen. I spent four months before that with John wonderin' what he saw in me, but not ready to question it and lose him. Don't get me wrong, it wasn't perfect, but he made me feel important and gave me hope that I could have something different from the life I was facing if I stuck around under my mama's control. So when he promised to get me out of my mama's house and a whole bunch of other things that he just *knew* he could give me once we got to Austin, I believed him. I believed all of him. I know now that I naively gave him my blind trust because I felt like he was the only way out." I inhale and hold the breath deep in my belly for a pause before blowing it out slowly. "It wasn't all bad. I met Lucy and Luke because of it. I also lost a lot of me in the process though. A lot of me that I didn't find again for almost six years. He drank excessively, yelled more often than not, and, toward the end, used his fists."

Clayton's quiet, but I can see my words are costing him. I give him a look, asking silently if he wants me to keep going. At his nod, I do.

"He got mad about some beer one night and sent me out to get it. Long story short, I got into a pretty bad wreck on the way back. A drunk driver slammed into me and I spent a few months recovering. But it was because of that accident that I was finally able to get away from him. I spent a week in the hospital before Lucy and Luke picked me up. I knew I had my chance and we had it all planned out. They were taking me to their place to finish my recovery and Luke got all my stuff back. It wasn't until a few weeks after moving in with them that I realized just how good my chances of making a clean break were. The man who hit me worked for some big auto chain and his company wanted to settle out of court. The settlement money was enough for me to come back here and open The Sequel, and I lived in the apartment above it for five years, until the fire."

"You haven't dated since?"

"No. I haven't felt safe until . . . you. I don't think you'd hurt me, if that's what you're thinkin'. Not like him."

"Fuck me," he breathes, his forehead dropping to mine. "I don't deserve someone as sweet as you, Linney. I really don't. But that's not gonna stop me from keepin' you. Words are weak, darlin', it's actions that mean somethin' when it comes to a man's character. I promise I won't ever lay a hand on you. My temper can burn bright, sweetness, but *never* do you need to fear me causin' you harm like that. We might fight, talk to each other with heat, but I'll never hurt you. Fuck, Caroline," he says, his hands framing my face with such gentle reverence I gasp. "How anyone could harm a hair on your head, I'll never understand."

"I know you wouldn't hurt me. I saw that in you from day one. Why did you look so mad back at the diner?"

He looks away, his hands going back to my legs but this time on the outside of my skirt.

"Clayton?" I probe when he doesn't answer.

"I'm gonna ask that you trust me now, sweetness. Trust that it's nothin' you need to be concernin' yourself with. Me wantin' to protect you will always be limitless in its reach."

"You're askin' me to give you somethin' I've only given to two people."

"I'll never make you regret trustin' me."

I search his eyes but see nothing except sincerity. He has no idea how much power he's asking me to give him. But my dark cowboy won't twist my trust into something ugly. He's a good man—always kind to others, humble in his pride, fierce with control, and worthy of respect. My heart feels the safety within his promise. My mind recognizes our connection without doubts.

It's time to drop the rest of the weights that hold me captive. My breathing is rapid, but I feel sure about my decision. I lift my hands and press them against his chest. He closes his eyes on an exhale when I drag them up to wrap around his neck. When those emerald orbs finally lock back on me, I press against him and bring him close enough for me to press my lips against his.

His fingers dig into my flesh the second my mouth opens, and I lick the seam of his lips, a groan coming from deep inside of him rumbling around us. When our tongues slide against each other, he pushes his hands under my skirt again and goes straight to my hips. With one strong pull, he's got his hips flush with mine, and the thickness of him presses tightly against my sex. I whine, wiggle, and pray that he gives me some friction. Our kiss changes when he starts to smile against my mouth. If anyone were to see us, toothy grins pressed together, I can only imagine how insane we'd look.

For the first time in my life, I don't care what anyone else thinks—I'm just happy this man makes me feel safe, shows me how to be bad, and breathes new life back into me with every small step of us exploring. If this is how strong we are after such a short time, I can hardly wait to see what comes next.

12

CLAYTON

"More Girls Like You" by Kip Moore

- ★ -

"You look good. Haven't seen you without that ugly-ass serious mask on in a long time."

I look away from Midnight, one of the best stallions on my ranch, and raise my brow at my brother. I just finished riding the property, letting Midnight go all out and take complete control of our ride. I forgot how fast the old horse could go when he wanted to show off.

"What the hell are you talkin' about?" I ask Mav after giving my horse one last brush.

"You've got the girls goin' nuts. I swear to Christ, you're gonna put one of them in labor the way they're actin' like you datin' is the most excitin' thing goin' on in their lives. They keep freakin' out that you're gonna get spooked and ruin it."

"You're fuckin' kiddin' me right now with that shit?"

He grunts and shakes his head. "Just repeatin' what they keep yammerin' about. Figured you should know that your love life is gonna make you an uncle sooner than you reckoned."

I flip him off before guiding Midnight back into his stall. I do a quick check of the feed to make sure everyone did their work today. Not that I need to worry about how things are run here. I've been stepping back more, and it's been refreshing. I trust my staff here implicitly, and by doing so, I free up more time to be with Caroline.

I never thought there'd be anything in this world that would have me wanting to spend less time on the ranch, but three weeks with her and I'm finding my happiness is directly connected to her and no longer to the ranch. She brings out a protective side to me that has only ever been shown to my siblings and the ranch. We spend as much time together as our complicated schedules allow, but it's never enough. For the first time in my life, I wish I had some sort of normal career where I could take her on the kind of dates she deserves instead of us "dating" here at the ranch for dinners, movies, and just generally spending as much time together as possible. I've been getting her in my bed most nights, something I did the second I found out she was staying at the fucking motel in Law Bone. In the past few weeks, she's only spent a handful of nights there, and each of those nights I spent unable to sleep, worrying about her. Between my responsibilities here on the ranch and her helping out at Hazel's, we get little time even for our unconventional, ranch-bound dates.

"Heard you ran into Jess the other day," he says, twisting his Stetson between his hands.

"Don't remind me."

"Also heard she's been running her mouth 'bout y'all bein' back together."

I stop in my tracks and look over at Maverick. He places his hat on his head and walks over to stand next to me.

"You're gonna want to get on top of that shit. That woman was evil when you were fuckin' her, but you and I both know she's not ready to believe it's over forever, regardless of how much time has passed."

We walk in silence toward the house, his words weighing heavy in my gut.

"Does Caroline know about Jess?" he finally asks.

"Yeah. Told her that night of the baby shower when she had dinner here the first time."

He mulls over my words while straddling his ride home, not starting it up yet. "The girls know about Jess tryin' to get back with you. They know she's cornered you once and tried a few more times unsuccessfully. They're worried about you dealin' with that as a brother, but they're worried about what could happen to Caroline if

Jess manages to tear y'all apart. You've got my wife and our sister actin' like worried hens and it's startin' to piss me off."

I clamp my teeth together as my breathing speeds up.

"Don't like hearin' that, do you?" He turns the key on the four-wheeler, shattering the silence. "You should probably let her know that your ex is sniffin' around again before she thinks you're keepin' it from her for some reason other than protectin' her feelin's. There won't be anything good that comes from her findin' that out from someone else." With that, he hauls his ass back to his own house.

I never regretted selling him back Leighton's family land when they got together. I didn't need it, the Davis ranch being as huge as it is. But it's times like these, when he takes advantage of being so fucking close by coming by to stick his nose into my life, that I question the sanity of my choice. Even the five hundred acres of our combined land don't provide enough distance when he gets a hankering to start handing out advice.

It's been a long-as-fuck week for Caroline now that the rebuild is under way on The Sequel, and the last thing I want is to bring this shit up tonight, but I know Maverick's right. I'm not blind to why Jess started this bullshit again. She's always made it clear she wants to get back together, and it's my fault for not being more definite in my refusals. Now that she knows I'm seeing someone, it's worse than ever, and seeing how Caroline's mama—Jess's boss at the salon—was with her the last time she tried coming on to me, it won't be long until it gets back to my girl. And the *last* thing I want is her thinking that I was keeping that from her.

Fuck.

I pull my phone out of my back pocket and pull up the last text she sent me. She stayed at the motel last night, not wanting to drive in the storm we had roll through after leaving Hazel's. I didn't sleep for shit and my mood has been terrible, but when her text pinged through early this morning, I almost came in my pants. All day I've been dealin' with the promise built off that message, and I finished my work twice as fast as normal.

Her small, perfect tits fill the screen of my phone and I groan when my cock throbs. We've been playing this game for a week now, teasing each other every chance we get, but never going further than heated kisses and feeling each other up like two horny teenagers. I've been craving her body since I last took it close to three months ago, and that need has only gotten worse since we've gotten together. When she sent me her first sexy text, I almost died, but when she sent me the first naked picture of her body, I was pretty sure I actually had. There is something hot as fuck seeing my shy and timid Linney opening up to me like this—giving me something that I know she's never given any other man.

And now it's likely going to be even longer before we get down to business again. I don't see her wanting to ride my cock after I tell her my ex-girlfriend grabbed my crotch in the middle of town yesterday.

Regretfully, I close out the picture of Caroline's naked chest and stomp through my house to shower. Thoughts of my good girl being bad make my jeans get painfully tight around my erection.

Ten minutes later, I've just started palming my cock when I feel it.

That zap of energy that sparks from top to toe when Caroline is near.

We could be back in that pitch-black motel room and I would know exactly where she is.

I keep stroking myself, waiting to see what my good girl is up to.

When I hear the curtain move, the rungs gliding almost silently against the pole, I smile to myself and release my cock, letting my hand join the other one pressed against the tile, letting the hot water roll down my neck and body. My ears strain to listen in an effort to try and figure out her next move.

But it never comes.

I'm half convinced I was imagining her, but I can still feel the hum of awareness on my skin, so I wait. Then, from my position leaning forward against the tile, I see the very tips of her purple-painted toes in the space between my braced feet.

Jesus fuck.

She's been less and less shy with me over the past few weeks, but never this forward. We have dinner together as often as we can, always ending up on the couch, but it's been me who'd make the first move to pull her into my lap and kiss her until we were both wound the hell up. I've been waiting for her to let me know she's ready for more, something I told her a week after finding out about her punk of an ex. I wanted her to make sure she was ready, because the next time I get my cock in her tight pussy, I won't ever let her go. "I know you're there, darlin'," I admit, and my smile grows when she screams and those tiny feet jump back.

"Dang it, Clayton!" she gasps breathlessly.

I push off the side of the shower and turn, expecting to find her covering as much of her body as she can, but when I finally see her I almost swallow my tongue. My cock jerks, and my smile drops with my jaw.

There she stands, every inch on display. I don't know where to look first. Her hands are on her hips, long tanned legs are spread apart, and her fiery temper is on display, all while her pussy is bare and begging for my tongue. I can't eat apple pie anymore because of that sweet pussy. Licking my lips, I move my gaze up, over her flat stomach and right to her tits—perfect little handfuls of flesh that heave with her heavy breaths, her rosy nipples hard from my attention. By the time I force my eyes off of her chest, any annoyance she felt at getting caught sneaking up on me is gone.

My girl wants to be bad and she isn't afraid to show me.

Her lightly tanned skin is flushed red with arousal, her eyelids growing heavy as the same need I feel takes her over.

"You tryin' to sneak up on me, Linney?"

She bites her lip and nods.

"Are you sure you want to take this step? I told you, once you give me this gift again, I'm not gonna give it back. We're gonna stop explorin' and start plannin' a future."

"I know," she whispers, stepping a little closer.

"Baby." I drawl the word out lazily, taking my own step forward when her eyes close at my endearment. "Caroline, I mean what I say. We've been goin' slow for almost a month, darlin'. You ready to admit what's happenin' here?"

Her eyes open and there isn't a lick of doubt in those beauties. "We were gonna happen the second you tried to kill me with your horse."

I grab her as her giggles echo around us and pull her naked body into my arms. "Sweetness, we were gonna happen the second you sat your ass down on a barstool and told me you were a good girl."

"Hey! I *am* a good girl!"

Her tiny hands hit my shoulders and I close mine

around her hips and lift her effortlessly off her feet. Her legs wrap around my back and I feel her lock her feet above my ass. My cock, having no trouble letting her know he wants to say hello, settles in the middle of her sex. Her back hits the shower wall and I flex my hips, dragging my thickness through the hug of her wet lips—their dampness having nothing to do with the shower.

"Yeah," I breathe, needing to be inside her more than I need air. "I know you are, darlin'."

She leans forward and starts peppering kisses all over my chest and up my neck. My hips rock steadily as my cock slowly glides through her wetness. I need to be inside of her, but not until I hear what I need to hear.

"Tell me, Caroline."

Her kisses stop, mouth on my jaw. When she looks up at me, I don't miss the meaning in her eyes. It tells me she's just as lost in me as I am in her. The shyness that I normally see is nowhere to be found.

"I'm ready to be yours," she says with confidence and hunger. "Please, Clayton, make me yours."

All rational thought vanishes as I take her mouth in a bruising kiss. I press her against the tile with my hips so that my hands are free to roam that gorgeous body. Her legs tighten and her mouth gets greedy. When I palm her tits, the small weight of them perfect in my large hands, she moans into my mouth and starts to rut against my length. I can feel the wetness of her arousal coating my cock, and I start moving with her until we're frantic for more.

It isn't until I lift back and enter her with one long thrust that I realize why she feels so fucking good.

"Condom," I breathe heavily.

"Pill," she answers, her head falling against the wall with a thump as she starts to roll her hips. With a deep breath, I realize just how much trust I have in her, no doubt filtering in whatsoever at her assurances of using birth control.

My eyes cross. "Goddamn, Linney, you keep moving like that and I'm not gonna last."

She hums but picks up speed.

"You want me to move, baby? Want to be bad with me?"

"Please," she whines. "You're so deep. I'm so full."

I bite her collarbone and pull my hips back so just the tip of my cock is kissing her entrance. She makes a low sound of protest as she digs her nails into my shoulders, her eyes pleading.

"You want me to fuck you hard or love you slow?"

"Hard first, slow later." Her feet tighten on the top of my ass, trying to get me back inside of her. "Clayton!" she begs.

I lean forward, nose to hers, and smile wickedly at her. "Tell me to fuck your pussy then, darlin'. Give me the words."

Her brown eyes go wide, but she doesn't stop trying to

push me back in. She wants to say it, but that little bit of shyness left when she's with me holds her back. So, I give her a teasing shallow thrust and arch my brow. Her chest heaves and those nails bite in again.

"Fuck me, honey. Fuck me hard."

"Motherfucker," I gasp. Hearing her say those words sends shock shooting right through me.

Then I fuck my girl until my ears are ringing from her screams and I've drained almost three months of frustration and want into her tight body.

We don't get out of the shower until I wash every inch of her and she returns the favor. I came so hard I'm sucked dry. My cock shouldn't be hard this soon, but I already want her again. Hell, I wanted her again as I was groaning out my release. But I know that before I allow myself to take her again, I need to get our talk over with. I'm not sure what she'll do when I tell her my nasty ex is sniffing around, but I'm not going to take her again while the shadow of Jess is hanging around me. I hope like fuck that after I tell her, she'll still want me to love her slow, like I promised.

"Let's get in my bed so I can feel you in my arms, Linney?"

She glances up from drying off her legs and frowns. "Why does your voice sound like that?"

"Like what?"

"Like you've got the weight of the world on your shoulders." She stands and regards me before her eyes open wide and her jaw drops. "Oh my God! Am I bad? Was it . . . not good?"

I sigh and point to my cock, my still-hard cock. "Darlin', my body is already beggin' to get back in you and I don't think it can be missed that I almost fucked you through my shower wall."

"So I'm not bad then?"

Having had enough of this space between us, I grab her gently by her shoulders and pull her to my body. My cock jumps the second her soft belly presses against it. "I've never felt anything better than what I get when you give me you."

Her whole body goes soft and she smiles up at me. Her hands on my chest start to roll across my skin until she's looping them around my neck. "Then what's on your mind, Clayton?"

"I need to tell you somethin' that happened and I would rather do it with you naked in my bed so I can keep my word and love you soft after."

A small worry wrinkle forms on the skin between her brows, but with a deep breath she nods and lets me lead us to my bed. She climbs in first, sitting on her knees and watching me as I drop the towel I had knotted at my hips. Not once does she hide her naked body, and I know that means she's more worried than she lets on.

"Come here, Linney," I request softly once my back hits the headboard. Her eyes go from my face, down my body, and up again before that worry between her brow grows. She sucks in a wobbly breath, but scoots forward. I take her face gently between both hands.

"What's goin' through your mind?" I question her.

"You've got me worried."

My thumbs rub against her soft cheeks before I lean in and press a soft kiss to her lips. "I'm sorry, darlin'. I don't want you worried, I just didn't want to put off talkin'."

Her tiny hands shake as they move from my shoulders to my neck, one on each side as she studies me. "Is this about John?"

Fucking John. I should've assumed he'd be her first thought, seeing as she hasn't brought him up since I asked her to trust me when it comes to that douchebag.

"No, I haven't seen him since that afternoon in Wire Creek."

"Oh."

"You been worried about him?"

She shakes her head. "Not really. He hasn't called in a while and I think he got the picture that we're together, so I don't expect him to now."

"What do you mean he hasn't called in a while?" Jesus Christ, I didn't even think to ask if he's been in contact with her since they split up.

She shrugs. "He called a few times after we were done, but stopped for a few years. He called me more recently, but the last time was the night I met you."

"You'd tell me if he did, right?"

Her head moves in my grasp as she nods. "I would, but he won't, since I changed my number the next day."

Somewhat pacified, I drop the subject.

"What's goin' on, honey?" she asks with concern when I don't say anything.

"You know my ex?"

"The one who tried to trick you into more?"

"Yeah. That one." I shift my hands, wrapping my arms around her body to pull her closer, needing to feel more of her skin against mine. Her hold on my neck slips for a second before she adjusts her arms and her fingers press into my hair. "I've run into her a few times since we started this thing, but other than runnin' her mouth, she hasn't done more, until two days ago. When I saw her, she cornered me, and before I could get her to move, she grabbed me in a way only you should be grabbin' me."

"Where?" Caroline asks, her eyes no longer worried now that they're burning with rage.

"It didn't last long, but I know people saw before I could stop it and I didn't want you to hear it from someone else."

"*Where* did she touch you, Clayton?" she asks again.

"Fuck," I breathe, dropping my head against the wooden frame.

"She touched this part of you, in the middle of town?"

I nod, clenching my jaw when she stops moving and I lose the sensation of her wetness caressing my body.

"And what did you do when she touched what isn't hers anymore? When she touched what's mine?"

I look back at her, shocked by the brazen words, still expecting to see her anger but there isn't any to be found. Her eyes are dancing but no longer spitting fire. Curiosity, maybe, but her trust in me is clear as she waits for me to explain.

"I grabbed her wrist and told her never to do that shit again, but whether she actually heeds that is another story."

Caroline nods, lifting one hand to run through my hair as she studies me. She repeats the process again as the silence ticks on before leaning forward and pressing her lips to mine in a quick kiss.

"Does she know you're seein' someone?"

I nod, my grip tightening just a hair, her body pressing more firmly against mine. "I told her, and seein' as I said I was buildin' the future I hadn't wanted with her with you, I'm thinkin' she got the point. I made sure she knew that not only do I dislike her disrespectin' the woman I'm buildin' a life with, she doesn't have a chance of makin' that life with me."

Her eyes, which were locked on my lips while I spoke, jumped to mine. "What?"

"What part, darlin'?"

"I'm not sure," she gasps.

"Caroline," I murmur with a smile.

"Well," she starts, scooting her bottom closer and rubbing against me, smiling when I groan. "I'm not happy that happened, but I think I like knowin' that you said all that to her. She doesn't deserve your kindness after what happened, even if it makes me a bitch to say so. I mean, I understand if you told her that to get her off your back and all. We haven't really put titles on us or anything, I mean. Is that what was botherin' you? That I might think you wanted for us what she hoped to get from you before y'all broke up?"

"I think it bothers me more that you think I wouldn't want that."

She deflates in my hold, just a tiny bit. "You were clear when we talked about it how you felt about marriage. Even if we were at that point where we'd be talkin' about it, I know where you stand."

"Stood, Linney. I'm not standin' there anymore."

"What?" she breathes.

I smile, leaning my face closer, and take her mouth in a deep kiss. She grabs ahold of my hair, pulling slightly, and sighs into my mouth. I kiss her slow, moving my tongue against hers in lazy glides. Her hips start moving against mine in a dance of pure torture. Each time she presses forward, I thrust up off the bed, and it doesn't take much of that for us to become too breathless to continue kissing.

"One of these days," I tell her as I roll her onto her back, "I'm gonna have a talk with you about our future." My hips lift and I reach between us to guide my cock into her body. "And darlin', I'm gonna have one hell of a different way of explainin' my thoughts for our future than I did back then. Until that time comes, you just let me love you slow and fuck you bad."

13

CAROLINE

"Close" by Ryan Kinder

- ★ -

The second he starts moving inside of me, I know this is different from any other time. Our night at the motel had been fueled by lust and the mystery the darkness created. It had been frantic, both of us knowing we only had that night. Earlier, in the shower, it was just as rushed, but driven by the need, our tantalizing past few weeks. This though . . . this is a profound kind of coupling. With every slow thrust I can feel the words he knows I'm not ready to hear. But, as I look up into his clear eyes, I hope he can see what I'm not ready to say.

I'm quickly becoming dependent on what's building between us, and after hearing what he just said, I know I'm not alone.

I could go the rest of my life with nothing more than

what he's giving me now as long as I continue to feel wholly and completely adored by him. I might not have tons of experience with relationships, but I do know what we share is special. He hits a spot deep inside me and I push my head back on a moan.

With each lazy thrust into my body, I feel him battering down the remnants of the walls I've put up. With each precious kiss, he promises me a future without hurt. When he looks deep into my eyes and plunges into me, I clamp down and come so hard it steals my breath. And when he starts picking up speed, taking me harder, I drag my nails down his back and feel my orgasm bleed into a second. With my moans echoing his, his come shoots into my body, and I know I'm going to give him every bit of myself until he has it all.

I close my eyes with a smile, my legs falling from their tight hold on his hips, and rub his back lazily.

"You hungry?" he questions when my stomach's grumbling breaks the afterglow.

I hum my answer, but don't move to actually do something about it and let him go. We both groan as he slips free.

"Come on. Let me feed you, darlin'," he jokes with a smile when my stomach continues talking.

He tosses me one of his shirts with a handsome smirk, watching me closely as I cover up. I can only imagine the blush covering my body under his watchful gaze, but it isn't from feeling shy. When he groans a complaint over losing the sight of my naked body, I feel the heat of arousal and pride knowing I can make a man as perfect as Clayton Davis come undone like that.

I push my hair out of my face and smile up at him. He says something under his breath about never letting me wear clothes again before pulling his jeans over his own nakedness. He has to tuck his still-hard length down before zipping them up, leaving the button undone.

"That can't feel good," I muse, pointing out the impression of his erection clear through the worn denim.

"It's not, but if I don't get us both fed, I won't have the energy to do anything about it later."

"You sound like I'm a sure thing," I joke.

"Prayin' you are, darlin'. I'd live in that sweet pussy if I could."

I gasp, swatting his abs. He only smiles bigger and pulls me to my feet, kissing me hard. When we finally manage to leave his bedroom and get some food, it's almost nine at night. I have no idea how two hours passed so quickly, but I shouldn't be surprised by his stamina. I know from our first night together he can go until I pass out from his lovemaking.

"I think I'm goin' to sell when the rebuild is finished," I tell him after taking the last bite of my sandwich.

He doesn't look away, frowning slightly.

"I've been thinkin' about it a lot these past few weeks and, well, I don't really want to be livin' forty-five minutes away anymore. I used to think bein' that far from Pine Oak was a good thing, but now, not so much."

His face gets soft when my explanation sinks in. "What are you thinkin'?"

"The buildin' next to the hardware store is openin' up. The lady who owned it doesn't want to deal with the trouble of ownin' a business now that she's gettin' older, so I was considerin' opening back up there."

"Miz Jordan's? The florist?"

"Yeah," I answer quietly, looking at my plate knowing he's likely thinking the same thing I did when I found out that was the only place in town available for rent.

"Darlin', that's right next to your mama's salon."

"I know."

"Not that I don't think you could handle it, but Caroline, that woman bein' that close to you makes me feel a whole lot of unease."

I nod, looking away from the intensity in his gaze and pushing some of the chips left on my plate around with my fingertip.

"I love the idea of you bein' closer, darlin', especially if that means you're goin' to be doin' it sooner than later, but I'd be lyin' if I said I was okay with puttin' you that near to her."

"There's nowhere else, Clayton. I've looked. I wanted to know all my options before I brought it up to you. I want to come home, not just because of us, but because I don't feel safe in Wire Creek either. Being here, well, I don't need to constantly worry."

He frowns. "I thought they ruled the fire an accident."

"According to the report, but I'm not sure."

He steps around the island and pulls me into his arms. "Why do you think it wasn't an accident, Caroline?" I can see the concern written all over his face and in the tense set of his shoulders.

"I think someone's been tamperin' with things. Materials are goin' missin' and yesterday Joe, the contractor, told me some of the electrical he had finished was pulled out. How would that even happen?"

"I'm not sure," he says thickly.

"We only passed inspection because Joe worked through the night to fix the issue, but somethin' in my gut is tellin' me I shouldn't go back there. I wanted to talk to you before I put a for-sale sign in the window and start lookin' for somewhere else to open up again. Whether that's here in Pine Oak or maybe in Law Bone, either way, I don't want it to be in Wire Creek anymore."

"Don't buy the Jordans' old place. It might look like the only option now, but havin' you that close to your mama isn't gonna happen."

"I'm goin' to have to look at Law Bone, then, and the only thing I found there was clear on the other side of town. Not that I'm lookin' for a new space based on the distance to your place, but . . . uh." I stop when he flashes me a wide, toothy smile. "What?"

"Linney, I think we need to start basin' your search off how far it is from the ranch, so don't get embarrassed when you say it because, darlin', I agree."

"Now that I'm going to sell, Clayton, I need to find somewhere to live that isn't a motel. I can't use the ranch as my base when I might find somethin' to rent that's on the other side of you, but close to a potential space for the store."

He throws his head back and laughs. "How many nights have you been at that shitty motel, darlin'?"

I shrug. "It's been two months since the fire and I started stayin' there not long after that. I don't know exactly how long though."

"Let me rephrase that. How many nights since we started explorin' us have you *actually* stayed there?"

"That's different, Clayton. We haven't exactly had tons of time to get together between me bein' busy durin' the day either sleepin' or monitorin' the build, and you've got a busy schedule of your own here. By the time I get a few hours in at Hazel's and get here, it's been so late I either fall asleep or you insist I stay."

He steps closer, smiling down at me with the most open expression of affection. "Darlin', it might've started out that way, but I haven't wanted you anywhere else for weeks than in my bed. You want to make up one of the guest rooms as yours, do it, but I think it's time we both admit this is your home."

"Clayton," I breathe, not knowing how to respond to him.

"I've got an idea about the store, but I need to check

some things out before I get your hopes up. Until then get the place in Wire Creek on the market, check out of that goddamn hotel for good, and get your sexy ass where it belongs."

"It's too soon," I weakly argue.

"Then put your clothes in one of the guest rooms instead of mine!"

"But—" I start, only to stop speaking when his hand covers my mouth.

"I wouldn't be sayin' it if I wasn't sure, Caroline. You don't need to be in that motel. You didn't want to stay with Luke and Lucy, and I think we both know that under this roof is where you belong."

"I . . . okay," I agree, not letting myself look for reasons to keep arguing against this.

"Okay," he parrots with a grin that makes my heart pick up speed.

"If you change your mind though—"

"No way in hell that's gonna happen, sweetness."

"This is insane."

His chest rumbles as he laughs low and deep. "I think we're pretty good at doin' things with a little insanity, darlin'. That's half the run of our ride together. I never know what's comin' next and I'm not findin' it a bad thing to give up control if I've got you with me doin' so."

There aren't any more words after that as his mouth

takes mine in a doozy of a kiss. By the time he has me passing out from exhaustion, there isn't a single concern on my shoulders anymore, and I go to sleep with a smile on my face all because of the man who is slowly becoming my everything.

14

CAROLINE

"Happy People" by Little Big Town

- ★ -

"Let me get this straight," Quinn says, folding another baby blanket and placing it on Leighton's coffee table. "Clay, my allergic-to-anything-resembling-commitment brother, is not only in a super-committed relationship, but also livin' in sin with his girlfriend?"

Leighton snorts, throwing some tiny yellow baby socks at her best friend's head. "You make it sound so scandalous, Q."

"And you aren't shocked?"

"Well, no, not really," Leigh answers, looking down at her lap, but not before I see the smirk on her face.

"It's only been two months!" she exclaims.

"So what?"

I stop petting Leighton's giant cat, Earl, and chime in.

"We've technically known each other our whole lives. I had a crush on him before I started datin' John. I guess it's just our time now." At my words, they both look over at me with jaws wide open.

"You had a crush on him back in high school?" Leigh questions with a smile.

"You hussy!" Quinn laughs. "He's six years older than you."

"What?" I blush. "He's the most handsome man I've ever known."

"That's so sweet." Leigh sighs dreamily, wiping her eyes as they fill with tears.

I gape at her in shock when she starts crying harder. Hoping to find some sort of help from Quinn, I'm utterly flustered when I see her crying as well. "Uh," I hedge.

"What the fuck is goin' on?" a voice thunders behind me.

At the sound of her husband, Leighton waves him off and sniffles loudly. "Stop growlin', cowboy."

"Did you hear?" Quinn cries toward her brother.

"Hear what?"

"Caroline moved into the ranch house."

Maverick stops in his path and turns slowly to assess me. I haven't gotten very close to the middle Davis child, but I also haven't spent tons of time around him since Clayton and I stated dating. The few interactions we had were brief, and he studied every move his brother made with me. What I hadn't gotten in the months since Clayton and I started dating was his younger brother smiling freely in my direction. It's so shocking I can't do anything but stare at him.

"Well, I'll be," he finally says, his grin growing even wider. "I bet that bitch Jess isn't too happy about this news."

I shake my head.

"What's *that* mean?" Quinn questions, sniffling loudly.

"Just what I said, Hell-raiser."

"Why would what Jess thinks even be relevant right now?"

"You must not have been hearin' the gossip flyin' around town. I know Leigh told you about it because she said you were goin' on and on about how nasty Jess is."

Quinn looks at Maverick like he's grown a second head. "She mentioned Jess was sniffin' around Clay, not details! I've been stuck at home on bed rest for a whole week, asshole. How am I goin' to get the good gossip when I can't even waddle my ass into town?"

Leighton laughs, finally dry-eyed. "I forgot to tell you what I heard when I was at the PieHole last week. Sorry, Q. I got distracted when you started talkin' about your cervix and everything."

Quinn's eyes go from Leighton's to her brother's, over to mine, then back to Leighton's when no one goes to explain further. "Well! D, don't just sit there. Give me the goods!"

I sigh but don't say anything.

"It really isn't a big deal. His ex put her hands on him in the middle of the day smack-dab in the center of town. Jana told me that he grabbed her hand off his crotch the second he realized—a second too late, I should add—that she was goin' to touch him there. She didn't hear what he said, but rumor has it that it was somethin' about her bein' a used-up slut that he wouldn't touch with a ten-foot-long cattle prod, even if he wasn't madly in love."

"I think you're embellishing it just a little, Leigh," I add, rolling my eyes to hide the fact that my stomach is going nuts at the mention of love.

"She isn't far from the truth," Maverick says, sitting down next to his wife and rubbing her stomach. She looks at him and smiles before placing her hand on top of his.

"How is that woman still even sniffin' around? They've been broken up for years and I know he isn't stupid enough to have gone back even for a quickie, seein' as she's been with half the town."

Leigh hums in agreement when Quinn stops talking. "Did he ever say why they split in the first place?"

They look at Maverick first, but he doesn't glance away from his wife's belly, ignoring them completely.

"Uh," I stammer, "I love you two and all, but if you haven't heard it from him before now, you aren't gonna hear it from me."

I might've gotten back the friendship that was broken when I left town after high school, but my loyalty will always be to Clayton now.

I ignore the annoyed glances they both shoot me and meet Maverick's gaze. I'm not sure what I expected, but a wink followed by a low chuckle damn sure wasn't it.

"You know!" his wife snaps accusingly. "You hadn't even come back to Pine Oak when he was datin' her."

"Didn't have to live in Pine Oak talk to my brother, darlin'."

"Well?" Quinn probes, looking at her brother.

"Yeah, right, Quinnie. And don't y'all be givin' his girl any shit for bein' faithful to her man. If Clay wanted y'all to know his personal shit, he'd tell you. You both know damn well you wouldn't say a thing if the roles were reversed, so give her the respect of doin' the same."

They stay mute as he leans down to kiss Leighton's belly before pressing another kiss to her lips. After rising from his seat, he walks by his sister and pats her head. Leaving the room, he shuts the back door softly. The girls share a look, then glance at me in shock.

"I think," Quinn breathes, "you just got a Maverick-size stamp of approval."

"She totally did," Leighton agrees with a smile.

Earl licks my hand and meows, clearly sick of me not petting him anymore. I lean back, fighting a grin. Five minutes later, he's not too happy with me when

Leighton shoos him off my lap so I can help her carry all the newly washed and folded baby items to the nursery. Quinn, knowing she'd be pressing her luck if she got off the couch since she's ready to pop, doesn't come.

"You seem happy," Leighton muses in the nursery.

"I am," I confirm with a smile.

"I haven't said it, but I'm really happy that you and Clay are together. It's not just that he's good for you— you're good for him. He's always been super private about his personal life, but I hope you know that both Quinn and I are here if you ever just want to talk to your girls about things. I respect the fact that you might never do that too, just so you know. We might be nosy, but Mav wasn't wrong."

"I'll keep that in mind, Leigh."

"A little advice from one girl who fell for a Davis to another: just don't ever tell Quinn about your sex life or you'll never hear the end of it. That girl is as weird as it gets when she finds out about that stuff."

I chuckle. "Noted. Don't ever tell Quinn how good her brother is." My eyes widen when I realize what I just said. "What are the chances you'll forget that?" I ask Leigh.

Her whole belly moves as she laughs softly. "Not even a little bit, but don't worry, I won't say a word. I've got a cowboy of my own, so I know how to keep quiet."

When we go back into the living room, Quinn is

asleep on the couch and Earl is curled up in a tiny space between her belly and thighs. A large cat, some breed Leighton called a Maine coon, there's no way he can be comfortable with his back half hanging off the couch, but he's purring away regardless.

"I'm goin' to let y'all rest and head home," I tell Leigh, feeling my heart skip a beat at the idea of home being the ranch. "I promised Clayton today I'd finally let him teach me how to ride."

I give her a hug, promising to call later, and walk out to my car. It'd be quicker if I knew the four-wheeler trails, but I don't mind the short drive. It's hard not to love it when every turn gives me the most beautiful views of Pine Oak's backcountry. Miles and miles of green pastures.

Every stretch of the road on the Davis property is lined with a stark white fence. Clayton explained that when his father had been running things, they had cattle roaming their lands. The Davises raised some of the best, but it was a business Clayton never saw for the future of the ranch. Since they no longer use the majority of their land for cattle, they farm out unused parts of those pastures for hay so that they can gain that resource for the horses.

Clayton tells me he owns pastures that have some of the best views in all of Texas, but since you have to travel by horse to get there, I haven't seen those yet. He's been working so hard to get me comfortable around the big beasts, but there's just something about those huge black eyes watching your every move that makes me uneasy.

I honk at Drew, the ranch foreman, when I see him working on one of the fence rails near the turnoff from Maverick and Leigh's road to ours. He pulls his hat off and waves it in the air before wiping his brow and bending back over to continue his work. Not far after that, I see two other hands do the same, and I give them a honk of my horn as well.

Right before the turn into the ranch house, I see a few cows in the distance, smack-dab in the middle of the road. The rancher who owns the land on the other side of the road has so many head of cattle, they're always dotting the landscape, but this is the first time I've seen wayward cattle making a break for it.

I continue down our drive, reaching for my phone in my purse. I pull up Clayton's number and give him a call, climbing out of the car while it rings.

"Linney," he answers in that deep way of his that's almost breathy but too manly to be called such. The sound goes straight through me, bathing my whole body in warmth.

"Hey, honey." I smile into the bright sun, walking up the porch steps and into the house. "I know you're busy, but I wanted to let you know some of the Larkins' cows are makin' a break for it. I saw them when I was turnin' in farther down the road."

"I'll give Todd a call."

"I figured you would. Are you goin' to be home for supper tonight?"

I can only imagine how tired he is, seeing that he left before sunup this morning to deliver some horses to a buyer out in Tulsa, Oklahoma. He made it sound like no big deal, but I can't imagine making a five-plus-hour drive one way and not being wiped by the time I got home.

"I should be at the ranch in about an hour, darlin'. Why don't we head into town for something?"

"Are you sure you don't want to just have a relaxin' night at home? You've been on the road all day."

He laughs. "No, I want to take my girlfriend out. Might not be as fancy as what we'd get if we drive into Dallas, but I don't take you out enough as it is."

"Clayton," I say with a smile, "you know I don't need all that." And I don't. I know he's busy with things at the ranch and his hours are long and taxing. I don't want him working his tail off all day only to get home and think I need him to take me out in order to show me a good time. All I want is to be near him. There're no distractions when you're getting undivided one-on-one time.

"I know, darlin', but I'm still feelin' the itch to show you off."

I roll my eyes, walking through the house toward the stairs so I can go get ready now that it looks like we're not going to be staying in.

"I was just visitin' over at Maverick and Leighton's. I

know Quinn is on bed rest, but why don't you give Tate a call and see if he'll okay a trip to town for dinner? I'll ring Leigh and see if she and Maverick want to join. They don't have much time left before the babies are here. As much as I love our time with just the two of us, I think we should have a family dinner before the little ones come."

A noise comes over the line that makes me pause in pulling off my leggings. "I like hearin' you refer to them as family."

"Well, they are your family, Clayton. What else would I call them?" I laugh awkwardly.

"And seein' as we're buildin' our future, they're yours too, Linney."

"Clayton." I gulp.

"Don't go sayin' my name like that when I'm too far away to do somethin' about it. One day soon, we're gonna sit down and talk so you know exactly what I see for us down the road and I can make sure you don't have any doubts as to where I'm standin'. Get ready, baby, I'll be home soon."

He hangs up before I can say anything else, but since he's rendered me speechless, that's just fine with me. I'm not stupid: I know he wouldn't have moved me into his home if he didn't see a future for us, but knowing how his last relationship ended, I worry he might not want the same things for his life as I do for mine—a family. There isn't much in this world that would make me willingly give up what I have with Clayton Davis, but the fact that he doesn't want kids might just be one of them. Which is the very reason I've been dreading the moment he wanted to have this talk.

What will I do if he only changes how he feels about marriage but not children? Can I stay with a man who can only give me his love but not his babies? I'm honestly not sure.

15

CAROLINE

"Tennessee Whiskey" by Chris Stapleton

- ★ -

"Would you stop?" Quinn snaps, yanking her husband's plate back toward her so she can continue to pick off it, having already polished off her food. "Do you want to be the reason your child starves, Starch?"

He smirks, his handsome face more boyish than those of the other men at our table. If I wasn't already tumbling head over heels for a certain dark cowboy, I might find Tate Montgomery attractive. He shrugs and I hear Leighton snicker from across the round table. My gaze moves to her and she winks before mouthing something about waiting for it. I frown in confusion before she points to the two Montgomerys.

"Grease, there's no way my baby is starvin' in there," he jokes, pointing to her very big stomach. I know he meant it harmlessly, but judging by the expression on Quinn's beautiful face, she doesn't feel the same way. "Now, don't go lookin' at me like that, Quinn. You know that's not what I meant."

"Oh really?" she asks, crossing her arms over her chest, which is no easy feat, seeing as she's top-heavy *and* belly-heavy.

"You know I love your body," Tate tells her sincerely, but she doesn't stop leveling him with a glare.

"You mean the body that keeps growin' as big as a house, keepin' your baby from starvin' because I'm storin' food in there for him, or somethin'?"

Tate looks up at the ceiling and I hear Leighton chuckle a little louder.

"Give it a break, Hell-raiser," Maverick mumbles around a forkful of barbecue. "You know damn well he didn't mean what you're implyin'. Just because you're in a shit mood, don't take it out on your man."

"He's the one who put me in jail!"

This time, Leighton doesn't keep her hilarity down. She starts laughing so hard, I can't stop watching her belly with worry that she's shaking her baby up in there. Surely it's not good for it to move that much. "He didn't put you in jail, Q! Don't be such a drama queen."

Quinn turns her narrowed eyes at Leighton. "You aren't the one stuck talkin' to herself while her husband is off playin' inside other women's vaginas."

My eyes widen and I feel my cheeks heat as heads

start turning in our direction. Maverick has his fork frozen halfway to his mouth, staring at his sister in shock. Leigh is hooting even harder now. Tate, having clearly heard this many times, just looks down at his plate with a smirk. When I look up at Clayton, he's wearing the same expression as his brother.

I try to ignore the stares as Quinn continues to grumble about her vagina-poking husband, but it's almost impossible when it feels like the whole place can't take their eyes off our table. I'm used to the curious looks when I'm out with Clayton or even the girls, but they're never as bad as when all six of us are together. When you factor in Quinn's shameless way of saying whatever is on her mind, it really does feel like we're on display.

"You get used to it," Maverick grumbles, and I look to my right to see him studying me with understanding. "Took me a while when I got back to Pine Oak. I forgot what it was like to live in a town where everyone treated other people's lives like a soap opera."

"How do you ignore the stares?"

He shrugs. "You just stop carin' what they think. Only person whose opinion matters to me is my wife's. They're gonna think what they want regardless of the truth, so you might as well just pretend they don't exist."

"But doesn't it bother you when you hear them talkin' about you and it's not true?"

His mouth moves, not into a full smile, but it's not a hard line anymore. "They're not ever gonna spread the truth when they can stretch it and fill in the less interestin' parts with lies. You just live your life and make sure you keep yourself happy. The rest of that shit can go to hell."

I lean back in my chair and look around. Just like Maverick, everyone eating with us is oblivious to the stares from the tables surrounding us in the packed restaurant. Just like when we're at the PieHole or even grabbing groceries, people have no qualms about gawking.

The Davis family is Pine Oak royalty, so it shouldn't be a shock, but for someone like me, who isn't used to it, it's a struggle. I never did look at the attention with such an untroubled and relaxed mind-set as Maverick does, though. In my mind, I'm still afraid of what they think, but in reality, what does it matter? I've got a great man, his family welcomes me with open arms, and other than the uncertainty of where I'll reopen The Sequel, life is perfect.

I turn to see Clayton regarding me in silence and feel the last tiny part of unease fall to the wayside. A wide smile forms on my face, and I direct all the newfound freedom I feel at him. It's his affections, after all, that have shown me how to complete the puzzle inside of me—that have allowed me to finally shed the past and start living.

The chatter at our table fades away when I see his eyes flash. I know we haven't said those three special words, but when he gives me this unguarded focus, I have no doubts that they're there.

I never stood a chance at keeping my heart from him. Not when he makes me feel like nothing is impossible.

"Hey! Earth to the lovebirds," Quinn yells across the table, breaking the moment with her snapping fingers. "Did you tell her yet?"

"Shut up, Quinnie," Clayton scolds, frowning at his sister.

"What?" She glances around, taking a bite of her husband's sandwich. "You didn't say it was some big secret."

"What are you talkin' about?" I ask.

Clayton sighs, glaring at her a second longer before turning to look at me. "I planned to surprise you later, but since my sister has a mouth the size of Texas, might as well do it now."

"Oh, come on! You didn't tell me not to say anything. How was I supposed to know?"

"I don't know, Quinn, maybe because I said don't tell Linney so I can make sure it's what she wants before you get excited?"

She waves a hand in the air. "Potato, potahto, big brother."

Clayton sighs, but smiles at his sister.

"Well, now that you two got that out of the way, how about one of you spill the beans so everyone else—including Caroline—can know what's goin' on?" Leigh jokes.

"I have a place I think would be great for The Sequel," Clayton tells me.

Of all the things I thought he'd say, *that* didn't even cross my mind. My heart picks up as happiness fills me to the point of bursting with the knowledge that even with how busy he's been, he's been looking for something better than the Jordans' place next to the salon.

"Really?" I gasp with excitement.

"The buildin' next to Davis Auto Works went up for sale a few years back. We bought it with plans to either use it for storage or expand, but never really had time to deal with either. I think you'll find it's perfect, but I wanted to run it by Quinn before I said anything. The last time we talked about it, we'd decided that D.A.W. didn't need anything bigger, and the setup we have now for storage works. I had every intention of listin' it but never got around to it. Feels like one of those meant-to-be things, sweetness," he explains with a shrug of his shoulders, downplaying just how huge this actually is.

"You want me to buy it from you?" I question, excitement bubbling through me even more. "I'd love to see the space, but I trust you. Given that it's in my budget and all."

His face gets soft and he gives me his knee-weakening grin. "Linney, you think I'm gonna take a single penny from you, you've lost your mind." Clearly seeing the argument forming, he raises a hand and closes it over my mouth. "Another one of those things we're buildin', darlin'. The Sequel is a part of you, and *you* are a part of me. You get that fire bubblin' over the teacup and I'm gonna have fun showin' you another way to toss that sass around."

My mouth moves, but he doesn't take his hand away, so the words just come out garbled.

"You gonna let me do this if you like the space?"

I shake my head and narrow my eyes.

"You need me to love you bad and change your answer?" he smarts off with a low rumble of his voice, eyes dancing with amusement.

I pause long enough to show him that I'm not unaffected by that in the least. He throws back his head, a booming laugh rocking his body before he drops his hand.

"You are *not* givin' me a buildin'," I finally say when he quiets down. "You can't just give someone somethin' as big as a buildin' and think that's okay."

He leans toward me till we're nose-to-nose and effectively kills any chance I had at arguing logic with him. "Caroline Michaels, you gave me back a life worth livin'. The way I see it, a buildin' isn't even close to big enough to make us even."

Everyone laughs when I lean back in my chair and shut my mouth. Even being the butt of their laughter, I don't feel the old feelings of nervous unease. Not now. All I feel is contentment so deep in my bones I don't think I'll ever be afraid of my own shadow again.

I'm finally living a life free of trepidation and wild

with adoration. Who would've thought that one night with a dark cowboy would heal my soul of fear?

I'm still riding the high of having my own space thirty minutes later when we leave the restaurant, Clayton and I following the other two couples. His arm is over my shoulders, pressing me tight to his side as we walk. I have one behind his back and one resting against his abs. When we stop next to his truck, I lift the hand off his stomach and bring it to his neck, pulling him down and pressing my mouth to his. He doesn't pause, deepening our kiss instantly. I hear the others talking as they move to their vehicles, but don't pull away. When Clayton turns us and moves my front to press more firmly against his, with both his hands on my bottom, I smile against his mouth and lift my head to look up at him.

"What was that for?" he asks, his voice thick with the same pleasure I feel shooting through me.

"Thank you," I answer simply.

His expression changes into one that makes my heart pick up speed. He's gazing down at me like I just gave him the world in the palm of my hand. His eyes are shining bright, the swirls of green so luminous that they look like the clearest emerald stone. His whole face is smiling. One hand leaves my butt, grabs the hand not holding his neck, and pulls it to his chest. His heartbeat hits my palm with a frantic tempo as his gaze holds mine.

I open my mouth to give him every last piece of me, but before I can, the magical moment is shattered. I hear my name called in a vile tone that belongs to one woman and one woman alone. Only unlike the last time, I don't feel the same panic that had me bolting—not with Clayton's arms safely enveloping me.

"Well, well, looks like some things never change. Left town a whore and come back as one. At least you're movin' up in the world now that you've wrangled a Davis man."

I can hear the slur in her voice, but I don't let that excuse her behavior. She'd say the same thing if she were sober.

"What the fuck did you just say?" Clayton seethes angrily.

"I'm talkin' to my daughter, not you."

"No, you're talkin' to *my* Caroline, not yours. She isn't anything to you."

Since I haven't turned yet, I see Quinn and Leighton with their husbands gaping at the scene my mother is creating. When I look up at Clayton, his rage making the muscles in his jaw clench and jump, I frame his face in my hands and force him to look away from Misty Michaels.

"I need to do this without you actin' like my shield, honey." I see the refusal on the tip of his tongue but shake my head before he can voice it. "I *need* this to finally move on."

His chest swells with a deep breath and I know it costs him, but he nods sharply. I turn, his grip only loosening enough to allow me to face her before tightening again.

He'll give me his silence and allow me to fight my own battle here, but that doesn't mean he's won't make his support known.

I address her in a strong and clear voice. "What do you want?"

She sneers at me, teeth bared, making her weathered face look as evil as I know her to be. "That's no way to speak to your mother."

"You're right," I agree. "But you stopped bein' that a long time ago. So I'll ask you again, Misty. What do you want?"

Her head jerks back as her scowl deepens. "You little ungrateful bitch!"

Clayton's arm spasms, and I know he's close to losing his mind. I reach behind and pat his thigh. I can see a small crowd forming near the restaurant's entrance, but I don't care that people are openly gawking. I'm not going back to the woman who was afraid of what they thought. I'm not the one in the wrong here.

"I'm waiting. Say what you need to, but know this is the only chance I'll allow you the freedom of doin' so."

"I shoulda had the doctor suck you outta me the second he told me I was pregnant. Now I'm stuck with my whore daughter and her disrespectful tongue. You should be thankin' me for keepin' you."

I lean my head against Clayton's chest and laugh. "You have some nerve callin' me a whore when you can't even recall who knocked you up in the first place." I lower my voice, not wanting the whole town to know by morning what I say next. "I've been with two men in my life, *Misty*. One who almost broke me because I was naive enough to think he could follow through on his promise to help me get away, and one who healed me after the first did his best to ruin what you hadn't already. Seein' that the latter is also goin' to be the *last* man I give myself to, I'd say I'm pretty dadgum close to sainthood. You want to believe I'm a whore, then you do so, but when I crawl into bed at night with the man I love with every fiber of my bein', I'm gonna do that knowin' that my life is finally perfect and your opinion no longer matters."

I watch the woman who gave birth to me, the same one who never gave me any love afterward, sputter in shock. I've never spoken back to her. I didn't when I was growing up, still under the impression that I wanted and needed her love. I didn't when I was a teenager, seeking out the wrong company in an attempt to fill the void she created. And I didn't when I begged her to save me. I carried the burden I felt with her inability to care about me for nearly thirty years, but no more. Never again.

"Do me a favor," I finally say when she continues to look confused that I'm not breaking under her verbal abuse. "Pretend you had that abortion. When you see me, Clayton, or anyone else in our family, act like we're invisible. Look right through us, Misty, because we're goin' to do the same to you."

I turn awkwardly in Clayton's stiff grasp and hug my

arms around him. I can feel the power of his fury in the tension-filled muscles that are flexed hard. I ignore her, hoping she'll just leave. With my cheek against his chest, I hear her attempt to speak up.

"Shut your goddamn mouth." Clayton rumbles venom-filled words that seem to explode from deep in his gut. "You don't want to find out what happens if you continue this, Misty. Don't fuck with me, because I will end you if you even so much think about *my* Caroline."

I squeeze him tighter, not in fear or panic over the confrontation with the woman who used to make me feel those things, but to reassure him that I'm fine. When he finally relaxes his body slightly, I know she's left. I keep hugging him for another second until I feel a little more tension leave his body—only then do I look up at him.

"It feels good to forget," I whisper, knowing he under-stands what I'm saying when his anger vanishes instantly. I'd thought he was speaking out of his ear when he ex-plained how he moved on from his own mama's hurt, but not anymore. She'll never deserve my forgiveness, so I'm going to forget her instead—just like he did his.

"Uh, guys?"

Clayton turns us together at Quinn's voice. She looks over the bed of his truck and gives a tiny wave. I scan the other three people at her side and frown when I get to her husband's pale face.

"I don't mean to interrupt what I'm *sure* was about to get interestin' and all, seein' that you just admitted you love my big brother at the same time you put your mama in her place so brilliantly, but my water broke five minutes ago and my vagina-pokin' husband has seemed to forget every year of medical school, because I'm not sure he's breathin' anymore."

16

CLAYTON

"The Fighter" by Keith Urban & Carrie Underwood

- ★ -

"Any news?" Caroline asks, handing me the coffee that she got from the cafeteria.

"Nothin' since the last time Tate came out and said she was about to start pushin'. That was almost three hours ago, Linney."

She grabs my free hand and gives it a squeeze. "These things take some time, honey. She's in good hands. I know you're worried."

"I hate knowin' she's hurtin'." God, just the thought of my baby sister—someone I spent my whole life, until she married Tate, protecting with everything in me—being in pain cuts me deep. I glance over at Maverick, seeing the same worry etched in his face. I can only imagine his is amplified because his wife will be in the same position soon. "It's too soon," I finally whisper, feeling fear claw at me.

"She's only four weeks early, Clayton. I know they had her on bed rest, but they told her they wouldn't stop labor if she went early; they just wanted to give her as much time as they could. They're both goin' to be fine."

My hand shakes as I lift my coffee and take a sip of the black brew. I lean forward in my seat, elbows to knees, and hold the cup in both hands. This is why I crave control. Knowing what will happen, how I can manipulate situations to ensure the outcome I find most favorable, and avoid anything that can cause harm. There isn't shit I can do except let God's will work, and it's tearing me apart.

"How about we talk about what happened back in the parkin' lot of Pit's," Caroline offers in a soft voice.

Just thinking about what happened after supper makes me burn with a whole new rush of conflicting emotions. I'm so fucking proud of her for standing up to her mama, but I hate that she ever had to. I've never wanted to harm a woman before, but Misty has me itching to ruin her.

"Linney," I tell her softly. I knew from her violent reaction months ago from just hearing her mama call her name that her childhood wasn't a good one. I don't want her reliving that just because she thinks she has to give me more.

"I know I don't have to, but it's important to me that you know what I said was true. That what she thinks of me isn't what I am."

I turn my head, not moving from my hunched position. "You think I could ever think of you like that?"

She shrugs, picking at her coffee cup. "I spent my life thinkin' that just because she thought I was a whore, I must have been. It's why I never really dated—until John, that is. I didn't dress provocatively or give people a reason to think that, so as I got older, I realized it was just another way for her to make sure I knew my place in her life." She takes a deep breath. "I'm sure you realize after that confrontation that I was far from planned. She hadn't wanted to stick to Pine Oak, but when she got pregnant with me, there was never a chance she'd make it to some big city and be discovered. Her words, not mine. I have no idea why she kept me, but she did, and because of that she blames me for ruining her grand plans."

"And your father?" I question, sitting up and turning toward her.

She shakes her head, but when her eyes connect with mine, I see the clearness within them. They no longer hold pain, hurt, or care regarding her upbringing.

"She never knew who he was. She had a different man every week while I was livin' with her; I don't imagine it was any different leadin' up to her gettin' pregnant."

"It doesn't bother you?"

"It used to. I think that's just another reason I desperately sucked up any attention John gave me back then. He was the first boy who paid me any mind, and when he promised me a way out from under her thumb, I took it. And I continued to take it, because I believed that was all I deserved."

"Darlin'," I mumble, wrapping my arm around her and pulling her closer, needing that contact.

"I don't feel that way anymore," she continues meekly. "I know now that I was stuck mentally, believin' all the garbage she projected onto me. I might still have times when I get uneasy or shy over too much attention, but it's not like it was then. You have no idea what you've given me, all because you pushed me to look past that fear and explore somethin' I didn't dream I could have."

This woman brings me to my knees. Watching her become stronger each day has been nothing short of humbling.

"I don't need her. I never did. I'm the person I am now because I was too strong for her to break me. I survived her, I survived him, and now I'm bein' gifted you. I meant what I told her, Clayton. Until the day comes that you might not want me, you'll be the last one I give myself to. All of me, I'm yours."

I open my mouth to tell her just how much that means to me and how she's out of her fucking mind if she ever thinks that day would come, but before I can, there's a commotion that pulls my attention away from her.

"I'm a daddy!" Tate bellows with a huge smile, his

chest heaving as he stands in the middle of the waiting room with his hands on his hips.

I turn back to Caroline, but she shakes her head with a nod toward Tate. "Later. We'll finish this later, honey."

Knowing she's right but hating that she has—twice now—given me the words that prove how much she cares for me without me returning them, doesn't feel right. I need to wait to tell the woman who stole my heart weeks ago that I love her when I can take the time to prove it, and as much as I dislike it, that isn't now. I fucking hope she can see the truth in my eyes. I bend toward her and kiss her quickly before standing and grabbing her hand at the same time. We both walk over to Tate, Maverick and Leigh already at his side.

"He's perfect," Tate says with a beaming smile. Realizing that my sister just gave me a nephew, I feel like someone punched me in the chest. "She's the strongest woman I know, thought that before, but after witnessing her bringin' our son into the world I know just how true that is."

"A boy!" Leighton exclaims. She looks up at Maverick. "A boy, Mav!"

"Heard Tate, darlin'," he answers, his voice thick with emotion.

When he looks at me, I see the same overwhelming emotions I'm feeling in his gaze. I swallow what feels like a golf ball and nod. Mav's eyes close and I clench my jaw, but somehow we both manage to get ahold of ourselves, but fuck, it takes one hell of an effort for me to keep from crying like a goddamn baby. I'm so happy for our sister that I feel like I might combust.

I can't believe my baby sister is a mama.

"Y'all ready to meet your nephew?" Tate asks, looking every bit the proud papa he is.

I keep Caroline's hand firmly in mine while we all follow Tate down the hallway. We wait while he pops into Quinn's hospital room to make sure she's decent, but not even a second later he's back and ushering us in. Leighton is first, moving as fast as she can. If I wasn't feeling like I was about to break down and cry, I'd find her waddling that quick funny as hell. Mav follows, stopping to slap Tate's shoulder in silent support.

"Go on, honey," Caroline urges when I don't move from my spot in the hallway.

Before stepping into the room, I release her hand and pull Tate forward. His hug in return is just as tight as mine. "Congratulations, Tate."

"Thanks, Clay. Means a lot."

There's so much I want to tell the man who broke my sister's heart years ago, but I release him and nod instead. He's made her happy since coming back to Pine Oak, and that's all I've ever wanted for Quinn.

Leigh is bawling her head off when we step into the dimly lit hospital room, looking down at Quinn as she smiles at the bundle in her arms. When I look over her shoulder and see my brother finally lose the war over his emotions with wet cheeks and a warm smile, I stop trying to hold mine in and suck in a heavy, choppy breath. Quinn glances up from her son and smiles at me, her chin wobbling like crazy.

"Come meet him," she requests softly.

My vision gets blurry and I step to the side of her bed and get my first glance at the next generation of our family.

"He's an impatient one, but healthy as can be, with lungs stronger than you've ever heard. Doc checked him over and said that for bein' a month early, he's perfect." Quinn lays him down on her thighs, tucking the blanket around his tiny chin to give us a better look at the baby who looks like the spitting image of his parents. "Grayson Ford Montgomery just couldn't wait to meet the best family in the whole wide world."

"He's perfect," Caroline whispers, and I squeeze her hand.

"Oh, Q," Leigh cries softly. "He's the most handsome thing I've ever seen."

"Did good, Quinnie. Did real good."

My sister looks from Mav, when he finishes speaking, and blinks up at me with watery eyes. I reach out, roll my fingertip across Grayson's tiny forehead, and take a rough pull of air into my lungs. His lips purse and his nose scrunches, but his eyes stay shut.

"So proud of you, Quinn," I finally mutter, unable to

resist my new nephew's silky smooth skin and caressing his cheek with my fingertip again.

"Here," she chokes on a tiny sob, lifting her son up toward me.

Caroline jerks her hand away, but with the tiny life being placed into my arms, I don't dare look and see if I can read what's going through her mind. The second I'm holding the seemingly weightless bundle, I never want to give it up. Feelings so foreign to me are hitting hard.

"Jesus, Quinn," I breathe, staring down at Grayson.

"I know, Clay. I *know*."

He isn't even my own son and I already know I'd protect this child with everything I have in me. Knowing that, I can't even fathom how a parent could ever feel anything but unconditional love. I don't have to guess that both my brother and sister are thinking the same thing. We might not have had a mama who cared or a father who could until it was too late, but this boy and any children born into our family will never know that kind of pain. He's got two parents who love each other and will love him fiercely, but he's also got two uncles and the women in their lives who will do the same.

I bend at the same time I lift my arms up and press my lips to Grayson's tiny head before handing him back to his mama.

When I'm finally able to look away and at Caroline, I'm not sure how to read what I see in her eyes. For as long as I can remember I've known I'd never bring a child of my own into the world. The way I'd been raised hadn't shown me anything positive in the way of having my own children. Looking at the woman I can't imagine a life without, with the reminder of what my nephew felt like in my arms, makes me want to be able to see something other than what I've always believed.

17

CAROLINE

"Sunday Morning" by Parmalee

- ★ -

I climb into bed and pull the covers up over my bare legs. I can hear Clayton as he moves through the house, locking up and setting the alarm. He's been quiet since we left the hospital. To be honest, I'm glad for the silence. Watching him holding Quinn and Tate's son shifted something inside of me, something I hadn't been sure was there. Something I hadn't even been sure I had even wanted until I met Clayton. Knowing his past, I was completely unsure if the man I was building a future with wanted the same thing.

Children.

I never thought about that for myself.

Why would I? I was raised by a woman who hated me, hardly tolerated me, and had been one of the main reasons I desperately traded one nightmare for another. I went from living with her hate to just surviving another's. I never would have brought a child into that. Luckily, John had been meticulous about protection and I had never had to deal with that problem.

I've never experienced the positive love of a mother, and I'm not sure that's something I capable of, but seeing Clayton with a baby in his arms and a look of pure, tender love, I started to hope.

I know, though, that if that's something Clayton doesn't want, I will never have it, because there will never be another man for me. My heart only belongs to one man and without him, I'll never bring a child into this world. Knowing that, it feels like a dark cloud has settled over a special night.

"I could hear you thinkin' downstairs, Linney." I jump at the sound of Clayton's voice, so lost in my thoughts I didn't even notice him enter the bedroom.

He starts unbuttoning his plaid button-down, pulling it off and grabbing the white undershirt he had on underneath and yanking it off too. His belt clanks on the floor in the silence after he toes his boots off and then, in one fluid motion, he's got his jeans and boxer briefs off. I don't look away when he straightens and hooks his hands at his hips, studying me with silent consideration.

"We've got two choices, sweetness." His brow is furrowed, but other than that he appears calm. I know my dark cowboy better than that, though. He's holding his control close to his chest. "We can either finish what we were talkin' about in the waitin' room earlier or . . ." He looks down, shakes his head, and, with a heavy breath, glances back at me. "Or you can tell me what I saw in your eyes when you watched me holdin' my nephew."

"I . . . Clayton." My thundering heart jumps into my throat and I feel my lips press together tightly. He waits, but without being able to find the words I need to continue, I lift both my shoulders, silently telling him I need his guidance, because I honestly don't know if I can pick one over the other. Not when I could be getting his love in one breath and losing a piece of my heart in the next.

He steps forward and rounds the bed. I track his every movement until he's standing next to my side of the bed. When his hands leave his hips, I glance down and watch with wide eyes as they both slowly come toward me. He pulls the covers from where I have them tucked into my hips, baring my legs. He makes a sound of disapproval when I start to pull the shirt of his I stole—like every night—to sleep in over my panties, halting me instantly. When he takes my ankles in his strong grip, I close my eyes, not even shocked when he pulls me gently down the bed until my back is no longer against the pillows propped up against the headboard. Even in the heaviness of the moment, his strength is something that amazes me.

His hands push between my legs at the knees and spread them to the side. Then his heavy weight blankets me. Legs between mine, hard length against my panty-covered center, and naked chest over my cotton-covered one. My hands move of their own accord to rest on his back at the same time his arms go under my shoulders, pushing his fingers into my hair and cradling my head in his hands.

"Open your eyes," he orders, and I do so instantly.

His face hovers above mine, eyes searching but guarded. I don't have to guess what he assumed correctly I was thinking back at the hospital, but I know without a doubt that I need him to know one thing before I confirm it.

"I love you," I utter on a whispered breath.

I literally feel my words as they hit him, physically, as his whole body seems to grow larger and harder at once. The fingers tangled with my hair spasm. His chest pushes into mine as it puffs out. And the part of him that fills me with a beautiful pain swells against my sex.

"I love you," I repeat loudly and fiercely, fueled by his reaction. This time, his eyelids droop and his forehead falls to rest against mine. That wide chest of his starts to move rapidly when his breathing speeds up.

"I love you, Clayton Davis."

Then his mouth is on mine and his tongue plays with mine without pause. He kisses me so deeply that my eyes cross and I swear I can feel the earth move. There's so much passion in this kiss, my legs come off the bed to wrap around his hips and my arms tighten around his torso. I frantically try to get closer. We continue to pour

our feelings into that kiss, both of us growing more desperate with each caress of tongues and swallowed groans. When he rips his mouth free, it takes me a moment to shake the intoxication of it off.

"It shouldn't be possible to love you as much as I do, Caroline Michaels, but every single day I feel that grow into somethin' I reckon few ever are blessed to feel. I knew close to four months ago when you sat down next to me that there was somethin' powerful between us. Had no doubts a month later that connection was somethin' I was foolin' myself into thinkin' I could forget about when it snapped into place. And, my sweet Linney, it wasn't long after that that I realized I was made to love you."

He shifts his grasp, his hands coming out from under my head and his thumbs wiping the tears from my face. My whole body shudders as I suck in a wobbly breath.

"I need to know the rest, darlin'," he says with care.

"I'm afraid to give you the rest, Clayton."

He shakes his head. His handsome face relaxes and openly projects his affection. "Nothin' should ever make you afraid, Linney. Not when it comes to me and damn sure not when it comes to our love. I never want you feelin' the fear that keeps your thoughts from me."

My chest smooshes against his as I take a deep and calming breath. "I—I want that," I finally admit.

He holds my worried gaze, not reacting. "You want what?"

"What they have."

I finally lose the brightness of his emerald gaze when his eyes slowly flutter closed. A rush of air fans my face a second later. I hold myself still as my heart pounds in anxious beats.

"Please say somethin', Clayton," I plead when he doesn't move or speak.

"I don't want her here," he finally says, confusing me instantly.

"What?"

"She has no place in our bed, but I also can't let you go long enough to move our talk from this spot."

"Who are you talkin' about?"

"Jess."

My whole body jerks as his ex's name slams into my brain. Confusion as to why he's bringing her up now of all times blends into a hurt I feel slice deep.

"God, Caroline, you're killin' me." His hips press into mine as he shifts his body to rest his elbows in the mattress. "Look at me, baby."

I hadn't realized I stopped. Looking back into his beautiful eyes again, I see the pain inside of them.

"She was pregnant. Right after I finally broke things off, all her schemin' paid off. When she told me, I was going to step up. In my gut, I knew I didn't want that baby, but I would've been there and done my best to give it a good life. However, I wasn't gonna give her what she thought she could trick me into." A slash of pain goes through his features as he grows heavier on top of me, and I know where he's going, hating that woman even more. "When I refused her when she said we should get married right away, makin' it clear to her that would *never* be an option, she knew she'd miscalculated drastically. I never in my life thought she would kill my baby because of it though."

"Clayton," I gasp, moving my hands to cup his strong jaw. "Honey."

"It cut me to the quick, but even though I felt like a piece of my heart had been ripped out, I struggled with feelin' relieved as well. It's fucked-up, I know that, but with her selfishness, I wouldn't be forced to have her in my life because she had my kid."

"I'm so sorry," I tell him, my tears returning.

"I had a mama who couldn't love me and a father who didn't want to until he was dyin'. I didn't know my grand-parents. The only real love I felt was toward my brother and sister. And with them, I saw what havin' shit parents did to kids. I grew up knowin' I didn't want to bring a life into the world without knowin' I'd be capable of what my parents weren't. That didn't change when she killed my baby, Caroline. I can't explain what it felt like holdin' my sister's baby in my arms, but even lovin' that boy instantly, if I didn't have you, I would never want that for myself. You make me *need* everythin' I never wanted."

A giant sob bursts from my lips.

"I told you we were gonna have this talk." He gives me a brief kiss. "I told you that what I wanted for our future would be different from what I wanted with her. I could live without anyone in this whole damn world, but you . . . I couldn't go on without you. I'm a man who knows what he needs, Linney, and that's you. I won't waste time when I know in my marrow that you're made for me to love. Ask me, baby. Ask me what roads we're traveling on."

"Wh-what roads?"

"The ones that collide together and form one indestructible path. One day, one day real damn soon, that road is gonna give you my name and give us a family that will never doubt what parents' love feels like. We both had a rough start, darlin', but there isn't anything we can't weather together. I knew it was time to cowboy up the second my good girl gave me her bad and together we made magic."

I'm crying so hard now, he had to stop talking softly halfway through that. I can see his smiling face, so full of love for me, through the tears swimming in my eyes. I blink frantically, but the tears keep coming. Not even when his lips drop to mine and we drown in each other's kisses do they stop. My sobs echo around the room as he undresses me, only slowing when he pushes himself into my body. By the time he's given me every thick inch, I finally stop crying. The passion between us is a soothing balm to my tears, which dissolve in the overpowering joy tipping me over the edge as I lose myself in the all-consuming sensation of the man I love loving me slow.

18

CAROLINE

"Humble and Kind" by Tim McGraw

- ★ -

You know the old saying when something feels too good to be true, it probably is? Well, there's no doubt to its validity in my eyes. Not after I wake up the next morning and the bubble of perfect love that had formed around Clayton and me pops. Only, when Clayton wakes me up this morning with worry hanging off him like a coat and tells me there's been another fire, the tears don't come. When I call Luke and hear him confirm what Clayton told me, I just feel a sad acceptance of what it means. There's no fear. No panic. Just the knowledge that whatever follows will be okay because I have Clayton to help me find my way through it.

The Sequel is completely gone.

What had been rebuilt and put on the market was just a pile of ash now.

There's also no doubt in anyone's mind that this fire was intentional. No matter what the report said about the first one, everyone now knows that one had been as well. What we don't know, though, is why.

"Talk to me, Linney," Clayton asks with a hint of desperate worry in his tone.

"What do you want me to say?"

"Jesus, baby, you just found out that someone intentionally set fire to the old store and you don't even look upset."

I shrug. "I'm upset, but not because it's gone. It was just an empty space. My dreams aren't tied up in there, and my happiness is not something I can only find in the pages of the books I sold. A few months ago, this probably would have felt a lot different, but then I went explorin' and I've got a path full of somethin' I never dreamed of. I'm stronger now. Too strong to let this break me."

"Fuck, I love you."

A small smile forms on my lips at his words. "The thing that bothers me now, even though I hate thinkin' that someone else might not be able to make a dream of my old space, is that I don't understand why *I'm* bein' targeted. Even though Luke said there was another fire across town at another business, I can't help but feel in my gut this is personal."

"What are you thinkin', darlin'?"

I sigh, shrug, and shake my head. "Do you think . . . Could this be John?"

A flash of anger crosses his face. "Do *you* think it could be?"

"I honestly don't know, Clayton. The John I knew years ago wasn't a good person, but he was an angry drunk who preferred to use his words and strength to hurt someone. He wanted people to know he was powerful in that way. Hiding behind a fire doesn't make sense. I just can't see him wakin' up one day and decidin' today is a good day to become an arsonist."

"Just because he didn't show it then doesn't mean he didn't have more malicious intent hidin' away and waitin' to come out."

"I know, I know. But it just doesn't feel like somethin' he'd do. If he's even still in town, he'd corner me somewhere before he'd hide behind a fire and not let me know he was the one who took more from me. The man I knew would've left no doubt it was him."

Clayton drops his head, looking down at his boots.

"What?"

A little pit of unease opens in my gut when he just shakes his head.

"Clayton. Tell me what's goin' through your head."

"Goddamn," Clayton grunts. "You knew him as a boy, Linney. You don't know him as a man."

"I was with him for close to six years. I might have

started with him when he was a boy, but he was a man when I finally left."

"And you haven't seen or really talked to him in close to another five, darlin'. People change, and you might not know the man that he is today."

I take a calming breath. Placing my palms on the counter, planting my feet on the rungs on the barstool at the kitchen island, I arch my brows at Clayton.

"I asked you to trust me," he finally answers my unspoken silent demand that he continue.

"I do, but I don't need you keepin' somethin' from me because you think I need you to protect me from him. He can't hurt me, even if he is the one behind the fires. He'll never touch me again." The confidence I'm starting to get used to rushes through my body. I can tell the second Clayton realizes that while I trust him completely, I won't back down from this conversation.

"Son of a bitch," he grunts under his breath, studying my face before shaking his head and continuing. "I've had problems with him for a while, Caroline. A lot of those problems are ugly, and I wanted to spare you that shit."

"What did you tell me about the ugly in our past, Clayton? I got you and you got me; all of that stuff we've dealt with in our lives just helped us get to this point. So stop thinkin' I can't handle it and let me show you how strong your love helped me become."

"Fine," he grinds out unhappily. "I've known John

Lewis since his family moved to Pine Oak. He was a middle school punk then, as I'm sure you know, but his arrogance didn't turn dangerous until years later. I never liked him, but I didn't hate the man until more recent years. It started when Jess used him to attempt to make me jealous. Didn't bother me that she was carryin' on with him, but him tryin' to pick a fight with me got real old, real quick. He mighta had a drinkin' problem when you left him, but he developed a drug problem on top of that when he came back to Pine Oak."

"How long has he been back?" I ask, unable to stop the chill that trickles down my spine just thinking about him being so close to where I've settled, even if he never made an attempt at making me aware of that. Just thinking about how easy it could have been for him to inflict pain on me makes my heart race.

"Way I figure, right after you left him. Dates seem to match up."

"I never knew."

"Darlin', he was so strung out, I don't think he knew which way was up, let alone that you were only a half hour, forty-five minutes tops, away."

"Tell me the rest, Clayton. I can see all over your face that there's more."

He runs his fingers through his hair, his naked chest flexing as he does. "He was supplyin' drugs to some of the newer hands here on the ranch back then. I busted him myself when I came back from a night ride checkin' the property after a nasty storm to find him in my fuckin' barn dealin'. He was so high, but he was even more reckless. He took off before the sheriff got here, but not before his strung-out ass took out a fence *and* killed two of my horses on his way out. He didn't even slow, Linney. Blew right through them in his daddy's jacked-up truck. First time I've seen him since was that afternoon outside the diner in Wire Creek. I know he went to jail, heard rehab followed, but I'm not ready to eliminate him from the list of suspects who could be responsible for this just because he supposedly got help."

I shake my head, shocked by what he's telling me.

"I should've told you, but after you confided how bad things were when you were with him, I didn't want you havin' more reasons to fear that man. Not when I had hoped to protect you from that."

"You really think it's him?" A tremor hits me and I shiver, making Clayton push off the counter and walk over to me, pulling me from my seat and into his arms.

"I don't know, darlin', but I'm not goin' to assume it isn't." He presses a kiss to the top of my head and tightens his soothing embrace. "I'm sorry I kept that from you, but I'd do it again if I felt like I could keep you from shakin' like you are right now."

I shift closer and press my face against his chest. Clayton's scent fills my lungs and calms my racing thoughts. "Thank you for tellin' me, honey. I don't like hearin' it, you're right, but it makes me thankful I got out and got another chance at happiness. I'm not convinced it's him, but I'm also not convinced it isn't."

"I'm not gonna let anythin' happen to you. You know that, right?"

"Yeah, honey. If it's all the same to you, I'm goin' to hold off on startin' the process of openin' The Sequel here in Pine Oak. I know Luke doesn't need help at Hazel's anymore, but I'm goin' to give him a call and see if I can work in the—" I stop talking when I feel the man holding me growl, the sound in his chest vibrating against my cheek.

"You ain't workin' in that bar, Caroline. I respect Luke, and your friendship with him and Lucy, but I won't have you workin' in Hazel's when I know how rowdy that crowd is."

"Luke won't let anything happen to me, honey."

"Luke can't watch you *and* run that place at the same time. If you're worried about money, don't be. You never have to work another day if you don't want to."

I untangle myself from his hold and narrow my eyes at him. "I will not sit at home and do nothin' while you bust your tail all day, Clayton Davis. I'm not an idle woman, but even if I were, I won't be like *her*." I poke him in the chest, the thought of his vile ex and how she just wanted to use him for his money making me see red at his implication that I should be a kept woman and live off his hard work.

He wraps his hand around my finger when I poke him

one more time, and I almost melt into a puddle when he smiles that devastating grin of his. "Calm down, darlin'. You know damn well I don't think you're with me for my money. If you want to keep busy until you're ready to open the store here in town, you can take over the accounting for Davis Auto Works and here on the ranch. I hate dealin' with that shit, so you'd be doin' me a favor."

He had already successfully dashed my ire with that smile, but learning that he trusts me with something so important to him—his ranch and family business—a whole new emotion hits me, and hits hard.

"Clayton," I breathe.

"Don't go givin' me breathy Claytons now, sweetness," he warns, pressing against me and pulling me close by the hips so that I don't miss his erection.

"I really wanna be bad with you right now," I shame-lessly admit, feeling a rush of arousal curl low in my belly and wrap around the base of my spine.

"Fuck, I love you," he rumbles, bending enough to pull me into his arms. My legs go around his body and my eyes all but cross when his hardness presses firmly against my aching core.

"I'd love to help take some work off your plate. I won't have you payin' me, but I meant it when I said I wasn't an idle woman."

"You keep givin' me this greedy-for-my-cock pussy and I'm pretty sure you'll be the one payin' me."

"You're naughty." I giggle, speaking against his neck,

kissing my way across his skin, and feeling the heat of his words bathe me in intoxicating pleasure. I rock my hips, wishing my lounge pants weren't in the way. "I love it when you show me your bad."

He hums, his fingers tightening on my bottom when I bite the thick column of his neck. Even with my pants and his jeans between us, my belly starts to flutter. My hips rock and roll quicker as his hold on me turns just a hair shy of painful. Thinking about his hands leaving bruises on my tender skin oddly only makes me hotter. His erection rubs me in the most toe-curling spot, and from that contact alone, I drop my head back, seeing the ceiling for just a second before my eyes roll back and close; then I come with his name on my lips.

"God fuckin' damn, that's the hottest thing I've ever seen, darlin'. You comin' from just rubbin' yourself against my cock, fuck," he groans, pulling me harder against his erection, pressing firmly against my sensitive sex and making me whimper. "My good girl doesn't need any help bein' bad anymore, does she? I'm about to love you so hard, you'll think I'm still inside you for days. So vividly that you'll take one step, feel what my hard does to you, and come from just the thought of me takin' you alone."

"Yes," I mewl. "Please."

"Go get in our bed. I want you waitin' for me, spread so wide, offerin' me that sweet pussy so I can eat my fuckin' breakfast in bed. I'm goin' to call Drew and let him know I'm takin' a sick day."

I jump down from his hold, my whole body alive and craving his promises. I don't even spare him a glance before I'm sprinting through the house, tossing my clothes as I go, and following his every command. Then, true to his words, he joins me a few minutes later and spends the day showing me just how delicious breakfast in bed can be.

19

CAROLINE

"Make You Mine" by High Valley

"**I**'m gonna kill her."

Lucy makes a snarling sound in her throat, backing up Leighton's threat without words.

I keep my mouth shut but grab Leighton's hand before she can leave the table at which Jana had told her, firmly and without room to argue, to "sit down and not move from that spot" not even five minutes after walking into her bakery. I feel the wide-eyed stares of the people in the shop around us, but it oddly doesn't bother me, proof that I really am becoming stronger. The only thing I care about in this moment is the nasty woman causing a scene inside my boyfriend's sister-in-law's bakery. His very, very pregnant sister-in-law's bakery. And that woman is going to find out just what the new me is capable of.

"You might think you've got him," Jess continues in a snarky tone. "Hell, you might even keep his attention for a little while, but he'll be back. He always comes back. No woman stands a chance at changin' that."

"You stupid bitch. Smartest thing he ever did was scrape you off, and he wasn't stupid enough to come back to you once since then. You can be damn sure he isn't gonna do it now," Leighton snaps with fury in her words.

"We have a history!" Jess shrieks, her beautiful face turning hideous and revealing her true nature.

I stay silent and study Clayton's ex. Jess really is lovely, I'll give her that, but she's the kind of woman who thinks that beauty is the be-all and end-all. The type that *only* has their beauty going for them and it really doesn't get them as far as they're convinced it does. Every time she throws more nasty words around, her shoulders start shaking with temper, her long blond hair swinging. Her blue eyes are cold, calculating, and full of vicious evil. She's taller than me and bustier than me, with curves I'll never have.

And I've never felt more beautiful.

"Your desperation is embarrassing," I finally say, low and steady, not backing down when that evil gaze homes in on me.

I stand and step in front of Leighton when Jess moves forward. Her eyes track my movements like a predator hunting its prey. Before Clayton, I would've curled into myself and backed down instantly under the weight of her stare and impending confrontation. Now, though, I'm ready to take this horrible woman on, and there's no way in hell I'm letting her close enough to Leighton to have even a slight chance of harming her or the baby.

"How does it feel to have my sloppy seconds?" she mocks.

I roll my eyes. "Bless your heart, honey. You really believe that, don't you? Insinuatin' a man as incredible as Clayton Davis could ever be sloppy seconds to any woman is pathetic and insultin'. You might think what you had with *my* man is worthy of bein' some second-hand, used-goods kinda love, but that handsome cowboy has never loved another woman until me. You were just a way to pass time until we found our way to each other."

She moves closer, stepping on my sandal-covered feet with her boots and making a shooting pain jolt through my body when she rolls her weight onto my toes. I don't give her the pleasure of flinching, though. I hold myself strong and true, unwilling to give her the upper hand.

"I was pregnant with his baby," she hisses, thankfully low enough that the people eating farther away can't hear.

Again, I don't react. Not even when I hear Leighton gasp as the secret Clayton kept from his family unfolds. I see Lucy start to stand in my peripheral vision, but I wave her off.

I might not care what the gawkers around me think anymore, but I won't allow Jess to hurt Clayton by bringing something so painful to light.

Moving my face closer, I sneer at her. "Correction, *bitch*, you tricked him and then *killed* his baby. Even if you ever had a chance at experiencin' the beauty of his love, you were dead to him when you showed him how nasty he already knew you were by doin' that."

I can tell she hadn't planned on me knowing the truth, but when her hand comes out and cracks against my cheek, I lose the upper hand.

"That is enough!" I hear Jana bellow from behind the counter.

"I'm fine, Jana," I call in her direction, pressing my hand against my cheek and not looking away from Jess.

"I'm gonna kill her," Leighton grumbles, repeating her threat angrily behind me, but thankfully, she doesn't move. I feel her knees bouncing against the back of my legs, so I don't need to turn to make sure she's still sitting. I'm not going to have another pregnant woman go into labor because she got too excited at the crazy that keeps invading my life.

"You can have that hit, Jess. I'd be mad too if I lost someone as amazin' as Clayton, but honey, you never did deserve him. I want you to really listen now. I'm gonna marry that man. In fact, he can't wait to get his ring on my finger. I didn't have to trick him into wantin' that. When the day comes that I'm blessed enough to share somethin' as beautiful as a child we created with our love, I'll be thankin' my lucky stars to have a gift that incredible. And we'll have that baby, Jess. It will be one that we both enjoy the hell outta workin' to get—without tricks and lies. We're gonna raise a house full of babies on that ranch. Babies we would have tomorrow, we want that blessin' built from our love that bad. Both of us. And sweetheart, I'm gonna keep lovin' Clayton so hard he'll feel that long after we've both left this earth."

"You stupid bitch. Clay doesn't believe in marriage." She cackles, the sound evil and malevolent, either not hearing me or really believing, after years of not having him, that Clayton might be pining away for her.

I press my hand against her breastbone, pushing her out of my face. After I get her a step away from me, I pull my phone from my back pocket and bring up Clayton's name. I hold up a finger in Jess's face and wiggle it a little before pointing down at my phone and tapping the speakerphone button. Ringing fills the shocked silence at the PieHole and this time I don't care that our audience is making an attempt to get a little closer and hear us better.

"Hey darlin'," Clayton answers, his voice soft and happy. I picture him smiling that heart-pounding smile and my own grows.

"Honey," I answer lightly, not wanting him to hear just how tense I am, but I should've known he'd hear it anyway. My cowboy knows his woman.

"What's wrong, Linney?"

"Nothin' I can't handle. You have a second?"

I hear him speak to someone, hear him moving around

a moment later before the click of a door shutting comes over the line. "Always got a second for you, baby."

"I don't want to keep you, I know you've got the doc out there checkin' on things."

"It's fine, Linney. Just finished with the last foal. I've got time before we move on to the fillies and colts."

"All right, honey." I pull the phone away and whisper to Jess. "Listen carefully." When her eyes flash, I pull the phone back up and address Clayton again. "You wanna get married, handsome?"

"You free in an hour, sweetness?" he answers immediately.

"I'm a little tied up right now, but I think an hour could be doable."

"I'll meet you at the courthouse then."

I laugh, feeling his love through the line wrapping me up in a cocoon of happiness. I don't even care if this didn't start out serious. I can't think of anything better than being his wife. I want this. As crazy fast as it is, I think I knew he was my forever the second he bought me a whiskey and promised to show me bad. "Only if you promise to start working on giving me those babies we both want right after our date at the courthouse."

The rumble of his deep chuckle comes through the line and I find my smile growing even bigger until my cheeks burn from the sheer insanity of my grin.

"My girl's got an itch to be bad?"

I hear Lucy and Leighton start snickering as heat

crawls over my skin. I might be ready to ignore the busy-bodies and nosy old biddies, but I bet any woman would blush hearing Clayton Davis make an announcement like that to a roomful of people. Difference is, I don't even care anymore. Let them know how much I love being a bad girl.

"I like the way you think, honey," I say softly, my eyes on the red-faced woman a foot in front of me. "But I think I'll take lovin' you slow before you love me bad."

"I love you, Linney," he drawls slowly in the erotic way that only Clayton can achieve with the deep raspy tones of his voice.

"I love you, Clayton."

"Linney?" he calls before I have a chance to say good-bye.

"Yeah, honey?"

"You let Jess know if she ever comes near you again, not even my woman callin' and givin' me her sweetness will be enough to keep her safe from my anger."

The woman in question jerks her head and gapes at the phone in my hand. I'm not even surprised that he knew about her being here. There isn't anything that gets by him, especially when it comes to my well-being.

"There won't be a safe place left in Pine Oak for her if she pulls that shit again," he says, the fury in his words unmistakable.

"You're on speaker, Clayton," I tell him, not taking my eyes off Jess.

"Good, baby. Maybe she'll heed my words this time

and not twist them up in her head to be whatever crazy shit she's convinced herself of this time. You enjoy your time with the girls, but when you finish you better get that sweet ass home so I can get my ring on your hand."

"What?" I gasp.

His deep, low laughter is the only answer I get before he disconnects the call with his parting shot still ringing in my ears. He doesn't just shock the nasty woman who interrupted my girl time though. He also floors me as well. I had been joking. I wanted to put his awful ex in her place, but the second the words left my mouth it became something else. I can't help but feel a little anxious over what will happen when I go home. I don't know if he's serious but hope he is, even if it makes us both crazy. When you know, you know. But the part of me that's completely owned by him can't stop the rush of pure pleasure I get when I think that he might have been planning for this if he really does have a ring.

"Holy cow," Leighton gasps breathily.

"Oh my *God*!" Lucy screams.

"I knew that sexy brooder would be a scorcher!" Jana bellows from her position behind the pie displays. "Just knew he'd give it real good."

With a pounding heart that has nothing to do with the showdown I just went through, I give Jess one last arch of my brow and let my whiskey-filled teacup boil over one more time. "Get out of my face, Jess. Get out of Leighton's place. And learn something from today."

I turn, my ponytail slapping across her face, and return to my seat at the table I had been sitting at before she stormed into the PieHole and started throwing her crap all over the place.

Clapping my hands, I look between Leighton and Lucy. "So, where were we?"

20

CAROLINE

"No Matter Where You Are" by Us the Duo

When I pull into the drive to the ranch, butterflies erupt in my gut. It's still early in the afternoon, so I know Clayton isn't going to be in the house, but that doesn't ease my nerves, but with the size of the Davis ranch, finding him is going to be like hunting for a needle in a haystack. I pull my car into my spot next to Clayton's truck and lean back against the headrest, closing my eyes, thinking about what could be waiting for me. The steady breeze from my air-conditioning cools my overheated skin in the process.

As anxious as I feel, I'm not going to be shy and timid about it. Not anymore. Even if he was joking, I have no doubt it'll one day happen for us. I'd be lying, though, if I didn't admit that I'd be disappointed now that the thought is in my head.

I want to be his.

I want him to be mine.

In the forever way that binds us legally and in the eyes of God.

I want to spend the rest of my life with Clayton Davis while he gives me bad and gives me the power to find myself with the confidence his love provides me.

A loud pounding pulls me out of my thoughts with a scream. My knees slam against my steering column as I almost come out of my skin. My eyes snap open and my hand flies to my chest as I look out the driver's-side window. My heart is still thundering in my rib cage, the lingering rush of panic from being caught off guard while I daydreamed still making it hard to focus.

Clearly having had enough of my wide-eyed staring, Clayton thumps his cowboy hat brim as he studies me through the window. With his hat farther up on his head, I can see his face clearly without shadows. His brows are pulled tight in confusion, but a small smirk is curling his lips. He shakes his head a few times, that smirk turning into a full grin, before reaching out to pull open my door.

I still don't move. I can't even blame it on the fact that he scared the crap out of me while I had been in la-la land. Nope. I don't move because he's looking at me in a way that has sucked the air out of my body and melted all my bones.

"Linney, love," he rasps, "you look cute as hell right

now, but I need you to stop lookin' like shock's got you trapped and get outta the car so I can get you in my arms."

"You scared me," I whisper, shaking my head in the smallest movements. So much for being a big brave girl. I was a fool to think I could handle a conversation of this magnitude without feeling a little trepidation.

"I noticed that, darlin'."

"You don't sound upset about it." I huff out a breath and cross my arms over my chest. Clayton's eyes move down and I follow his gaze to see that my flowy tank is giving him one heck of a show, the shirt's front now pulled low with my arms being crossed. The tops of my breasts and some of my white lace bra peek out of the wide scoop neck. I roll my eyes when he still doesn't look away, uncrossing my arms and pulling the material up. "A gentleman wouldn't have looked, Clayton."

"Sweetness, when it comes to you there isn't anything gentlemanly about the thoughts that constantly keep me company."

"Well . . ." I trail off, not having a good retort. "I didn't even show you much. You'd think I didn't keep you satisfied the way you're reactin' to a small glimpse of my boobs. Next time I'm tryin' to throw a fit, you could at least not be all swoon-worthy and distractin'."

"Linney, all it would take for me to react and be ready to feel your heat around my cock is you walking into a room. You don't need to give me a tease. But the lace was a bonus. . . ."

244 - Harper Sloan

"You're incorrigible." I sigh with a smile, turning off my car and getting to my feet between the car and Clayton's body when he doesn't move to give me more space.

His hands come up, fingers brushing against my cheeks. I rest mine at his waist and tip my head up to study my dark cowboy as he gazes at me. His eyes devour me, his hands not idle as he drags his fingertips down the column of my neck and down my bare arms until he reaches my elbows. Then he repeats his trail back up until he's holding me with his palms right under my jaw. He pushes his fingers lightly into my hair as best as he can with it up in a ponytail, and his thumbs rub against my cheeks with slow glides that awaken every inch of me.

"Hey," he whispers in a bold tone that makes his already deep voice sound a few degrees deeper. Velvet and sandpaper.

"Hey," I parrot back, sounding like I just ran a marathon. The way he's looking at me right now, *this* is something I've never seen from him. This, right here, is my dark cowboy giving me everything silently. Himself, his love, our future. All of it is shining bright down on us. The warm buzz that travels over my skin has nothing to do with the summer Texas sun high in the sky.

My fingers flex, doing nothing more than move against his stone-like muscles, as I make no attempt to gain purchase on his skin. My feet shuffle forward until I feel the toes of his cowboy boots. My hands go behind his back as I press my body against his and tip my head up. His back flexes under my touch, but other than that, he doesn't move an inch. Just gazes down at me, holding me gently.

"I got a lot I want to say about your call earlier, Caroline," he tells me softly. "You've got my head all twisted up, though, and I can't figure out if now is the time to say even half of the shit that's rollin' around without freakin' you out. But you brought it up, and now I don't think I *can* sit on it any longer."

The rapid tattoo of my heart has my breathing speeding up, but with his bright green eyes showing me nothing but the enormity of his love, I feel it—the fearlessness that only Clayton brings out in me.

"It's time," I rush without hesitation.

His face gets soft and he bends slightly to press his lips lightly against mine. He doesn't deepen the kiss, just gives me a brief peck before lifting his head a degree as he keeps his eyes locked on mine. "Yeah?"

"Oh, yeah." My breathy affirmation is met with his eyes flashing with pleasure, the corners of his mouth tipping up, and the laugh lines around his eyes coming out. He adjusts his hold, his hands falling down a little until his palms are resting against either side of my neck.

"You . . . God, Linney," he drones, shaking his head but still smiling. "First, you're okay?"

Knowing instantly he's referring to the fact that I had words with his ex, I nod. "I'm fine, honey."

"When I got word that Jess was at the PieHole throwin' her shit around, it wasn't pretty. I almost took off Drew's head when he reminded me I couldn't do a single thing with the doc out lookin' over the horses and two buyers out from Montana. I didn't give one a damn about my responsibilities here when you are and will always be more important than anything else. If you hadn't called me when you did, I woulda been there in a second, not givin' one fuck about how much money I'd lose walkin' away from those Montana folks."

"I'm fine," I stress, hoping he understands that I mean it.

"I know. I just can't seem to help myself when it comes to you, darlin'. The thought of you feelin' anything other than happiness and love isn't somethin' I enjoy too much."

I tighten my arms around his body and lean up on my toes to attempt to get closer than our height differences allow, wanting him to really see me clearly.

"Clayton Davis, you've given me nothin' but happiness for over four months now, and I have no doubt you'll continue to do so for a long while, but there'll be times that even *you* can't control everything. Life might toss us some ugly. But I'm ready to take it on now if it does. Trust that I'm not goin' to break just because some of that ugly tries to creep around us."

"Trustin' you has nothin' to do with me wantin' to protect you and keep you safe from all of that, Linney."

"And that, honey, is what makes me feel like I'm strong enough to take on anything. Knowin' that you care that much, that you'll be there to keep me from trippin', gives me the confidence to finally live free of fear and worry.

There isn't a dadgum thing on this green earth that has the power to douse that. Not anymore."

"You want the rest?" he asks after holding my gaze for a few minutes, the weight of my words rolling over us.

I nod, his thumbs rubbing against my jaw as I do.

He releases his hold on my neck, drags his work-roughened hands down my skin until he's got my wrists in his hold, and unwraps my arms from around his body. Silently, he places my palms on his shoulders and leans down. The brim of his hat drags over the top of my head while he continues to get so close I can feel the heat of his lips against mine.

"Hold on," he rasps, confusing me.

When he grabs me at the back of my thighs and lifts, I squeal out in shock before wrapping my arms around his neck and pressing my chest into his face in order to keep my balance. Miraculously, I manage to stop acting like a weirdo long enough to grab his hat as it's knocked off with the force of my freak-out. Keeping my legs tight, I lift my chest out of his face and release the arm holding his hat to place it back on his head. When the hat blocks my view, I pull it back off and plop it on my own head. Mindlessly, I use my free hand to run my fingers through his thick, unruly hair. His body moves as he laughs softly and my hand freezes in its third pass.

"You look good in my hat, darlin'."

I shrug, the movement making his hat fall down over my forehead.

"Though I should probably get you one that fits better," he jokes.

I lift my hand back off his shoulders to adjust the too-large hat. Not wanting the anticipation to get thicker, I ignore his joke. Mentally, I take one last swing at the walls I had used to protect me for my whole life and give the man holding me everything. I know he sees the enormity of my feelings written all over my face when his whole body jolts and his eyes darken. "You've got me now, handsome. Time to give me the rest."

He starts walking, not looking away from me and me not looking away from him. When he turns us from the house and toward the stables, I frown in confusion.

"Trust me?" he questions, not missing a beat, knowing me well.

"Always," I answer emphatically.

His chest expands with my answer like that one word was everything to him. He enters the stable that houses his personal horses. I don't ever make it my mission to come in here with all the black-eyed beasts, but I know enough about this place that when he stops at the last stall, chills break out.

Onyx.

I know very little about him, but I heard Clayton and Drew talking about him and what I discovered broke my heart. He's a pure black Arabian horse that Clayton saved. I don't know all the details, but something along the lines of Onyx's old owners sold him for meat in exchange for cash. When a shipment of horses was stopped on its way to Canada, one of Clayton's old friends called him for help in placing the fifteen horses on their way to slaughter. No one wanted Onyx, so Clayton loaded him up and brought him back to the ranch.

That was about three months ago, and according to what I've overheard, Clayton spends every spare second he isn't needed elsewhere working with Onyx. When I first came here I remember seeing Onyx from a distance as he bucked and bucked, going wild in his desire to be left alone and even though I feared him immensely, I felt drawn to the beast.

I feel the horse's eyes on me as Clayton brings us farther in, and I shiver in his arms.

"You doin' all right, darlin'?"

I nod, not trusting myself to verbally answer without fear in my voice.

"I wouldn't bring you in here if I didn't think Onyx was ready to finally meet you."

I jerk my wide eyes from the black beast and look at Clayton. "What?"

"Knew the second I saw Onyx he was meant for you. He's a fighter. Hell, he'd fight the wind if he thought it was tryin' to get in his way. He's beyond loyal to those he lets close though. You earn that from him and he'll protect you from everything and anything. Includin' that damn wind. I knew the second I found him that there was only one person a warrior like Onyx was built for."

Shocked by his words, I can't do anything but drink in my handsome man's serious expression. When I feel something nudge my back, I jump in Clayton's arms. His whole face grows soft and full of affection.

"Told you," he grunts, tipping his chin in the direction behind me.

I turn, finding Onyx close to my back, his eyes focusing completely on me. When I don't move, he bumps me again with his nose and makes a show of blowing air through his nostrils. Clayton turns us so that his back is to Onyx, allowing me to study the beast without turning my neck so harshly. Something in the way the horse is looking at me sends a rightness-filled calm through me. I lift one hand and slowly move it toward Onyx. His tail swishes, and before I have a second to let myself fear him, he bumps the tip of his nose against my palm. He does this twice more before I find myself smiling at his antics and rubbing my hand against the slope of his head. If he were a cat, I imagine he'd be purring loudly.

"He likes you," Clayton says softly, kissing me against my neck. "I've been waitin' for this moment, and darlin', I had no doubts that you two would click instantly. You haven't been around horses enough to understand, but you've just become the most important person to him and all you did was give him your trust. Onyx and me . . . we've got that in common. All it took was one touch from you and you became our everything."

I keep caressing Onyx, but feel emotion grow into a thick ball in my throat. "Honey," I breathe, not capable of more.

"It sounds like a pile of shit, but I promise you, Linney, I mean everything I just said."

"He's just a horse. A horse that just wanted to be petted."

Clayton laughs, his hilarity jolting my body. "Darlin', in the time that Onyx has been here, he hasn't willingly let a soul touch him. He tolerates what's needed to cool him down after a ride, and that's usually done with a lot of bullshit from him. I can feel him itchin' to buck even me, someone he likes slightly more than toleratin', right off when I'm walkin' him."

I lift my hand from Onyx and frown at Clayton. "You're basin' this all on the fact that he nose-bumped me a few times?"

"No, I'm basin' this on the fact that he came to you, asked for you, and even now is tryin' to get closer to you."

I turn to glance at the horse and see that Clayton wasn't lying. He's pushing himself as far into the opening in his stall door as he can get. When he realizes that isn't working, he becomes agitated. I reach out to press my hand against his nose again, gasping when he stills instantly and presses gently against my hand.

"Trust me?" Clayton questions again.

I look away from Onyx and nod, feeling a rightness click into place.

"I'm goin' to let you go so I can get the horses ready. You okay with that?"

My heart warms, knowing that he's kept me in his arms for the past five minutes because he knew I was fearful of being this close to an animal I don't understand well enough to not fear. I press my lips to his before nodding.

"Then let's get ready for our first ride together, darlin'. Those roads collided and it's time we check out the new path before us."

Oh, wow.

Reluctantly, I slowly lower myself with his help until I'm standing and watching as Clayton gets Onyx and Dell, his horse, ready. When Clayton opens Onyx's stall, the horse walks to my side instantly and doesn't leave his spot next to me. His solid mass presses against me in a soothing way. I don't even realize I'm running my hands over his coat, loving the feeling of his powerful softness, until he makes a sound that makes me think he's enjoying the attention. For the first time, I feel no fear being near one let alone two horses, but I have a feeling that has a lot to do with Clayton and my trust in him, even if I feel the connection to Onyx that he was speaking about. When I look at Dell, a horse I know has the most even temperament and calm nature, I shiver and push my side into Onyx, who huffs air out. Maybe Onyx doesn't scare me as much because, him being solid black, those seemingly all-knowing eyes aren't so noticeable. Dell, though, is the opposite of Onyx. Dell is pure white. The way his eyes contrast against his coat makes them look even more arresting.

"I know, big guy," I tell Onyx softly, still looking at Dell. "He creeps me out too."

Clayton chuckles. I ignore him and keep talking to the horse at my side. "I should tell you, I don't know a lick about horses, but I promise to respect you. Just . . . I don't know, try and not go crazy and buck me off you. I don't want to break my back and have to be put in a home."

This time Clayton bursts out in a deep belly laugh.

"What?"

"God, I have no idea what I'd do without you in my life."

"That's good. Maybe that means you won't ship me off to live in a home when I break my back and become a burden."

Watching him tighten something on the saddle before turning, I drink him in. His full lips are smiling, the shadow of his facial hair along his jaw making him look rugged and sinful. But it's the brightness shining from his eyes that holds me captive.

"There will never be a day that I won't have you in my arms when I wake, Caroline. I don't care what's thrown at us in this life, me needin' to care for you will never be somethin' I look at as a burden. I'll spend every second of every day showin' you that I deserve that honor." He steps closer and lifts his hat off my head, placing it opening side up on a shelf near us. "Even if you get thrown from a horse and break your back—even then will I love every second that I'm blessed with you in my life."

I feel my chin tremble and I know if he keeps going, I'm going to burst into tears.

"You ready to take a ride with me, darlin'?"

I swallow thickly, my chin still fighting with my emotions, and nod.

Clayton moves to help me mount Onyx. Knowing that he wouldn't be putting me on the back of this horse if he wasn't confident in the animal's abilities eases some of my nerves. I listen intently as he continues to explain everything I need to know as Onyx waits patiently for me to climb onto his back.

"Left foot in the stirrup and pull your body upward. Take your time and swing your other leg around. Just hug his back with your legs and slip your other foot into the stirrup. I'll hold his reins, but he's well trained, darlin', and I suspect he'll be statue still while you get sorted."

"He's not gonna just take off with me danglin', right?"

I'll give Clayton credit, if it weren't for the slight twitch of his lips, I wouldn't know how bad he wants to laugh at me.

"Trust, darlin'."

"Trust. Right. I do."

"Then get your hot ass in the saddle, baby. We've got plans."

It takes me two tries to get myself up and into the

saddle. True to Clayton's words, Onyx doesn't even flinch, letting me get myself positioned with my back straight and orienting myself to balance with my weight centered to my bottom like I was told. Clayton walks around and makes sure my legs are in the proper position, giving me a few tips as he does.

"When we start ridin', keep your toes up, ankles stable, and your heels pointing downward. You let Onyx lead."

"What do I do with these?" I ask, holding up the reins he just placed in my left hand.

"That is how you steer. A gentle touch against Onyx's neck will signal the movements that you want. Move across his right side to go right and left side to go left. Keep them in your left hand, right hand on the saddle. We'll work on all of this another time, but even though I know he'll guide you without help, following me, I still want you to know what to do on the off chance that he decides to show off."

"Okay." I gulp. "Right for right and left for left. Seems easy enough."

"If somethin' happens and you need him to move quick, grab the reins in both hands and gently pull or squeeze in the direction you need him to go. It's not often that it happens to our horses, but if you need to emergency steer him, that's how."

I nod, filing that information under *let's not think about what could happen that would require emergency steering*, and give Clayton a nod. "How do I get him to turn on?"

His lips twitch again. "Squeeze with your legs and let him know you're ready."

"That's it?"

He nods. "Yeah, baby, that's all it takes."

"You'll be close?"

"Always, Linney. Always."

21

CLAYTON

"I'm Gonna Love You" by Jamie Lawson

She's a natural.

You'd never know she's never ridden or that before this, she'd been afraid of every horse she encountered. Her smile is huge, carefree, and full of life. The only time I've ever seen her looking more beautiful is when she's under me and gasping out my name.

We've been riding about ten minutes, but five into it she let go and I quickly changed our course so I could watch her longer.

It didn't take me long to get everything I needed in order. I texted Leighton shortly after I got off the phone with Caroline earlier and asked her to give me a heads-up when Caroline was on her way home. Luckily, by then I'd finished with the doc and successfully sold eight horses to the buyers who had come down. Drew waved me off when I asked if he needed help, but the crooked grin on his face told me he was doing it more because he knew what I had planned and not because he didn't actually need help.

The rest I'm hoping like hell Maverick took care of. Otherwise I'm going to be winging it and not giving Caroline a fraction of the romance she deserves. I can't remember a time I've ever cared about that, but I want to give her memories that have her feeling our love for the rest of our lives.

Moving my hips, I lean back slightly. Dell instantly slows his trot. I wait, giving Onyx time to follow my lead, pleased as hell when he does so without hesitation. I hear Caroline gasp, but keep my eyes on Onyx while he follows Dell to the tie-off post. Dismounting, I loop Dell's reins around the post before taking Onyx's from Caroline and doing the same. Both horses stretch their necks to drink from the large watering basin as I move to her side and, with my hands on her hips, help her to her feet. Only when she's grounded do I look over her head.

This spot has always been my favorite within all our acres: the peak where our land is the highest and the trees are few and far between. From here, you can see part of Maverick's land to the west, where he has a few housing structures for the riders enrolled in his rodeo school. The other side is all Davis land. Nothing but green earth and blue skies. Untouched by any man and unblemished by any structure aside from the fence that used to keep cattle locked in.

"I used to come out here when I needed to get away. When my pops was drunk out of his mind and fightin' with anyone who would look at him. When Quinn's cryin' got too much to bear, knowin' I couldn't fix what hurt her or bring the only person she wanted back. And when Maverick left town, I found myself out here more and more. Wouldn't do anything more than just look out across our land, focusin' on nothin' and wishin' more than anything I could've protected them more. This was the only place on this ranch that felt like home to me, even after my pops passed away. Here the only thing I had to worry about was myself. Still, after he passed, and this place became all mine, I never felt like it was home unless I was out here." I pause, walking over to the table that Maverick set up for me, grabbing the bottle of red wine sitting atop it and filling the two glasses placed next to it. "I felt like that my whole life, Linney. Never findin' peace in my own house, on my own land, long enough to let me find *my* home—my sanctuary. It wasn't until a beautiful good girl, lookin' to be bad, sat down next to me in a dirty bar. There you were, surrounded by drunks and bikers, lookin' like you stepped out of the pages of a magazine—you were pure temptation. That moment, before we even left Hazel's, I felt like somethin' had snapped in place deep inside my chest. I found my sanctuary—my *home*—that night in your arms. I found it and almost lost it forever after just one night. You'll never know how thankful I am that I got my second chance. Knowin' that we might never have found this if I woulda let my stubborn pride keep me from findin' you—that kills me."

Her wide brown eyes stay locked on mine when I stop talking and hand her a glass of wine, then take a sip from my own glass.

"One day, we're gonna bring our children here, Linney, and you're goin' to sit on a blanket between my legs while they run all over this damn hill. Laughter will echo across our land while we bask in what our love created. There'll never be a day that I don't love you. Not one. I wasn't plannin' on you, baby, and I know you weren't plannin' on me, but sometimes what we need to finally feel whole is what we least expect. You are that for me."

"Clayton," she whispers, tears filling her eyes.

"Just a second, darlin'," I interrupt, bending to kiss her nose before taking our glasses and placing them on the table next to the picnic basket.

"Clayton," she repeats softly; this time I hear her tears in her voice.

"Sweetness, one second." When I turn, seeing the worry in her eyes, I take her face between my hands gently. "What is it, Linney?"

She swallows, her whole head moving in my grasp as she does. Her mouth moves, opening and closing, but no words come. I relax my grip and bend to press our lips together. It doesn't take long before our kiss turns hungry and I regretfully pull my mouth from hers.

"You good?" I ask with a smile that grows when her eyes don't open for a few more pounding beats of my heart. Finally her lashes flutter, and she looks at me in a daze.

"I just . . . I don't want you to think that I expect you to . . . I don't know! I mean, I was jokin', wantin' to let that nasty woman know she was wrong about you, but the second the words left my mouth I . . . I'm freakin' out here, Clayton!"

There really is no way to describe what it feels like when all the pieces of you that had been out of sorts your whole damn life start to click together. When all those years of twisting them up because you couldn't figure out what you were missing are unraveled in an instant when you find what your purpose in life truly is. For me, I knew my place was here on the ranch and that my protection and love went to my siblings and only them. Because of my parents, I knew allowing myself to find what Maverick and Quinn had would be something too risky. I had resigned myself to that life, only recently feeling like I was spiraling, with my siblings no longer needing me. But then I met this woman and those pieces started shifting until I knew without a doubt that my crazy, shy, wild-when-she-wants woman was my purpose. My reason for waking and my reason for breathing. The woman who made the risk of loving her unquestionably worth it, because with her love, that risk is really just a reward. I would have done this weeks ago, but it wasn't until today that I knew it was time. I take her hands in mine and wink when her eyes grow a little wider. Not looking away from her, I drop to my knee. Her hands jerk in my grasp as she watches me. I inhale deeply and start putting mental pictures of this moment away so I'll never forget what it looks like to ask for forever with the person who holds your purpose.

"Caroline Lynn Michaels," I start, having to pause when a lump of emotion crawls up my throat before continuing. "There will never be a time in my life, yours, and whatever waits for us beyond that when my heart won't beat a little quicker because of what my love for you does to me. You came into my life and showed me how wrong I'd been about so many things without even tryin'. I never wanted more for myself than what I had runnin' the ranch and seein' my family thrive, but then your love made me need things I hadn't ever allowed myself to think of before. Without you, there isn't anything here on this earth worth findin'. Not a goal I can set for my life that would mean anything to achieve. My purpose. Everything I could possibly achieve. It's all you now. You've turned my house into our home, put me back together when I hadn't even realized I'd been broken, and given me so much more in four months than some people will ever get in a whole lifetime. We burned our way through our own paths in order to find this road we're travelin' on now together. I only hope I'm able to give you back a fraction of what you give me. I was made to love you, Caroline, and there isn't anything that would make me happier than you becomin' my wife. Marry me, Linney. Marry me today, tomorrow, or the next day, and let me spend the rest of our lives provin' that I deserve the honor of you."

"Oh, God," she cries, her whole body shaking with her soft sobbing. The tiniest sounds come from her while she struggles to compose herself.

I release her right hand, keeping hold of her other, and reach into my pocket to pull out the ring I bought almost four months ago. Right after our second dinner at the ranch. I knew then, just like I knew when I stupidly denied it to myself the night I met her, that she's my forever.

When the sun catches the diamonds, Caroline stops trying to control herself and cries harder. I place the ring against the tip of her ring finger and wait, looking at the diamonds as they reflect thousands of colorful prisms in the sun, feeling my own eyes burn, knowing that this moment will forever be one of the greatest triumphs in my life. Her body shudders as she sucks in a choppy gasp, and I glance up just in time to see her looking down at our hands with her chin quivering and more wetness starting to pool in her eyes. This time, there are no sounds, just her tears running silently down her cheeks while she watches me intently. A lesser man would feel some dread over the prolonged silence from the woman he just asked to be his wife, but not me. I know what she'll say. I've known for months now that her answer would be yes, no matter when I asked. It's what drove me to the jeweler to begin with, needing this ring to be ready when the moment came. Confident as I was, I knew she'd be like this. She wouldn't be the woman I love if she didn't need to work through the overpowering emotions slamming into her. If I need to kneel here until the sun dips below the trees, I'll do it. I'll give her all the time in the world to give me—us—the beginning of everything.

By the time we leave here tonight, I'll have my ring on her finger; our bellies will be full with the food waiting for us; and there'll be grass stains on our clothes from when I love my future wife slow and soft under the blue skies, endless green pastures, in the spot that was my only salvation for thirty-five years. Used to be—not now. Not with the love of a damn good woman showing me my way.

Her hand pushes forward in my hold with a sharp jerk, the movement causing the ring to slide down to the middle of her finger, stopping at her knuckle. I'm unable to look away from the big round stone surrounded by tons of smaller diamonds, what it symbolizes hitting me with a maelstrom of emotions. None of them bad, either. No panic, like I had felt when this was almost forced on me by my ex. No fear when I think about my parents' marriage. Nothing but excitement for what my future with Caroline holds. I swallow thickly before glancing back up at her. Her silent tears are still cascading down her tanned cheeks, but she's giving me a huge, blindingly happy, toothy smile. Even though I knew it in my gut, seeing how happy she is and knowing those tears are because she's *that* happy, I feel my own expression break as my joy is given free rein.

"Yes," she finally answers in a small whisper so soft that if there had been some wind, it would have carried her word away with it before it reached my ears. Awe present in her hushed tone, her stare is locked on our hands as I slide the ring the rest of the way down her slim finger. She continues to look down, only giving me her eyes when I lift her hand and press a kiss against the ring. I hold my lips there, watching her chest shake as she pulls in rapid breaths. It's the pure, unmasked joy lighting every inch of her that has me silently vowing I'll do everything in my power to make sure she never loses that happiness while we love each other for the rest of our lives.

I climb to my feet, bending down to dust the dirt off my knee, before stretching to my full height. Caroline looks so tiny standing before me, holding her hand out in front of her face as she admires the ring.

"You look good wearin' my diamonds, Linney, love." My voice must have broken the spell she had been hooked in, because her head snaps up and she jumps. When our gazes collide, I see she hadn't really stopped the crying like I thought. "You're killin' me with the tears, darlin'."

"I'm *so* happy, Clayton Davis." Her whole body

shakes as she gets choked up. I can't help it when my chest puffs slightly. I feel damn good about being the reason she's feeling this way—even if it's coming with some tears.

"How about you get in my arms with your mouth on mine and show me just how happy you are?"

She doesn't hesitate. She jumps, and her arms go around my neck at the same time her legs circle my hips. My hands instantly go to her sweet ass, pulling her closer and keeping her right where I want her. The heat of her pussy is unmistakable against my hard cock, even with the layers keeping us apart completely. She peppers my face with kisses, her soft lips moving frantically as she covers me from forehead to jaw. When she lifts her head, after pressing one last kiss to the side of my jaw, I expect her to finally give me her mouth. Instead, she tips her head back, and shouts up to the sun and the bright blue sky, her back arched, with her tits right in front of my face, while holding on with her hands hooked together behind my neck. Her body bounces, excitement flowing, and I groan when I feel that movement milk some pre-come from my needy cock.

"My dark cowboy is goin' to be my husband!" Caroline shouts. Her whole body quivers with excitement as she looks back at me. "You're goin' to be my husband, Clayton," she tells me, her lips curled in a beautiful, happy smile.

"You're gonna be my wife."

"Oh my God!" she starts bouncing and I almost fall to my knees as pleasure zaps up my spine.

My fingers clench, grabbing her ass cheeks and pushing her roughly against my cock, stilling her movements instantly and groaning loudly. I hiss when she manages to wiggle just a fraction against me.

"Keep that up, sweetness, and I'm gonna strip us down and forget about our dinner so I can fuck my love into you with the sun shining down on us."

She moans, her cheeks turning a light shade of pink.

"You want that, baby?"

Her thighs clamp tighter around my hips and her fingers dig into my shoulders. The bite of pain just makes me crave her more.

"Linney, love. You want me to feed you or eat you?"

"Oh, God," she whimpers.

"Give me the words, darlin'. Tell me what you want. I'll give you the world, but you gotta use the words to ask for it."

"You," she breathes heavily. "I just want you."

My chest vibrates with the hungry sound of approval that bursts free and I lean my head toward hers as she moves to meet me halfway. Our mouths are already opening before our lips press together. Her tongue glides against mine in a slow caress. Her hands drag up my neck as we both give everything we have. Her moans meet mine as our tongues dance. Our bodies become frantic as she rolls her hips and I flex my ass to push my length harder against her, needing, craving more.

I have to rip my mouth from hers, unable to wait any longer to feel her heat hugging me tightly. Caroline starts to kiss and lick down my neck and that sound fills my chest again—a mix between a groan and a growl that her intoxicating body brings out in me. I see the thick flannel blanket Maverick placed under the small two-person wooden table. The huge swath of red-and-black material gives me all the space I need.

"As much as I hate to say it, you're gonna have to get down."

"No, honey," she hums, licking me from my collarbone to my ear before taking a tiny bite with her teeth, nipping me and making me falter as the shock of it creates waves of pleasure through my body.

"Linney," I grunt when she sucks the flesh she just nipped into her mouth. "Get down and get naked, *now*," I hoarsely command, quickly losing the battle with my control. I can already feel my balls pulling tight, ready to explode and not giving one shit that the only place I want to pour myself into is the woman drunk with arousal and high off happiness.

I don't waste a second seeing if she's heeding my demand. My fingers curl in my shirt and I give it a tug. Buttons scatter all around as I pull it and my undershirt off and reach for my belt. When I see Caroline moving just as frantically as I am, not even hesitating to strip out here in the open, I clench my jaw and pray for control. Her small, perfect-handful tits are free and jiggling slightly against her chest as she wiggles her jeans down, kicking them in the direction of her boots and hooking her thumbs into her white lace thong. Her hands freeze, though, and I lick my lips before looking up at her.

"You're too dressed," she pants, rubbing her thighs together.

Knowing she's desperate for me to ease her ache between her legs sends an animalistic need bursting through me. I tear my clothes off wildly and so fast that when I'm taking the few steps separating us, she's still standing there with her thumbs hooked in her underwear. Her breath rushes from her lungs when my body collides with hers and I take her mouth again. My hands turn her head as I deepen our kiss and moan in her mouth when her soft belly presses against my cock.

It doesn't take much before I know I'm seconds from coming, and I'm not going to do that shit on her stomach. Shifting our bodies, I grab her hips and lift her. Her legs hook behind my ass and she slams her center against my cock. Her wet heat slides against my shaft as she rocks her hips and mewls a knee-weakening moan. Our bodies move without prompting until I'm on my back, her knees at my hips, and her hand circling as much of my cock as she can while lining the tip up with her entrance. She pauses, and my eyes practically cross when her heat kisses the tip of my cock. When she doesn't move past that, I look up at her face.

"Fuck me," I breathe. The sun, high in the sky, casts a

glow around her naked body. The brilliance of the bright light hitting her back makes it seem like little beams are shooting around her. She looks like a fucking angel. I have no idea what I did to earn the love of this woman, but I'll never take it for granted. "Get on my cock, Linney, and ride me. Show me how much you love me and take what you need."

"Oh, Clayton," she gasps, her chest heaving with her rapid breaths.

My hands move until my thumb is pressing and rolling against her clit as the other goes to her tit. She inhales with a hiss, her eyes slits as pleasure takes hold of her. I pinch her again, a little harder, before soothing the tight bud with my thumb.

"Take me. Give me you while I give you me. Show me what having my ring on your hand makes you feel."

She drops down, impaling herself on every inch of me. Her eyes squeeze shut and her mouth drops open. She's only taken all of me at one go once, and that was after I had fucked her with my mouth until she came over and over. Even as wet as she had been after that, she still couldn't take all of me. But with the lips of her sex pressed against my pelvis, she greedily takes every inch, her hands curling against my abs as she begins to fuck my cock. Pulling herself up and dropping back down, she rakes her nails over my skin in a burning path. I keep thumbing her clit, her walls fluttering against my cock, milking me.

"I'm not gonna last, baby," I groan when I feel her wetness on my balls and her pussy start to tighten to the point of pain before sending me rolling into blinding pleasure. "Fuckin' hell," I moan, taking her hips and thrusting up as she starts to scream out my name, clamping down on me with her wet heat. I pull her hips down and flex my ass to feed her all of me while I start coming with a shout. I hold her firmly against me, not willing to lose any part of our connection, and lift off my back to take her mouth while she milks her release.

She falls against my chest and I grunt when the movement slides my cock a little deeper, closing my eyes when I feel another burst shoot deep inside of her. The tension from my release finally drains out of my muscles a minute later, but I keep my hold on her hips so I don't lose her heat. We lie there in comfortable silence, the only sounds our ragged breathing as we both come down. Every few minutes my cock, still more hard than soft, twitches inside her, making her moan. Caroline shifts in my grip, bringing her hands to my chest as she pushes against me to lift up. As soon as there's some space between our bodies, she looks from my face to my chest. She starts moving her hand in small degrees, staring at her ring, and I can only guess that the sun hitting her ring is the reason she's doing so. I watch her beautiful face as she smiles, still looking at her hand.

Then her hand drops, but her smile grows.

"Oh my God," she gasps, giggling a beat later, the ring forgotten as she points to where the horses are grazing, patiently waiting for us. "Dell . . . he's all white, Clayton!" My fingers tighten when I feel her laughter in the walls of her pussy, still surrounding my cock. "You," she snorts, unaware of what she's doing to me. "How did I not see it before! You rode in on your white horse, knocked me on my butt, but saved me in the end. My knight in pressed flannel and Wranglers."

"You're a nut, darlin'."

Her giggles multiply and I can't help but join in. "I'm goin' to make a whole section on hot, flannel-wearin', white-knight cowboys when I get The Sequel back open. Just you wait."

Her body rocks against mine as she continues to laugh softly, looking at our horses again with a tiny shake of her head. Unable to stand it anymore, I thrust my hips. Her giggle quickly turns into a whimper.

"I love you, Linney," I tell her, giving her a few more thrusts.

Her soft brown eyes darken and her lips take on a smile that will forever be branded in my mind. The sun is still swirling around every inch of her as I look up from my spot on the ground. She's never looked more beautiful than she does in this moment, joined with me as we start our forever.

"Never gonna stop lovin' you, Caroline."

Her breath hitches. "And I love you, Clayton. Always."

22

CAROLINE

"Forever and Ever, Amen" by Randy Travis

- ★ -

"**I** don't want to wait," I tell him, helping him pack up the rest of our lunch. He stops folding the blanket we finally climbed off of to actually eat the lunch I was cleaning up, but seeing the material in his arms against his naked chest makes me want him all over.

"Wait for what, darlin'?"

I place the last empty storage container into the basket before looking back at him. The rush of him loving me is still surging through my body and mingling with the euphoric high I've had since he knelt in front of me, making me feel as if I could take on the world and win it. And right now, becoming his wife is just as grand in my mind as owning the world would be.

"To become your wife," I answer confidently. No

more, not with him, will the shy Caroline Michaels hold back because of her insecurities.

His shoulders move in silent laughter. "What makes you think *I'd* want to wait?"

"That's usually what happens, honey. Man asks woman, woman spends every waking moment planning her dream wedding until months of stress and preparation form the most perfect day that you'll ever experience."

His lips twitch before he smiles his heart-stopping grin. His green eyes squint as his smile grows. "Darlin', you planning on takin' that long?"

I shake my head. "Well, no."

"How long you need?"

I tilt my head, thinking about it, but don't get far before he starts laughing deeply. He tosses the blanket on top of the picnic basket a second before his arms are around me. The light peppering of hair against his rock-hard chest tickles my palms and I regret getting dressed before we ate when my nipples harden. I love the feel of his chest hair against my skin as he takes me.

"Linney?"

"Hmm?" I answer, rubbing my hands over him.

"How long do you need?"

"For what?" I lick my lips when I feel him grow harder, the length of him no match for the denim covering it.

"Baby." He laughs.

I blink, looking from his chest to his face. "Don't laugh at me, mister."

"You loved me hard, Linney, then you still let me take you slow. My cock shouldn't have anything left, but with you lookin' at me like that it damn sure does. How about you answer me and I can get you home, in our bed, with my cock buried deep."

I feel his words dance through my body, lighting a fire of need in their path, wetness dampening my panties.

"I forgot the question," I tell him honestly, breathless for him.

"How much time," he starts, pressing his mouth to mine quickly, lifting his head to smile down at me, "do you need to plan our weddin'?"

"None," I hum, pressing myself closer and shifting my hands to glide over his skin until I've got a palm against each side of his neck and my face tipped up to look into his. "I don't need any time, Clayton. I just need you."

"Baby," he responds thickly.

"I don't want anything big, Clayton," I say. "Your family, Lucy and Luke. That's it, honey. I don't want to wait weeks, months, years. We've both wasted too much time in our lives while we dealt with our ugly in order to find our beauty. I don't need to continue to waste time now that it's even more precious. I just want you. You and me and whatever blessings we find together."

"You sure you don't want somethin' big?"

"Why, Clayton? You have your brother and sister, their families, and I have Lucy and Luke. There aren't grandparents; my parents and yours didn't have siblings. I don't want the town turnin' our weddin' into somethin' crazy because they're just nosy. All we need is a small ceremony, our family together, and us."

He drops his forehead to mine, smiling. "I like that, Linney."

"I don't want to wait," I reiterate.

"Then don't. I wouldn't have asked you to be my wife if I wasn't ready to make that happen. You aren't the only one not wantin' to wait, darlin'. I don't want you lookin' back and wishin' you had some big weddin' though either."

"I would never."

"Then, Caroline, don't wait."

"The whole town's goin' to think you knocked me up. They went crazy when news got out about us livin' together, I can only imagine what they'll think when they hear about us bein' engaged."

His eyes flash, something I don't quite understand flickering there for only a second before vanishing. I feel his heart thundering against my chest as the silence continues. His throat bobbles when he swallows.

"Clayton?"

He clears his throat.

"I don't want to rush you," I finally say when it becomes clear he isn't going to stop staring at me mutely. My words get his attention, but I keep going. "I'd marry you tomorrow, but I don't want to rush you."

"Tomorrow will still be longer than I care to wait."

"What?"

"Caroline," he breathes, "I've had that ring for damn near the whole time we've been together. I had you one night and it took everything inside of me to walk away. I might be a foolish man, but when I saw you at the girls' baby shower, I knew I wasn't strong enough to walk away a second time. Every single day since, I've been ready, and every day from this moment will feel like it's not soon enough. Trust me when I say there isn't a damn way to rush somethin' that every second you don't get it feels like a lifetime."

"Oh," I say lamely.

"Take the time you need to plan the weddin' you want. Small, big, or in between. Just don't take *that* much time, darlin'."

"I won't," I mutter.

"That's good, Linney. That's damn good."

He lets me go with a short kiss. Silently, we finish cleaning up and stacking the things he'll pick up later on top of the table. I take one last look at the land around us and feel lighter than I've ever felt in my life. His words from earlier return and I can almost see our future kids running around the green grass. One day, one day that's going to be ours, and I can't hardly wait for it.

The ride back to the ranch is a lot easier—Onyx proved himself to be trustworthy already. I imagine it will take some time for me to get over my fears, but I no longer look at Onyx as part of that. He's been patient with me and I know, deep down, that Clayton was right when he said there's a bond between the dark beauty and me. During the time I'll have to wait to reopen The Sequel, I hope to learn more from Clayton when it comes to riding. A horse as perfect as Onyx deserves that.

We pass a few ranch hands working with a couple of Clayton's newer horses in the riding course that's set up between the Davis personal horse barn and the huge one that houses their stock, for lack of a better word, on the way back. Ignoring them, Clayton continues until we both have our feet on the ground and I've finished the last task that he's coached me through in getting Onyx ready to go back in his stall.

I caress the horse's neck, not really ready to leave. "I'm goin' to be back in the mornin', handsome."

Clayton laughs. "Handsome?"

I look over my shoulder at him. "Uh, yeah. Look at him."

"Such a nut," he mutters, walking Dell down to his own stall.

"Clay," I hear someone call from outside the barn right before one of the younger cowboys comes in. His eyes go straight to me but shift back to Clayton when Clay makes a disapproving sound deep in his throat. "Sorry, Mr. Davis. Drew had to run to town and you didn't bring your phone or the radio, but your brother's been callin'."

"For how long?" Clayton questions, walking to me and taking my hand before heading toward the younger man. He pauses to grab his hat, placing it back on his head while waiting for a reply.

"Reckon 'bout a half hour ago, maybe close to an hour now."

"Thanks, Tim," Clayton says, walking right out of the barn and toward the house.

"Is everything okay?" I quicken my pace to keep up with his long legs but feel like I'm more jogging than walking.

"He knew what was goin' on, darlin'. Only reason he'd be callin' is if it's important. Seein' that Leighton is so close to havin' the baby, I'm guessin' that's why."

"You'll get to your phone quicker if you go ahead, honey," I rush out, pulling my hand from his hold. "Meet you in the house. I'm goin' to run to my car and grab my phone so I can call Quinn."

He nods sharply, turning to continue up to the main house. I quickly snatch up my phone before sprinting back toward the house. I pull Quinn's name up and press the phone to my ear before I even reach the porch steps.

"Are y'all on the way?" she questions when the call connects.

"About to be. Is everything okay?"

"I think so. I haven't talked to Maverick since he called to say it was time. We had to wait for Jana to get to the house so she could watch Grayson. Tate's tryin' to get some information with his doctor magic."

Clayton comes barreling down the hallway, phone to his ear. "That Quinn?"

I nod. "Here's your brother, Quinn."

His breathing is harsh when he takes the phone and places it to his ear. "Quinnie?" Whatever she says to him must ease some of the worry, because his shoulders loosen up and he closes his eyes before exhaling slowly. "We're on the way."

He hands me back my phone and visibly struggles with his emotions. "I'll never be able to hold my shit together when it's you about to have a baby. I feel like I'm too big for my skin right now. I've watched those two fight for this moment for damn near our whole lives. Knowin', like us, they could have never found it because of that shit they had to deal with in order to do so. This baby of theirs is somethin' we've all of us been waitin' for so long to meet. I can't imagine, feelin' this much over their child, what you givin' me one of our own will do to me. Never, not until you, did I ever want this for myself. To my knees, Linney, thinkin' about somethin' as perfect as our future children brings me to my knees."

"Oh, Clayton." I wrap my arms around him and hug him tight.

"I don't want to wait either, darlin'," he says against my temple, his head bent and his arms around me. "There's nothin' better than travelin' with you and doin' it in a way that we don't waste a second of our time hesitatin' in takin' what we want. You've got two weeks. Two weeks, and I'm not goin' to wait any longer than that."

"Two weeks," I echo breathlessly.

"Not a day more."

By the time we make it to the hospital, Tate was able to find out that Leigh was being prepped for a cesarean section. Her baby is just too big and the natural birth she's been hoping for is out of the question. Tate assured both Quinn and Clayton that they had nothing to worry about, but even with him explaining how common this is, it's still major surgery. That was almost three hours ago, and even Tate has some worry in his eyes now.

The tension in our area of the waiting room is thick, but when the doorway opens to reveal a crying, smiling Maverick, that tension vanishes instantly. I look over at Tate and smile, both of us letting the two waiting Davis siblings go to their brother first.

"Congratulations," Tate says after Clayton and Quinn reach Maverick's side.

"Huh?" I respond in confusion, not taking my eyes off Clayton. When he grabs his brother by the shoulders and pulls him into his arms, I feel the burn of tears start. When both of them drop their foreheads to the other's shoulder, Clayton's hat falling carelessly at his feet, and both their arms tighten as they embrace, I know I'm not going to be able to keep my tears in as I witness such strong men be overcome by their emotions. Then, as if they practiced the move their whole lives—each man lifts the arm closest to where Quinn is standing out. She moves instantly, all but diving into their embrace with her arms going around each brother.

"They've been through a lot of shit in their lives," Tate whispers, moving to the seat next to me. "Thick and thin, those three have been each other's rocks through the worst of it, only sharing that responsibility recently. Maverick findin' Leighton. Quinn and me. Now you and Clay. Lot of time has passed since they were young kids livin' a shit life without the love of anyone other than each other, but when you get right down to it, they're always goin' to need each other's support."

I blink furiously, trying to get my stupid tears to back off, but when Maverick lifts his head and looks at me with his piercing emerald eyes swollen and wet, I feel them start to fall. His don't stop, but he smiles at me with a small nod before bending his head back to his brother's shoulder.

"Felt that when Gray was born. There's no way to explain what you feel when your child is born. Not sayin' that my son's birth wasn't as important, but for them, this is so much more. Me and you, we weren't around for all of it, but you know as well as I do that they had a dark childhood. Leighton was there. She loves my wife as a sister. Your man as a brother. And her husband owns the rest of her heart. Those three, they finally have it all, and more importantly, they know it. Makes moments like this hit a little harder because there was a time they all thought this would never happen."

"Their gifts," I whisper.

"Pardon?" Tate asks.

I look away from the huddle across the room and smile at Quinn's husband. "It's their gift for all that ugly they survived."

I don't think I really believed Clayton when he told me that months ago, but there are no doubts now. I've seen it in Clayton during the course of our relationship, but never as clearly as I do today. I spin the ring on my hand, loving the weight of it, and grin when I realize just how much of a gift *my* Davis has received today.

"Yeah, you get it."

"I do, Tate. I totally do."

"Like I said, congratulations." He taps my hand, stilling my fingers.

"Thanks," I breathe, opening my mouth to say more but snapping it shut when I see the siblings release each other and turn to us.

"That's our cue."

We both stand and walk over to them.

"I knew it!" Quinn exclaims with a shake to her voice when her husband reaches her side. "Since I was six years old, Tate. I've always known it."

I glance at Maverick, seeing him look down at his boots, but not hiding the smile on his face. Clayton pulls me to his side and I wrap one arm around his back, place my other hand against his hard stomach, and tip my head up to look at him. His eyes are wet and red, but his smile is huge.

"I've got a niece," he tells me in a soft voice full of happiness.

"I knew it!" Quinn cries out again. "What's her name?"

Maverick looks up, his lips tipping even further.

"Promised Leighton I'd let her tell y'all."

"Well, bucko, what are we waitin' for? Take me to my niece!"

Maverick smiles at his sister and we all follow the new daddy down the hallway. Clayton's been quiet since his brother came into the waiting room, but every time I glance at him he just smiles, so I leave him to his thoughts, knowing he's anxious to meet the newest member of his family.

We stop behind Maverick when he reaches a closed door. James, their last name since he took Leighton's when they married, is written under the room number.

"She's still tired but didn't want to wait," he rumbles low, looking down at his hand on the doorknob. "I'd keep y'all here with us all night, but I'm askin' because I need this time with my wife and daughter. Please, keep it short tonight."

"I swear, if you don't get your tail outta my way, I'll take you out."

"Quinn, I mean it."

I look at her as she rolls her eyes. "I know you do, big brother, and I think you understand that I get you. Now get out of my way so I can see my sister and hold the niece you denied me for years, and *then* I'll leave."

Maverick nods at his sister as Tate and I laugh lightly when she starts pushing into the room before the door's even open all the way. Clayton hangs back while Tate enters, causing Maverick to glance his way.

"I spent ten years worried you'd never come home," Clayton tells Maverick, his words low. "Ten years I felt nothin' but fear that I'd lost my brother because I couldn't protect him enough to keep him here. I'm so happy for you right now. Seein' you overcome all that pushed you away and kept you gone to find what you were always meant to have . . ." He pauses as his arm tightens around my shoulders. "You made it possible with all that for me to be able to see what I was meant to have. I'm so fuckin' proud to call you my brother, Mav."

"I'm just goin' to . . ." I point toward the open door and try to step out from under Clayton's arm.

His head tips down to look at me. "Don't you dare move."

"We're all gettin' what we were meant to have, brother," Maverick says, breaking the staring contest I had apparently entered with Clayton as we both look to him. "You'll be in my shoes sooner rather than later, I reckon." He steps closer to his big brother and lowers his voice. "Don't let me hear you say you didn't protect me again, Clay. You've always done that. You did it when I was a kid, when I left, and you continued doin' it when you look care of Leigh when I didn't. I overcame all that because I had the love of a good woman and the support of you and Quinn. Don't forget it was *you* who helped me see my way to her. Means the world to hear you're proud of me, seein' that you were the man who taught me how to be one myself."

I don't hesitate to step away from Clayton when Maverick finishes, walking into the hospital room and leaving them to have the rest of that moment privately.

An hour later, much to Quinn's irritation, the four of us walk out of the hospital, leaving Leighton and baby Laelynn Quinn James resting peacefully in Maverick's strong arms.

23

CAROLINE

"All My Ex's Live in Texas" by George Strait

- ★ -

I wave at Marybeth Perkins and back out of the grocery store as quickly as I can without making it look obvious that I'm trying to get away from the sweet, but extremely nosy, older woman. I could tell she was itching for some gossip with the way she kept looking at my stomach. I knew this would happen the second our engagement news started circulating. What should've only taken me fifteen minutes, tops, took close to an hour. Everyone, and I do mean everyone, I encountered asked me a million questions.

It's been almost two weeks since Clayton asked me to be his wife. I've spent every second of that time planning our wedding and going between our home, Maverick and Leighton's, and Quinn and Tate's. Since both couples have such tiny newborns, I didn't want them coming out to our place. It was just easier to go to them. Plus, this way I get tons of time cuddling babies without having to fight off someone else in order to do so.

Lucy's been out a few times, Luke as well, but we've had little time to get together like we normally do. They understand, and I know both are happy for me.

"Caroline."

I freeze, my body locking tight.

"Please," the voice continues. Instead of making me feel uneasy, though, the broken tone in his pleading gives me what I need. *He* doesn't get to feel broken here. *He* doesn't have that right, seeing as he's the person who did everything in his power to ensure *I* was the broken one.

I suck in a cleansing breath before turning. "What do you want, John?"

He looks terrible. The once handsome man I knew is long gone. His hair is a little too long. His eyes are bloodshot and sunken, with shadowy bags under them. And he's lost weight. Not too much, but enough that I know he's not taking care of himself.

"I'm so sorry," he rushes out, looking around frantically. "So, so sorry."

"I moved past needin' to hear that a long time ago, John."

"It wasn't supposed to be like that," he continues like I didn't even speak.

I cross my arms and arch a brow, not willing to turn my back and continue loading the car, but I realize my mistake when John's panicked eyes drop. I glance down and see that my left hand and big diamond ring stick out like a billboard announcing my relationship status.

"Is that . . . Are you . . . to Clay Davis?"

"Why does it even matter to you?" I sigh, shaking my head. "You have no say in my life, John. You haven't for years. Why now, after all this time, is tellin' me you're sorry so dadgum important?"

He keeps shaking his head, not looking away from my ring. He mumbles something I can't hear under his breath before looking up at me with worried eyes. "I loved you, you know," he finally says. "I don't know what to do now."

Clayton's words about John being on drugs filter through my thoughts when I realize how odd he's acting. Knowing what I do about his past here in Pine Oak and having firsthand knowledge about just how violent he can be, I should be blind with fear. Heck, months ago I would have been. But I've come too far to let him push me right back into that person who was afraid of living.

"I want you to leave me alone. I want you to leave Clayton alone. And if you're goin' to be livin' in Pine Oak too, then I want you to avoid us at all costs. I survived what you did to me, John. I made it through that, and even though it took me a while to find my reward, I have it, and I'm not goin' to let you try and dirty that up with everything that is *you*."

He opens his mouth to say something, but I release my arms and hold one up to stop him silently.

"I don't want to hear your apologies, because they mean nothin' to me. Just like you. Do you understand that, John?"

He shakes his head sadly, looking down. "I loved you."

"No! No, you didn't. You loved owning someone who feared you. You loved the power of breakin' me. You loved *you*!"

"You're wrong, Caroline. I've done everything for you."

I snort. "You must be delusional."

"Don't marry him. I won't be able to save you."

This time I laugh in his face. "You? Save me? You're a riot."

"I tried," he says, but stops and shakes his head.

"You inflicted pain. Don't get that mixed up. It's been years, John. I've finally moved on and I'm so happy, it's ridiculous. You're sorry? Great. If it's my forgiveness you want or need, then you'll be waiting for a while. You can't give forgiveness to someone you've forgotten. And you, John, are just a forgotten memory."

I turn my back and load the last four bags into my trunk before shutting it and walking the buggy back to the return. When I start walking back to my car, I don't see him anywhere.

The first thing I do when I climb into my car is grab my phone and call Clayton.

"You on your way, darlin'?"

"I just ran into John."

Silence.

"Clayton?"

"I heard you," he answers with venom in his tone. "He touch you?"

"What? No, Clayton."

"What did he want?"

I sigh, then tell him what happened, trying to remember what John had said, but knowing I probably got some of it wrong. Still, even though it was pretty harmless, I can tell Clayton is about to lose his mind.

"He wanted to apologize. It doesn't make any sense to me, why he'd feel that's somethin' to be done so many years later, but nevertheless, he did. He startled me only because I wasn't expectin' him, but Clayton, I didn't feel anything but done. I don't fear him or what he did to me anymore."

"He could've hurt you," Clayton finally says, letting me know what's really upsetting him.

"He didn't. And I'm not the weak little girl who won't fight back. I've got all the reasons in the world to fight, and if he had been stupid enough to try and touch me in the middle of Main Street, I guarantee I wouldn't have been fightin' by myself for long."

He grumbles under his breath.

"We're gettin' married tonight, Clayton Davis. Don't you dare let this put a cloud over our weddin' night. It happened, it's done, and you know about it because I didn't want you hearin' it from someone else. I'm fine, and in just a couple of hours, we're goin' to be husband and wife. No one can stand in the way of that kinda happiness."

"Get home, Linney. Get home and no more of that shit about me not seein' you before tonight. I need to see with my own eyes that you're fine."

I smile, leaning my head back against the headrest. "I'll see you in our spot tonight, and not a second earlier."

I laugh outright when I hear him bellow out his complaints before I can disconnect the call. Not wanting to make him suffer too much, I quickly take a picture of myself and text it to him, happiness and love written all over my face, my smile big and my eyes dancing. I place my phone on the passenger's seat and back out of the lot to head over to Leighton's place, ignoring the chimes announcing texts that don't stop coming in the whole way to her house.

Not wanting to be distracted, I leave the phone on the seat and walk to the trunk to grab the bags.

"I've got it," Maverick says, making me scream.

"You need a bell," I gasp, holding my hand to my chest, my heart pounding from being snuck up on.

"Leigh's waitin' on you," he tells me, bending over to

scoop up all of the bags and trudging into his house, leaving the front door open for me.

"Well, then."

Earl is the first to greet me when I step into their home. He's sitting on his large rump in front of the baby swing. The huge, kind of scary cat gives me a look that, were he human, would express disapproval, his brow arched and a frown beneath his whiskers.

"Hey, Earl," I greet, stepping up to the swing to look at little Laelynn as she sleeps peacefully. I reach out, wanting to move her blanket down a little so I can see her adorable dimpled chin, but jerk it back when Earl hisses and swats at my ankle. "What the heck," I whisper, frowning at the cat.

"He's a little protective of Laelynn." Leigh giggles, scooping up her huge cat as he hisses and wiggles to get free. "Stop it, you big baby."

"So . . . I'm just goin' to go get changed, then," I tell her. "No offense, I'm sure he means well, but I'm pretty sure your cat could kill me, and as much as I love your daughter, I don't want to die."

Leigh laughs, dropping her cat to his feet. He pads back to his spot and settles in to sit guard in front of the swing.

"Quinn's feeding Gray and Lucy is gettin' dressed. Luke and Tate went up to get everything finished. I think Maverick is on the way back up there. He just happened to be checkin' in on things when you drove up."

"I feel like there's somethin' I should be doin' other than gettin' dressed."

"There is *nothin'* you need to be frettin' about, sister."

My heart warms and I smile at my old friend, soon to be my sister-in-law. "It's really happenin'?"

"You betcha ass it is! Come on. We've got a weddin' to get to and a bride who isn't ready yet."

All thoughts of John and our bizarre run-in are forgotten while my three closest friends help me get ready to marry the man of my dreams. By the time Luke comes back to let us know everything's ready and that the groom is waiting very impatiently, I've been buffed, fluffed, painted, and sprayed. He takes one look at me in my simple, floor-length lace dress and turns to walk back out the door.

I look over at Lucy, seeing her watery smile, and blink furiously to keep my tears from ruining my makeup. I glance at Leighton and Quinn, seeing them wearing the same simple coral sundresses that we all agreed on as their bridesmaids' outfits. All three are wearing brown cowboy boots, and their hair is braided simply to rest over one shoulder. Quinn's holding Grayson, dressed in a miniature version of what the guys are wearing— a black button-down and dark washed jeans. With Laelynn being only two weeks old, there wasn't anything close to the girls' outfits that fit her, but I bet Leighton tried anyway.

"Okay," Luke says, walking back in.

"You okay?" I whisper, walking to his side and hugging him.

"Yeah." He swallows thickly. "I'm just real damn happy for you, Carrie."

"Caroline," I correct with a laugh, not the least bit serious.

"I'm honored that you asked me to give you away, sweetheart."

"Don't make me cry," I warn.

Luke laughs but lowers his head so the girls can't hear him. "I knew five months ago when you sat next to Davis at Hazel's that this would happen. You both looked like you'd been zapped. I'm always here if you need me, but I couldn't be more pleased with the man you've chosen to be your husband."

"Luke," I murmur, my vision getting wonky with the tears filling my eyes.

"Enough of that," he exclaims, clapping his hands and rocking on his booted feet. "You ladies ready? Because there's a man up at the top of that hill who's about out of patience to get his bride in his arms."

Quinn gives me a quick hug before walking out and climbing into the front of the golf cart, next to Tate in the driver's seat. Lucy follows, thankfully having said much of the same that her brother did the night before and sparing me the tears. She winks before settling in.

Leigh is last out the door, holding the pink bundle of her daughter in her arms. "You ready?"

"God, yes," I answer emphatically.

Her grin is as huge as mine, I'm sure, as she walks to the cart and climbs up to sit with Lucy. Tate gives a wave before driving off slowly, careful of the precious cargo, in the direction of the Davis property. I look up at Luke and, with just him there, finally let loose some of the pent-up excitement. My hands go up in the air with the bundle of wildflowers held tight in my hand, and I shake my hips as I dance in a circle on Leighton's front porch.

"I'm gettin' married!"

"Not if you don't stop dancin' around, you aren't. Come on, crazy girl, your man is waitin'."

I drop my arms and turn to him, my cheeks burning from the enormous grin on my face. "This is it, Luke. This is my forever."

His eyes get soft and he grabs the hand not holding my bouquet. "No one deserves it more."

"Thank you, Lucas," I tell him after he helps me into the golf cart. "Thank you for bein' there for me all these years. You didn't have to be, but you were. I just want you to know how much your friendship means to me."

He taps my nose with his finger and grins. "You're family, darlin'. I didn't have to, but I wanted to. That's what family does. That will always hold true. Even with you gainin' a husband I know will protect you completely, I'm always gonna be here if you need me."

I reach out and grab his hand, not trusting myself to answer him without breaking down like a baby, and squeeze. Luke gives me a nod, then presses his foot down and takes off on the trail that will bring me to my forever.

24

CLAYTON

"It Took a Woman" by Craig Morgan

- ★ -

"**J**esus," I hiss, feeling my heart try to burst out of my damn chest when I see Caroline step down from the golf cart and smile at Luke as he walks around to hold his elbow out for her.

She looks like one hell of a vision. Her dress makes her tanned skin glow, the bright white lace hugging her small frame like it was made just for her. The low-cut neckline highlights her small breasts—and the fact that there is no way she's got a bra on. Her long, dark hair is pulled up into some messy curly bunch at the base of her neck, exposing each delicate inch.

It's her face, though, that holds me captive, openly projecting her happiness to everyone who is with us up on the hill that I used to run to when I needed to feel grounded. The same hill that I made love to her on two weeks ago when I asked her to be my wife. If you'd told me years ago that I'd be marrying the love of my life right here in this spot, I would've laughed you right out of Pine Oak.

She and Luke start to walk down the flower-petal-covered path that'll bring her to the gazebo I built in our spot. I did as much of the work as I could myself, but with limited time to give her something perfect, I had to get help. Drew and I pulled a few of the boys off their normal duties and with the help of my brothers as well, we created something I have no doubt will be standing for many years to come. The large, square base covers the expanse of where I got on my knee, the roof keeps us covered, and the low walls around the opening she's walking up ensure I can keep loving her out in the open while giving us some privacy.

With each step she takes toward me, I have to fight the need to rush to her. Feeling a nudge against my arm, I reluctantly look away from Caroline. The handkerchief in Maverick's hand silently gets passed to mine and I wipe the tears I hadn't realized I was crying. Caroline takes the last step into the gazebo and pulls the material from my grasp, wiping my eyes for me with the most serene expression on her beautiful face. When she's done, I take it from her and return the favor when one tear of her own slips down her cheek.

"Oh, God," one of the girls sobs.

I hear some more sniffles, but I can't look away from Caroline to see who is crying. My eyes don't leave hers once while Judge Allan—the only person available to marry us on a Wednesday night—speaks out for the small group to hear clearly. The whole ceremony is a fog for me, my focus only on Caroline as my heart pounds happily. I slip my band on her finger without breaking our gaze, and she does the same. The second the solid weight of my wedding band registers, I feel my control slipping and my eyes watering. She doesn't miss it either, but I reckon she's too busy holding her own emotions in check to do much about it. It isn't until Judge Allan tells me I can kiss my bride that I move.

My hands frame her face and my feet take a step closer until I bend and take my wife's mouth in a slow, deep kiss. I have to force myself to pull away, but when I look down at Caroline—*my wife*—and see the dazed stare in her dark eyes I smile and drop my forehead to hers.

"I love you. I loved you before you were my wife and I'll love you long after my last breath. Thank you, Linney, for blessin' my life."

She hiccups out a soft sob, closing her eyes and tightening her arms around me. "Heavens above, Clayton Davis. You're an incredible man. You own my heart, honey. Now and forever."

I move my mouth to her ear, making sure no one can hear me, and grin when she sucks in a breath. "I'm gonna be bad with my wife tonight."

Her hand that's resting on my chest trembles slightly before her fingers grip the fabric. Leaning back, I wink down at her and place a quick kiss against her forehead.

Judge Allan signs the papers to make us legal before waving us off and taking one of the golf carts back toward the ranch where he left his truck. He knew we wanted this moment to be as private as can be, shared between family only, and I'm thankful he doesn't stick around, giving us this moment before our marriage news spreads through town.

And spread it will.

I have a feeling that by the time I wake up in the morning with my wife in my arms, the whole town is going to know Clayton Davis finally settled down.

"What's up, sista!" Quinn hoots, her voice carrying in the vast open space around us. I frown at her when she pulls Caroline from my arms and wraps her in her own. The brat just sticks her tongue out at me when I reach for Caroline again. "Someone is goin' to need to learn to share. She's not just yours, big brother."

"Like hell," I grunt.

"Oh, be a good boy, Clay. Sharin' is carin', you know."

I narrow my eyes at Quinn. Before I can say anything, Caroline smiles at me over her shoulder, her eyes dancing with mischief.

"Yeah, honey . . . be a *good boy*."

I arch my brow, place my hands on my hips, and smile

at her. Her eyes widen the second she realizes that, by trying to play me, she's about to get it right back.

"Darlin', need I remind you how much you love it when I'm bad?"

"Clayton!" She hisses, her cheeks turning pink.

"Oh, really?" Quinn gasps with mock shock. "Someone's been holdin' out on us, Leigh!"

"I'm goin' to get you for that," Caroline whispers, closing her eyes and shaking her head when Quinn and Leigh continue teasing. "I'm goin' to tell them you've got a butt fetish."

Tossing my head back, I laugh loudly and pull her into my arms. "Linney, that's not exactly a threat, considerin' I most definitely love your ass."

"That's not what I meant!"

"I might need to show you just how much I love it later," I continue, ignoring her. Her eyes darken and I pull her tighter against me. "Knew you loved me bein' bad for you."

I expected her to ignore me, but instead she holds my gaze—pink cheeks and all—and shrugs. "I don't think there's a single thing in this world that I don't love when it comes to you, Clayton."

"Feelin's mutual, Linney, love."

"We're goin' to head back to the house and start gettin' the food out," Maverick says, stepping closer with his daughter asleep against his chest. "Give y'all some time alone."

I nod. "Thanks, Mav."

He lifts his chin, looks down at his daughter, and kisses her on the top of her blond head. I glance at my niece and feel the tug in my chest. Until Caroline, I never wanted that—what my brother has right there in his arms. I shoot my eyes over to where Quinn is fussing over her son while he grunts in his father's arms. One more glance at Laelynn, and I feel a burst of determination rush over me. I want that. I want children with the woman who owns my happiness, love, and life. I need it. More than that, I want to prove that I can be what my parents couldn't be.

Maverick clears his throat, pulling my eyes from his daughter. My normally stoic and closed-off brother gives me a whole hell of a lot without words when I lock eyes with him. He gets it. The need that's coursing through my veins right now. One corner of his mouth tips up. He adjusts his daughter so he can pull one hand away, placing his large hand on my shoulder. Caroline steps to the side; then my brother has one arm around my back and his head next to mine, voice low. "Real happy for you, Clay. You deserve everything you've gotten and will get with Caroline. You know what kinda peace lovin' her gives you, but just you wait until your woman blesses you with your firstborn. No fuckin' feelin' can compare to the love that grows from that for your child, and for the woman you never imagined possible to love more. Just you wait."

Fuck me.

I clench my jaw, press my lips to my niece's temple, and lift my head to nod at Mav. He doesn't need me to acknowledge his words, not when we both know he isn't wrong.

True to his word, Maverick corrals the small group into carts to head off to his house. The sound of their chatter lingers behind them long after they disappear around the trees that keep Mav and Leigh's property mostly hidden. Caroline steps into me, her front against mine, and wraps her arms around my waist. Resting my chin against the top of her head, I close my arms around her.

"I can't wait to get you back home," I confess softly, my hands caressing the bare skin completely exposed from just below her shoulders to the top of her ass, showing the dimples at the base of her spine. "Is this clasp the only thing holding your dress together?" I continue, flicking the tiny stretch of fabric that goes across her shoulder blades.

"Pretty much." She giggles, pressing herself even tighter against me. "I think it's more for extra support in keeping the front from showing too much."

I pull back a little and look down at the front of her dress. My fingers trail from the strap in question over her lace-covered shoulders, and down her front. The deep V of her neckline stops below her chest, mid-stomach. Sticking my pointer fingers into the lace at the bottom of the V, I glide them up toward her breasts. The bottom swell of her tits is silky smooth as I slide over the flesh. Her teeth bite her lower lip when my fingers finally move to her nipples, and she moans low. I roll each tight bud before pulling both fingers out of the fabric. Her chest moves rapidly.

"Tonight, tonight I'm goin' to love my wife bad and not take this dress off until I'm done." I bend, my tongue coming out to lick her from the bottom of that V and up the middle of her chest until my mouth is at her ear. "I can't wait to feel all this lace against me while your silky heat sucks me dry."

"Oh, God," she breathes.

"One day, when our family isn't waitin' for us, I'm goin' to bring you back up here and we're goin' to break this gazebo in."

Caroline places her hands against my chest and lifts up on her toes. "I like the sound of that, honey."

With a groan that seems to come from deep in my body, I take her mouth in a deep kiss. Her lips open instantly, ready for me, and our tongues slide against each other. With her body pressed tight and her hands at the back of my head, keeping me close, I feel surrounded by her love. She whines when I shift us and my erection pushes into her belly. My hands move and I bend, taking her ass in my palms and lifting her as I stretch back up. Her dress keeps her from wrapping her legs around me, but her arms adjust to wrap around my neck, deepening our connection.

I've never felt more whole than I do right now. High above my land in a place that's always meant something to me, with the rest of my life in my arms.

I've got it all. I truly have it all.

25

CLAYTON

"Ain't Nothing 'Bout You" by Brooks & Dunn

"**M**ore."

I breathe in, the scene and taste only becoming more addicting when I do. How she can taste like the sweetest apple pie ever baked, I'll never know, but fuck if I'm not going to enjoy the dessert of her.

"Please, Clayton," she gasps, the breathy sound turning into a scream when I bite her swollen clit between my teeth before hollowing my cheeks and sucking hard.

Her hands fist in my hair, pulling me closer as she grinds against my face. I look up her body, seeing her lost in pleasure as she writhes against our bed. The stark white of her wedding dress against our dark gray sheets reminds me that only hours ago this woman became mine for life. I growl against her, causing her to yelp, and press my left hand against her pelvis to keep her hips on the mattress.

In the dim glow from the lamp on my nightstand, the black metal on my ring finger can't be missed. Seeing that symbol of our union only drives the need I'm feeling to take her grow to insurmountable levels. It's undeniable, primal, the forceful urge to consummate our union in the most carnal of ways taking on a life of its own.

Dragging my hands up her torso, I take her breasts. The fabric of her dress catches on my callused hands, but it doesn't stop me from flexing my fingers against the small weight of her tits. She moans low and deep as I continue to play with her, her wetness covering my chin. Flattening my tongue, I lift my head and then lick her from opening to clit, dragging my tongue around the bud, then moving back down. Her flavor bursts on my tongue, making me hungry for more. The heady scent of her swirls around me as my balls tighten. Running the tip of my nose over her sex, I inhale and feel my chest vibrate as the satisfying aroma of her arousal fills my head.

"Look at me," I demand, stilling my hands. She rolls her head from side to side but doesn't give me those brown eyes. "Look at me, Linney. Watch me love the fuck outta my good girl. See what it does to me to drink from your pussy. To know that I'm the one your body comes to life for."

"Oh, God," she gasps.

"Look at me *now*," I growl.

Her head lifts slowly as she obeys. Her hair, no longer contained, tumbles around her face and over her chest. The ends tickle my hands against her breasts. Her eyes, so dark they almost look black, plead with me through hooded lids, and incoherent mumbles leave her mouth. Her kiss-swollen lips part as she starts panting, needing this as much as I do.

Opening my mouth wide, I close my lips around her pussy and stick my tongue into her entrance. Thrusting as deep as I can before lifting my head back slightly to lick her again, I hold her gaze and suck, flick, and lick her pussy until her eyes flutter closed and she screams out my name as her orgasm slams through her.

Releasing her breasts, I drag my hands down her body, and with one more closed-mouth kiss to her pussy, I turn my head and wipe my mouth against her thigh. Her legs fall open as I lift my shoulders from between her legs and climb up her body, thankful I stripped down before following her into bed. I glance at the clock on the nightstand and smirk.

"You look smug," she pants drunkenly, out of breath and making my cock jerk, knowing I'm the reason she's trying to catch her breath.

"I just made you come three times and even though I had your pussy wettin' my lips for over an hour, I want more."

"My heart is always goin' to be racin' around you, isn't it?"

I smile at my wife as my hips start moving, gliding

my thickness through her slickness, not entering her. She hisses each time the tip of my cock bumps her sensitive clit. "I hope so, darlin'." Keeping my pace, I watch her dress move against her chest while I rock her body with my teasing. Her small tits jiggle slightly each time I thrust against her. The delicate fabric that goes around her shoulders to meet the strap across her back strains with each heavy breath. I wonder how hard I'd have to take her for those tits to break free of the fabric.

I come up on my knees and drink her in as I stroke my cock. The long skirt on her dress is bunched at her hips, her sex glistening in the low light, and those brown eyes I love are watching my fist as I work my length. When she moves quickly, it takes me a second to realize her mouth is suddenly around my cock and her tongue is swirling against the tip. Her hand wraps around mine, squeezing my stalled grip, and when I don't move, she hums against my flesh. I grunt, clench my cheeks, and with my free hand brush her hair out of her face. Her hand squeezes me again and her eyes meet mine.

"Fuck me." I hiss, seeing clear as day in those dark depths the pleasure she's getting from sucking my cock.

My hand moves, letting her hold guide the movements as we start stroking the hard, needy flesh. Her mouth takes as much of my length as she can, which isn't much, before swirling her tongue around me to repeat the process. It takes every ounce of my control to not come, but when I feel her teeth scrape against the underside of my cock, I see stars. With a bellow, I release my hand from her hold and hook her under her arms and toss her back against the bed. My body covers hers instantly and my mouth drops to hers. The sounds coming from the two of us are hungry as our tongues dance together.

Lifting my hips, I feel her arm move between us, and without any encouragement, she feeds my cock into her body. She screams out with the first hard stroke, but because of how long I primed her with my mouth, she has no trouble taking me completely. The shock of her pussy strangling me from tip to base is almost enough to have my come shooting deep into her, but I hold on and rumble a warning when she wiggles her hips.

"Please," she begs.

"Don't move," I demand through thin lips, feeling a tiny burst of pre-come leave my cock. "Fuck." I drop my forehead to her neck and try to measure my breathing and get ahold of my body.

"Clayton Davis, if you don't start movin' now, I'm goin' to knock you on your ass and move for you."

"Caroline Davis, if you don't stop movin' and let me have a minute, I'm gonna spank your ass and then move for you."

"Yes." She exhales, her eyes widening and her pussy clenching greedily and flexing against my cock.

"Goddamn," I blow the word out with a hiss.

Pushing the thoughts of her liking the sound of me spanking her from my mind, I start to move, slowly gliding through her, in deep thrusts. Her nails scrape against my back, her mewls echoing and mingling with my low grunts, but it's her slick heat rippling against my cock that almost does me in. I drop my mouth to her neck and start to kiss up the slim column until my lips are moving along her jaw. The whole time, my hips start to pick up speed. By the time I've covered her mouth with mine, she's frantic, her hips surging off the bed to meet mine, our damp bodies slapping together, and her voice becoming hoarse as she screams out her release. Between the incredible feeling of her pussy clamping down on my cock and the expression on her face when she does, I can't hold myself back any longer.

Planting my hips against hers, the tip of me as deep as I can get, I feel my stomach clench and my balls draw up. My mouth opens over her shoulder and I bite her against the tender flesh while emptying my release deep into her body. I lift my mouth when the last tremor shakes up my body and lick where there are indentions of my teeth.

"I love it when you're bad with me." She sighs.

"Did I hurt you?" I ask, panting and staring at the mark I've left on her flesh—a mark that only makes me want to put more all over her. Logically, I know it's going to disappear before we wake up in the morning, but I can't deny loving the fuck out of seeing it—wishing it was to stay.

"Hurt me? God, *no*." She moans the last word when I

start to slip free from her heat, that sound turning into a low whine when I pull the rest of the way from her body.

I glance down at my cock, the wetness of our combined releases covering every inch. She whimpers, the pitiful sound making me smile. She isn't the only one who wishes we could keep our bodies connected. When I look back up at her, all flushed skin and bright eyes, I feel like the luckiest bastard in the world.

"Thank you."

She frowns and searches my face. "For what, honey?"

I inhale and shake my head, feeling my lips move as I grin down at her. "For lovin' me. For givin' me you. For wantin' me. Never thought I would have this, Linney, but now that I do, I know I'll never be able to live without it. So"—I kiss her slack lips—"thank you, baby."

Her chin wobbles and she blinks rapidly. "Clayton," she hiccups. "Honey," she sniffles. "Never, *ever* do you need to thank me for doin' what I was made to do. You have no idea what you've done for me, do you?"

When I don't speak, she gives one more sniff before giving up and letting the tears fall, smiling through them up at me.

"You, honey, you saved me. You healed me. You gave me purpose in a life that I had given up on. You've given me strength, confidence, and a fearlessness that only grows with your love. Don't thank me for doin' what comes as natural as breathin' does, honey."

"Linney," I rumble thickly.

"You brought me back to life," she continues.

"Stop, darlin'."

"Showed me just how beautiful my days could be."

"Caroline."

"Offered your silent protection, my white knight, while I faced my demons."

"Baby," I try again, her words making my throat get thicker and my eyes burn.

"Loved me bad and gave me forever."

"Fuck," I grunt, my mouth covering hers so she'll stop talking. I don't even attempt to hold back the wetness falling from my eyes in tune with my pounding heart. Getting emotional because your other half loves you isn't something I'll ever be ashamed of. Not when I never thought I would have this.

I keep my mouth fused to hers while I strip her carefully of her dress and, with her silky-smooth skin pressed tightly to mine, love my wife slow. Our moans and pleading gasps are swallowed as we kiss. The slick silk of her chest rubs against mine as I continue the slow tempo of my hips.

With her words still echoing through my mind, the last thought I have before the sensation of loving her becomes too much is that she's wrong. It was she who brought me back to life.

- ★ -

My ringing phone pulls me from a deep and sated sleep. Caroline curls into my side as the ringing continues and I pull her closer while burying my head in the crook of her neck, content to ignore whoever is calling. I groan when the ringing picks up not even a second after it stopped, but it isn't until I hear Caroline's phone join in that I move.

"Clayton?" she asks, confused.

I roll and grab my phone off the nightstand, jabbing the accept button. "Yeah?"

"Clay."

"What, Mav?"

"The gazebo," he starts, releasing an aggravated breath. "It's gone, Clay."

"What the hell do you mean, it's gone?" Sleep instantly vanishes as my brother's words wake me up as effectively as an ice-cold bucket of water tossed over my head.

"Trey was out on a late ride tonight. He does that shit after a long day—don't ask me why he goes this damn late. He said when he went west, all was quiet. About an hour later, before he could even see where it was comin' from, he noticed the glow of somethin' burnin'. He tried, Clay. Rushed back to grab the extinguisher here, but by the time he got back up the hill, there wasn't anything left."

I swing my legs over the side of the bed with a heavy exhale. I click on the light and brace my elbows on my knees, looking down at the floor. I feel Caroline press against my back, her hands rubbing my arms in silent support. Fuck, I don't want to tell her. I'll rebuild it, no doubt about that, but it won't be the same. I know that, even without telling her and confirming it.

"He see anyone else out there?"

Maverick's silence tells me all I need to know.

"Who?"

"Calm down, brother. You gettin' pissed isn't gonna help shit."

"I'll be there in five." Knowing in my gut that he didn't tell me who it was for a reason, that reason pressing herself against my back, I shake my head and look down at my feet.

"What is it, honey?" Caroline's question breaks the silence, worry in her tone.

"Fuck." I hiss, knowing this is going to put a dark cloud over our wedding day. "I need you to trust me, darlin'. I don't know much, but there was a fire and I need to go meet Mav and find out the rest. I'll tell you everything when I get back, but stay put while I go get answers."

"You're scaring me," she whispers, her voice shaking. "Was anyone hurt?"

I turn and reach for her, pulling her into my lap. "No, Linney, I don't think so. Trey, Mav's uncle, found it and did his best to put it out. I don't want to scare you, darlin', but I need you to stay here and let me handle this. Until I know more, I don't want you leavin' the house."

She nods, but I can tell she isn't happy about me leaving her with no answers.

"I'll be quick and I'll keep my phone on me."

"Is . . . is there more? Is everything okay?"

"Everything *will* be okay."

Her eyes search mine for a beat before she nods and pulls a choppy breath in. "Be careful," she whispers.

"Always."

I climb from the bed and start getting dressed. The whole time her eyes follow me. I see her wrap the comforter tighter around her body and I hate knowing she's worried. She isn't stupid, my girl. She's likely connecting the dots, just like I did when Maverick mentioned a fire. We haven't had a single break in finding the person who set her bookstore on fire twice, but judging by what Mav didn't say, I have a feeling that's about to change.

The question is, will finding those answers do more than give Caroline the closure of knowing the truth? I know she's no longer the scared and shy woman I first fell in love with, but this situation is worthy of a little fear. I just pray that fear guides her to rise through the aches.

"I'll be back," I promise.

She nods. "I'll be ready."

She'll be ready. Fuck me, this girl. She means it, too. I can see her building herself up, steeling herself for whatever news comes back with me, ready to take it on. She isn't building walls, not like she used to do. She's building her emotional army. Even with the shit I'm about to go handle, I can't help but feel pride witnessing just how far my shy and timid Caroline has come. I honestly believe she could take on the world. My Linney, she's always been so much stronger than she gave herself credit for, but just as our love saved me, it helped her see that. I have no doubt about it.

"Yeah. Yeah, you will be."

"I love you, honey."

I bend over the bed and kiss her soft and quick. "I love you too."

26

CAROLINE

"The House That Built Me" by Miranda Lambert

A fire.

Clayton said *was*. Past tense. There had been a fire, not that there still was one. That's something I've been holding on to since he left ten minutes ago. I locked the front door behind him and watched through the living room window as he rushed across the grass and into the detached garage that holds the golf carts and quad bikes. A few minutes later, he's tearing through the night on the back of one of the quads. I expected to see some sign of the fire close, but seeing the direction he's headed makes no sense. The land between our house and Maverick and Leighton's holds nothing. Unless the fire was at his brother's. God, I hate not knowing, being afraid for the family that already owns my heart.

There's no way I'll be able to go back to sleep.

It was just a little past midnight, I think, by the time we finally fell asleep earlier. I lost track of how long we spent loving each other, but the last time I saw the time, it was close enough to midnight that I'm fairly sure that's when we passed out. Glancing at the clock above the oven, I wince. Fifteen minutes till two. No wonder it feels like I just fell asleep—I literally did.

Needing to keep my mind occupied, I start the coffee maker and then go to the fridge to pull some breakfast food out. We haven't eaten since the dinner at Maverick and Leighton's after the ceremony, but even then, we didn't eat much. Even if we hadn't been anxious to be alone, we couldn't keep our hands—and mouths—off each other long enough to eat anyway. I don't even think either of us finished half of our food before we were making our excuses and rushing home.

Not knowing how long he's going to be, I decide to start putting together a quiche. Nothing crazy, but at least it'll keep me busy. If it weren't the middle of the night, I would call one of the girls to talk me through my worry. I take my time cutting the onions and bell peppers, the mindless task not taking my mind off my worries at all.

"This isn't workin'," I mumble, dumping the diced bits into the bowl.

I grab the piecrust I had already prepped and start to add all the ingredients, my eyes moving to the clock every five minutes or so. I blow out a breath, pick up a handful of peppers and onions, and scatter them on the bottom of the pie tin, covering the crust completely. As satisfied as I can be with my mind in such a jumbled state, I pick up the egg, cheese, and spice mixture and pour that into the crust.

Picking up the quiche, I turn from the island and start to walk to the double ovens. Two steps in and the deafening sound of glass shattering breaks the silence. I scream, my whole body jolting in fear. The pie tin hits the floor, the sticky yellow contents splattering my bare legs and the area all around me. I glance down, confused, seeing the mess before another sound by the back door reminds me what startled me enough to drop the quiche in the first place.

"Hello, Caroline."

The heinous heat in those two words slams into me, and without looking, I know this is going to be bad. I just hope and pray that whatever happens here, Clayton won't be harmed.

"Look at me, you stupid bitch!"

I fill my lungs with a deep breath and say a silent prayer. Then I look up from my egg-soaked mess and into the evil glare of Clayton's ex, Jess. Jess, who is pointing a gun in my direction with wild hair and even wilder eyes.

This is it, Caroline. Time to fight for the beauty you've found. No more letting fear win. Not now. Not when it isn't just your life that's in jeopardy here.

"Clayton's going to be back soon," I tell her, proud of the calm I don't actually feel in my voice.

She tosses her head back and laughs sinisterly. The gun jerks in her hold while she takes obvious enjoyment out of her crazy thoughts. "Oh, no, he won't. I made sure he'd be busy for a while."

"What did you do, Jess?"

My worry for Clayton barrels into me, but I push it aside . . . for now. I focus on where I am in the kitchen and weigh my options while hoping to keep her distracted with questions. If I can just move a little to the left, I can reach the knife block.

"What did *I* do? You've got to be kidding me."

"No." I shake my head. "I'm not kidding you."

"You've got some nerve, whore. You show up, move in on my man, and even though I was nice enough to give you a few warnings, you still didn't listen! Not even when I finished what I didn't accomplish the first time."

"*You* set those fires?" I take a step back slowly when she looks away briefly.

"God, you're dense. Of course I did. I would've taken care of you with the first one, but he assured me you weren't worth it. He said you wouldn't stick around. HE SAID I WOULDN'T HAVE TO WORRY ABOUT YOU AND MY MAN!" She wipes her mouth as spit falls down her chin. "He said all you'd need was a little warning and you'd be too scared to leave the house. WHY DIDN'T YOU LISTEN!"

Good heavens, she's insane.

"Who, Jess? Who said that to you?" I take another step back, my heart thundering in my chest when I almost slip on the sticky mess at my feet.

She moves away from the broken back door, kicking the rock she must've thrown through the window out of her way. As the barrel of her handgun gets closer, I feel panic rising in my throat.

"John, you dumbass. He seemed to think you wouldn't be a threat. One fire, he said, would be enough to make the timid little turtle go back into her shell. I thought he was right. You didn't come sniffin' back around *my* man for a while. But, then you had to go and fuck it all up, didn't you? Shoulda trusted my gut the first time I saw you with Clay at that piece-of-shit bar. Shoulda slit your throat when you left that motel, like I wanted to."

I shake my head, blown away by what she's saying. "The motel?"

"The first time I saw you with my man. I left it be because you stayed away and I gave you some time to make sure you wouldn't go sniffing back around what is mine. I knew Clay would get bored of your used goods. I knew he'd come back to me. But then you had to go and move your trash into *my* house with *my MAN*! That's when I knew you needed more of a reason to run far away from Pine Oak—and Clay. John didn't want to help me again, but he did when I reminded him who was in charge. No matter what we did, you didn't take a hint. You were supposed to leave!"

"You and . . . John? Y'all were the ones messin' up things with the rebuild of my store?" It takes everything in me to keep my voice calm as the panic starts to flow quicker. I just need to keep her talking. Keep her mind distracted. One more step. My hand slowly moves behind my back and I wait until I have an opening, finally being close enough to grab a knife, but not wanting to get shot when she realizes what I'm up to.

There's no way I'm going to give up without fighting to keep the beautiful life I have—I've got too much to live for.

"He didn't want me to, but I had to finish what I started. Saw right through his stalling and realized he wasn't really on my team. Stupid motherfucker. You know, I'd hoped it wouldn't come to this. Now I'm goin' to be cleanin' up your blood in my kitchen. You dirty everything up. I should just light this place up so Clay and I can move on without your filth." Her chest heaves and her eyes narrow as her face gets bright red. "You just couldn't leave though, could you! Even with your stupid fuckin' store gone, you still didn't go. NO ONE WANTS YOU! You're nothin' but a paid whore now, moochin' off my man and livin' off his dime. There isn't anything for you here!"

"You're wrong," I whisper, wincing when the unhinged madness in her eyes amps up. In my inability to keep from defending what Clayton and I have, I might as well be throwing out a challenge to this madwoman.

"I'm wrong?! I'm WRONG?! You did NOT just say that. There isn't shit for you here! All you are and all you'll ever be is a warm hole."

"How did you get Clayton out of the house?" I hedge, knowing I need to steer her into something a little safer than my relationship with Clayton so I can get out of this kitchen alive.

She grins, evil and wicked, clearly proud of herself. "That dumbass ex of yours." She laughs, the sound nothing short of vile. "You know, all he wanted to do was apologize. Stupid bastard. I finally realized what he was doin' when he tried to stop me tonight. The whole time he's been tryin' to stop me—I just didn't realize it until today. Slipped up, he did. Told me you had a diamond on your finger—*my* diamond—and that he was fuckin' happy for you. Fool. Found out not long after that Clay married your dumb ass tonight. John couldn't hide it any longer. He was just blowin' smoke up my ass, protectin' you the whole fuckin' time by keepin' me from doin' what I wanted to do all along. Always had a reason why we shouldn't hurt you. Well, joke's on him since he damn sure can't protect you with a bullet through his brain."

"My God," I gasp, not dwelling on the thought of John being dead, but recognizing just how far past sane this woman is. There will be time later, when I make it through this, to reflect on everything she's said tonight—and I *will* make it through this.

"I made sure to leave Clay that stupid fuck as a present. Left him right next to the ashes of that ugly gazebo I hear you married my man under."

My heart clenches. Clayton worked so hard building that in our spot. "He's not goin' to forgive you for this, Jess. You might think hurtin' me is the answer, but he'll hate you more than he already does if you go through with this."

"HE LOVES ME!" The gun jumps as she waves it in my direction, spit flying from her mouth as she growls. "You don't know anything!"

"I know everything!"

"Clay loves me. He always has. He was comin' back to me!"

"He hates you! The second you killed his baby, you made it so he wouldn't ever feel anything more than hate when he thought about you. When he finds out what you've done, he'll do one more than just hate you. He'll forget about you. Because that's what MY husband does when someone wrongs him and doesn't deserve his forgiveness."

"Shut up!" she screams, shaking her head and banging her free hand against the side of it.

Taking advantage of the insanity inside her bubbling over, distracting her enough that she lowers the gun just enough so it isn't pointed at my head anymore and her eyes are no longer wildly hunting me as though I were prey, I lift my hand and grab the first knife handle I reach, pulling it from the block behind my back.

"All he had to do was give me *that* diamond and I wouldn't have had to take care of the problem."

"The problem?" I gasp.

"He didn't even want a fuckin' little snot-nosed brat. He said he never wanted them, but I knew he'd marry me if I was carryin' his child—then I could take care of it and we'd still have each other."

My hand tightens on the knife, my anger for the wrongs she's done to Clayton taking on a whole new life. "You *bitch*! He would have loved that baby. Even with you bein' stuck in his life because of the child y'all shared, he would have loved it. You're right, he definitely didn't want to have a baby with you, but he would've been the best damn father. Who knows, maybe he would've come around, but you'll never know, because you killed his child."

I see it in her eyes the second she decides to pull the trigger, that insane glint that's been dancing there since she broke in turning into something feral. I move on autopilot, jumping to the side and diving behind the island. Before I fall to the floor, though, my arm flies out and over my head as I release the knife. I don't even know if I threw it toward her, but it was the only thing I could think of. Fighting a gun with a knife leaves little room for options.

My thigh burns and I cry out when I land hard. My ears ring, the blast from her gun so loud that I feel its power in my bones. My body slides and slips against the eggy mess on the floor as I back toward the hallway. I had expected her to be on me the second I moved, but when I hit the hallway and press my back against the wall, all I hear is silence. Well, muffled silence. Between the gun going off and my thundering heartbeat, I can't hear much over the bounding tempo of my racing heart and my gasping breaths.

Think, Caroline. You can't just sit here and wait for her to come back for you. Fight.

The gun safe.

Clayton showed it to me a few weeks ago. Gave me the code, but I didn't think anything of it. I listen for movement, but still don't hear much of anything. However, when I go to stand, I realize why my leg is burning, and it has nothing to do with landing on it wrong. There's a small puddle of redness forming under my leg. Now that I've noticed, the bullet wound's pain becomes all but unbearable.

Linney, fight. FIGHT, baby!

Gritting my teeth, I do the only thing I can and rally. I wipe my hands on my shirt before placing them behind me and turning from the wall. Unable to put weight on my leg, I start scooting back with my good leg, pushing my body down the hall toward Clayton's office. The red trail against the hardwood floors is unpreventable, even if it's basically an arrow telling Jess how to find me.

Once I reach the office, it takes me a little while to remember the code, but finally the metal door pops and swings open. I take in the different guns inside, but, not knowing anything about them, I just grab one and pray it's loaded. I start moving back toward the door but pause to look down at the gun I'm holding, remembering the safety that Clayton had mentioned. He hadn't been teaching me how to use the gun, merely mentioning how, if I needed it, I would have to click the safety off.

"Where the fuck are you, bitch!"

"Oh, God," I pant, blinding white fear slamming into me. "Where the heck is it?" I turn the gun around in my hand, finally seeing the small button. After making sure it's off, I try to move behind his desk, but the fire in my leg makes it hard to breathe without it throbbing.

"I'm goin' to find you and gut you from your nasty, used cunt all the way to your chest so I can rip out your heart and stuff it down your throat."

I raise the gun, leaning my back on Clayton's desk and try to calm my racing heart. I hear her moving, swearing as she does.

I look down at my still bleeding leg. *Shit.* Using the desk, I pull myself up from the floor and hobble as best I can to the attached bath, cracking the door and placing the tip of the gun between the gap in the direction of the office doorway. I hear her as she moves down the hall, her words incoherent as she rants and slurs. My vision is getting gray around the edges, and I know time is not on my side.

"Gotcha, bitch," Jess yells, jumping into the office doorway and searching the room wildly. "The fuck did you go?"

My hands don't even tremble as I adjust my hold on the gun and wait. She takes three steps into the room, stopping right next to where I'm hiding, and with one last slow exhale, my vision now a dull black, I pull the trigger.

27

CLAYTON

"Sometimes I Cry" by Chris Stapleton

- ★ -

Pulling up to the still-smoking remains of the gazebo, I park next to Mav's four-wheeler and cut the engine on mine. I expected Sheriff Holden to be here, but not the three other patrol trucks pointing their headlights toward the ash- and ember-filled space that I'd married Caroline in hours before.

What I also hadn't expected, was the body of John Lewis to be here.

"What the fuck?"

"Shit, Clay," Mav answers, blowing out his breath. "I know you thought it might have been him, but fuckin' hell."

I don't look away, my eyes struggling to make sense of what's before me. John Lewis, the man who deserves whatever hell is waiting on him, lying half burned on my property. "What did he do? Start the damn fire and fall in?" I ask no one in particular.

"Not sure, son," Holden says, coming to stand next to me. "Your brother tells me that there's a connection here?"

I nod, looking away and at the older man. "He's my wife's ex. There's not one good thing about what he shared with her either. Not to mention his history of erratic behavior from a few years ago."

He clicks his teeth, looking back down at the body. "That's right. I remember that. Such a shame, those horses of yours."

"I hadn't seen him after that until a month or two ago when I was pickin' up Caroline in Wire Creek. Didn't say a word to us, but saw him there watchin' and not hidin' it one bit."

"Has he contacted your wife?"

"Shit," I hiss, looking away from the dead man. "Earlier today. I don't know everything that was said, but she mentioned him approaching her briefly. Shit just got busy with the weddin' and I haven't talked to her about it since."

"Tucker says he saw them outside the grocery earlier yesterday."

I glance in the direction he's pointing to see the younger police officer. He dips his chin but doesn't say anything.

"With all due respect, Sheriff, I hope you can understand how it slipped my mind, seein' that aside from us sayin' I do, there wasn't much time to talk about our day."

"I didn't mean anything by it, Clay. Just pointin' out that this clearly wasn't a spur-of-the-moment thing if not even twenty-four hours after approaching your wife, he's here."

"What the hell was burnin' somethin' down in the middle of my property goin' to prove anyway? It doesn't make a lick of sense."

"I understand your wife's store in Wire Creek had some fire issues as well recently?"

I scoff. "You could say that. Someone tried to burn her inside of there the first time. Shit got tampered with while she was in the rebuildin' stage, and the second she put the place on the market, they came back and sparked it up real good. That wasn't long before when she officially moved in to the ranch."

Holden bobs his head, listening to me while one of the younger cops writes some notes down.

"Coroner's here," someone mumbles.

I glance up at Spencer Russell, the town's coroner, as he climbs down from his truck. The man's old as dirt but wise as hell. He walks toward our huddle and shakes hands with Holden and Mav before getting to me.

"Nice night for a barbecue?" he cryptically jokes, grunting out a belly laugh while walking toward John's body.

Mav snickers under his breath and I see the sheriff shake his head, a small grin on his lips. I keep my silence. It's not like John being behind all this isn't believable. But Caroline's words about how he wouldn't have hidden behind the fires echo through my mind. That's why I'm having a hard time believing this is clear-cut. Someone like John Lewis would have made his point in an irrefutable kind of way. He would have been in your face and proud, hungry to see the fear he had produced. What he wouldn't have done was spent months hiding behind fires and petty construction-site mischief.

"Well, well," Spencer mutters, using his gloved hands to turn John's head. "Y'all see a gun anywhere round here?"

Ice-cold dread fills my veins.

"No, sir. We checked the area real good when we got here, too."

"Linney," I wheeze, already turning and running back to the four-wheeler. I toss my leg over the seat and reach for the key. Before I can fire it up, the unmistakable sound of a gunshot echoes through the night. "Caroline!"

"Clay!" I hear bellowed at the same time my engine kicks over. Before I can get the four-wheeler into gear, my brother is jumping on the back rack with his legs hanging over one side. I don't spare him a glance, flipping my wrist and gunning it back to the ranch knowing he'll hold on but not giving a shit if he falls off. I need to get back to my wife.

"Kill it back behind the barn," Mav yells into my ear.

I nod, changing gears and picking up speed. When we come into the clearing that the house is in, I flip the lights off and drive to the back of the barn and turn off the four-wheeler, running toward the house not even a second later. I don't look to see if my brother is following; the only thing I care about is making sure Caroline's okay. My feet have just cleared the top step of the porch when I hear the second gunshot and all rational thoughts vanish. I lift my boot and kick the front door, the wood splintering as the lock gives. Shouldering the broken door out of the way, I stand in the doorway, my eyes searching and my heart praying.

"Clay," Mav whispers, pointing to the red smear that looks like someone dragged a body down the hall.

"Caroline!" I scream, rushing forward and following the trail, Mav hot on my heels. I hear more footsteps rushing up the porch and I have no doubt that Sheriff Holden didn't waste a second following me.

"No," I pant, coming into my office and seeing a nightmare coming to life. My world stops spinning a second later when I see through the cracked door of the office bathroom the delicate hand lying limp—the hand adorned with the rings I had put there.

"Holy hell," someone says behind me.

I jump over the very dead woman on the floor in the middle of my office, noticing that not only is her head missing, she's got a knife sticking out of her chest, directly under her collarbone.

My girl fought.

"Linney, love?" I sob, pushing the door open enough to get into the bathroom. "God, darlin'." My knees slam into the floor and I reach out to check her pulse, feeling instant relief blast through the dark pit of dread that had settled over me when I find one, though it's weak. "Get an ambulance here, now!" I bellow out. "Stay with me, baby. You stay with me, Linney."

I rock her in my arms and pray, plead, and beg. My throat burns and my eyes sting. I bury my face in her neck, breathe her in. Her limp body is heavy in my arms, her face drained of color.

"Ambulance is five out," Mav says, his own voice betraying his calm outer appearance. He grabs a towel off the rack and presses it against her leg. "She's gonna be okay, Clay. Believe it. Ain't room for any other outcome."

I shake my head, my tears falling faster. I don't say a word. Not while my brother helps to stop the blood flowing from her leg, pulling my shirt she's wearing down to cover her underwear. When the paramedics burst through the door and take her from my arms, though, I break. Break into so many pieces that I know if something happens to her, I'll never put them back together again.

The stretcher makes her look even tinier than normal. The men work on her for only a second before rushing down the hall. I jump from the floor and sprint after them.

Mav grabs my arm, stopping me from getting to the ambulance. I turn and punch him in the face when the ambulance door shuts, one of the men yelling out that they're on the way to the hospital in Law Bone and taking off without me—taking my *everything* away from me.

"Get in the fuckin' truck," Mav demands, spitting and wiping his split lip with the back of his hand.

He stomps toward my truck, not looking to see if I'm following. We both climb in, and he punches the gas while I hunch forward to push my hands through my hair. Silence and the sound of my engine speeding through the night ring in my ears, the vision of Caroline lying in a pool of blood, lifeless, etched in my brain.

"She's gonna be okay, Clay."

"I'm nothin' without her," I mumble, feeling the pain of my words like a knife to the heart.

"Stay strong. She needs you fightin' too."

"If she doesn't—"

Mav slams his palm against the wheel and bellows a string of curses. "Shut the fuck up. You've got another ten minutes before we get to the hospital, and I fuckin' swear, you better fix your shit by then. You're doin' her no good already placin' her in the ground when she fought to make sure you never gotta know what it's like to not have her. You fight, knowin' she's doin' the same."

I blow my air out and lean against the seat, closing my

eyes and doing my best to bat the fear back. The vision of Caroline as I saw her last makes it hard, but finally we pull up to the emergency room entrance, and I'm out and rushing into the brightly lit waiting room.

"Caroline Davis. My wife. She was brought in by ambulance."

The young nurse nods before typing something into the computer in front of her. "She's here, but I don't have any news right now. If you have a seat, someone will be out as soon as they can tell you more."

"I need to be with her," I tell her frantically.

She gives me a sad smile and shakes her head. "I'm sorry, sir. It's hospital policy."

"Come on," Mav says, taking my shoulder and turning me to walk over to one of the empty seats.

And we wait.

We wait and I pretend my world isn't ending.

28

CAROLINE

"Wake Up Loving You" by Old Dominion

- ★ -

The heavy weight against my hand is the first thing I notice.

The warmth from that weight, the second.

With the cobwebs in my mind, though, it's hard to register much of anything else.

Slowly, the rest of my body starts to connect back with my groggy mind, the weight on my hand forgotten when the burning sensation in my leg comes into focus. I groan and try to open my eyes.

"Linney," I hear whispered, but the only thing I can focus on is the pain in my leg, which is getting more and more intense with each passing second. "Darlin', please calm down."

"Hurts," I moan, my voice gravelly and thick, like I just woke up.

"God, baby."

"Carrie, stop fightin'. You're safe. Calm down before you hurt yourself more."

At Luke's words, my body stops moving. I hadn't even realized I had been thrashing against the bed. My eyes are still not opening, but more around me registers now. I hear sniffles, some farther from me than others and some right next to me. I hear the beeping of machines and soft, pleading whispers at my side.

Clayton.

Knowing he needs me just as much as I need to see him is what helps me to push the cobwebs away and take control of my mind and body. It takes a couple minutes, but I finally pry my eyes open. I blink frantically as my pupils adjust to the dim light. Luke is standing at the end of my bed, his sister in his arms while she cries against his chest. I turn my head when I see movement to see Maverick in much the same position with Leighton, standing under the TV mounted in the corner. Next to them, Tate is standing behind Quinn, his arms around her shoulders as she wipes her eyes.

Then, when I look away from them, my handsome husband fills my vision.

His hair is wild, like he's done nothing but run his hands through it. The stubble that had been on his jaw when we went to bed is even darker now. And his red, swollen eyes look like they're glowing as he openly and silently cries. Tears spill over his lashes and fall down his face before landing against our joined hands resting next to my side. He doesn't look away, doesn't dry his tears. He just stares at me, breathing heavily, like he can't believe I'm right in front of him.

"Hey," I whisper.

His eyes shudder closed and he sucks in a jerky breath before dropping his forehead against my belly. He shakes his head as his strong shoulders hitch as he loses whatever control he'd been holding tightly to.

"Clayton," I plead, my heart breaking over seeing my strong husband falling to bits in front of me. "Please, honey."

He mumbles something against me, the words muffled. I look around the room, frantic to get help in easing his pain, but I see not one dry eye as they witness the strongest man we all know unable to keep himself together any longer.

"Cl-Clayton," I wobble out, my chin quivering and my eyes filling with tears. "You're breaking my heart." My chest literally feels like someone is pulling my heart from my body with each second that passes.

His body shudders and I hear him suck in a breath. "I thought I lost you," he admits, lifting his head and looking down at our hands. "I saw you there, blood everywhere, and knew if I lost you I'd be losin' myself too."

"I'm okay," I gasp, needing him to stop. "I'm here."

"There's nothin' for me on this earth without you by my side," he continues. "She almost took you from me."

I choke on a loud cry as it bursts from my throat. I gasp for air, but I can't stop wailing. Through my tears, I see Clayton jump to his feet, and then his hands push under my shoulders as he pulls my upper body off the hospital bed and into his arms. I wrap my arms around him the best I can with the IV and cling to him, soaking his shirt while he drenches my gown, the early-morning events coming to a head as we hold each other.

"I'm so sorry," he mumbles against my neck after we both calm.

"For what?" I question, opening my eyes. The first person I focus on is Maverick. His jaw clenches and his eyes are just as wet as I imagine mine are.

"I should have done better at protecting you."

I gasp, pull back, and stare up into his tortured eyes. "This is *not* your fault. No one, not even you, could have seen this comin'. You *did* protect me, honey. All I heard in my mind was your voice remindin' me to fight. Your strength filled me up without you even bein' there. I remembered you tellin' me where you keep your firearms, and that gave me a chance. You might not have been there, but it was you nonetheless who protected and saved me."

"It's because of me you were in this situation to begin with, Caroline."

I frown. "No, it was because of your crazy ex. Don't you dare take this on, Clayton Davis."

"Linney," he breathes.

"Don't you Linney me. We're both victims here. And she does *not* get to win. Not now. Not ever."

I see my words take root, the despair in his eyes lifting. His forehead comes to mine and he rocks against me, shaking his head. "I'm never gonna let you out of my sight."

"I'm thinkin' that's not goin' to be a hardship, honey."

"I've never been more scared in my life. If she wasn't already dead, I'd fuckin' kill her myself."

Knowing I'm the reason Jess is dead doesn't even faze me. It was either her or me, and I'm not about to feel guilty that I battled for the beautiful life I've earned. Maybe one day I'll feel differently, but I doubt it.

"Why am I here?"

He exhales, his eyes looking pained again. I hate that, but I know it's unavoidable if I want to know what happened.

"When she . . ." He sucks in a deep breath. "When she shot you, the bullet lodged deep enough in your thigh that you lost a good bit of blood. They stitched you up, and the doctor assures me that, aside from the scar, you'll have no lastin' issues. But the bump on your head is what's got you here for the night. When you passed out, you hit the edge of the toilet on your way down."

"And the rest?"

"That's it, darlin'. Stitches, fluids in your IV, and monitorin' you overnight, and they assure me you'll make a full recovery."

I search his eyes, feeling my brows pull in. "What aren't you tellin' me?"

He searches my eyes before dropping his head and shaking it slowly. "John was part of this."

My shoulders droop and the tension I felt in them drains away. "I know."

"What do you mean you know?"

"Jess admitted it." I look down at my lap. "I know he's dead. And I know she did it too. I'm not upset he's gone, but knowin' that, in his way, he tried to stop her doesn't exactly make me feel good that he died doin' so."

"And him? What did he say to you?"

Pulling my head back, I look into his face, confused by his question. "Pardon?"

"I forgot about it until I stood over his body and told Sheriff Holden that John approached you yesterday afternoon."

"Oh, that," I whisper, nodding. "I wasn't keepin' it from you, Clayton. Things were just, well . . . He was the last thing on my mind when I was gettin' ready to marry you. I only had room for happiness and it slipped my mind."

"I'm not mad, darlin'. I just want to know what he had to say. Piece this shit together the best I can."

I search my mind, replaying everything I can remember. After what Jess said, some of John's confusing words make more sense.

"He tried to stop her," I finally say after the silence stretches on. "It didn't make any sense when he came up to me in town, but after what she said about him, I get what he'd been tryin' warn me about."

"Explain that to me."

I sigh and recount everything from when I was starting to cook, to when Jess broke the door, and every word she had to say before what happened in the office. I know it costs him to sit here and not react. The tic in his jaw muscle and the twitching of his left eye betray the calm he's trying to project. Once I tell him everything, I take a gulp of air and lean back, instantly exhausted.

"I don't give a shit that he thought he was protectin' you. He should've gone straight to the fuckin' cops when he realized what Jess was up to instead of helpin' her with some misguided belief that he was doin' it to keep you safe. There's no fuckin' gray line, Linney. You could have died tonight, regardless of what he tried to do leadin' up to it. You could have been lost to me forever, and I'll take your life over theirs any day."

"I wasn't justifyin' his actions. I agree with you, but even though he failed, he tried."

"And failed. All that matters is that he failed."

I nod. "Our ugly isn't goin' to touch us anymore."

He closes his eyes and his nostrils flare while he composes himself. "Nothin' but good's gonna touch us, darlin'."

I nod, resting my head against the pillow with a yawn. Clayton leans over me and presses his mouth to my forehead. I blink up at him and smile. "A honeymoon might be a good idea now," I slur, exhaustion pulling me under.

"Seein' that we're gonna be mighty busy in the next handful of months, I think you're right."

I hear some feminine giggles but give in to the tiredness and fall asleep, knowing that I'm safe, Clayton's safe, and there isn't anyone else out there who can hurt us.

29

CAROLINE

"My Best Friend" by Tim McGraw

"**W**hat?!" I screech, looking at the doctor like he's lost his mind.

I woke up ten minutes ago when the doctor and the evil nurse who'd been torturing me all night clattered into the room pulling some equipment. Okay, so she hadn't been torturing me, but each time she came in to wake me up, it sure did feel that way. Logically, I know head injuries aren't anything to take lightly, but I'm exhausted and sleep is the only thing I want.

"Pardon?" the doctor questions, looking up from the chart in his hand.

"I get that I bumped my head and all, Doc, and I'm not tryin' to tell you how to do your job, but maybe we should be checkin' my noggin . . . or better yet, yours, because nothin' you just said makes sense."

Clayton's manly chuckles tickle my fingers and I glance away from the doctor to see my husband hiding his smile behind the hand he's been holding all night.

"Mrs. Davis," the doctor says, and I look over from Clayton to narrow my eyes at him. "Tracey's monitored you all night and we have no reason to believe that further testing is needed regarding your injuries. I've given your husband your care instructions and he knows what to look for in the event that more medical treatment is needed—which I'm confident won't be the case."

"So you're just goin' to let me leave without makin' sure the head you've kept me here all night for is fine?"

Closing the chart, the doctor crosses his arms over his chest and smirks. I'm not sure what he thinks is so dadgum funny. At this point, I wouldn't mind knocking him over the head. When his grin grows and two dimples appear, I make a mental note to find out if he's single. He's young, clearly successful, and handsome—though not as handsome as Clayton. Perfect for Lucy, even if I want to shake some sense into the crazy-talking man.

"We wouldn't let you leave if there was even a slight concern, Mrs. Davis."

"Well, clearly there's somethin' wrong with my head, Doc. I'm hallucinating, hearin' things or somethin'! Either that or I'm dreamin', because there isn't any other reason you'd be standin' there with Nurse Pokes-for-fun, tellin' me I'm pregnant." I take a deep breath, my eyes widening. "Oh, my God! I'm losin' my mind, aren't I? The fall knocked somethin' loose and you're about to ship me off to a home!" I turn my head to look at Clayton. "I don't want to go to a home!"

His shoulders shake as he laughs at me. "Linney, love, no one is puttin' you in a home."

I narrow my eyes at him. "Well, maybe we need to put him in one, then," I snap, pointing at the doctor.

"Maybe it'll be easier if we show you, hmm?" the evil, poking-me-all-night nurse says in a sugary sweet voice.

"Show me what?"

"Your baby." She smiles and I stare, my mouth hanging wide-open.

I stop arguing and, with a huff, lie back on the bed. There's no way I'm pregnant. I haven't missed my period. Aside from the whole being-shot-and-passing-out thing, I feel fine. I haven't been sick, tired, or sore.

Clayton sits up straighter when the nurse holds up some long, ET-looking finger and starts covering it with a condom. I frown when the doctor starts moving the sheets from my legs, taking the condom finger from the nurse. My hand is squeezed at the same time the doctor starts explaining to me that he's about to insert the finger into my vagina.

"Whoa!" I swat at his hands when he moves my gown. "You can keep your kinky alien probe away from me, mister."

"Mrs. Davis." He sighs, his lips twitching as he obviously tries to keep from laughing at me. I'd like to see him be all calm and doctorly when someone wants to stick a long, skinny, condom-covered piece of plastic inside of him! "This is the most accurate way to determine how far along you are. Your numbers are high, but that could mean one of quite a few things. My guess is you're somewhere between six to nine weeks along, which means this is the only form of ultrasound we can actually see the baby with."

"This is such a waste of time. I haven't even missed a period!" I pull the hem of my gown down, covering my naked sex. If I could reach the blanket, I'd put that back over me as well.

"Some women, though few, experience their cycle throughout their pregnancies. I know this might be a surprise, but I assure you there's no way we aren't going to see a baby."

"Linney," Clayton huskily whispers.

I stop glaring at the doctor and look at my husband. His stubble has grown out even more, the black shadow highlighting his strong jaw. The lips that can drive me wild curve, a small and happy smile across his mouth. His dark-as-night hair is still a mess, but instead of seeing the raw pain that had been in his green eyes last night, all I see is a whole lot of love and even more . . . hopefulness.

"Had a little more time for this to sink in, darlin',

and I get you not believin' the good doctor, but please, baby . . . let them show us what our love created."

The wind in my sails evaporates instantly and I study my husband, the emotions written all over him infectious as a flicker of hope starts to ignite inside of me.

With a nod to the doctor, I follow his instructions as he embarrassingly bares me, then inserts his ET finger into my sex. It's uncomfortable as hell, but I keep my eyes on Clayton and hold my breath. I watch his face as his eyes go wide and stay trained on the monitor. Tiny wrinkles form between his eyebrows as he concentrates.

Then his hand convulses in mine and his whole face goes soft. I've seen what my husband looks like with love shining bright, but this . . . this is something I've never seen on his face. It's as if his heart jumped from his chest to beat right behind his blazing bright eyes. Wonder, love, and pure elation beam out at me. My own heart starts to pick up speed when I realize there's only one thing that could make him look as if the world is being handed to him.

"Amazin'," he says softly.

I feel lightheaded as my head rolls against the pillow to look in the direction of Clayton's stare. I see the doctor's face first. He arches a brow and smiles smugly. The nurse is beaming, but I let my attention pass over her and fall on the monitor.

"Oh my God," I gasp, my eyes burning as a beautiful kind of bliss slams into me.

The doctor reaches out and presses some buttons, then the quiet room fills with what can only be described as the sound of muffled hooves racing.

"What is that?" I whisper, not looking away from the monitor, my grip on Clayton's hand tightening.

"That, Mrs. Davis, is your baby's heartbeat."

"Oh," I breathe.

"Strong and healthy. You're measuring right at eight weeks, and everything with the baby looks just fine."

"But . . . are you sure? Nothin' is wrong after last night?"

The doctor shakes his head. "Not a thing. The baby is nice and protected in there, Mrs. Davis."

"A baby." I shake my head, smiling so big my cheeks hurt, and blink rapidly to clear the tears even though I know it's fruitless to try. "Honey, a baby!"

"Heard the doc," Clayton says, his voice thick and even deeper than normal.

I look at him, seeing the same things I'm feeling in his eyes. "Can you believe it?"

"It's our beauty, darlin'. 'Course I believe it."

"We're havin' a baby," I cry, the image of him swimming now that my eyes are full of happy tears.

"I'll print some images for y'all and get out of your hair," the doctor mumbles.

I don't pay him any attention, not when my husband is looking at me like I've just given him the greatest gift. We continue to stare at each other, ignoring the other two in the room. I don't even flinch when the doctor pulls the probe free from my body and drapes the sheets back over my legs. I hear one of them mention that the pictures are on the table next to my bed and that they'll be back shortly with my discharge papers, but I don't look away from the blazing green orbs that have me transfixed.

When the door clicks signaling their departure, Clayton pounces. My hand falls from his grip and lands on the mattress with a soft bounce the same second his lips land on my mouth. If I thought our kisses before were magical, I was wrong. He devours me and fills me with so much love that I'm drunk on it. This is the kind of kiss you only experience with the person who holds the other part of your soul. With every swipe of his tongue, I feel like my heart is swelling, every swirl and sweep feeding my very being. His panting breaths against my face fill me with the all-consuming power of his love.

And I give him just as much as he's giving me.

The knowledge that our child, one who is wanted and loved already, is growing healthy and strong inside of me is nothing short of incredible. Our love, while it flickered to life with a brilliant boom, grew into what we're sharing right here—perfection.

"You're goin' to have my baby," he finally says in awe after pulling his lips from mine.

"I'm goin' to have your baby."

"Everything, Linney, love . . . your love gives me *everything*."

I hiccup a sob, smiling at the man who owns my love. "You're wrong, honey. *Our* love gives *us* everything."

"This is it, darlin'. This is our forever startin', with nothin' and no one standin' in the way of what kinda beautiful we create. Told you before and I meant it then just like I do now, the ugly we had to face to get here only made us unbreakable. Havin' you and our child as my reward for makin' it through mine only makes it all the sweeter. From this moment on, we're not lookin' back and I'm gonna love you so bad you won't ever have a day without knowin' your husband is everything because of you."

"Oh, Clayton."

"Thank you, darlin', for takin' that seat next to me, makin' that crowded bar feel empty with your shy smiles, takin' a chance on us, and, in the end, givin' me life."

I'm openly crying now. I couldn't have held it back if I wanted to. Not with him giving me so much.

"I love you, darlin'," he rasps, his lips pressing against my forehead.

"I love you, too, honey. So much."

Epilogue
CAROLINE

"Holdin' Her" by Chris Janson

- ★ -

I lower the camera and smile. It's moments like these that make me want to pinch myself. Moments that fill my every day, giving me a life that's so unbelievably beautiful it doesn't ever seem real.

"Pretty sure you've got a million pictures just like that one, Linney love."

I scrunch my nose at my husband, turning the camera in my hands and bringing up the image I just took on the screen. "I could have a million more, Clayton, and it still wouldn't be enough."

He grunts out a few low chuckles. "You're a nut."

"Whatever, honey."

He stands and I lean my shoulder against the door-frame to watch him. His head dips once he's on his feet, pressing a light kiss atop our daughter's head. Her tiny little rosebud mouth purses, but she doesn't wake up. His eyes close, lips still pressed against her head while he takes a moment, like he always does. Never fails, he works hard all day and the first thing he does when he comes home is strip his shirt off, wash his hands, and hold our daughter to his chest until she's asleep; then he kisses her sweetly and breathes her in.

Since before Harlow was even born, Clayton would end his day much like this, only with his mouth against my belly and our daughter kicking against his touches.

My pregnancy was the kind that women dream of. I was happy, full of energy, hungry for my husband's touch, and hardly gained any weight. Of course, when you have a man like Clayton Davis showering you with his love, there isn't a snowball's chance in hell you'll feel anything other than pure bliss.

Not everything has been sunshine and rainbows. In the year since the fateful night that almost stole this from us, we've continued to move forward—but it was the early days when we both were frantic to erase the memories of that night that put a dark cloud over the beginning of my pregnancy.

The first thing he did was buy an RV—not just any RV either. This was the luxury of luxe, grander than some homes. And after he pulled it down the drive and parked it in the grass away from the house, he told me we were moving in—temporarily—to his deluxe home on wheels.

I didn't argue with him because I could see it in his eyes, the wild hunt for control driving him.

So we moved into the RV.

And we lived in it for almost four months while Clayton put all his responsibilities on hold so he could oversee the complete renovation of our home. I didn't need to ask to understand why. I knew why he needed that. Even if it was to erase what Jess had done, I have a feeling he was also banishing the ghosts of his childhood as well.

The first time I saw all the hard work he poured into our home, I cried for an hour. Not only had he gutted and updated everything, he'd turned the spare bedroom closest to ours into the most heavenly nursery I've ever seen outside of a showroom.

The nursery had me crying for another hour.

While our house was being renovated, he also hired someone to rebuild our gazebo. This time he created a wraparound porch outside the structure with a freestanding hammock and an outdoor table. We've had a few dates in our spot and not once has our time out there been anything short of perfect. All the painful memories from that night are completely eradicated.

What we didn't do though was worry about The Sequel. Not until six months ago, when I was entering my last month of pregnancy. I hadn't been sure that I wanted to reopen my store, but in the end, Clayton helped me see past the sadness I've been associating with rebuilding. I think a little part of me hasn't been sure I could reopen without continuously looking over my shoulder. I knew Jess and John were gone, but with so much of their evil being connected with the store, I had a hard time seeing past it.

Until Clayton.

Until my husband reminded me that we've got nothing but beautiful now.

It didn't hurt that he reminded me while filling me with his cock and loving me slow.

"She's out," Clayton says softly, standing in front of me and startling me out of my thoughts.

I lean to the side and look around his delicious naked torso to see the blanket-covered bundle in the middle of the dark gray crib. When I straighten and blink up at Clayton, nervous flutters start to fill my belly when his smile grows.

"You got somethin' for me?" he questions, smiling.

"Maybe," I hedge, a nervous giggle breaking free.

He tilts his head and studies me.

"Come on, honey," I request, placing the camera on top of Harlow's dresser and taking his hand in mine. He follows as I pull him from our daughter's doorway and into our room. I drop his hand when we reach the middle of our room and turn to him. My eyes roam from his chiseled chest, over his defined abs, and down his denim-covered legs to his bare feet. I take a deep breath and smile at the floor before looking up at my husband.

"Strip, handsome."

His eyebrows shoot up, but he brings his hands to his buckle without questioning me, making quick work of shucking his pants and briefs, standing to his full height in all his naked glory.

With a wink, I reach down and pull my sundress up and over my head. My breasts bounce free, reminding me that they've taken on a life of their own since having Harlow. Clayton's eyes burn as he looks down at them. He's made it no secret that he loves the changes our daughter brought to my body—especially my breasts. Anytime they're out, he's licking his lips and staring, and with a breastfeeding four-month-old, they're out often.

"On the bed."

Silently, he walks around me, not without reaching out and grazing my thigh with his fingertips. He climbs into our bed, right in the middle, and lies down with his arms up and hands behind his head.

I climb up on the bed and shuffle my knees forward until they're pressed against his hip. He watches me intently with his emerald gaze, his erection bobbing when my eyes look down at it. When I lick my lips, he groans.

As much as I'd love to sit here and drink him in, I need to feel him. Shifting, I climb over him, spreading my legs and sitting back on his knees. His eyes look down his body and straight between my legs, his nostrils flaring wildly. My hands go to his thighs and I start moving them, caressing him slowly while leaning forward until his cock is right at my mouth. My tongue comes out and licks him. He hisses but doesn't move. God, I love the taste of him. Opening my mouth wide, I take him as deep as I can and lift one hand up to work his shaft while flicking the head of his dick with my tongue. I hum when I taste his salty essence, moving my other hand down and between my legs. I don't take my eyes off his, wanting him to see the pleasure I get from using my mouth on him. I also know what he looks like when he's about to come, and right now, as much as I love it, I want him inside me when he does.

Removing my mouth with a loud pop, I start to crawl up his body.

"I've been waitin' all day to give you my bad, Clayton Davis." I place my hands next to his head and lean down, placing my mouth close enough to his to feel his hot breath as he pants. My pussy glides against his erection, making me moan. "You're goin' to sit there and let me give that to you. You're goin' to keep your back on the bed and let me take everything. I want to feel you, so deep, Clayton."

"Fuck yes," he hisses.

"You gonna sit there and let me give you my bad while I love my husband?"

"Baby," he breathes.

I lift my hips, moving one hand to his abs, the other wrapping around his thickness, moving my body until he's kissing my entrance. I swirl the blunt tip around my wetness, moaning when he hits my clit. My head rolls while my body burns with need. Then I stop my hand and drop my hips, impaling myself on him. He shouts a deep grunt that turns into a low moan when I roll my hips again. We don't look away from each other as I begin to move, both our mouths open. Our heavy breathing fills the room. He lets me drive as I take his body, using my legs to pull my hips up and drop down. Each time he hits that sweet spot deep inside of me, I feel myself growing wetter and wetter. I won't last much longer.

Feeling it build, my body trembles. "Help me," I beg, moaning when he takes my hips in his strong hands and starts lifting me, pulling me down, and thrusting up from the bottom. My cries turn wild when he quickens the pace. "I'm goin' to come, honey," I breathe, my vision getting hazy as fireworks start to explode behind my eyes. I clamp down on him and cry his name out, his own groan of completion echoing around us.

I fall to his chest, sucking in air as my body comes back to earth. His heart thumps wildly against my cheek and I smile.

"I would've put money on us makin' another baby just now, but . . . seein' that you took care of that weeks ago, I'll just enjoy the practice."

He jolts under me, the hands that had been roaming my back stopping, and I lift up to look at him. His eyes are wide, happy, and wet.

"You tellin' me my baby is growin' in there?"

"Yeah honey," I sigh, tears slowly cascading down my face and landing on his chest.

"You tellin' me I'm goin' to get more beauty from you?"

I sniffle and nod.

"Linney, love," he breathes, kissing me deep and quick.

"Are you happy?" I ask, knowing he is, but still worried about my handsome husband.

"God, yes."

"Good, honey. I am too. So happy. Tate did a scan and said everything looks perfect."

He frowns slightly. "Tate? Darlin', how long have you known you were carryin' my baby?"

I shift, making both of us groan from the connection we haven't broken. "A few weeks. I didn't . . . I, well, I wasn't sure if it was a good time to tell you before now."

His face gets soft and I know I don't need to clarify. Three weeks ago, the day I found out I was pregnant again, Clayton took a call from his brother, and after he said hello, he didn't speak again. Not during that call, or for hours and hours after. He ended his call, placed his phone on the counter, and walked out the back door. It wasn't until four in the morning that he came back. I listened from our bed while he moved through the house, seeing his shadow enter Harlow's room before coming into ours with her in his arms. He got into bed, made sure our girl was situated, and reached over to pull me into his chest.

With my daughter's face close to mine, the heart of the most important man in both of our lives beating under us, he told me that his mother had passed away. I kept my mouth shut but tightened my arm over his body. He didn't say anything else about it, just kissed my head, then Harlow's, before all three of us went to sleep.

And until today, I hadn't been sure how to tell him that I was pregnant because I wasn't sure if he was handling his feelings over his mama.

"I understand why you didn't tell me, but darlin', you don't need to worry. I didn't have her in my life for a long time. I don't miss her, haven't in a long time."

"You haven't talked about it though, Clayton. I've been so worried about where your head's been that I wasn't sure if it was a good time to tell you about the baby."

He tightens his hold on me, and his lips form a tiny smile. "I let her go that night. I left because I didn't want her—even the thought of her—in our home with our daughter. The only thing I could think of, even now, is how anyone could walk away from their children. When I think of Harlow, there isn't anything I wouldn't do for her. I'd die for her—you—and any children we have. When I think of my mama now, the only thing that goes through my mind is how thankful I am that, because of her inability to love her children, I know I'll never be what she was. She didn't have what it took to cowboy up and live each day for someone else. But I do."

"I've been so worried."

"I know, darlin', but I wasn't keepin' it from you. I meant what I said: she doesn't have a place under this roof."

I nod, understanding what he's saying. "Okay."

"Okay." His smile grows, teeth flashing, and the corners of his eyes crinkle. "You, Caroline Davis, are the best thing that happened to me."

I rock my hips, my happiness mirroring his. "Ditto, honey, ditto."

His hands move from my hips to my lower belly. "Just when I think I couldn't love you more, you go and give me more beauty. Give me your mouth, baby, and let me love you slow this time so I can show you how much you givin' me another baby means to me."

I squeal as he flips us and moan when he starts slowly gliding his hard length in and out of my body. He takes his sweet time, not breaking the steady rhythm he's built. His eyes hold mine and his lips part only a breath above mine. I'm surrounded by and filled with the man that owns me—heart and soul—as he loves me slow and steady. My heart pounds against my chest, calling out to his, and with his name leaving my lips on a whisper, I tumble over the edge. Clayton follows me not even a minute later, turning our bodies, keeping us connected, and wrapping his strong arms around me.

"Never dreamed that this existed. You fill me with so much, darlin', that a lifetime will never be enough for me to repay that."

"Far as I can tell, honey, it's me who gets filled to the brim. I reckon if we both keep tryin' to repay the other, there won't be a day that passes where we aren't ridin' high."

"I'll love you forever and always, Linney."

"And I'll be lovin' you right back forever and always, Clayton."

- ★ -

Fifteen years later

High on the hill located on the back end of Clayton and Caroline Davis's property, there isn't a face without a smile on it. The painful memories that used to haunt the three Davis children are a distant memory. Each in the arms of his or her spouse looks down from the gazebo that's stood through six tornados over the years and only grown since the eldest Davis realized just how important this spot had become not just to his wife, but to his family, as their children run, laugh, and love. There hasn't been a day that happiness didn't sound from the Davis property for the past fifteen years.

Clayton Davis looks from his two daughters over to his son, wrapping his arms a little tighter around his wife, knowing that without her, he wouldn't have this wonderful life. Glancing over his wife's head, Clayton takes a second to appreciate the same contentment-induced happiness on his brother's face.

Maverick, not having missed the attention of his brother, turns to meet his gaze. Gone are the hard lines and stoic disposition. His wife made it impossible for him to keep his old flinty edge throughout the years. But it was with the birth of each of his children that whatever pain he had left inside of him vanished. With a year separating each of his four daughters, something inside of him changed forever, but it was when his son was placed in his arms that Maverick Davis finally found out what it was like to have the world. There are days when he wakes, the house still silent, and he's slammed with just how lucky he truly is. His heart swelling, his wife pressed tight to his side, and his house full of the children his wife blessed him with. Seeing what he feels on those days in his older brother's gaze, he smiles even wider.

Both the Davis boys look to their left and down at their baby sister tucked tight to her husband's side. Her youngest son leans into his mother with his hand wrapped around her belt loop and her hand rubbing his raven-black hair. It was a long road for Quinn Montgomery and her husband to have the last of their four boys. She struggled through two miscarriages but never gave up, knowing that they weren't whole. It was during those days that Quinn got quiet and her smiles came less and less. When her husband delivered their last baby almost six years ago, she changed. Holding their miracle in her arms, Quinn had laughed so loud that her family heard her outside of her birthing room, her laughter sparking something in each of them that well and truly made them realize how far they had all come.

And that's how Clayton and Caroline, Maverick and Leighton, and Quinn and Tate . . . came home.

Acknowledgments

As always, to my family. Your support, love, and understanding is the reason I'm able to continue living my dream. Without the four of you, I would be lost and my words would have no meaning. Knowing my three daughters are never allowed to read Mommy's books, I doubt you'll ever see this: but I every time you ask about what I'm writing, I hope your dreams are weaving knowing that the sky is the limit.

To my team at Pocket Books, especially my fabulous editor, Marla. Thank you for giving me this chance. Thank you for believing in me. Thank you from the bottom of my heart for showing me that anything is possible. Even seeing your books at the grocery store next to someone's forgotten bag of pasta!

To Danielle Sanchez, the best publicist a girl could have. Honest to God, I would be lost without you. Thank you for always being there, even when I'm in another country and confused about life.

To the two girls that were with me every step of the way during each book in this series. You both know how much I love you, Felicia and Lara. Felicia, don't expect more . . . I've dedicated a book to you already and feed you from my minifridge. Lara, what can I say, other than Clay's yours.

To Marisa Corvisiero, thank you for everything! And I do mean everything. I can't believe that this series is over, and I can't wait to see what other trouble we can get into together.

And lastly, to my amazing readers. Every word I write is for you. Each dream I pen. Each love I create. I love you all.